EISENHOWER'S SPUTNIK MOMENT

EISENHOWER'S SPUTNIK MOMENT

THE RACE FOR SPACE
AND WORLD PRESTIGE

YANEK MIECZKOWSKI

CORNELL UNIVERSITY PRESS
Ithaca and London

First published 2013 by Cornell University Press

Printed in the United States of America

Library of Congress Cataloging-in-Publication Data

Mieczkowski, Yanek.
    Eisenhower's Sputnik moment : the race for space and world prestige / Yanek Mieczkowski.
        p. cm.
    Includes bibliographical references and index.
    ISBN 978-0-8014-5150-8 (cloth : alk. paper)
    1. United States—Politics and government—1953–1961. 2. Artificial satellites, Russian—Political aspects—United States.   3. Sputnik satellites—History. 4. Astronautics and state—United States—History. 5. Eisenhower, Dwight D. (Dwight David), 1890–1969. I. Title.

    E835.M47 2013
    973.921092—dc23
                                        2012029157

Cornell University Press strives to use environmentally responsible suppliers and materials to the fullest extent possible in the publishing of its books. Such materials include vegetable-based, low-VOC inks and acid-free papers that are recycled, totally chlorine-free, or partly composed of nonwood fibers. For further information, visit our website at www.cornellpress.cornell.edu.

Cloth printing   10 9 8 7 6 5 4 3 2 1

For

Yasuko Kawakami
(1927–1944)

Echi Kawakami
(1900–1989)

Tadeusz Mieczkowski
(1885–1965)

CONTENTS

LIST OF ACRONYMS AND ABBREVIATIONS

ABM	Anti-Ballistic Missile
ABMA	Army Ballistic Missile Agency
AEC	Atomic Energy Commission
ARPA	Advanced Research Projects Agency
CEA	Council of Economic Advisors
CIA	Central Intelligence Agency
FY	Fiscal Year
HEW	Health, Education and Welfare
ICBM	Intercontinental Ballistic Missile
IGY	International Geophysical Year
IRBM	Intermediate Range Ballistic Missile
NACA	National Advisory Committee on Aeronautics
NDEA	National Defense Education Act
NRL	Naval Research Laboratory
NSC	National Security Council
ODM SAC	Office of Defense Mobilization Science Advisory Committee
PSAC	Presidential Science Advisory Committee
SAC	Strategic Air Command
SCORE	Signal Communication by Orbiting Relay
TCP	Technological Capabilities Panel
TVA	Tennessee Valley Authority
USIA	United States Information Agency

Introduction

"Now, so far as the satellite itself is concerned, that does not raise my apprehensions, not one iota."

President Dwight D. Eisenhower sounded calm at an October 9, 1957, news conference, five days after the Soviet Union launched Sputnik, the world's first satellite. When a reporter asked about national security concerns "with the Russian satellite whirling about the world," Eisenhower tried to dispel any notion that the new object in the heavens should cause alarm. He insisted that a satellite represented a scientific development, not a military threat.

The satellite might have genuinely caused him no fear; or he might have been trying to dampen political damage by downplaying it. Skeptical reporters peppered him with questions. One asked whether American scientists erred by "not recognizing that we were, in effect in a race with Russia," thus failing to give the U.S. satellite project top priority and speed. Another queried whether Eisenhower could "give the public any assurance that our own satellite program will be brought up to par with Russia or possibly an improvement on it." Still another asked "why we seem to be lagging behind the Soviets."[1]

What a difference a week made. The previous week, Eisenhower had given a press conference that reporters praised "as one of his best ever," recalled William Ewald, an Eisenhower speechwriter and biographer.[2] Most questions that day centered on the Little Rock, Arkansas, school desegregation crisis, and the president handled each question deftly. He emphasized "respect for the law" and specified that federal troops were "not there as part of the segregation problem. They are there to uphold the courts of the land."

But the perception of leadership had been a problem for the former five-star general since he became president in 1953, as the press and pundits faulted him for passivity. At the October 3 press conference, one journalist challenged Ike, saying that "some of your critics feel you were too slow in asserting a vigorous leadership in this integration crisis."[3] After Sputnik, the matter of Eisenhower's assertiveness as president became a central issue in newspapers and politics. The space race intensified questions about Eisenhower's presidency and highlighted critical issues of the 1950s: world prestige, economic strength, national security, science, education, and American ideals. With U.S. politics roiled by concerns ranging from race relations to nuclear warfare, Sputnik served as a focal point for criticism and a political weapon for Eisenhower's foes on the left and the right.

Sputnik was one of America's darkest Cold War moments, at least as the press portrayed it. The United States was caught unawares, and the Soviet technological triumph signaled the apparent superiority of the USSR's rocketry and weapons systems, scientific prowess, and political leadership. In a contest between different systems of government and ways of life, Americans had assumed that theirs were better and would someday prevail. Sputnik bludgeoned that confidence, and the media bemoaned America's vulnerability.

As this book will show, the Sputnik uproar was more apparent than real. It was the press and politicians who generated noise, capitalizing on the event for attention and electoral gain. The Sputnik "panic" showed the divergence between popular opinion and elite voices, a chasm that some historians have tried to close by describing the public as fearful and traumatized by Sputnik; that characterization generated a myth that has continued through the decades. Yet this myth also holds important truths and insights regarding not only the Eisenhower presidency but also world prestige, the state of space exploration and science education in the United States, and the federal government's role in promoting both.

This book addresses the perception and reality of Sputnik within three critical frameworks. First, Sputnik tested Eisenhower's leadership. The satellite sent shock waves through various levels—in the closely connected areas of international affairs and military competition, in domestic political bat-

tles, and within party politics, as both the Democratic and Republican parties anticipated the 1960 election. All three levels intersected in the years
after Sputnik. On balance, the satellite was more a political threat to Eisenhower than a military one to the nation. Yet the manufactured perception
of a weakened America had a powerful domestic impact. It allowed younger,
more agile politicians to generate publicity, making startling claims about
America's defenses and enhancing their presidential ambitions. The contrast
between the principal aspirants to the White House—Democratic Senate
Majority Leader Lyndon Johnson, Senator John Kennedy, Vice President
Richard Nixon—and the sixty-seven-year-old president became striking.
In many ways, this book revolves around not just one but four men who
occupied or would occupy the Oval Office, examining how they flowed in
Sputnik's slipstream and how their personalities, quirks, and political calculus shaped their reactions to the satellite. Johnson especially orchestrated
the post-Sputnik fallout to work in his favor, grabbing headlines with spectacular quotes, leading a Senate investigation into American "preparedness,"
and gaining credentials as a statesman. But all three politicians appreciated
Sputnik's significance and pledged to do something about it. They urged
more federal commitment to rockets, national defense, and science. Their
more energetic, visionary responses to Sputnik made Eisenhower look like
a stodgy, marginal player in a fast-paced game.

Sputnik thus ripped off the veneer that critics claimed covered Eisenhower, exposing a part-time, golfing president who allowed the Soviet Union
to surpass the United States. A health crisis in November 1957 further undermined Eisenhower's presidency by raising doubts about whether he was
physically competent to execute the office and mirroring what seemed an
anemic America, which contrasted poorly with a Soviet Union surging behind its bombastic leader, Premier Nikita Khrushchev. Sputnik had been
a gamble for him, and he reaped rich rewards when it paid off. His boasts
became credible and his desires feasible. He wanted another meeting with
Eisenhower, he announced; he got one, which garnered worldwide attention, leveled the playing field between the two nations, and began a Cold
War tradition of superpower summitry. In a sense, these changes all started
with Sputnik, and they happened at Eisenhower's expense.

Delivering yet another blow to Eisenhower, the economy sputtered in
1957–58 and then again in 1960. The 1957–58 recession prompted thump-
ing Democratic victories in the 1958 midterm elections, which handicapped
Eisenhower further and stood as an omen for the 1960 presidential election.
By 1958, Eisenhower's principles and priorities seemed in question—his fiscal conservatism, national security strategies, cordial congressional relations,

and methods to maintain America's global reputation. He was a wounded president. Yet this book will show how his principles and priorities continued to guide his decisions after Sputnik, acting as a polestar he could continually follow during crisis.

Every presidential term has tough times, and deft presidents learn to stage comebacks, even improbable ones. A diminished reputation, in fact, provides powerful incentive for presidents to redeem themselves. Facing an onslaught of criticism after Sputnik, Eisenhower's White House at first fumbled. Then the president launched a counterattack. The shift in his leadership was real, and its results magnified Eisenhower's presidential legacy, often in unexpected ways. He used the new medium of television to speak to Americans about the country's defenses, acquiesced to new military programs, and forged new bonds with the scientific community. He cooperated with Congress to give direction to America's space efforts and more federal support for education. He also assumed an ambitious schedule of foreign trips to parlay his popularity into a better U.S. image overseas. In taking these actions, Eisenhower went beyond his comfortable role as statesman and became a barnstorming diplomat; he also helped to forge institutions that seemed inimical to his earlier notions of federal power and good governance.

The creation of critical Cold War institutions is the second framework for analyzing Sputnik and its aftermath. NASA and its sister institution, the Advanced Research Projects Agency (ARPA), were the direct results of Eisenhower's efforts to reassert America's space and military superiority. To stimulate science instruction and its attendant gains in research and technology, Eisenhower approved the National Defense Education Act, one of the twentieth century's landmark education bills. He reformulated the panel of presidential science advisors into the Presidential Science Advisory Committee (PSAC) and enjoyed perhaps the closest relations with the scientific community of any president. These institutions and actions transcended Eisenhower's term in office, ensuring that his post-Sputnik energy would reverberate over ensuing generations.

Then there was the space race itself, this book's third framework of analysis. The scope of scientific achievement during Eisenhower's presidency was astonishing. American satellites were technological marvels, far superior to those of the Soviet Union, and they yielded data that changed scientists' views on the earth and solar system. While Eisenhower was in office, satellites also achieved breakthroughs in communications, navigation, and meteorology. In addition, by his presidency's conclusion, America was orbiting more satellites than the Soviet Union—in fact, more than three times as many. Eisenhower even agreed to back the country's first program to send humans into space, Project Mercury. Thus, the notion that the United States trailed the USSR in the space race made for a dramatic, foreboding news story—and the media trumpeted it—but it was false. Although he has received little credit for it, the real truth was that Eisenhower's space initiatives were impressive.

Eisenhower's policy responses to Sputnik constituted fine achievements, and one reason observers overlooked them was his leadership style, which was characterized by quiet effectiveness and incremental strides rather than headline-grabbing leaps. His actions took place almost in shadow, away from the media's center spotlight, and failed to attract attention. Furthermore, these developments ran contrary to some of his stated policies and even clashed with his principles. For example, he initially opposed a civilian space agency, yet he changed his mind and fostered NASA's founding. Wary of connecting military and civilian projects, he ended up inaugurating an ambitious missile-building program—the fruits of which became clear during the Cuban Missile Crisis—that linked scientific research with military applications. He also supported satellites for ostensibly open scientific research, but a powerful ulterior motive was reconnaissance. Indeed, the secrecy surrounding spy satellite programs such as Corona, whose espionage contributions became known only after Eisenhower left office, suggests another reason why his presidency received too little credit for America's space program. Corona illustrated Eisenhower's relentless focus on national security, his foremost concern. These Cold War contributions became declassified only decades after the Cold War ended, and the benefits they bestowed on the country's defenses raise Eisenhower's achievement level far higher than his contemporaries—and even later historians—judged. Ultimately, what Eisenhower accomplished laid the groundwork for many dividends in security, surveillance, and science. They also enhanced the military-industrial complex against which he warned in private and, by 1961, in public. The contemporary media accounts and political manipulation of Sputnik's aftermath have occluded this complicated legacy.

Within his own time, Eisenhower got to see some rewards. After a post-Sputnik plunge, his standing with Americans recovered, and as he prepared to transfer the presidency to Kennedy, his popularity and principles were largely restored. Yet even as public affection for him rebounded, the questions of leadership remained. When Eisenhower left office, media assessments from both the left and the right carped about his record. The *Washington Post* said that he failed "to supply decisive leadership in domestic and foreign affairs" and "to use the full powers of the Presidency in a period when nothing else suffices." The paper called the president "an extreme economic conservative with an overly finite view of what the Nation could afford." Calling Ike a "miserable" president, the conservative *National Review* said that Khrushchev took advantage of Eisenhower's "lethargy, indecision, and ignorance." The liberal *New Republic* compared Eisenhower to Calvin Coolidge, calling both men "capable of building Nothingness into an immense success."[4]

For all of Eisenhower's achievements, he never fully grasped the concept of prestige. For him, it was vital that the economy recovered from the 1957–58 recession and continued to act as the world's free-market showcase for prosperity. Similarly, he never publicly dispelled the myth of the "missile gap" even though he held reconnaissance evidence showing how baseless were claims of Soviet superiority in rockets. Rather, he rested serene with the knowledge that the United States was far ahead of the USSR in missile numbers and technology, and he kept quiet about it. Capitol Hill critics who cried for increased defense spending were wrong; in reality, America's defenses were "awesome," as Eisenhower put it, and he made sure of it. Yet by eschewing the game of prestige, Eisenhower created problems in domestic and international politics. It was no mere accident that the politician who seized on this issue most deftly, John Kennedy, nabbed the Democratic nomination and ran an aggressive campaign, placing Republican nominee Richard Nixon on the defensive. Kennedy's victory revealed the domestic costs of failing to recognize the significance of prestige. In the international arena, prestige translated to power; it was political and diplomatic currency, yet Eisenhower dismissed one means at his disposal—the space race—to enhance America's Cold War standing and secure imaginative methods to woo and wed allies, old and new alike.

One way of describing the Cold War, then, is as a *prestige race*. It was a competition whose terms were hard to measure; winners and losers were not always clear-cut, nor were the means for enhancing world prestige obvious. Still, the prestige race was a defining aspect of the Cold War, and the world carefully watched the superpower competition. The contest for prestige permeated the space saga, because the desire for a greater international reputation motivated space exploits. Space was not just about science and a new frontier; concerns about national image suffused the contest. Eisenhower had firm ideas about bolstering America's world standing, and his views clashed with those of political rivals who vied to succeed him. After Sputnik, Kennedy, Johnson, and Nixon shrewdly jumped on space as a political issue, and their stances revealed much about their character and ambition. During the 1960 election, Kennedy and Nixon vigorously sparred over space and the related concept of world prestige. At the time, America had the edge in the space and arms races, even if the public was unaware of it. But the country seemed to be losing the prestige race. The fault, Kennedy charged, lay with the Eisenhower administration.

The resulting drive to recoup America's prestige fomented one of history's sharpest disagreements between a current and former president. Once in office, Kennedy challenged America to land men on the moon. Eisenhower groused that his young successor was pulling a "stunt" that was just plain "nuts." The nation could enhance its prestige in more constructive ways, he insisted. This book will illustrate how Eisenhower's and Kennedy's conflicting views epitomized differences in their personalities, economic philosophies, generations, and politics. And although Kennedy's sensational goal of landing Americans on the moon had merit, NASA's subsequent efforts to fly manned space vehicles, especially the shuttle, also confirmed the wisdom of Eisenhower's views.

The space race began more than half a century ago, when America struggled against a formidable military and ideological adversary. That race ended with a U.S. victory. Yet the prestige race has transcended the Cold War, and it will continue to define world relations. It will prod and sometimes trouble Americans, especially as they face twenty-first-century challenges from emerging economic competitors (such as the BRIC countries—Brazil, Russia, India, and China). As this happens, the Sputnik story will remain a trope that Americans can repair to, looking for inspiration and answers. Indeed, new versions of the "Sputnik moment" abound. In 2011, *Newsweek* magazine reported that China had introduced the world's most powerful supercomputer, a development that chagrined U.S. engineers who assumed that such a prized possession would belong to their country. The magazine called it "a Sputnik moment." Earlier that year, President Barack Obama delivered a State of the Union address during a paralyzing economic downturn, and he mentioned an incident of which he had no firsthand recollection, being the first chief executive born after Eisenhower's presidency. He invoked the Sputnik launch and its effects—a defeat that the United States transformed into victory. "This is our generation's Sputnik moment," Obama said of the country's debilitating recession. The satellite dazed Americans, and "we had no idea how we would beat [the Soviets] to the moon. The science wasn't even there yet. NASA didn't exist," he said. But the United States invested in science and education and unleashed a flurry of technology that stimulated economic growth, and eventually, the Americans beat the Soviets to the moon. What seemed like a debacle instead marked

America's great Cold War moment, and Obama—like presidents before him—sought to draw from that well of historical purpose to energize present-day efforts. Understanding that moment and its complicated legacy requires being attuned to the concept and significance of world prestige.[5]

The Sputnik launch was a seminal twentieth-century event, and it helped to define Eisenhower's legacy. Although the small satellite might not have raised his apprehensions by "one iota," it changed his presidency. It induced a severe test of his leadership; yet from that moment grew significant accomplishments, many reflecting his principles and priorities.

PART ONE

Sputnik

 **CHAPTER 1**

What Was the Sputnik "Panic"?

Eisenhower enjoyed his home in Gettysburg, Pennsylvania. In 1950, when he and his wife, Mamie, had purchased the property, a bucolic piece of land that was once part of the Civil War battlefield, they had planned to retire there. They remodeled the house, and the residence assumed greater importance after the president's 1955 heart attack, when doctors advised Eisenhower to avoid the high altitude of the First Lady's home state, Colorado, where they had liked to vacation. So the couple began to use their Gettysburg house and 496-acre farm as a getaway, going there almost every weekend. It was just twenty minutes from Camp David, and the scenic drive from Washington to southern Pennsylvania was relaxing. Once at the house, the Eisenhowers had plenty of creature comforts. They particularly enjoyed the home's back room, with its expansive glass ceilings and walls, which gave a marvelous view of their backyard and drenched them in sunlight on nice days. There they would sit, with Ike typically reading or painting and Mamie watching television.

For the weekend beginning Friday, October 4, 1957, Eisenhower returned to Gettysburg, anticipating pleasant diversions from the grind of his presidential duties. He could watch over a herd of prized Angus cattle, which provided steak for barbecues where he cooked and entertained. He could go trapshooting, golf, or paint. Eisenhower was looking forward to these diversions when he received a telephone call from Washington. Something big had happened in the Soviet Union.

The news first hit the United States on Friday evening, just after six o'clock. The event's epicenter was a desert in the Kazak Republic, east of the Aral Sea, site of the Soviet Union's rocket launch complex but an area so barren and remote that NASA engineer James Oberg remarked after a visit, "If Earth has any human settlement halfway into outer space, this is it." The spot was secretive, and Soviets called their spaceport "Baikonur," after a distant mining town; the deceptive name was part of an attempt to keep their space activities concealed, even though American U-2 spy planes had detected the spaceport's construction. Near the rocket launch-pad, a group of Soviet engineers and military officials shoehorned themselves into a small, bunkered room, listening anxiously to radio receivers. The room was so quiet with anticipation, one colonel later recalled, that the only audible sounds were people breathing and radios crackling with static. When they finally heard beeping over the radio, the room erupted in cheers.[1]

The Soviets had fired an R-7 ICBM rocket that carried the world's first artificial satellite, "Sputnik" (abbreviated from *Iskustvennyi Sputnik Zemli*, meaning "artificial fellow traveler around the earth"), and the beeps confirmed that it was orbiting the earth. Sputnik was simple: just a small, shiny aluminum sphere, 22 inches in diameter—about the size of a beach ball—with four metal antennae protruding from it, two of them almost 10 feet long. Its scientific payload was meager: a radio transmitter, batteries, and temperature gauges.[2] But for its role in history, Sputnik was gigantic. It had ushered in the Space Age.

Scientists debate where "outer space" begins, but some peg it at roughly 100 kilometers, or 62 miles, above the earth's surface. The rocket that launched Sputnik consisted of three stages, with the third stage reaching 142 miles in altitude before the satellite (essentially, a fourth stage) separated to begin orbit. The satellite raced around the earth at 18,000 miles per hour, the speed needed to counteract gravity and achieve orbit, at a maximum altitude of 560 miles. Every hour and a half, it made a complete orbit.[3] To maximize its propaganda value, Russian scientists directed the satellite to circle the earth's most populated areas. They had polished its metal surface to reduce friction heat and increase reflection of the sun's rays, making it more visible. Astronomers tracked its path, and at dawn and dusk Americans nationwide strained to see it, visible as a glowing dot arcing across the sky. Radio operators in Riverhead, Long Island, were the first to hear Sputnik's eerie "beep . . . beep . . . beep." One NBC commentator dramatically announced, "Listen now for the sound which forever more separates the old from the new." The satellite also created a cascade of events that nearly paralyzed Eisenhower's presidency.[4]

 ## "They're Miners and They're Peasants"

George Reedy, an assistant to Senate Majority Leader Lyndon Johnson and later his presidential press secretary, recalled that Sputnik's launch hit Americans "like a brick through a plate-glass window, shattering into tiny slivers the American illusion of technical superiority over the Soviet Union." Before Sputnik, Americans had looked down on their adversary, ridiculing crude, clunky Russian equipment prone to breakdowns. "How do you double the value of a Soviet car?" went one joke. The answer: "Fill up its gas tank." According to another wisecrack, the Soviets could never smuggle a nuclear bomb inside a suitcase because they still needed a good suitcase. Harry Truman, who dismissed Russians as "those Asiatics," once predicted, "Do you know when Russia will build the [atom] bomb? Never."[5]

The cartoonish vituperations had a point: the Soviet Union had formidable military strength but a backward economy. Just two months before Sputnik, *Fortune* magazine reported that the Soviets "want to slow down the arms race, at least for a while, because the U.S. pace is too stiff for their existing technical resources to match." Soviet technology and workmanship were suspect. Premier Nikita Khrushchev acknowledged that in the past Soviet helicopters "weren't too reliable, and we had quite a few accidents with them," prompting recommendations that he avoid flying in them. During the Korean War, spectacular dogfights featured American-built Sabre jets battling Russian-made MiG-15 fighters. The Soviets enjoyed a fearsome reputation in aircraft design, and in some respects the MiGs outperformed the Sabres. Overall, though, the U.S. warplane's superiority was clear. After a North Korean pilot defected, U.S. engineers examined his MiG-15. Chuck Yeager, the World War II ace and test pilot, commended it as "a pretty good fighting machine" but noted that it was "a quirky airplane that's killed a lot of its pilots." The MiG had a host of mechanical problems, and the North Korean defector warned against activating a fuel pump that could destroy part of the plane. Before he flew the Soviet jet, Yeager recalled thinking, "Man, that thing is a flying booby trap, and nobody will be surprised if I get killed."[6]

Aware of poor Soviet technology, disdainful of their political and economic system, Americans underestimated their Russian counterparts. The mere notion of the USSR trumping the United States in a scientific endeavor seemed far-fetched. Hans Bethe, the Cornell University physicist who worked on the Manhattan Project and served on Eisenhower's Presidential Science Advisory Committee, recalled that before Sputnik, Americans "were terribly conceited. We thought only we could do great [scientific and engineering] achievements."[7] In fact, during the twentieth century, Americans had grown used to being first, and they bathed in the glow of prestige that accompanied historic technological firsts.

After World War II, the United States enjoyed an atom bomb monopoly and unparalleled economic and military strength. Rivals such as Japan and Germany lay ruined, as did former superpowers Great Britain and France. Had any of those countries launched the world's first satellite, the effect on the United States would hardly have been severe. They lay prostrate enough that Americans felt sorry for them.

In a way, the Soviet Union had also been vanquished during World War II, suffering tremendous losses even though on the Allied side. Nearly thirty million of its people died, and Adolf Hitler's troops inflicted great physical damage when they invaded Russia. The country was "flat on its back" after the war, recalled Spurgeon Keeny, an arms control expert who worked for the Defense Department's Office of Research, Development, and Engineering. In August 1945, when Eisenhower visited Moscow, he remembered that "damn near all [Josef Stalin] talked about was all the things they needed, the homes, the food, the technical help." As Eisenhower flew back to Europe, he crossed a ravaged Russia, with not a single house standing from Moscow westward.[8]

As a result, Americans grew accustomed to thinking of Russians as a backward, beaten people, an impression that lasted into the 1950s. One of the most crippling problems that Soviet citizens endured was a housing shortage so severe that entire families lived in one room of an apartment. Conditions in Moscow were so bad, Americans learned, that the question "Is the bathroom free?" was actually inquiring whether someone lived in it. One New Yorker recalled that when Sputnik was launched, "the public mood was, 'How could this happen to us? How could we be second to the Russians?'" They seemed little more than a "cold people in a cold land," he remembered. "They're not scientists—they're miners and they're peasants. . . . How could they beat us?" Sputnik came as a big surprise. Ralph Nader, the future consumer advocate and third-party presidential candidate, was a Harvard Law School student at the time of the launch, and he remembered that the news "hit the campus like a thunderbolt."[9]

It should not have been so. Although ravaged by World War II, the Soviet Union was still America's rival, an economic competitor with growth averaging a spectacular 11–12 percent during the early 1950s.[10] Russians could achieve technological breakthroughs, and Americans had already raced against them in various arenas. Using stolen secrets, the Soviets implemented a crash program to develop weapons of mass destruction, exploding their first atomic bomb in 1949 and first hydrogen device in 1953, just one year after America's H-bomb. Americans suddenly "recognized that we did not have a monopoly on scientific and engineering developments," Bethe said. The atomic and hydrogen bombs, horrifying yardsticks of scientific progress, intensified American feelings that their Cold War rival offered stiff competition. Moreover, the 1950 capture of German scientist Klaus Fuchs in Britain for funneling atomic bomb secrets to the Soviet Union led some Americans to assume that the Russians were privy to all U.S. secrets and stepping-stones to development. "Suddenly people said, 'Everything we know, the Soviets now know,'" Keeny commented.[11]

During a 1956 visit to the Soviet Union as a Senate Armed Services Committee member, Henry Jackson observed the paradox of a supposedly backward country that could achieve breakthroughs. He noted that Soviet living standards lagged far behind those in the United States, and few Soviet citizens had cars or modern home appliances. "Daily life in Russia is still drab and largely without comforts," he wrote. "One sees deprivation on every hand—in the stores and on the streets, in people's clothes and in their homes." Soviet infrastructure was primitive; Jackson noticed that "many of the airfields in the Soviet Union lack concrete or hard-surface runways. Sod or grass runways are quite common."[12] Yet Jackson believed that the backwardness belied a latent capacity for progress. Ironically, the poverty of its people allowed Russia to make industrial gains. "Just because civilian consumption is held down, a large proportion of Russian production can be reinvested—notably in new machines," he believed. "The Kremlin ploughs the standard of living of the people into new capital equipment."

Moreover, Jackson noted, the Russians relished a race. "On my trip I found the Russians constantly talking in terms of industrial competition with us," he said. "The Russians think in terms of only one probable outcome to this competition—beating us. . . . Of course, beating us industrially is a polite way of saying that they intend to achieve a position where they can have their way in the world." Jackson also saw schools emphasizing math, physics, chemistry, and technology, and he visited a large observatory whose director said that "they expected to view from this observatory the new satellite that is to be launched by the Soviet Union."[13]

What Sputnik Signified

The notion of a "race" with the Soviet Union permeated Cold War thought, and it applied not only to space but to nuclear arms. On August 26, 1957, the USSR proclaimed that it had tested an intercontinental ballistic missile that flew more than 4,000 miles. That successful test encouraged Khrushchev to give final approval to use the ICBM rocket to launch a satellite, in effect getting two propaganda victories for the price of one. To the United States, the ICBM test plus Sputnik demonstrated that Russia indeed had rockets powerful enough to launch nuclear weapons that could reach Western Europe or even North America. A scientist working on the U.S. satellite project acknowledged that Sputnik signified that "the Russians must have the intercontinental ballistic missile as they claim." Before Sputnik, U.S. intelligence had predicted that the Soviets would have an ICBM around 1961–62.[14]

Sputnik confirmed what many Americans suspected and the media reported: the Soviet Union led the United States in rocket technology. According to one poll, half of all Americans believed the USSR did lead. Sputnik "validated Khrushchev's very bellicose statements about missiles," recalled Eugene Skolnikoff, the staff secretary for PSAC. "In the summer of '57 he was saying a lot about how ballistic missiles of the Soviet Union could swamp the United States, and no one believed him. . . . And Sputnik, in one fell swoop, validated it."[15] But Eisenhower argued that Sputnik represented only a scientific achievement, not a military threat, a diminution of U.S. strength, or a change in world power. Still, its military value was clear. In addition to the rocket, the scientific information on the earth's atmosphere would help in plotting ICBM flight paths. Senate Majority Leader and Texas Democrat Lyndon B. Johnson, then one of the country's most powerful politicians, warned that soon the Soviets "will be dropping bombs on us from space like kids dropping rocks onto cars from freeway overpasses." A future Senate majority leader, Democrat Mike Mansfield of Montana, said, "What is at stake is nothing less than our survival."

Khrushchev, for his part, gloated as he watched "our potential enemies cringe in fright." One Cold War race was the contest for world prestige, and as Sputnik leapt into space, it also jumped over America's international image. One Texan wrote to Johnson that the Soviet Union had "gained as much prestige as we have lost." But he added that "this matter of prestige isn't so terribly important . . . but Russia's domination of space, perhaps, has sinister overtones. All of the newspapers have carried articles stating that the moon, and space, could be a formidable base for super-weapons. To sum it up, the general opinion seems to be that 'he who controls space controls the world'"—a phrase that Johnson later unleashed with great political panache.[16]

A land with geographic security, America now seemed suddenly vulnerable. By 1957, the Soviet Union had had the atomic bomb for eight years, but the primary means of delivering it was bombers, which U.S. forces stood a good chance of intercepting and destroying. Not so with rocket-powered missiles. Republican congressman Gerald Ford of Michigan commented, "We Middle Westerners are sometimes called isolationists. I don't agree with the label; but there can be no isolationists anywhere when a thermonuclear warhead can flash down from space at hypersonic speed to reach any spot on earth minutes after its launching." Rockets, launched thousands of miles away, were the most deadly delivery mechanism known to man, and Sputnik, flying over the United States, proved the Soviet threat. It was not the satellite itself that was disturbing but more the rocket that put Sputnik in orbit.[17]

Throughout history, nations have clashed over new frontiers—on land, on water, or in the air—and control over vistas have signified world dominance. The British navy's command of the oceans once represented the most visible symbol of England's empire, while America's own Great White Fleet paralleled the U.S. rise to world power in the early twentieth century. Air power and jets enabled the United States to achieve even greater military strength. Space was the newest frontier, and after their success in flight, Americans might have assumed that they would be the first in space, too. [18]

Sputnik shattered that assumption and represented a revolution, too. Warfare would now rely not just on tanks, ships, and planes but more on science, and America's lead might no longer be secure. During World War II, Americans drew the connection between science and security, witnessing how technology could either enhance or threaten freedom with breakthroughs such as proximity fuses, radar, and the atom bomb. But it was Hitler's V-2 rockets that terrorized Great Britain, and amid the Cold War, Sputnik gave rise to statements implying that the Soviet Union and its allies would similarly use its regimented science training and technical achievements to threaten the free world.[19]

Further developments threatened. After Sputnik, a *New York Post* headline blared as if in warning, "Soviets say MORE COMING." *Newsday* concluded that there was one question "the U.S. did not express, but which fearfully came to mind: What else were the Russian scientists working on?" One possibility, influential columnist Walter Lippmann speculated, was that "the Soviets will have operational missiles capable of neutralizing the allied bases in Western Europe and the Middle East," which would force America completely to reformulate its foreign policy.[20]

No one knew precisely what would come next, and secrecy shrouded Sputnik. At first, the Soviets released no pictures of their satellite, so even its appearance remained a mystery; only on October 9, five days after the launch, did the Russians distribute a photo. Scientists were uncertain about how long Sputnik could stay in orbit; some predictions said thirty years (in reality, it lasted just ninety-two days, reentering the earth's atmosphere and disintegrating on January 4, 1958). Speculation ran rampant about the satellite's composition, power source, and the meaning of its eerie "beeps." Moscow boasted that Sputnik beamed back valuable data but gave no details. Detecting changes in the beeps, some American scientists figured that the electronic pulses represented a code but had trouble guessing its importance. "It's hard to tell if it represents real information," commented John Hagen, the scientist who headed America's satellite program. Indeed, when strange events happened while Sputnik flew overheard, it took the blame. A Schenectady, New York, man claimed that it was the satellite that had caused his garage door to open mysteriously.[21]

James Killian recalled that two aspects of the satellite troubled him: "Russian," meaning a blow to America's pride, and "184-pound." Sputnik's remarkable weight shocked Americans. A planned American satellite was to weigh just 21.5 pounds. Scientist Joseph Kaplan expressed awe at Sputnik's weight. "This is really fantastic, and if they can launch that they can launch much heavier ones." The Soviet figure was so stunning that some government officials doubted its accuracy. Rear Admiral Rawson Bennett, chief of naval operations, belittled Sputnik as a "hunk of iron almost anybody could launch" and questioned its real weight.[22]

Eisenhower was skeptical, too. At a National Security Council meeting, he asked aides about a report that someone had misplaced a decimal point in reporting the satellite's weight. Speaking to reporters, he conceded that "if it is 180 pounds, I think it has astonished our scientists; I would say that." He later wrote, "The Soviet achievement was impressive. The size of the thrust required to propel a satellite of this weight came as a distinct surprise to us." U.S. rockets produced a maximum of 150,000 pounds of thrust, while the rocket that put Sputnik in orbit, Eisenhower learned, generated 200,000.[23] In truth, it was more. The R-7 rocket that boosted Sputnik into orbit had almost one million pounds of thrust. For the rest of the 1950s, the impact of powerful Soviet rockets left a deep impression worldwide. The Soviets, people concluded, led America in space because they had more powerful rockets, and that conclusion proved nearly impossible to erase. Bigger implied better, and those who subscribed to this notion concluded that the Russians had a superior satellite.[24]

In truth, the Soviets had no choice. They launched their rocket from a higher latitude than Florida's Cape Canaveral, on the same parallel as North Dakota, and thus they had less spin from the earth's rotation to act as a natural boost to the rocket. Years later, another reason for Sputnik's weight became obvious. The Soviets could not miniaturize their scientific devices as American scientists could; ironically, their satellite's size reflected crude technology. Jokes about gigantic Soviet batteries were standard Cold War fare, and Sputnik had three of them, with zinc chargers that weighed 122 pounds—two thirds of the satellite's total weight. John Townsend, Jr., a scientist working for the Naval Research Laboratory, commented that none of the early Soviet satellites were sophisticated. They used "common metals, not lightweight alloys. They used radio tubes instead of transistors. . . . Later, when I was in Moscow and saw the hardware, it was clear that they had brute-forced everything." Over the long term, scientific and technological advances mattered most. Yet in the strange alchemy of world publicity, the Soviet contraption's sheer scale attracted awe, even though the smaller American space devices were more advanced.[25]

Eisenhower knew that launching such a satellite into orbit was a significant technical accomplishment, but firing off nuclear warheads required much more rocket thrust. Sputnik's weight "was not commensurate with anything of great military significance, and that was also a factor in putting it in [proper] perspective," General Andrew Goodpaster, Eisenhower's staff secretary, recalled. But media outlets leapt to more ominous conclusions. England's *Manchester Guardian* commented that the Soviet Union "can now build ballistic missiles capable of hitting any chosen target anywhere in the world."[26]

That was wrong. In reality, aiming a rocket across thousands of miles to a specific target was more complicated than shooting a satellite into space orbit. Eisenhower's military experience had taught him that perfecting a weapon as complex as the ICBM would take years, even if the Soviets had successfully tested one. Moreover, Soviet missile guidance systems were still crude. Khrushchev admitted, "It always sounded good to say in public speeches that we could hit a fly at any distance with our missiles. Despite the wide radius of destruction caused by our nuclear warheads, pinpoint accuracy was still necessary—and it was difficult to achieve." In fact, the R-7 proved impractical as an ICBM: it took hours to fuel, needed to be moved aboard railcars, and was vulnerable to U.S. bombers. It was hardly the breakthrough it seemed. Later, Khrushchev confessed that the R-7 was shaky; its value, he said, was only in the prestige race, as "a symbolic counter threat to the United States" because it was otherwise unreliable.[27]

Scientists and defense experts knew that dropping a bomb from a satellite was impossible, too, because any object released from a satellite would not drop to the earth but go into orbit. Deputy Defense Secretary Donald Quarles informed Eisenhower at a meeting two weeks after Sputnik that the United States itself already had military rockets powerful enough to launch 500 pounds into orbit, and the president knew that the United States outpaced the Soviets in guidance systems. That information appealed to Eisenhower's interest in the big picture and in understanding all the pieces. He liked to examine "relative probabilities," as he put it. As long as the United States had enough deterrent capabilities and abilities to respond to a Soviet first attack, he said, the enemy lacked "total capabilities." Sputnik changed none of this picture; Eisenhower remained confident that America's defenses remained effective. "We still can destroy Russia. We know it," he declared at a cabinet meeting two weeks after Sputnik was launched.[28]

 ## A Press and Political Panic

In June 1957, *New York Times* correspondent Max Frankel reported from Moscow that the Soviet Union planned to launch artificial earth satellites "before the end of 1958." As Frankel later recalled, his story "faintly hinted at the derision we Americans still felt for Soviet technology," as he wrote that the first satellite "will be of some undisclosed size and will circle the earth at some undisclosed altitude." He continued, "The scientists suggested that their models would be superior to the United States satellite but insisted they had no desire to compete with Americans for the first launching." Frankel's editors buried the story inside the newspaper.[29] The condescension and blasé attitude set the stage for a media uproar and national wake-up call.

The Soviet government newspaper *Izvestia* said that "hysteria" gripped America in Sputnik's wake. But the vast majority of Americans did not panic after Sputnik, nor did the satellite generate any deep fear among the populace. As authors Matt Bille and Erika Lishock have written, "It has become accepted that Sputnik generated widespread panic among the American people. . . . In fact, there is no evidence this took place." Some politicians admitted as much, although they were eager to capitalize on the political fallout. In Texas two weeks after Sputnik, Lyndon Johnson said, "I am not trying to scare you today because I am not very scared myself. I don't believe you are either. There have been no signs of panic that I have detected among the great mass of our people."[30] Still, Johnson and other politicians were all too eager to seize on the event.

Occasional remarks indicated that some individuals felt fearful. At a dinner party in Washington, Budget Director Percival Brundage tried to brush off Sputnik by saying that it would be forgotten within six months. His dinner companion replied that "in six months we may all be dead." In a street interview, one woman commented, "It gets the American people alarmed that a foreign country—especially an enemy country—can do this. We fear this. We fear that they have something out there that the majority of people don't know about."[31] But the president refused to feel fearful of or defeated by Sputnik, and many Americans, especially those involved in science and engineering, did the same—and even felt some cold rage. Working at the time for the Army Ballistic Missile Agency in Huntsville, engineer John Twigg acknowledged that he felt angry because "it was frustrating to us to have had a rocket that could have done it before the Russians did." Charlie Mars was a college student who felt "mad" at Sputnik's launch, he recalled, because "we should have had the technology to be first." Mars's anger impelled him to become an electrical engineer; he later worked on Project Apollo and the space shuttle.[32]

Most public opinion data revealed no trepidation. *Newsweek*'s "Listening Post" survey of national public opinion concluded, "There was concern, but no panic" among Americans. In Boston, a *Newsweek* correspondent reported, "The general reaction here indicates massive indifference." The *Milwaukee Sentinel* relegated Sputnik to page two; first-page coverage was on the city's hosting the first game of the World Series.[33] When Eisenhower held a press conference on October 30, only one reporter asked a question that dealt directly with outer space.

Polls conducted after the launch of Sputnik suggested that Americans took the event calmly. For the standard query about "the most important problem" facing America, only 6 percent cited Sputnik or missiles, while another 7 percent mentioned defense and preparedness. A plurality—29 percent—brought up integration and racial problems. One Gallup poll found that 61 percent of Americans still believed that the next great scientific breakthrough would come from the United States, not Russia. Some samples revealed apathy. The Public Opinion Index showed that 40 percent of those surveyed gave Sputnik little thought. In a Minnesota poll, 69 percent believed it mattered little that the Soviets were "ahead of the United States in sending up a satellite," while a Georgia man remarked that the Soviets had "a gadget whizzing around out there somewhere. So what? Are they going to bomb us tomorrow? I don't see the connection."[34]

Future NASA administrator T. Keith Glennan noted that after Sputnik, people grew "preoccupied with the progress of the World Series, or the standings in the pro football league, or the shabby disclosures of the TV quiz show investigations." The media, though, showed inordinate interest in the hot new topic because Sputnik made good copy. Glen Wilson, a member of Johnson's Senate staff, recalled, "The newspapers, of course, played it up quite vigorously. It was front page stuff practically every day for weeks."[35] Eisenhower's critics blamed him for America's world embarrassment. Walter Lippmann wrote in his syndicated column that because the president was "in a kind of partial retirement," no one led America in the space race, and the country likely trailed the Soviets in the ballistic missile race.[36]

Media outlets played up the angle of a "space race" that the United States had lost. *Newsday*'s page-one headline proclaimed, "Russia Wins Space Race"; NBC newscaster Chet Huntley commented, "The Russians, who have a constant feeling of inferiority in the modern world, became terrifically elated when their country was able to win the race in getting a satellite up into space." Arnold Frutkin, who later became a NASA associate administrator, recalled, "The media was just hysterical on the subject, and . . . the people in the Eisenhower administration spent a hell of a lot of time denying that there was any race on. They wanted to treat it as a more routine thing." But the White House found that "the press insisted that we were in a race. So you're in a race whether you want to be or not."[37]

With media rumors speculating about how far the Americans trailed the Soviets in the race, some observers saw a wide gap. As perspicacious a journal as the *Economist* wrote that "there have been hints of [Soviet] new rocket designs and new kinds of missile fuel which suggest that the Americans are not only lagging behind but in certain respects may not yet even be on the same road." Consequently, the magazine predicted, "it is almost certain to be a Russian" who would land first on the moon.[38] Other media stories dwelled on the satellite's destructive potential, which reflected the themes of vulnerability and survival reverberating throughout the Cold War. The *Atlanta Constitution* urged Americans to rally together "to meet the outside challenge which threatens our very existence." To Montana's *Lewiston Daily News*, Sputnik furnished "grim proof that the Reds have solved the fundamental missile problems and that this nation and the Free World are now under Soviet sentence of death." *Newsweek* devoted a special section to "Satellites and Our Safety," while *Time* concluded, "The military threat posed by Sputnik is immense, immediate and sobering."[39]

Two days after the launch, CBS aired a television special on Sputnik in which anchor Douglas Edwards commented, "One meaning very quickly read from the launching of the satellite is an ominous one. This is that the Russians have licked some of the toughest problems of rocket propulsion, the basis of the so-called ultimate weapon, the long-range ballistic missile." Edwards ended the broadcast by stating that "the course of United States policies in the competition with Russia has been severely shaken."[40]

More than media topics, Sputnik and space became political issues. Meeting in mid-October, the International Affairs Seminars of Washington reported, "If there was any trauma following the Russian sputnik, it occurred in Washington and not among the general public. Washington, for its part, took its cue from the newspapers and other issues makers." Some politicians may have sincerely seen a crisis, believing America to be imperiled; their precise motives were impossible to divine. But others recognized that Sputnik presented an opportunity, because Eisenhower was now politically vulnerable, and they pounced. Adlai Stevenson said, "I see nothing wrong in acknowledging Russia's accomplishment. But I see a great deal wrong with kidding ourselves. Not just our pride but our security is at stake."[41]

Sputnik marked the start of a concerted political offensive against Eisenhower that lasted for the rest of his presidency. He had an uneasy relationship with politicians, complaining that they "have a habit of making me ill—mentally and physically!" He railed against "those damn *monkeys* on the Hill," and Edward McCabe, an associate special counsel in the Eisenhower administration who acted as a liaison between the White House and Capitol Hill, recalled that "Congress, as an institution, had no great regard for Eisenhower" and that its members "were looking and hoping that he would slip on something" to give them a line of attack. After Sputnik, William Ewald observed, Democrats finally "had a focus and a theme." Democrats could gain traction against the popular president by portraying him as indifferent or negligent. Sputnik stripped the general of his reputation for wisdom in military matters, and the criticism was more harsh and personal than any he had faced.

After Sputnik, for the first time Eisenhower's popularity slipped below 60 percent and remained there almost continuously for the next year and a half. In the South, a region still smarting over the Little Rock desegregation crisis, Sputnik gave its residents another reason to dislike Ike. One Eisenhower advisor recalled the week after Sputnik as a "prolonged nightmare. Any number of people—from the Pentagon, from State, and from the Hill—were dashing in and out of the President's office. Each new visitor had a longer face than the one before."[42]

The combination of Little Rock and Sputnik emboldened critics to attack Eisenhower with a vigor unseen during his first term. They had special interest in space, both for constituents' projects and their careers. One assistant to Defense Secretary Charlie Wilson observed that Sputnik affected legislators "like heavy drinkers hearing a cork pop." For months, members of Congress had charged that the United States lagged behind the Soviet Union in the arms race, specifically in developing guided missiles. In a February 1957 appearance on NBC's *Meet the Press*, Stuart Symington said, "I don't 'believe' that the Soviets are ahead. I state that they *are* ahead of us."[43] Now congressmen had the space race as an issue, too.

Representing Missouri, Symington had the McDonnell-Douglas Corporation's interests to keep in mind, and Senator Henry Jackson had constituents to cultivate, too. During his lengthy Senate career representing Washington State, Jackson fought so hard to secure government contracts for Seattle's Boeing Aircraft Company that he became known as the "Senator from Boeing." He knew what space meant to Boeing, and he wanted Eisenhower to assume "personal responsibility for making sure our ballistic missile effort is speeded up." Calling Sputnik "a devastating blow," Jackson implored, "This is a life and death matter for our country and the free world, and it should be so treated at the highest levels of our government. Critical decisions must not be left to subordinates," an obvious dig at Eisenhower's alleged habit of delegating the bulk of his work to the White House staff.[44]

Other politicians poured out a mix of invective and dire warnings. Senators called for an investigation by the Senate Armed Services Committee into the lagging American satellite and missile programs. The Democratic Advisory Council, which included former president Harry Truman and Adlai Stevenson, criticized the administration's "dangerous and foolish complacency" and charged that it failed adequately to support American scientists.[45]

The intense media and political scrutiny even forced one Eisenhower defender to change his tune. At first, two days after the Sputnik launch, Republican senator Jacob Javits of New York minimized it. "There was no race to launch the satellite between the USSR and us, unless we create one now, which is directly contrary to our policy," he maintained, adding, "We too shall launch a satellite in due course, and we hope with even more significant results. Right now it is an occasion for congratulations, not bad temper, that a new era is inaugurated to pierce outer space." Yet later that month, perhaps sensing the intense political fallout, Javits's tone became more urgent. He called Sputnik "the most serious challenge to us since the end of World War II," an incredible remark since it implied that the satellite overshadowed even the Berlin blockade, Soviet development of the atom bomb, and the Korean War. On another occasion, he implored, "I urge such a crash program as we need to deal with our defense against any possible Russian Intercontinental Ballistic Missiles and other missiles."[46]

Meanwhile, industry, the military, and scientists hoped to gain more money for space research and hardware. Just as with politicians, genuine concern might have been a motive, but so was opportunism. Aerospace media hoped to ratchet up circulation with space stories, especially those that scared the public. Scientists, although preferring to think of themselves as above the political fray, succumbed to the temptation to capitalize on Sputnik. Hans Bethe recalled that scientists felt that "we had been mistreated before; we thought we should get back into some relationship with the government." Physicist Herbert York remembered that "there were a lot of people . . . in industry and the services and everywhere, who were trying to use the Sputnik event and the psychology that followed it to their advantage. So there were all kinds of people pressing Eisenhower to buy this program, buy that program, do this, do that." York confessed, "I did it myself. I was director of the [Lawrence] Livermore Laboratory when Sputnik went up. We were always trying to get more money." York recalled that when a U.S. senator visited him from Washington, he arranged to have a recording of Sputnik's "beeps" play in the background as they discussed his laboratory budget.[47] Always unabashed, rocket scientist Wernher von Braun said, "There is a crying need for more money for basic and applied research . . . for development of bigger booster engines." At a post-Sputnik press conference, Eisenhower drew reporters' laughter when he cracked, "I have never seen any specialist of any kind that was bashful in asking for Federal money."[48]

Military officers dreamed of fighting wars from space or ruling earth from the heavens. Some military officials used Sputnik as an opportunity to warn Americans, perhaps with the ulterior motive of garnering more federal funds for defense. Army Secretary Wilber Brucker blamed Congress for cutting the defense budget and talked of "the urgency of this critical hour." He warned, "In this age, complacency is a luxury we cannot afford. In order to meet the Soviet challenge . . . we must squarely face all the unpleasant facts and make a sustained effort to build stronger than ever."[49]

These were precisely the reactions Eisenhower wanted to avoid. The Sputnik "panic" was not a public panic but a press and political one. The media, military, politicians, industry, and scientists formed a mass of interests that exaggerated Sputnik's importance, with the ultimate effect of generating support for space and defense programs. The country, Eisenhower feared, would spend money it did not have on programs it did not need. Sputnik showed that some Americans were breathing what Killian called Cold War "vapors," which caused them to react disproportionately to Sputnik. The military's efforts to take advantage of the situation especially upset Eisenhower. "He got very angry," Goodpaster recalled, "whenever the armed services went into public print with rivalry or when they were trying to whip up a sense of danger in order get additional weapons or when people came into the White House to propose a crash program."[50]

Sputnik also showed the media at its worst, and the *Nation* magazine regretted its brethren's eagerness to take advantage of a hot topic. The *Nation* noted that "each week a publisher must look for new ways to build circulation in a culture screaming with hucksters' calls. It is all right for journalists to be constantly racing press deadlines, but when they begin to share their professional headaches with the readers, they give the nation a continuous case of ideological jitters." The Sputnik panic showed the classic schism between the elite opinions of publishers and writers and true public opinion. But the media clamor also generated genuine concerns.[51]

◗ American Materialism and Eisenhower Complacency

As a technological achievement, Sputnik should have impressed Third World nations the most. Instead, it had the greatest impact on the United States, and the country's allies noticed that. London's *Daily Telegraph* believed that Americans "are not suffering from a crisis in technology but a crisis in confidence."[52] Sputnik reversed the world's two great superiority and inferiority complexes. The Soviet Union, battered after World War II and laboring under the shadow of American technological and military superiority, now seemed supreme, while the United States felt inadequate. The satellite struck down national verities. America, the wealthiest nation on earth, was supposed to be the world's technological leader. But in space, the United States had nothing. A tiny satellite forced reappraisals of American materialism and Eisenhower complacency.

Eisenhower recalled during his retirement, "While in governmental councils the Russian accomplishment caused no apprehension respecting national security, the psychological effect upon the entire country was drastic." Some Americans felt a sense of wounded pride. After Eisenhower gave reassurances that Sputnik posed no military threat, the *New York Post* editorialized, "We agree with Ike that the Russian sputnik up there can't hurt us. It isn't armed, it apparently isn't likely to fall on us." But, the paper added, "Despite his reassurances, the country remains uneasy. For the first time we know what it feels like to be a have-not nation. We have no sputniks, and all the rationalizations of all our leaders . . . [do not] alter that fact." Bothering the *Post* (which was a liberal paper in the 1950s) was what it sensed in this apparent defeat: "We see poor planning, lack of imagination, underestimation of our adversary, faulty education, a lack of scientists. . . . We see a nation obsessed with material comforts, more adept at producing washing machines than sputniks."[53]

A leitmotif of 1950s America was the high standard of living and material wealth that made citizens proud of their country and willing to defend it against communism. Sputnik soured those feelings. The satellite transformed material comforts from symbols of excellence into signs of surfeit, revealing not achievement but vapidity. Conceivably, that softness could provide fertile ground for communists to plant their system and spread it.[54]

In the late 1940s, Eisenhower himself had wondered whether Americans focused excessively on luxuries, saying, "Maybe we like caviar and champagne when we ought to be working on beer and hot dogs." Sputnik generated calls for new national priorities and a stiffer moral spine. Senator Styles Bridges of New Hampshire, an Armed Services Committee member and Republican stalwart (already in 1936, Republican presidential nominee Alf Landon had considered him as a running mate until strategists warned that Democrats would delight in the phrase "Landon Bridges falling down"), stressed that Sputnik should force Americans to reassess their values: "The time has clearly come to be less concerned with the depth of the pile on the new broadloom rug or the height of the tail fin on the new car and to be more prepared to shed blood, sweat, and tears if this country and the Free World are to survive." A writer in *Life* magazine urged Americans to become "more concerned about whether we will live in freedom than about whether we can afford a new car next year."[55] Even America's youth, normally optimistic, got caught up in the self-doubt. Brown University's student newspaper, the *Daily Herald*, declared October 4, 1957, "the day the United States became a second power." It said that the solution to regaining scientific and technological leadership "is not simple, and is probably not too pleasant. It necessitates some basic changes in our entire system of production and development."[56]

Some critics blamed the Red Hunt. During the McCarthy era, communist hunters targeted scientists and forced many of them to quit government jobs. Now, it seemed, America bore the bitter fruit of this episode. A Norwegian newspaper called Sputnik "the punishment for that vile and foolish persecution of a series of American scientists during the time of Sen. Joseph McCarthy." Former president Truman, defending himself against charges that his administration had failed to support space and rocketry, deflected blame onto the witchhunt. "We had a terrible attack upon the scientists of the United States . . . [who] were so much abused that we lost a great many of them," Truman said. "They retired and went into schools and other places and that is one of the main reasons why we are behind in this satellite proposition which the Russians have raised above the earth."[57]

Americans even uttered fears that their country's existence might end soon. George Price, a Manhattan Project scientist, believed that unless Americans "depart utterly from our present behavior, it is reasonable to expect that by no later than 1975 the United States will be a member of the Union of Soviet Socialist Republics." Other observers noted the contrast that as the Soviet Union triumphed in space, Eisenhower played golf at his Gettysburg farm. One *New York Post* reader concluded, "Thus do great nations perish." It was as if the Soviets' technical victory portended world revolution. Eisenhower later explained, "When such competence in things material is at the service of leaders who have so little regard for things human, and who command the power of an empire, there is danger ahead for free men everywhere. That . . . is the reason why the American people have been so aroused."[58]

Soviet Propaganda

Sputnik's beeps were more than just a signal for radio operators to track. They represented a Cold War signal, a sound the Soviets wanted the world to hear. Because countries could not readily use atomic weapons, propaganda and symbols became important weapons in waging the Cold War, and Sputnik was the ultimate propaganda coup. The Kremlin used it to imply that communism was the wave of the future: the Soviet Union was a technologically sophisticated as well as militarily powerful nation, and the world balance of power now favored communism. The Soviets now appeared focused, steeped in science and technology, and driven to succeed. In Spain, Soviet scientist Leonid Sedov drew a contrast between his country and the United States: "America is very beautiful, very impressive. The living standard is remarkably high," he said. "But it is very obvious that the Average American cares only for his car, his home, and his refrigerator. He has no sense at all for his nation. . . . Russians do!"[59]

Two weeks after the launch of Sputnik, the U.S. Information Agency's Office of Research and Intelligence compiled a confidential report, "World Opinion and the Soviet Satellite." The report read, "General Soviet credibility has been sharply enhanced." The USIA predicted, "This gain in credibility, which can be exploited by almost every aspect of Soviet propaganda, may in the long run be the most durable and useful gain accruing to the USSR from the satellite." Russia could employ its newfound psychological advantage, the agency believed, in two possible ways: "seeking a détente or attempting an expansionist venture." The USIA report predicted that one of the USSR's propaganda aims was to "make a very strong effort to create and deepen the impression that the satellite marks a new era, and to make its launching a sort of Great Divide."[60]

The Soviet Union made the most of it. The Communist Party newspaper *Pravda* (which meant "Truth") declared Sputnik "a victory of Soviet man who, with Bolshevist boldness and clearness of purpose, determination and energy knows how to move forward." Moscow boasted of great space exploits and weapons yet to come, while Soviet media condemned the American way of life. It pointed to segregation in the South, criticized the "social inequality" of American health care, and portrayed U.S. work stoppages as evidence of "bitter class struggle." The Soviet news agency Tass reported that the USSR would launch several more "larger and heavier" satellites and concluded, "Artificial satellites will pave the way to interplanetary travel, and apparently our contemporaries will witness how the freed and conscientious labor of the people of the new socialist society makes the most daring dreams of mankind a reality."[61]

When Sputnik roared into space, Khrushchev was at his vacation home in the Crimea, a province on the Black Sea's north coast, and he returned to Moscow. Interviewed by *New York Times* columnist James Reston, he breezily maintained that he went to sleep after hearing of the launch. He might have, but he was far from blasé about Sputnik. He used the satellite to lecture Reston: "It must be realized that the Soviet Union is no longer a peasant country," and he promised that his country would mass-produce missiles "like sausages." His braggadocio extended to subtle threats, as he warned about the prospect of war in the Middle East, staring down U.S.-backed Turkey. "When we let off our intercontinental ballistic missile, people said that it was a psychological trick and that we were out to create an impression. They did not believe us," Khrushchev said. "But we do not go in for bluffing. We are a serious people. . . . If war breaks out, Turkey would not last one day."[62]

In truth, Khrushchev had more swagger than sincerity. His country had no fully operational ICBMs, as it had yet to clear the guidance, fueling needs, and other technical hurdles to deliver a missile to a target. But in November 1956, while addressing NATO diplomats at the Polish embassy in Moscow, Khrushchev had launched into a tirade against the West and famously declared, "We will bury you." Sputnik gave credence to his claim, and as if to underscore his propaganda achievement, *Time* made Khrushchev its 1957 "Man of the Year." The Soviet leader, the magazine said, "outran, outfoxed, outbragged, outworked and out-drank" all Communist Party rivals. He outdid all foreign rivals, too, including the U.S. president.[63]

Eisenhower versus Nixon

With Sputnik, the United States suffered a blow to an intangible yet important Cold War entity: world prestige. Democratic senator Richard Russell of Georgia claimed that "Sputnik confronts America with a new and terrifying military danger and a disastrous blow to our prestige." Khrushchev knew it. His son Sergei said that the Soviet leader called Sputnik an "extremely significant and prestigious offshoot of the intercontinental ballistic missile. He emphasized that here we had succeeded in surpassing America. He dreamed of demonstrating the advantages of socialism in actual practice."[64]

Some Americans denied any damage. Democratic senator J. William Fulbright of Arkansas, chair of the Foreign Relations Committee, noting that Sputnik could not feed Russians, wrote that the satellite "was a trick, a kind of gambit. It does not convert anyone to communism. So far as real prestige goes, it is nothing." The reality seemed otherwise. Abroad, the media found space a dominant topic. *Wall Street Journal* correspondents reported that "Russia has earned a big boost in prestige and the U.S. has received a bad black eye in most of the world's more backward areas." A Gallup poll just after Sputnik revealed that America's prestige had fallen in six of seven foreign cities (New Delhi, Toronto, Paris, Oslo, Helsinki, and Copenhagen; only in Stockholm did America's reputation remain unchanged).[65]

At a National Security Council meeting six days after the Sputnik launch, Arthur Larson worried openly about diplomatic damage from the satellite. "We can't take successive [hammer] blows like this and always be behind," he argued. Larson had served as undersecretary of labor and then, since December 1956, as director of the U.S. Information Agency, which Eisenhower had hoped to turn into a public relations machine overseas, broadcasting American television and radio programs to popularize the United States. Larson was sensitive to world opinion of America, and he wanted to offer countries a positive, constructive message. He proposed "an all-out project" aimed at either hitting the moon, launching manned satellites, or establishing a space platform. He found little support, and Eisenhower wondered whether the country's resources could support such an effort. One administration member who did seem interested was Vice President Richard Nixon."

Nixon "hit the nail on the head," William Ewald recalled, by zeroing in on Sputnik's political impact. Nixon was far more attuned than Eisenhower to the political ramifications of space. His response was "almost the best" of the entire administration, Ewald said, because Nixon viewed Sputnik "as a challenge to America's scientific and engineering ability to stay abreast of what was going on in the world." Nixon warned, "We can make no greater mistake than to see this as just a Soviet stunt. We've got to pull up our socks and get with it and make sure that we maintain our leadership." At the same NSC meeting where Larson spoke, Nixon inquired about disseminating information from the planned U.S. satellite to interested countries, adding that doing so would be "a great propaganda advantage" for America.[66]

Nixon's political future influenced these thoughts. As the presumptive 1960 Republican presidential nominee, he would suffer most from a flaccid administration response to Sputnik. He wanted a vigorous reaction, and Eisenhower's sense of cool calm frustrated him, as did many White House actions as 1960 approached. Elliot Richardson, an assistant secretary in the HEW Department who later served in President Nixon's cabinet, remembered the vice president's angst over Eisenhower's indifference to political calculations. "Time and again I would see Nixon get up from the table after Cabinet meetings so tense that beads of sweat were standing out on his brow," Richardson said. "The cause of his tension was that he had to keep his mouth shut while decisions were taken that he knew would erode his political base for 1960."[67]

As John Kennedy did later with Lyndon Johnson, Eisenhower could have delegated more responsibility to Nixon in formulating space policy. Instead, Eisenhower's attitude toward Nixon was ambiguous, and he failed to use his vice president's energy and political insights on space. He had, after all, asked Nixon to head the Cabinet Committee on Price Stability for Economic Growth to popularize the notion that fighting inflation was vital to America's economic health and thus to its national security. But fighting inflation was important to Eisenhower; space mattered less.[68]

Eisenhower also had an uneasy relationship with Nixon. He expressed puzzlement that Nixon had few friends, never felt close to him, never invited him to the White House residence or the Gettysburg farm, and remarked that he could never figure out Nixon's "personal equation," a term he used to denote a person's essence.[69] The discomfort stemmed partly from the general's view of his ambitious young vice president as "too political," echoing Senator Robert Taft's characterization of him as "a little man in a big hurry." At times, Eisenhower had to rein Nixon in. In 1954, as the French colonial regime foundered in Vietnam, Nixon and Secretary of State John Foster Dulles urged the president to send ground troops to aid the French. Showing his trademark caution, Eisenhower refused, sparing the nation from an agony his successors did not. Later that year, before the midterm elections, Eisenhower gave Nixon a verbal spanking for his harsh campaigning against Democrats, which he worried would spoil their chances of gaining Democratic support in foreign policy.[70]

Looking to 1960, Eisenhower much preferred that a presidential aspirant like Nixon make his mark in another venue, as he had done, rather than climb the greasy pole of politics. He commented, "Well, the fact is, of course, I've watched Dick a long time, and he just hasn't grown. So I just haven't honestly been able to believe that he *is* presidential timber." For his part, Nixon chafed against the president's penury in budget matters. Ike was not political enough for him, and Nixon privately complained that the president shunted his views aside. Eisenhower "regards me as a political expert only," Nixon grumbled. "If I try to speak up on defense matters, say, from a strict military point of view, he says, 'What does this guy know about it?' So I put the case on a political basis."[71]

The divide between the president and vice president widened after Sputnik. The political aspect of space—which Nixon saw so clearly—was an Eisenhower blind spot. Cutting his teeth in the military rather than politics, Eisenhower was less attuned to the political leverage that some issues exerted. Larson commented that for Eisenhower, "in the scale of motivations for a decision, political advantage, the effect on votes and so forth, was not only very low on the list, it was absolutely non-existent. If you wanted to get thrown out of the Oval Room, all you had to say is, 'Look, Mr. President, this is going to cost you votes in West Virginia.' Well, you wouldn't get past 'West'—you'd be out."[72]

Despite the blinders on Eisenhower's political vision, in another respect, his focus was clear. He recognized what only Americans such as himself who had witnessed the Soviet Union firsthand could see. Sputnik aside, the country's economy and infrastructure could hardly compete with America's. *New York Times* correspondent Max Frankel recalled that he tried to reassure readers "by contrasting the spectacular success of Soviet rocketry with the pathetic poverty and inefficiency of daily life." Khruschchev's brag-gadocio could not fool Frankel. "I had stood face-to-face with the man at embassy parties, stared into his sparkling eyes, and followed the witty wag of his finger as he acted out the insecurities of his backward society. He pro-claimed a maddening faith in the ultimate superiority of socialist economies, but it was capitalist achievements that he envied and market incentives that he longed to unleash." Raymond Saulnier, who chaired Eisenhower's Coun-cil of Economic Advisors, traveled in the Soviet Union during the early 1960s and found that "the Russians are far from ten feet tall. They can con-centrate effort on selected goals with high-grade results; their achievements in space are evidence of this." But Saulnier added that "their production system as a whole, viewed as a means of meeting the full range of the na-tion's economic needs, is fundamentally an inefficient one."[73]

Eisenhower knew that. Still, given the reaction to Sputnik, he had to get America's satellite program off the ground.

CHAPTER 2

"The Most Fateful Decision of His Presidency"

Until 1948, Eisenhower had spent his entire adult life in the U.S. Army. Ready to leave and begin a civilian career, he toyed with the idea of teaching college history. His high school yearbook had predicted that he would become a Yale University history professor, and he certainly had witnessed history firsthand during World War II.

Instead of teaching at a college, though, Eisenhower became a university president, assuming the top spot at Columbia University in 1948. It was an odd match. Eisenhower had no doctorate and made no pretensions of being an academician. (He even joked that Columbia hired the wrong Eisenhower, having confused him with his younger brother, Milton, the president of Kansas State College.) At Columbia, Eisenhower's attainments were modest. Striving to put the university's fiscal house in order, he balanced the budget after years of red ink. But overall, Eisenhower's relationship with Columbia was unhappy. Having commanded armies and basked in world attention during World War II, he felt restless, and a university presidency seemed a hollow follow-up act. As a Kansas native, he felt out of place in New York City, and Mamie cared little for the metropolis.

There were other problems. The Columbia faculty looked disdainfully on Eisenhower. They thought his emphasis on civics was odd. They joked that he could read no more than one-page memos; otherwise, his lips would get tired. The interminable meetings, where faculty droned on in what they considered useful debate, bored Eisenhower. Even his relations with under-graduates were rocky; he once grew irate at their irreverence and threatened to boycott commencement ceremonies. As a whole, the university community was irritated that Eisenhower traveled so much, and when he was on campus, two aides strictly guarded access to him.

In 1950, Eisenhower was relieved when President Truman appointed him NATO supreme commander, enabling him to leave Columbia. Even though Eisenhower kept up contacts with many colleagues and liked revisiting favorite spots, he forged few lasting friendships at Columbia and felt little desire to return to New York City.[1]

In some ways, Eisenhower's uncomfortable relationship with his first job outside the Army served as a metaphor for civilian–military tension. After becoming president of the United States, Eisenhower experienced other clashes between the two worlds. One of the most confounding was the competition between civilian and military rockets, on the one hand, and a proposed space satellite, on the other.

The International Geophysical Year

Because Eisenhower was at Gettysburg during Sputnik's launch, White House press secretary James Hagerty handled the Washington press corps' questions. Despite his reputation for astutely managing news from the White House, like most administration members, he gave limp responses. Even when prodded by reporters, he refused to comment on Sputnik's military implications, stating, "The launching of the Soviet satellite is, of course, of great scientific interest. It should contribute much to scientific knowledge that all countries are seeking to gain for the world during the International Geophysical Year." Hagerty stressed that because the U.S. satellite program was linked to the IGY, it would not accelerate in response to the Soviet launch, especially since the administration "never thought of our program as one which was in a race with the Soviets."[2]

What Eisenhower valued more than a space race was a marriage of the American satellite effort to the IGY, an event that the International Council of Scientific Unions sponsored. With sixty-seven nations participating, including the United States and the Soviet Union, the IGY was to last from July 1957 to December 1958. "International Polar Years" had taken place in 1882 and 1932, but the IGY was devoted to more ethereal studies. Its timing was deliberate: the eighteen months (it was not really a "year") of 1957–58 covered a period of heightened solar activity, and the IGY aimed to let the world's scientists pool talent and cooperate to study the earth's geophysical properties, including its atmosphere, gravity, and climate.[3]

Two American IGY projects caught Eisenhower's attention. One was in the Antarctic, where a U.S. team was to establish three observation sites, which inspired the Soviet Union to mount its own expedition to the icy continent. The other was in space. Under the direction of the National Science Foundation, America planned to send a basketball-sized satellite into orbit and "promised to make information on the space vehicle available to the public," Eisenhower noted.[4] Given the uproar Sputnik generated, the satellite program's prosaic start appeared ironic in retrospect. On July 29, 1955, the Eisenhower administration unveiled the project, stressing that it was to be an open endeavor anchored to the IGY. Divorced from defense efforts, the program would share scientific results worldwide without fear of yielding strategic booty and take a giant stride in exploring the earth's upper atmosphere, using a multistage rocket, at a time when most data had come from single-stage rockets.[5] The news created no great impression on Americans. At a press conference one week after the announcement, no reporter asked Eisenhower about it. Some public responses expressed skepticism. One Louisiana woman protested to Eisenhower and called the satellite program a "hair brained [sic] scheme," writing, "This is about the most stupid bit of news out of Washington within my memory."[6] Yet Eisenhower "took sincerely the scientific motivation of the International Geophysical Year," Arthur Larson believed. The IGY "was supposed to be a totally friendly, non-competitive, scientific enterprise. And for the most part it was," Larson said. "But inevitably a certain amount of competitiveness crept into it. But that was never the intention in the first place."[7] Eisenhower wanted the American satellite program's results made available to all nations, including the Soviet Union.

Moscow timed Sputnik's launch to coincide with IGY conferences in Washington, which increased American humiliation. At the Moscow embassy, where Russians were hosting IGY scientists, the unsuspecting guests drank vodka, ate from a buffet, and enjoyed Russian hospitality. Suddenly, *New York Times* science reporter Walter Sullivan came over to William Pickering, the physicist who directed the California Institute of Technology's Jet Propulsion Laboratory. "What have they said about the satellite?" he asked. "What do you mean?" Pickering replied. Sullivan explained that his newspaper had received a Radio Moscow report that Russia had just launched a satellite. The two men approached physicist Lloyd Berkner, head of Long Island's Brookhaven National Laboratory, who decided to play the good sport. He stood up on a chair, clapped his hands, and announced to the room that he wanted to propose a toast. The room fell silent. Berkner then congratulated the Soviet Union for launching the world's first man-made satellite.[8]

The Soviets had played the event for maximum excitement, recalled Arnold Frutkin, the deputy director of the U.S. National Committee for the IGY, saying that "there's nothing that could be more dramatic than an announcement at the Soviet Embassy" of their country's launching the satellite. But Frutkin detected a different emotion among the American delegation of rocket scientists. Their disappointment was palpable, he said, recalling, "There was a visible crush in the room." The crestfallen U.S. delegation went back to the IGY headquarters on Washington's Nineteenth Street to discuss Sputnik's meaning. As they huddled in a room, not one of them talked of manned spaceflight. "I find that extraordinary, because some of them had manned flight on their minds," Frutkin said. Instead, the scientists focused on the Soviet satellite's political and world impact and on America's ability to launch its own satellites. They also knew that the United States had lost a historic opportunity. After a promising start following World War II, it was America that had been poised to launch the world's first satellite.[9]

U.S. Rocket Development

After World War II, rocketry development in the United States followed a twisted path that generated different offshoots, one of which led to the proposed IGY satellite. During the war, German technology became one of the envies of the world and laid the groundwork for the Space Age. Thousands of Germany's top scientists and engineers worked at Peenemünde, a remote research center on a Baltic Sea island. The Peenemünde workshop also harnessed the work of slave laborers, an emaciated force that toiled under subhuman conditions of sanitation and hygiene. Starvation and disease scythed them down at the rate of 150 per day. In this grisly environment, the Germans developed the V-2 rocket (which stood for Vengeance Weapon Two), a medium-range ballistic missile that they began deploying in September 1944.

It was a terrifying weapon. Until May 1945, when the war ended in Europe, Germans unleashed more than three thousand V-2s, most onto London and Antwerp, Belgium, killing 5,400 people. Although the German scientists had not perfected the rocket's accuracy, it still represented what American journalist Edward R. Murrow called "malignant ingenuity." Generating 56,000 pounds of thrust, its powerful boosters propelled the forty-six-foot-tall rocket faster than the speed of sound and to a range of 210 miles, with payloads of 2,200 pounds. Because of its high velocity, the V-2 caught victims by surprise; Londoners never heard them until they hit the city. When they struck, some residents thought the sound was exploding gas lines.[10]

The V-2 showed what a nation could achieve when a leader assigned a project high priority and relentlessly drove toward it. Hitler invested even greater importance and money in rockets than in an atom bomb, and when WWII ended, Germany led the world in rocketry, besting both the Soviet Union and the United States, the latter having funneled its scientific and military resources toward the bomb. Ominously, German scientists were preparing new vehicles to fly across the Atlantic Ocean and attack America.

But the Peenemünde scientists helped America. Before the war ended, as the Soviet Red Army approached Germany, many of them resolved to surrender to the Americans. They buried fourteen tons of V-2 documents in an abandoned mineshaft, stowed away rocket blueprints and components aboard railroad cars and motor vehicles, and ferreted themselves away in hiding places like a Bavarian ski lodge. On May 2, 1945, an American private in Germany spotted a man approaching on a bicycle. In accented English, the man said, "I am Magnus von Braun. My brother invented the V-2. We want to surrender." When the Americans captured Wernher von Braun, hiding in a forest near Peenemünde, at first they could not believe that this cheerful, good-looking, thirty-three-year-old man could be the brains behind the V-2. But von Braun was brilliant, and he had impressive skills as an organizer and administrator that complemented his forceful personality. An aeronautical engineer whose doctoral dissertation on rocket engines had such military value that the Germans classified it as secret, von Braun had grand dreams for rockets and spaceflight. When the first V-2 struck London, he remarked to a friend—probably half seriously—that it had hit the wrong planet.

Soviet troops took Peenemünde, but the rocket scientists' preemptive actions allowed the United States to claim the lion's share of V-2 paperwork, hardware, and brainpower. The German scientists impressed General Eisenhower, who sent a telegram to Washington: "The thinking of the scientific directors of this group is 25 years ahead of U.S. Recommend that 100 of the very best of this [V-2] organization be evacuated to [America] immediately." "Operation Paperclip" was the American effort to bring German rocket scientists to the United States after the war (so named because paper clips held together the documents of the German émigré scientists), and it netted America more, and better, scientists than the Soviets secured. In all, 120 German scientists came to the United States. The American military also boxed up V-2 rocket components and transported them by rail and sea to the White Sands Proving Grounds in New Mexico, bringing enough material to assemble one hundred V-2 rockets.[11]

Thus began a gestational phase for American rockets and satellites, and it exemplified how starkly the world had changed in just one year—and how serious the new competition was. The United States employed erstwhile enemies in a race against a new enemy, the Soviet Union, that involved leaps of technology that was the stuff of science fiction just a decade earlier. Von Braun led the Paperclip Scientists as they worked at their new home in White Sands, where they launched V-2 missiles beginning in 1946, making them instruments of science rather than weapons of mass destruction. In moves that foreshadowed the rapid American progress in space science during the 1950s, the rocket engineers put instruments—not bombs, as during World War II—into the nose cone, which parachuted to the earth for safe retrieval. These rockets made lasting contributions to science. In 1946, for example, they discovered the earth's ozone layer. The scientists also improved on the V-2 by making it the first stage of a two-stage rocket called Bumper. On February 24, 1949, the first Bumper was launched, attaining a record altitude of 244 miles and proving the viability of a two-stage rocket.[12] The following year the German rocket scientists moved operations to Huntsville, Alabama, which acquired the nickname of "Hunsville" but also became America's unofficial "Rocket City" (although no launchings took place there).

The United States tried to find a launch area for rockets, and Cape Canaveral, Florida, emerged as a premier spot. Located in the Deep South, where the earth's rotational spin gave rockets an extra boost, the Cape enjoyed good weather and seemed a region that avoided the hurricane season's ravages. Firing rockets eastward from Florida provided additional advantages: they flew in the same direction that the earth rotated, which gave them more momentum, and they posed less danger by flying over the Atlantic rather than over land.[13] On July 24, 1950, a Bumper rocket was launched from Cape Canaveral, inaugurating this area as a key player in rocketry and space.

Von Braun's team soon developed a V-2 on steroids, a bigger, more powerful rocket named Redstone (after the Army's Redstone Arsenal near Huntsville, which made chemical munitions and stored material during World War II), which delivered 78,000 pounds of thrust and had a two-hundred-mile range. On August 20, 1953, after journeying by barge from Huntsville to Florida, the Redstone made its first flight from Cape Canaveral. The rocket was the German scientists' labor of love, and it became a source of pride for the U.S. Army, too, eventually becoming the rocket that put America's first man into space. It was also an open secret. In July 1957, in an unusual publicity stunt, the Army propped up a Redstone missile in the upper concourse of Manhattan's bustling Grand Central Terminal. It was an awesome sight; commuters gawked at it, and the media reported that this missile could deliver an atomic warhead to a distant target.[14]

But von Braun had a more ambitious publicity stunt in mind: he pushed for permission to launch a satellite, and he hoped that the Redstone could do it. In 1954, he issued a report called "A Minimum Satellite Vehicle," in which he said that he could launch a satellite using available rocket components for just $100,000, warning that other nations—namely, the Soviet Union—were developing satellites. Von Braun had a gift for boiling down complex issues into a stark sound bite, and he wrote with urgency: "*It would be a blow to U.S. prestige if we did not do it first.*"[15]

Rockets were also vital for national security, but the military was downsizing and demobilizing after World War II, and Pentagon planners chose to rely more on bombers to deliver atomic weapons, blanching at rockets' cost and doubting whether bombs could survive atmospheric reentry. By the mid-1950s, though, scientists predicted that nuclear bombs would become compact enough to fit inside a missile tip, and the Soviet Union, determined to build on the military strength it achieved during wartime, worked apace on ballistic missiles.[16]

Von Braun later complained that "the United States had no ballistic missile program worth mentioning between 1945 and 1951. These six years during which the Russians obviously laid the groundwork for their large rocket program, are irretrievably lost." One of Eisenhower's science advisors, Jerome Wiesner, faulted America's "late start" in missiles.[17] While writing his memoirs in the 1960s, Eisenhower tried to set the record straight. Without mentioning Truman by name, Eisenhower singled out "the Executive" and "responsible political authorities" who pared back defense expenditures after the war and hurt the nation's nascent rocket program. Eisenhower noted that between fiscal years 1947 and 1953, the federal budget allocated less than seven million dollars for long-range ballistic missiles. He also blamed Congress for slowing down progress in missile development with budget cuts that "were serious and, to me, frustrating." Whereas defense spending on ballistic missiles stood at $3 million in Truman's last year in office, it leapt to $161 million during Eisenhower's second fiscal year as president.[18] As a result, Republicans claimed that they gave higher priority to national security. In 1958, when GOP congressman Gerald Ford of Michigan campaigned for reelection, he noted, "Our missiles and rockets program, long neglected by the Truman Administration, was literally lifted off the ground by increased emphasis and appropriations. The $3 million programmed for long-range missiles development in 1953 was boosted to $14 million in 1954, to $161 million in 1955, to $515 million in 1956, to $1.3 billion in 1957, and to some $2.5 billion in 1958."[19]

In May 1954, Defense Secretary Charles Wilson gave priority funding to the Atlas rocket, which was designed to become America's first ICBM. With a thrust of 360,000 pounds and range of more than five thousand miles, it could cross the Pacific or Atlantic oceans to attack other continents. To provide a backup to the Atlas, he also approved a second ICBM program, the Titan, and put the Air Force in charge of both.[20]

The Technological Capabilities Panel gave such rockets a boost. In 1954, Eisenhower asked Massachusetts Institute of Technology president James Killian to chair a forty-six-member committee to evaluate America's military strength vis-à-vis the Soviet Union's and assess the chances of a Russian attack. After meeting secretly for five months, the Killian Panel, as it was also known, produced its report, "Meeting the Threat of a Surprise Attack," and delivered it to Eisenhower in February 1955. The Killian Report urged the speedy, high-priority development of intercontinental and intermediate-range ballistic missiles. Reacting to these recommendations and reversing years of Truman administration policy, Eisenhower gave top priority to developing an ICBM to deliver nuclear warheads to other continents. The panel's report also recommended using aerial surveillance, including reconnaissance satellites, to monitor the Soviet Union and urged the Navy to develop its own missiles. [21]

The Killian Report carved the contours of Eisenhower's defense policy for the rest of his presidency. While the legendary NSC-68 casts a long shadow in postwar history—U.S. history textbooks usually discuss it, and many college students can cite its gist—the TCP report deserves as much attention. It was a Cold War game changer, its importance visible in the weapons and surveillance systems it inspired. It fostered the triad of missiles—the Atlas ICBM, Jupiter IRBM, and Polaris submarine-launched missile—that formed the backbone of America's rocket weaponry, and it accelerated IRBM and ICBM development on a "crash" basis. It led to the U-2, the secret Lockheed spy plane that began flying over the Soviet Union in 1956, America's most formidable espionage tool until spy satellites, for which the panel also advocated. The TCP report also strengthened relations between government and scientists and put Killian's competence on display, which later led Eisenhower to appoint him as the first presidential science advisor.[22]

The Killian Report also fueled the race that mattered most to Eisenhower. To him, ICBM development was crucial, and competition from the USSR forced him to run on a fast track. In 1955 he told Democratic senator

Clinton Anderson of New Mexico, who chaired the Joint Congressional Committee on Atomic Energy, "The earliest development of ICBM capability is of vital importance to the security of the United States. The Soviets may well have begun top-priority work on this weapon shortly after World War II."[23] Because the deployment of America's first ICBM was still years away, Eisenhower followed the Killian Panel's recommendations and gave the go-ahead for the Jupiter and Thor IRBMs, which would be ready sooner. While the Air Force was to develop Thor, the Army would guide Jupiter. With a maximum range of fifteen hundred miles, these missiles could not cross oceans, but they could be stationed in Europe, bringing the Soviet Union and other potential enemies within striking range.

Thus, Eisenhower approved "parallel development" for both ICBMs and IRBMs, a duplication that reflected his determination to beat the Russians in this race. Eisenhower's order to develop IRBMs was unanticipated, because the original thinking was that deploying these short-range missiles within the United States was useless, and their evolution would be natural outgrowths of the ICBMs. But once both Jupiter and Thor proved workable, Defense Secretary Wilson exulted that he felt like a man "who proposed to two girls, both of whom accepted." The order to institute the IRBM program reflected how serious Eisenhower was about making missiles for security. Normally, he rejected any parallel development or duplicated efforts as wasteful. But he was proud of the federal dollars he devoted to missile development and bristled when critics charged him with skimping on it. "*Look* at these lines," he said angrily, pointing to a chart outlining money on missiles. "Up to 1954, there's almost nothing—at the highest, nine million dollars in one year. Now look at *our* line—so damn high it goes right off the chart finally—$1,390,000,000."[24]

Atlas, Titan, Jupiter, and Thor all used liquid fuel (meaning liquid oxygen plus kerosene, for example). One problem with liquid fuel was that it had to be delivered to the missile only at the last minute to keep the oxygen cold enough to stay in liquid form. If an emergency forced an immediate launch, the long fueling process would be a handicap. But in December 1956, the Eisenhower administration approved a new IRBM program for the Navy, the Polaris, which would use solid fuels and be launched from submarines. The Polaris marked the fifth missile the United States was developing, and as a submarine-based weapon, it would give America's arsenal a launch vehicle that was mobile and almost impossible for the Soviet Union to find and disable. When Eisenhower turned over the Oval Office to Kennedy in January 1961, he knew he was giving the new president a tremendous boon in this new weapon. "You have an invulnerable asset in Polaris," he told Kennedy, adding for emphasis, "It is invulnerable."[25]

Growing Soviet strength forced Eisenhower to maintain this nuclear arsenal, which was powerful enough to deter the Russians from considering aggressive action. Unlike the late 1940s, the 1950s was a time when the Soviet Union hoped to match America's nuclear might. Eisenhower thus gave both ICBMs and IRBMs the highest priority and speed—making them "crash" programs—according them "all the resources that they could usefully absorb at any given time," he recalled, which included a substantial and quick infusion of money. The outcry after Sputnik ignored the emphasis that Eisenhower had placed on missile development and national security.[26]

The IRBM program also gave von Braun's Redstone new life because the Army's Jupiter used that rocket. To give the Jupiter operation more status, the Army designated the Huntsville team the Army Ballistic Missile Agency, which began operating on February 1, 1956, under the direction of Major General John Medaris. To test a missile's ability to survive reentry, ABMA developed a test vehicle called Jupiter C (short for "Jupiter Composite Reentry Test Vehicle"), which used the Redstone for its first stage, followed by two smaller, solid-fuel rockets for its second and third stages and a fourth inert stage. The Jupiter C was a research rocket, different from the Jupiter IRBM, even though they bore similar names, but both rockets symbolized a remarkable metamorphosis. With von Braun supervising the entire process, the original V-2 rocket, a World War II weapon of terror, underwent mutations from a Redstone, with a two-hundred-mile range, to the Jupiter IRBM, with a range of two thousand miles, to the three-thousand-mile range Jupiter C.[27]

Soon satellites entered the race. Just after the war, the Pentagon began to realize the military value of satellites, especially for reconnaissance. One of the TCP's recommendations was to develop a small satellite not expressly for reconnaissance but more to establish the principle that such vehicles could orbit freely overhead, regardless of political boundaries below. Eisenhower's eagerness to test this idea was a major reason he liked the IGY, which would further his surveillance objectives while providing the perfect cover of science and international cooperation.[28]

At a May 26, 1955, NSC meeting, Eisenhower reviewed a policy paper, which became known as NSC 5520, giving the official go-ahead for a scientific satellite project. NSC 5520 recognized that "prestige and psychological benefits" would accrue to whichever nation first launched a satellite, but more was at stake, and the often sly president knew it. The satellite would benefit science and be an open, cooperative project, but in addition to asserting free space travel over international boundaries, it would pave the way for future reconnaissance vehicles. This objective interested Eisenhower far more than a satellite's scientific contributions, and it later became one of his legacies. As he said at the meeting, "the big stuff" was not the scientific satellite but rather the prospect of an eventual spy satellite. He approved the project.[29]

Because all the service branches conducted rocketry research, the prospect of launching satellites intensified rivalries, which were already heated. Future NASA administrator Keith Glennan once observed a dinner toast between a Navy admiral and an Air Force officer that resembled "two little boys arguing over which of their fathers could lick the other." Each service wanted to be preeminent in the emerging field of rocketry. Yet rockets blurred the historic dividing lines among the services—the Army covering land, the Navy sailing the sea, the Air Force flying the sky. The Air Force had an obvious claim to rockets, since they flew. But the Army saw them as artillery, while the Navy envisioned their being launched from submarines.[30] Eisenhower resented the rivalries, repeatedly using the word "parochial" to chide the branches (to the point where advisors warned him to keep such a Catholic term out of his presidential language).[31] Before long, the services bickered over satellites, too.

Whose Satellite to Use?

Although the IGY was a civilian scientific endeavor, the Pentagon had jurisdiction over America's IGY satellite. The question was which military service branch should develop it. To evaluate three competing proposals for the American satellite, Deputy Defense Secretary Donald Quarles formed an eight-member ad hoc group eventually known as the Stewart Committee, after its head, Homer Stewart of the Jet Propulsion Laboratory.[32]

In September 1955, the Stewart Committee met to review civilian satellite proposals from the Army, Navy, and Air Force. The Air Force proposed to use its massive Atlas ICBM rocket to launch a satellite, but this option had problems. The Atlas had yet to be tested, and work on a scientific satellite could distract the Air Force from premiering the ICBM as a weapon. The Stewart Committee quickly dismissed the Air Force's offering.[33]

The Army proposal, Project Orbiter, had the perfect name and seemed more promising. It would be led by Huntsville's ABMA and use the Redstone rocket as a first stage, followed by three stages, the last containing a five-pound satellite. Orbiter promised to be ready to launch by January 1957. At the time, the Army claimed that this proposed launch date could match or beat any Soviet satellite into space. Yet Orbiter, too, had problems. Its puny, five-pound satellite hardly excited scientists, and it would record little data and be difficult for observers to see.[34]

The Navy's offer, Project Vanguard, was nonmilitary and advanced by the Naval Research Laboratory. Starting in 1946, the NRL worked on improving the old V-2, producing a rocket called Viking that it first launched on May 3, 1949, reaching fifty miles in altitude. The Vanguard would use the Viking rocket as a first stage, with two yet-to-be-developed stages plus a fourth piece that would be the satellite, which would go into a low orbit, 100–150 miles up. Slender and almost fragile looking, the Viking generated just 27,000 pounds of thrust, but its satellite had one advantage: better instruments. Vanguard was "ultra-sophisticated," as Arthur Larson said, weighing nearly forty pounds and loaded with advanced instrumentation and a revolutionary new steering mechanism. Von Braun said that Vanguard compared to the Jupiter C the same way a jet engine compared to a propeller-driven airplane. Although Vanguard had a smaller rocket than either the Air Force's Atlas or the Army's Jupiter C, its satellite promised to yield more scientific data while not interfering with missile programs.

But Vanguard had a huge drawback. It was a brand new vehicle whose upper stages did not yet exist; the NRL still needed to develop them and estimated the entire rocket would be ready no earlier than 1958. An ideal solution would have been to marry the Army's rocket to the Navy's scientific instruments, but Clifford Furnas, chancellor of the University of Buffalo and Stewart Committee member, later recalled that Army–Navy rivalry made that option impossible.[35]

To offset its inchoate state, Vanguard offered the virtues of sophistication and nonmilitary status. A civilian project, it was unclassified, which would allow scientists to disseminate information about it, in keeping with the IGY's open spirit, while the media could report on the whole system without opening security breaches. Vanguard's civilian nature was a clinching factor. In fact, in May 1955 the NSC weighed in on the matter, as NSC 5520 proscribed using a military rocket to power a scientific satellite. This directive underscored the importance of a boundary between rocket development for military missiles and rockets for peaceful, scientific satellites. It also drove the Stewart Committee in one direction.[36]

On August 3, 1955, the Stewart Committee made a decision that changed history. In a five-to-two vote, it picked the Navy's Vanguard as America's first satellite (one member missed the vote). Although Stewart voted for Project Orbiter, other committee members believed that Vanguard had more to offer science, including the Navy's proposals to track the satellite with radios and cameras. Defending the Vanguard decision after Sputnik, Eisenhower explained that "from the beginning the whole American purpose and design in this effort has been to produce the maximum in scientific information. The project was sold to me on this basis." Above all, the decision reflected the committee's desire to ensure the satellite's civilian character and avoid interference from the military. By contrast, Project Orbiter's use of the Redstone rocket could generate objections from other IGY nations and divert the Army's attention and resources as it developed the Redstone for national security.[37]

The decision boiled down to priorities. In Sputnik's aftermath, Eisenhower emphasized military rockets' primacy. "We got into this so-called satellite race strictly for scientific reasons," he said, adding, "We decided not to give the satellite a higher priority in 1955 because we had begun to pour big money into the missiles—the things that really count, at this stage." He recognized that Vanguard did not use the impressive technology military rockets had already incorporated, including the Redstone rockets that, as he later acknowledged, could have launched a satellite "sometime late in 1956, considerably before the Soviets." But Eisenhower was in no rush. He wanted to avoid distracting the Redstone scientists from progressing on national security work, and moreover, as "no obvious requirement for a crash satellite program was apparent, there was no reason for interfering with the [Vanguard] scientists and their projected time schedule." He also worried that using a military rocket would taint the civilian satellite and even hurt America's image worldwide.[38] Arnold Frutkin commented that Eisenhower "understood that people would fear the United States and fear the space program if it were clearly military in character, so they did their best to keep it civil. And I think that was brilliant." To do otherwise would play into the hands of Soviet propagandists who painted America as bellicose or sinister. Moreover, the decision reflected a long-standing American suspicion of the military and a desire to make it less visible, a wariness that dated back to the noisome presence of standing armies in the colonial era. Over time, the tendency to prefer civilian control had led to important institutional decisions, such placing responsibility for presidential protection with the Treasury Department's Secret Service rather than with the Army, thus preserving a more republican feel to the government.[39]

The administration had other reasons to separate the civilian and military satellite projects. Eisenhower anticipated the day when spy satellites would orbit the earth, Frutkin recalled, and he "wanted to establish that the first satellites were entirely peaceful and scientific and nothing for anybody to worry about. And that way, [the world] would become used to the idea of being under the eyes of a satellite and would not take it too seriously."[40] The IGY meshed comfortably with the Eisenhower administration's desire to establish the principle of freedom of space, because an IGY satellite would be unarmed. A purely scientific vehicle would pose no threat to the Soviet Union and would weaken the case for protests about overflight. During retirement, when explaining his reasoning in an interview, Eisenhower repeated this idea three times, once pounding the table with his fist: "What's more important than keeping space peaceful?" Yet Eisenhower also knew that he was, in essence, advocating a cause more dear to him, the ability to survey the Soviet Union from the sky above.[41]

Although the Stewart Committee's verdict was "thoroughly ill advised," as James Van Allen later said, Donald Quarles approved, and the Eisenhower administration ordered that Vanguard be a scientific program disassociated from the military, thus barring the Army and Air Force from developing satellites. (By also confining the Army to work on IRBMs, the Pentagon thus left it out of both the ICBM race and the satellite race.) "The American space program thus in no way began as a race or contest with any other nation," Eisenhower affirmed. Instead, it was "a gift to the scientific community of the entire world." Science trumped world prestige—for the time being. In November 1956, the NSC Planning Board predicted that the Soviet Union might launch a satellite before America did and conceded that the United States would suffer "prestige [loss] and psychological setbacks." But the Planning Board believed that America's satellite program would later make gains in world stature because of its superior scientific work, which would earn international recognition.[42]

In Eisenhower's mind, that view held firm even after Sputnik. Responding to Larson's suggestion at the October 10, 1957, NSC meeting that the United States needed a space achievement to maintain international prestige, Eisenhower acknowledged the idea's merits—which indicated he partially accepted arguments of world image—but added that the United States could ill afford vast programs that attempted to outdo the Soviets in all scientific areas. "We must, above all," he said, "still seek a military posture that the Russians will respect."[43] Eisenhower's Cold War priorities focused on national security, and he steered away from glamorous space projects—or, as he called them, "mere contests"—of little scientific value. At a White House meeting after the Sputnik launch he wryly commented, "I'd rather have a good Redstone than hit the moon. I don't think we have an enemy on the moon!"[44]

Larson maintained that if Eisenhower had perceived the American satellite effort "as a space race with the Russians, there were a lot of things we could have done. But we never treated it that way. We treated it as—exactly as it was—an educational and scientific cooperative venture." John Neilon, an NRL mathematician who worked on Project Vanguard, recalled that work on the satellite was "not a hurried thing, no crash development," and went at almost a leisurely pace. Eisenhower sensed that no American satellite scientist considered the program a race or ever asked to accelerate it.[45]

Still, Eisenhower regarded the project important enough to support it despite irritating price hikes. When National Science Foundation director Alan Waterman originally approached him about Vanguard, the scientist described a project costing $22 million, which would orbit a satellite the size of a grapefruit. In subsequent discussions, Waterman upped the figure to $60 million, then $150 million. Additional instruments would make the satellite the size of a basketball. The inflated expenses frustrated Eisenhower, yet he remembered that he "called in the Director of the Budget to tell him that we would have to find or obtain the money because I believed that it was the kind of experimentation that would have real value" for the country. He did this even though his treasury secretary recommended scrapping the program because of its rising costs. At a May 1957 NSC meeting, the president criticized scientists for trying to "gold plate" the satellite and festooning it with devices when the imperative was simply to get it into orbit for the "element of national prestige." In short, Eisenhower recognized the satellite's scientific value and even acknowledged a potential impact on world opinion, but he wanted to keep the effort within a fiscal perspective.[46]

The NSC aimed at a launch date of March 1958 for America's first satellite. To von Braun, that date was late, and he knew the Stewart Committee and Eisenhower administration had made a mistake. Vanguard had a superb design, true enough, but "this is not a design contest," he protested. "It is a contest to get a satellite into orbit, and we (the Army) are way ahead on this."[47] Von Braun was loath to give up on his dream. But while Vanguard lived, Orbiter seemed dead.

Civilian versus Military

In fact, after Eisenhower settled on the Vanguard project, America progressed well toward getting into space. It was developing a satellite without a specific government agency guiding the project. By contrast, the Soviet Union had the advantage of a political system in which the central government directed money, materiel, and personnel toward a goal, all of which well suited satellite development.[48]

Though Eisenhower resisted this viewpoint, a race was on. During retirement, he recognized his mistake, once reflecting, "It would have been easier, in hindsight[,] to have used the Redstone from the beginning" as a satellite launch vehicle.[49] At the Pentagon, normally flippant Defense Secretary Charlie Wilson expressed regrets, too. He acknowledged "the basic unfavorable fact that the Russians have been first" and conceded that the decision to make Vanguard "non-interfering with the high-priority ballistic missiles was certainly reasonable at the time, even though it may appear questionable in retrospect."[50]

Eisenhower's judgment to accept the Stewart Committee verdict was "the most fateful decision of his presidency," William Ewald believed. The president "knew *Sputnik* was approaching; he did not foresee its force." John Medaris called the attempt to separate military–civilian space efforts "a costly and ridiculous division of the indivisible." Some observers used harsher language. The decision was an "astonishing piece of stupidity," said I. M. Levitt, the director of Philadelphia's Fels Planetarium.[51]

Dividing civilian and military projects created a slippery distinction, because the line between them was fluid. "The IGY was in all essentials a civil scientific effort but it also was supported at many points by the military. It was the Navy that planned the Vanguard program," said Arnold Frutkin. At bottom, "the political idea was to have a program you could say was entirely for peaceful purposes. But because rocketry derived from . . . World War II technology, it was inevitable that there would be . . . points of military participation everywhere."[52]

Perhaps the most mordant postmortem came from a Russian. Soviet engineer Leonid Sedov later remarked to one of von Braun's colleagues, "You would have saved so much time, not to mention troubles and money" if America has simply picked the Redstone rocket to launch a satellite. The Soviets took a more efficient approach. Like Eisenhower, Khrushchev made the ICBM race his highest priority. On February 27, 1956, when he visited his country's secret missile laboratory, he looked skeptical when rocket engineer Sergei Korolev showed him a model of a satellite. A science stunt seemed lame, but the notion of a race with America piqued Khrushchev's interest, especially when Korolev assured him that it would not interfere with ICBM development. At last, Khrushchev assented. "If the main task does not suffer, do it," he said.[53]

Using the Redstone rocket, the United States could have easily sent a satellite into orbit before October 4, 1957, by as much as a year. ABMA's Jupiter C was a sensible backup, and knowledgeable insiders advocated its use.

In April 1956, PSAC executive officer David Beckler noted that even though the chances of the Jupiter C's success were small, "it might be in the national interest to attempt this shot if the feasibility, cost and non-interference with the IRBM program permit." Beckler specified that the Army's satellite would supplement—not replace—the Navy's Vanguard but would represent "an attempt to advance by as much as one year this historic event, anticipating an early Soviet attempt."[54]

Even the media knew ABMA's capabilities. In July 1957, writing an extensive profile of ABMA for the *Baltimore Sun*, Henry Trewhitt reported that von Braun's team could launch a satellite "almost left-handedly with army missiles already tested, while the Navy, which has charge of the satellite program, is still working on a system." The next month, the *St. Louis Post-Dispatch* reported, "The Redstone team almost overnight could put together the components to launch Vanguard, the earth satellite."[55] From both the media and Washington insiders, this judgment was resounding. In a titanic misstep, the Eisenhower administration failed to act on it.

Warnings Ignored

In his 1958 State of the Union address, Eisenhower stated, "Admittedly, most of us did not anticipate the psychological impact upon the world of the launching of the first earth satellite."[56] Nor had he sufficiently appreciated warnings that the nation launching the first satellite would achieve a great coup in world prestige. Yet, predictions about the psychological impact of a satellite launch began years before Eisenhower's presidency.

In 1945 the RAND Corporation was born as part of a Douglas Aircraft effort to study weapons technologies. (Standing for "Research and Development," RAND later became an independent think tank.) In 1946 the RAND Corporation issued a report estimating that an earth satellite would cost $150 million to develop, capture people's imagination worldwide, and serve in communications, observations, and future celestial journeys. RAND believed that the world's first satellite would generate an impact "comparable to the explosion of the atomic bomb." Prophetically, RAND observed that the nation that "first makes significant achievements in space travel will be acknowledged as the world leader in both military and scientific techniques. To visualize the impact on the world, one can imagine the consternation and admiration that would be felt here if the U.S. were to discover suddenly that some other nation had already put up a successful satellite." The United States, RAND estimated, could have such a satellite by 1951. On

October 4, 1950—precisely seven years before Sputnik—RAND released another report, commissioned by the U.S. Air Force, predicting that a successful satellite launch would have tremendous international significance. The event would be impossible to keep secret; assuming the satellite would be American, it advised making the launch a political event that the United States should carefully oversee.[57]

Other reports buttressed RAND's point. In May 1955, when the Office of the Assistant Secretary of Defense for Research and Development suggested that the United States launch a satellite as part of the IGY, it noted, "Considerable prestige and psychological benefits will accrue to the nation which first is successful in launching an artificial satellite." The technology involved in a satellite coupled with its missile applications, the report noted, "might have important repercussions on Free World political determination, especially if the [USSR] were to be the first to establish an earth satellite." Nelson Rockefeller, the special assistant to the president on governmental operations, added personal thoughts to the report. The grandson of oil tycoon John D. Rockefeller and future vice president had been responsible for World War II propaganda in South America and grasped that an artificial satellite "will symbolize scientific and technological advancement to peoples everywhere. The stake of prestige that is involved makes this a race we cannot afford to lose."[58]

Once the American satellite program kicked off in 1955, more warnings came. The CIA advised the Eisenhower administration to proceed quickly, as the Soviets raced to put their own vehicle up first. "The psychological warfare value of launching the first earth satellite," a CIA report suggested, "makes its prompt development of great interest to the intelligence community and may make it a crucial event in sustaining the international prestige of the United States." An August 15, 1955, memo by Army Lieutenant General James Gavin predicted "psychological damage if the Russians were first to launch." Yet none of these blandishments, nor the concept of a race with the Soviets, prodded Eisenhower enough. Ewald wrote, "In a ho-hum mood on January 24, 1957, [Eisenhower] and the National Security Council routinely discussed the Soviet Union's plan to put up an earth satellite—a plan known for nearly two years. They saw, they noted, they moved on to more pressing problems."[59]

What was notable was that the promptings came from all corners—not just national security agencies and the military but also civilian and political figures. In October 1956, Columbia University physicist and Nobel laureate Isadore Rabi wrote to Arthur Flemming, the director of the Office of Defense Mobilization, "Failure by the U.S. to launch satellites successfully during the IGY . . . would result in loss of U.S. scientific prestige that would be compounded by successful Soviet launching." An imploring voice came from Capitol Hill. In the summer of 1957, Democratic congressman George Huddleston, Jr., of Alabama publicly stated that if the United States failed to launch a satellite during the IGY or if another country launched a satellite first, America would "lose face." Because he had heard that Alabama's ABMA had rockets that could launch a satellite, he urged the Defense Department to give "more adequate consideration to using Army rockets developed at Redstone Arsenal to successfully launch the earth satellite."[60]

The satellite's potential impact on national defense was clear. In January 1957, David Beckler submitted a memo to Arthur Flemming that warned, "Failure to support an extended scientific satellite program could adversely affect our national security posture" in numerous ways. Knowledge of the upper atmosphere's properties was crucial to missile flight and military communications. The long-range weather forecasting that satellites provided would help military planning, too. The United States suffered a "vast ignorance of this region of space," Beckler warned. "It is because of this ignorance that we can ill afford to have an effective Soviet satellite program much greater than our own." Even the popular magazine *Collier's* recognized the relationship between the satellite and national security, editorializing in 1952 that the first nation to have a space satellite "will hold the ultimate military power over the Earth."[61]

Eisenhower gave such reports "specific and repeated consideration," Andrew Goodpaster recalled, but the president downplayed world prestige as a priority. Eisenhower took the matter "out of the psychological realm," Goodpaster said, believing that any public reaction to a space breakthrough "should be keyed to its true significance. What did it mean? It was a scientific achievement or a step toward a scientific achievement, but it told very little about anything of serious military import." Moreover, harkening back to his military experience, Eisenhower tended to be suspicious of the RAND report and others as "bureaucratically self-serving," Goodpaster remembered, as a ploy to gain more funding for the military's satellite projects.[62]

Beckler noted that Eisenhower "was not caught up with the whole idea that an artificial satellite would make that much difference as to who got there first." The reason Eisenhower dismissed warnings about a satellite's psychological impact "has to go back to his perception of the importance of this satellite," which he viewed through the prism of its military value. Beckler recalled "a general view that the space platform would not be a particularly attractive platform for carrying out military activity. You are not going to shoot down your enemy from a satellite." Beckler added, "So I think Eisenhower was pretty much thinking this was a scientific program and therefore did not deserve the kind of priority that would justify a very major investment. . . . He just was not keen on it." At a May 3, 1956, NSC meeting, Eisenhower even admitted that his enthusiasm for the Vanguard program was relatively low.[63]

Yet science and national security were intertwined, and Eisenhower's World War II experience made his failure to act on the connection odd. World War II proved a cardinal tenet of warfare, that science provided breakthroughs in weapons and tools crucial to victory. Eisenhower once said, "The armed forces could not have won the war alone. Scientists and businessmen contributed techniques and weapons which enabled us to out-wit and overwhelm the enemy. Their understanding of the Army's needs made possible the highest degree of cooperation." Anticipating further collaboration during peace, he added that integrating scientific programs with military efforts would "draw into our planning for national security all the civilian resources which can contribute to the defense of the country." The Soviet Union was boldly proceeding on this front, allowing scientific and military efforts to dovetail. As the CIA warned Eisenhower in 1955, the Russians had decided that "their satellite program can contribute enough prestige of cold war value or knowledge of military value to justify the diversion of the necessary skills, scarce material and labor from immediate military production."[64]

Eisenhower also understood the importance of firsts, which made his lack of peremptory interest in satellite development all the more curious. The United States had to be the first country to get an ICBM ready and working, he insisted; being first would have more psychological impact than having many of them, and he thus declined to order massive numbers. At a White House meeting five months after Sputnik's launch, Eisenhower—in discussing the importance of beating the Soviet Union in specific, selected areas—warned against getting bogged down in technical areas that would impede progress.[65] In fact, the allure of first place in a space race tempted him. In mid-1956, Goodpaster told Eisenhower that the U.S. satellite would be ready in late 1957 at the earliest, and more likely in 1958. When Goodpaster mentioned that a Redstone rocket could fire a satellite as early as late 1956 at a cost of just $2–$5 million more, the prospect interested Eisenhower enough that he asked Goodpaster to consult with Defense Secretary Wilson about it.[66] The inquiry was one of the ironies of the later Sputnik shock, Ewald recalled, because "he asked Andy Goodpaster, 'Check it out and see whether we can't speed this thing along and not have to wait another year to put up a space satellite.' "[67]

But Eisenhower's belief in the Stewart Committee's recommendations, coupled with his own military experience and judgment, proved insurmountable. The committee dug in, counseling in June 1956 that the administration refrain from launching a satellite using the Redstone. Stewart pointed out that the tracking equipment needed to monitor the satellite in orbit was not ready yet and maintained that an early launch "would seriously compromise the strong moral position internationally" that America had developed by presenting the Vanguard satellite as an open project. E. V. Murphree, a special assistant for guided missiles, worried that a Jupiter C satellite "would most surely flirt with failure" unless a development program preceded it, and it would divert ABMA resources, including scientists, from the missiles. Moreover, he argued that a Jupiter C launch would be one isolated space shot, whereas Vanguard was to be followed by at least five more satellites, and a 1956 launch was even before the IGY was scheduled to begin in June 1957. Stewart Committee member Clifford Furnas pointed out that if the Jupiter C program suddenly took over the American satellite effort, scientists would feel slighted, the Vanguard program's morale would suffer, and the move would wound relations between the military and science.[68]

Importantly, the administration rated science higher than speed. The NSC Planning Board, in a November 1956 memorandum, concluded that the United States could overcome any psychological or image gains the Soviet Union made with a first satellite by ensuring that the American IGY satellites contributed more to science. "And basically," Ewald recalled, "the Pentagon said they didn't think [trying to launch a first satellite] was a good idea. Andy [Goodpaster] went back to Eisenhower with it and there it died. And nobody was thinking of what will be the effect on public opinion if the Russians get there first."[69]

After Sputnik, complaints that Eisenhower had prevented America from winning a "race" aroused his temper. He scolded two Army generals, Holgar Nelson Toftoy and John Barclay, after they implied that Eisenhower and Wilson had blocked their efforts to launch an American satellite in 1956. Reminding them that he had deliberately separated the civilian and military satellite efforts, he said a space race was "exactly the wrong impression" to convey and instructed the men to use "no comment" to discuss satellites.[70] He later remarked that it was ironic "that we should undertake something in good faith only to get behind the eight-ball in a contest which we never considered a contest."[71]

"To make a mistake in judgment is excusable, but to make a mistake in preparation can't be excused," Eisenhower once said. Yet he had stumbled on both counts, misjudging the impact of the first satellite and failing to prepare an efficient satellite program. He wisely continued to support Van-guard despite cost increases, but given its psychological impact and implica-tions for national security, he failed to give the project adequate priority. Indeed, poor funding and a lower-priority status hampered Vanguard, which led scientists overseas to mock it as "Rearguard."[72] Further, from a political standpoint, by playing down prestige and a "first" satellite, Eisenhower weak-ened his presidential power. The post-Sputnik uproar nurtured doubts about his judgment and created a wellspring of pressure for crash programs and more spending. It was precisely what Eisenhower wished to avoid, and it cast a pall over his second term. That was a shame. He would have needed no special efforts to bolster his or America's prestige had he focused on win-ning the satellite race. As Arnold Frutkin commented, Eisenhower "would not have had to say a word if we had gotten the first satellite up. . . . He would not have needed any propaganda. The satellite would have made it all for him."[73]

Jupiter C and the Satellite Race

After the Stewart Committee decision to support the Navy's Vanguard, the Huntsville ABMA team was bitter but unbowed. Von Braun and Medaris badgered the Defense Department to ask that they be granted permission to launch a satellite using the Jupiter C—which they said they could do by January 1957—or be a backup should Vanguard fail. The Defense Depart-ment turned down each request. Medaris ruefully recalled that they made "a bargain-basement bid to make six satellite launchings for eighteen mil-lion dollars, pleading the desirability, at those low prices, of providing back-up assurance to the nation's prestige that was riding precariously on the Vanguard. . . . [W]e were told to go back and mind our own business."[74]

Still, ABMA continued to tinker with the Jupiter C, improving its nose cone so that it could withstand the heat of atmospheric reentry. These tests also enabled ABMA to keep a rocket ready to send a satellite into space in case the Vanguard faltered or the Defense Department finally acceded to Medaris's pleas. ABMA was using the Jupiter C as a potential launch vehi-cle, while the Pentagon assumed that it was testing an IRBM, which it was in fact doing. Medaris also kept two Jupiter C missiles in storage at Hunts-ville, ready to use if he ever received permission to launch a satellite.[75]

On September 20, 1956, ABMA successfully launched the first Jupiter C from Cape Canaveral. It landed in the ocean 3,350 miles from the launch pad, setting a distance record and gaining a maximum speed of 13,000 miles per hour. Even more important, its fourth stage had reached an altitude of 682 miles, another record—the highest any man-made object had ever gone. Achieving this altitude, it could have sent a satellite into orbit. Thus, September 20, 1956, could have gone down in history as the date of the world's first satellite launch. A mix of jubilation and disconsolation filled von Braun. Jupiter C performed "perfectly," he said, and "we knew that with a little bit of luck we could put a satellite into space. Unfortunately, no one asked us to do it."[76] In fact, before the launch, Medaris warned von Braun not to try to send up a satellite, even though he could have used the fourth stage for one. "Wernher, I must put you under orders personally to inspect that fourth stage to make sure it is not live," Medaris said.

In 1957 ABMA conducted two more Jupiter C flights, including an August 8 launch carrying a missile nose cone that reached an altitude of 300 miles. Recovering the nose cone in the ocean, ABMA found it in excellent shape. That was a remarkable breakthrough: in previous tests, the nose cone burned up during reentry, as it went from a no-oxygen environment to earth's heavy atmosphere at speeds reaching 15,000 miles per hour. Heat friction created temperatures hotter than those on the sun's surface, which would endanger a nuclear warhead. This time, the Jupiter C used a special ablative material that dispersed the heat, shielding the nose cone and preventing it from disintegrating; the ceramic protected so well against the heat that a paper letter within the nose cone survived intact. Its fall slowed by a parachute, the nose cone hit the ocean, discharged dyes to color the water, and released a buoy with a flashing light and radio transmitter. Aided by these devices, ships retrieved the nose cone.[77]

As it tested Jupiter C, ABMA also was developing the Jupiter IRBM, conducting its first successful flight on May 31, 1957. In all, ABMA conducted five tests of Jupiter. In June, the Air Force tested the Atlas missile, and it reached an altitude of 9,500 feet; a second test flight in September reached 14,500 feet. That month, the Navy also test-fired its Polaris for the first time, and in September, the Thor missile achieved its first successful test and reached an altitude of 1,300 nautical miles.[78] Contrary to popular opinion, 1957 was a banner year in American missile development—although after Sputnik, no one dared say so.

America's missile achievements showed that this race ran full throttle, and during the summer of 1957, the satellite race—which had far less urgency up to this point—heated up, too. Vanguard workers heard rumors that the Soviets were working on their own satellite, and they felt that "we better get ready to launch an actual satellite, for real, earlier," John Neilon recalled, and he and his colleagues began to work overtime on the project.

Yet at ABMA, even Medaris underestimated the Soviets, and one exchange showed that he retroactively overstated his own wisdom and actions in pushing for a first U.S. satellite. On September 27, 1957, ABMA engineer Ernst Stuhlinger approached Medaris and expressed concerns about an imminent Soviet satellite launch. "The shock for our country would be tremendous if they were the first in space!" Stuhlinger exclaimed. Medaris brushed his worries aside, saying, "Now look . . . don't get tense. You know how complicated it is to launch a satellite. These people will not be able to do it. . . . Go back to your laboratory and relax!"[79]

By coincidence, on the day of Sputnik's launch, the incoming defense secretary, Neil McElroy, happened to be visiting the Redstone Arsenal with a retinue of Army brass. McElroy, a six-feet-four-inch former Harvard basketball center, gave up his $285,000 yearly salary as head of consumer products giant Proctor and Gamble to accept the $25,000 annual pay as defense secretary, and he was about to undergo an on-the-job baptism by fire. Breathless with excitement, an Army public relations officer rushed over to von Braun and told him about the Russian satellite. Medaris recalled, "There was an instant of stunned silence. Then von Braun started to talk as if he had suddenly been vaccinated with a vitriola needle." He had warned that the Vanguard could never beat the Soviets, he said. "For God's sake turn us loose and let us do something," he pleaded. "We can put up a satellite in sixty days, Mr. McElroy! Just give us a green light and sixty days!"[80] But Eisenhower's reaction was far more restrained than von Braun's.

 **CHAPTER 3**

Eisenhower's Reaction to Sputnik

Eisenhower believed that the worst mistakes came during panics. "Don't make any mistakes in a hurry" was one of his favorite maxims. In 1955, he tried to tamp down tensions when a war scare rattled Asia, as China conducted bombing raids on the islands of Quemoy and Matsu. Eisenhower told reporters, "I have one great belief: nobody in war or anywhere else ever made a good decision if he was frightened to death. You have to look facts in the face, but you have to have the stamina to do it without just going hysterical."[1]

A man of discipline and self-restraint, Eisenhower was "exceedingly controlled" in temperament, William Ewald recalled. Personal habits exemplified this trait. For most of his adult life, he smoked four cigarette packs a day, and during World War II, he wrote to Mamie that his doctor had given him "a stinging lecture" for smoking so much. In early 1949, after a physician told him to limit his smoking to only a pack a day, he quit cold turkey. So confident was Eisenhower that he could resist smoking, he laid out cigarettes around his house, proving to himself that he could flout temptation lying everywhere before him.[2]

Eisenhower's self-restraint was also visible in his political conduct. As Fred Greenstein has shown in his seminal work, *The Hidden-Hand Presidency*, Eisenhower refused to "engage in personalities." Rather than publicly attack adversaries, even so hated a figure as Senator Joseph McCarthy, he bit his lip and waited for them to self-immolate.

Eisenhower also bridled himself at press conferences, professing ignorance or mentally meandering to avoid letting slip inflammatory statements that could exacerbate Cold War tensions. This performance came at the risk of looking ill informed and detached, but its purpose was caution. Better to be quiet or opaque than to say something controversial, Eisenhower believed, once saying that "a certain sphinx-like quality will do a lot toward enhancing one's reputation." At weekly cabinet meetings, he remained oddly quiet, doodling on a note pad until he decided to break his silence and offer a comment. "Sometimes he remained cautious even when he had a good reason to speak out," Sherman Adams, the curt and intense chief of staff, said of his boss. "Without his sense of restraint, some of the comparatively tranquil pages in the history of the United States during the Eisenhower years might have been written in blood and turmoil. The needs of the time seemed to call for a President of deliberation, one who even seemed to hesitate occasionally."[3]

After Sputnik, Eisenhower wanted Americans to exercise restraint, and his initial public reactions—and those of administration officials—tried in various ways to resist outcries, spread calm, or save face.

 ## The Administration Reacts

At an October 10, 1957 NSC meeting, Eisenhower recalled that during World War II, the Anglo-American strategy for defeating the Germans had faced heated criticism, and every German move brought panicked cries to change or drop the policy. "We never did abandon it. It was a good plan, a long-range plan that had been carefully worked out. We went on and won," Eisenhower said. Urging his staff to remain composed after Sputnik, he added, "There's no reason for hand wringing, just because the Russians got up there first—they're to be congratulated. Sure, we underestimated the propaganda advantages they would gain. But we've lost nothing of our national security, and we shouldn't change our scientific plan." Eisenhower pointed out that administration members would appear before congressional committees or the media. When they did, he expected them to support the U.S. satellite program, which had won NSC approval, he pointed out.[4]

Jupiter C's successes gave Eisenhower's administration confidence in the country's defense and scientific posture, knowledge that kept them calm after Sputnik. Arthur Larson recalled, "We could easily have placed an object in orbit with the old Jupiter. . . . We all knew this, and so you can see why at the White House we had no reason to see Sputnik as some kind of demonstration of Soviet superiority."[5] A comprehensive memorandum from the new defense secretary reaffirmed Eisenhower's confidence in America's strength. Russia had no lead over the United States in science or atomic weapons, Neil McElroy stated, noting that the Soviets' achievement "of a 'first' in placing a satellite in orbit should not be taken as the sole index of their overall scientific and technological capability." McElroy deemed that "[i]n total military strength, the U.S., in our judgment, is still distinctly ahead of the U.S.S.R., although the U.S.S.R. may be ahead in certain specific areas. In the non-military sector, there can be no question but that the U.S. is well ahead of the U.S.S.R." He also assured Eisenhower of "splendid" progress in the American ballistic missile program.[6]

All that was true. Yet despite Eisenhower's emphasis on America's strength, congressional critics and the media argued that Sputnik proved America's vulnerability, especially a lag in missiles, and the Eisenhower administration seemed caught flat-footed. The *New York Times'* James Reston wrote that the White House assumed that "social and political pressures within the Soviet empire would either destroy the Communist system or force it to modify its policies and accept Washington's proposals for disarmament, the unification of Germany and Europe, and the pacification of the Middle East." But Russian scientific and military advances challenged that posture, Reston maintained: "They are forcing reconsideration of the assumption that the Soviet Union is weak and may collapse of its own internal disorders."[7]

Against such reports Eisenhower's aides mounted a clumsy, shambling defense. Some tried to soft-pedal or even dismiss the Soviet achievement. Speechwriter Emmet Hughes said the administration resembled a busy man who looked up from a newspaper and then buried his face again in his reading. Clarence Randall, an administration economist, ridiculed Sputnik as "a silly bauble." Sherman Adams belittled the "Soviet satellites that sail over our heads and land on the front page of every American newspaper." He maintained that there was no space race between the United States and the Soviet Union because "science, not a high score in an outer space basketball game, has been and still is our country's goal."[8]

Charles Wilson chimed in, too. The outgoing defense secretary had a reputation for denigrating scientific research, once scoffing, "Basic research is when you don't know what you are doing" and saying that he did not care what made fried potatoes brown or grass green. Wilson had also derided space satellites. In 1954, when asked about American satellite progress, he replied that he had "enough problems on earth." As to the Soviets' putting the world's first satellite in orbit, he said, "I wouldn't care if they did." Now they had, and Wilson lamely described Sputnik as "a nice scientific trick" and no threat to national security. "Nobody is going to drop anything down on you while you're sleeping, from a satellite, so don't start to worry about what this satellite's going to do," he said. Wilson even denied that the launch indicated that the Soviets had an operational ICBM.[9]

Testifying before Congress, Secretary of State John Foster Dulles argued that one satellite was no benchmark of an entire economic system. He commented that "despotisms generally can achieve certain spectacular results which democracies don't achieve." Around the world, he observed, visitors could see products of regimented governments, such as the Egyptian pyramids or the Roman Coliseum, but he warned against competing against nation-states that used human labor to create such spectaculars. Dulles wondered aloud whether the cost of going to the moon was worth it and "whether it is possible for us to beat the Russians at it. They have a big start on us, you know, in this exploitation of outer space. . . . How much we want to spend in an effort to be second, I don't know." Newspapers slayed him. Calling Dulles "querulous" and a "tired old man," the *Nashville Tennessean*, for instance, blasted his "singular blindness to the new wonders of the world."[10]

The criticism Dulles received characterized the general reaction to White House statements, which assuaged no one. Adams later conceded that his "outer-space basketball" remark was inappropriate. "I was only trying to reflect the President's desire for calm poise," he wrote, "but I had to admit on reflection that my observation seemed to be an overemphasis of the deemphasis." The ineffective remarks only widened the perception that Eisenhower's administration failed to understand the Sputnik challenge.[11]

The comments underscored a larger problem in Eisenhower's presidency, his inability to rein in administration members' headline-grabbing remarks. Colorful comments mottled Eisenhower's policy goals and distorted his presidency. John Foster Dulles's strident statements, for example, proclaiming "brinksmanship," "massive retaliation," and containment's "immorality" dominated media reports and remain etched in histories of the era, even though these views contradicted Eisenhower's own. Earlier in 1957, Treasury Secretary George Humphrey gave a spectacular display of candor in which he criticized administration economic policy and warned of "a depression that will curl your hair." The colorful metaphor did incalculable public relations damage. Here again, after Sputnik, Eisenhower faced the fallout from wayward statements, adding to his woes.[12]

Goodpaster believed that administration members who derided the Soviet achievement "were probably reflecting what they knew to be [Eisenhower's] view," namely, that Sputnik was a scientific accomplishment posing no threat to national security. Eisenhower thought his colleagues' words would do no harm because he saw them as managers "rather than as a major source of policy," Goodpaster explained.[13] But belittling Sputnik was a poor tactic, and it came across as sour grapes. A more effective response would have been to offer generous—even fulsome—praise of Sputnik as a technological achievement. As Harvard University sociologist George Homans advised White House cabinet secretary Maxwell Rabb, "When someone has put something over on you, the only way to take the sting out of it is to *overdo* the praise, to snow the other guy under with it."[14]

Eisenhower carefully avoided disparaging remarks about Sputnik. Some administration members thought the put-downs were "the best way to control the wave of reaction," Larson recalled, "but it wasn't his way. He thoroughly appreciated the achievement." Larson said that "Eisenhower never underestimated the importance and seriousness of the achievement of the Sputnik as such. He fully appreciated what an accomplishment it was from the scientific point of view." Yet from a propaganda point of view, Eisenhower's understanding was wobbly. At first, he said nothing publicly, but he had to control the growing damage. His task was to convince Americans that his emphasis on science and national security was reasonable and right. His presidency depended on it, as did his popularity. In January 1957, as Eisenhower began his second term, his public approval rating stood at 79 percent. After Sputnik, it plunged twenty-two points.[15]

Shocked by the Shock

The post-Sputnik fallout shocked Eisenhower. He noted that Americans had ignored news that the USSR was about to launch a satellite, writing that "in the early part of 1957 the Soviets stated that they expected to orbit a satellite and in a later announcement gave some details of what they expected to do. . . . [T]he public paid no attention to this Soviet announcement." He remarked that on October 1, the *New York Times* had printed a front-page story describing a Soviet satellite. The article hardly caused a stir. Other publications, such as *Astronomer's Circle*, wrote about an impending satellite launch, but the Little Rock desegregation crisis absorbed the media's attention and overshadowed such reports.[16]

Eisenhower viewed the satellite like a lightning bolt outside the window—surprising, but no cause for alarm—and he later commented that the most troubling aspect about the satellite launch "was the intensity of the public concern." During a meeting with science advisors, he expressed bewilderment over the ostensible uproar. "I can't understand why the American people have got so worked up over this thing," he remarked. "It's certainly not going to drop on their heads."[17] Yet his three words "I can't understand" encapsulated his inability to heed the warnings about the prestige of the world's first satellite and grasp the media and political reaction. Eisenhower also expected better from those who knew better. Remarks such as that by physicist Edward Teller, the so-called father of the hydrogen bomb, comparing Sputnik to the Japanese attack on Pearl Harbor, distressed him. It was the spectacle of a scientist acting like a politician, Eisenhower later said. Conversely, he was dismayed at politicians and military men who suddenly tried to speak with scientific knowledge, making irresponsible and uninformed statements.[18]

Eisenhower hoped that Americans would remain as calm as he was. Larson recalled, "I can say with complete confidence that Eisenhower personally did not believe the orbiting of Sputnik was an occasion for alarm. What he did believe was that a lot of Americans were heading into an orgy of self-commiseration and inferiority as to our science, our education, our entire system." Viewing Sputnik through the lens of national security, Eisenhower saw it as he did other crises in his presidency that warranted cautious responses. "Whether it is sputnik or it's Quemoy or it's Korea or whatever it is," he later said, "what we have to do is to stand steady, as I see it, to be alert, to watch what we are doing, and to make certain that we know how and where we have to produce action if action became necessary. . . . [The] adequacy of our defenses is not going to be especially increased or strengthened by any particular sudden action in response to one of these moments of increased tension."[19]

Though Eisenhower misjudged Sputnik's psychological impact, he did not believe that the launch merited the self-pity and mourning that Americans "were beginning to wallow in—[the feeling that] everything about our culture was wrong, and everything about the Russians was ultra-smart, we were way behind. He knew better than that," recalled Larson. Editorialists and politicians suddenly saw huge holes in American science, education, and military strength where none existed. Eisenhower remembered that when the British discovered penicillin, Americans had expressed appreciation, and he was personally grateful that the antibiotic was available to his troops during World War II. "I heard no one complain that the English achievement belittled the quality of science in America," he said. When Larson suggested that the event might signal a time for the president to ask Americans to sacrifice after five years of prosperity, Eisenhower demurred. That kind of call, he believed, might exaggerate the threat that Sputnik allegedly posed.[20] Moreover, as Jimmy Carter's 1979 "Crisis of Confidence" speech illustrated two decades later, Americans felt uncomfortable with a president who blamed them for a spiritual crisis, especially when coupled with a call for tighter belts and a sense of limits.

To the *New York Times*, Eisenhower seemed outwardly unruffled. "Aside from seeing more of the scientists, the President has not materially changed his way of life in the days since Sputnik as compared with the days before," the paper observed. "It has not interfered with his golf games around Washington, nor has it changed his plans for the regular mid-November ten-day golfing holiday in Augusta, Georgia." Nor did Eisenhower seem compelled to dwell on the Soviet satellite. At an October 11 cabinet meeting, no one mentioned the satellite. Discussion of Sputnik at the three remaining October NSC meetings was conspicuous by its absence.[21]

The low-key response epitomized Eisenhower's leadership style. Disdaining what he called "desk-pounders" and fostering a public image of a relaxed president, he avoided publicizing intensive activities to convey the impression that the nation and the world were sound and peaceful without his having to toil relentlessly. Critics expressed frustration that Eisenhower conserved his political capital, construing his composure as complacency or a reluctance to confront harsh national security realities. "Because of the element of restraint running through all of [his] principles," wrote Larson, "it was tempting for Eisenhower's critics to try to apply to him the most ill-fitting label of all—'lack of leadership.'" In explaining how Eisenhower managed to preside over eight years of peace and international conflict resolution, Larson wrote, "It is easy for the activist to become exasperated with the slowness, subtlety, and undramatic character of the new kind of crisis management [in the nuclear age], and therefore also to have become impatient with its patient practitioner, President Eisenhower.[22] Critics thundered for a dramatic and urgent reaction to Sputnik; but Eisenhower understood the value of patience.

Many scientists and engineers, like Eisenhower, acknowledged the Soviet achievement with good sportsmanship. "We didn't expect it, so we were surprised," Hans Bethe admitted. "But we were used to recognizing good work wherever it occurs, and in this case, [Sputnik] was that." Robert Mackey, an electrical engineer working on Vanguard who later became the project manager for the Echo satellite, recalled that while most Vanguard team members felt disappointed, he and some other colleagues were excited about the Soviet feat and relished the competition, likening the situation to a football game in which the Soviets scored first but left the ball in America's hands.[23]

The sports analogy had merit. In a sense, the Cold War was a race or, more fittingly, a series of races. After a 1958 visit to Russia, U.S. Commissioner of

Education Lawrence Derthick commented, "The Soviet Union is like one vast, sprawling college campus on the eve of a football game with its great rival. That rival is the United States. The game is economic and cultural conquest of the world." As almost an athletic competition, the Cold War placed Eisenhower in a familiar role. Sports, especially football, had given a young Eisenhower his first taste of leadership and teamwork and allowed him to apply his determination and optimism toward tangible goals. These talents were especially critical given the agitated state of some members of Congress and the media, which troubled the president because it could filter down to the public. When asked what concerned Eisenhower most after the Soviet launch, Goodpaster replied, "the public anxiety, I would say."[24] The Sputnik panic tested Eisenhower's ability both to calm and rally Americans.

Meeting the Media

A presidential press conference had been scheduled for October 9, and the nation waited for Eisenhower's first public words on the Space Age. *Time* remarked, "To the man whose job it was to speak and act for the U.S. and the free world, it was a challenge to be met," for converging on the president were "all the frets, frustrations, and fears of a suddenly fretful and frustrated people." The evening before facing reporters, perhaps to work out his own frustrations, Eisenhower hit golf balls late into the night.[25]

To prepare for the press conference, Eisenhower asked his staff to dig up information, especially on guided missile development, to deflect any charges that he was weak on defense. He had no desire to disparage Sputnik, he explained to Detlev Bronk, the president of the National Academy of Sciences, but he wanted "to allay hysteria and alarm" by emphasizing that the satellite showed the Soviets had "a thrust mechanism" with power and accuracy but posed no threat to national security.[26]

The thirty-minute press conference became a virtual media feeding frenzy, as reporters queried the president repeatedly about Sputnik. Twenty different reporters asked questions; only two focused on Little Rock, the crisis that had dominated the October 3 press conference. Merriman Smith of United Press International began by reminding Eisenhower that the Soviets had a satellite and claimed to have fired an ICBM, "none of which this country has done," he noted, sighing heavily. "I ask you, sir, what are we going to do about it?" With careful detail, Eisenhower summarized the inception of the U.S. satellite program, stressing that he undertook it as an IGY contribution. He called Sputnik a "small ball in the air," maintaining that "the value of that

FIGURE 1.   Presidential press conference of October 9, 1957, five days after the Sputnik launch. Eisenhower showed an almost eerie calm, which reporters challenged. (Library of Congress, Prints & Photos Division, *U.S. News and World Report* collection)

satellite going around the earth is still problematical." He further argued, "I wouldn't believe that at this moment you have to fear the intelligence aspects of this," nor did it corroborate Soviet claims to an operational ICBM, even though it proved that the Soviets had powerful rockets.[27]

As for science and space, there was no race, Eisenhower maintained. The American satellite would contribute openly to the IGY, and that was that. "There never has been one nickel asked for accelerating the program," he said. "Never has it been considered as a race; merely an engagement on our part to put up a vehicle of this kind during the period that I have already mentioned [the IGY]." In light of the American project's scientific character, Eisenhower told reporters that when he received advance information on the Soviet launch, "there didn't seem to be a reason for just trying to grow hysterical about it." America's space program was progressing well, the government was expending much effort and money, and "I don't know what more we could have done," he said. The American satellite would be more sophisticated than Sputnik, he said, twice promising that it would provide "much more information."[28]

The plaintive statements indicated how Eisenhower felt he had done everything necessary to support America's fledgling space effort. On a deeper level, he likely "realized how bad was the analysis he was getting, and it wasn't just technical analysis but analysis related to his foreign policy objectives," commented Eugene Skolnikoff. That realization would lead to a change in Eisenhower's thinking that affected him for the rest of his presidency. On matters related to defense and science, he turned more to his own team of scientists for advice and relied less on ad hoc bodies like the Stewart Committee. Eisenhower's defensive tone also tried to convey his knowledge that the United States was far ahead of the Soviet Union. He wanted to say "that we had a very, very powerful military arrangement," William Ewald recalled, "and that we had nothing to fear on that score, and that we were going to maintain that leadership."[29]

Yet the president's performance failed to convince the media. Rather than shielding him from criticism, his arguments over budget money and scientific sophistication provided more slings and arrows for media and political opponents. The *New York Post* editorialized that Eisenhower had merely tried "to cover up America's scientific lag." Another newspaper columnist noted that he "displayed a curious earthbound preoccupation with money," repeatedly stressing the costs of satellite development: "his performance had the incongruity of Buck Rogers haggling about the fare to the moon." While Eisenhower expected the American satellite to provide more information than Sputnik, the columnist commented, "He did not explain how this would impress the Indians, Indonesians, and other uncommitted people who are currently awed by the Russian achievement. Do extra gadgets make up for being six months late?"[30]

Leading Democrats proved just as critical. Senator Hubert Humphrey ridiculed Eisenhower's "pseudo-optimism." Lyndon Johnson scoffed at Eisenhower's promise of a superior U.S. satellite: "Perhaps it will even have chrome trim and automatic windshield wipers." Michigan's Democratic governor, G. Mennen Williams, launched a doggerel broadside at the president:

Oh, little Sputnik, flying high,
With made-in-Moscow beep,
You tell the world it's Commie sky,
And Uncle Sam's asleep.
You say on fairway and on rough,
The Kremlin knows it all.
We hope our golfer knows enough
To get us on the ball.[31]

The press conference marked a low point in Eisenhower's relations with reporters. During World War II, he had been a media darling who charmed

FIGURE 2.   One of many Eisenhower critics in the media, the *Washington Post*'s Herblock saw the president's response to Sputnik as flaccid. (Herb Block Foundation)

reporters and used them in the war effort. But then he was a nonpartisan, patriotic general; as president, the charm wore off. He began to look askance at reporters, concerned that they were always hunting for a "sensation and a ready-made story," which caused "depreciation of the prestige of the presidential office." Besides betraying his testy feelings toward reporters, Eisenhower's press conference also reflected the pattern of his initial reaction to Sputnik. He stubbornly stood by his approval of the Vanguard program that divorced military and civilian rocket development, and he refused to alter "the present orderly procedure to produce an earth satellite."[32]

Meeting Scientists

On October 14, Eisenhower observed his sixty-seventh birthday, and it was his unhappiest yet as president. The charges of complacency, of an old, fusty leader who failed to inspire Americans and envision new national ventures, had a ring of truth. He appeared out of touch, unable to appreciate Sputnik's full value or—the criticism that stung him most—negligent over national security.

He turned to scientists for advice. On October 15, Eisenhower met with the ODM Science Advisory Committee, fifteen of the nation's foremost scientists who served as presidential advisers. He had scheduled the meeting before Sputnik, but it had new significance. He recalled that as he prepared to meet with the scientists he was "curious" to discover whether they "really thought that American science was being truly outdistanced," and he wanted to know whether they had any proposals to bolster U.S. science.[33]

Edwin Land, president of the Polaroid Corporation, told Eisenhower that the nub of the problem was the American attitude toward science. Whereas the Soviet interest in science was a "kind of social passion," Land said, Americans lacked that drive. He urged the president to act as a role model and inspire boys and girls in scientific adventure. Eisenhower expressed his willingness to do so, perhaps by making some galvanizing speeches. Because of Sputnik, Eisenhower noted, Americans "are alarmed and thinking about science, and perhaps this alarm could be turned to a constructive end." Isador Rabi, whom Eisenhower had known since his Columbia presidency, warned that the Soviets had science momentum on their side, having made great strides in only a few decades. Unless the United States made more progress, Rabi warned, the Soviets might overtake America, just as the United States had outpaced Europe within just a generation.[34] The group also urged more scientific cooperation with America's allies. Rabi stressed the importance of a presidential science advisor. At present, Rabi noted, no one gave scientific advice the way economists dispensed their counsel, and Eisenhower agreed, saying he needed guidance on projects such as the IGY.[35]

The meeting helped Eisenhower to formulate his public response to Sputnik. Although concerned, the scientists were neither pessimistic nor panicky. Had they responded in the exaggerated way that the media and politicians had, they might have lost Eisenhower's confidence, even led him to breed a suspicion toward them. Instead, their lucid thoughts provided a starting point in a policy reaction. Their emphasis on learning, for example, inspired the president to support federal aid to education, a notion he had resisted; the idea of a science advisor also grabbed him. As physicist Hans Bethe recalled, "It was a marvelous meeting, because Eisenhower understood every suggestion we made; he saw very clearly why it was a good suggestion."[36]

The meeting established a new link between the president and science because the group accurately framed Ike's image problem. He had often seemed estranged from scientists, once even disparaging them as "just another pressure group."[37] The White House needed a bridge to the scientific community, and the era's technological breakthroughs made increased contact vital. During their meeting with the president, the scientists had planted the seed for policy changes, from which grew a closer cooperation between the White House and their world. In the ensuing weeks, the ideas from the scientists' meeting grew into administration policy.

Just two days after the meeting, Eisenhower hosted Queen Elizabeth and Prince Philip of England. The royal visit was the thirty-one-year-old queen's first to the United States, and Eisenhower used the occasion to reiterate his belief that one satellite was no defining index of the Soviet Union's values. He said that "the total of the Free World's assets are so much greater that those of our potential enemy," and it was "ridiculous to compare their brains, their abilities in science, philosophical thought, or in any phase of culture or of the arts with the combined total of the Free World." Still, the Cold War demanded allied scientific cooperation. "Our scientists must work together," he urged. "NATO should not be thought of as merely a military alliance. NATO is a way of grouping ability—of our manhood, our resources, of our industries and our factories."[38]

The visit from the royals gave Eisenhower a respite from political assaults, and he enjoyed their company so much that when they left he stood waving at their limousine until it disappeared from view. Grinning broadly, he said, "If they'd stayed a day or two longer we'd soon be calling them Liz and Phil!" The visit also gave Eisenhower a chance to compare the British Sputnik moment with his own, and he learned that Britons had responded as he did. As he later reported, both the Queen and Prince Philip "were amazed at our press reaction to Sputnik. Each one, independently, told me so. They said that the people in London just gave it one day of excitement, then went about their business." That perspective revealed that international reactions were more congruent with Eisenhower's. In turn, Eisenhower's response comported with his principles.[39]

CHAPTER 4

Eisenhower's Principles

In 1948, at age fifty-eight, Eisenhower took up painting. British prime minister Winston Churchill had encouraged him to try it, and Eisenhower got his chance one day when an artist came to paint Mamie's portrait. The painter was about to throw away a canvas when Eisenhower salvaged it and decided to dabble himself. He was hooked. "For me the real benefit is the fact that [painting] gives me an excuse to be absolutely alone and interferes not at all with what I am pleased to call my 'contemplative powers,'" he once explained. At the White House, Eisenhower had a special room upstairs where he painted, often late at night before going to bed; he also quietly slipped away there during the day to retreat from the crush of presidential activity. The room, which overlooked Pennsylvania Avenue, had no ringing telephone so that Eisenhower could escape without being bothered. Sometimes, when James Hagerty went to the room, he found the president just sitting before a blank canvas, lost in thought.[1]

Eisenhower's painting reflected his protean interests. With a wealth of pursuits and pastimes, Eisenhower exemplified the versatile leader. Speech-writer Bryce Harlow called him the "compleat" president: "He was the most completely rounded American I shall ever know. Not a perfect man. He's more like the Olympic all-around athlete, decathlon—not the best in everything but best in most things, and therefore the finest athlete of all. That's Eisenhower. Personality-wise, ability-wise, motivation-wise, he was about the finest leader we've ever had." Budget Director Maurice Stans observed of Eisenhower, "Though not an economist, he was nevertheless interested in fostering the principles of a sound economy. Though not a businessman, he respected the contributions of competitive business to the nation's progress. Though not a legislator, he knew that the key to legislation was compromise."[2]

Though not a historian, Eisenhower had also shown a keen interest in history from childhood, and as a general and president, he repaired to the experiences of idols like George Washington and Robert E. Lee. He had a deep admiration for Abraham Lincoln and often quoted his speeches and aphorisms. He was also not a philosopher, but Eisenhower expressed many philosophical ideas for the country. He often spoke of "principles," once saying, "You must live by principles; principles, not expediency." Larson observed, "For almost every decision, whether earth-shaking or trivial, he appeared to have some underlying guiding principle into which he would dip in order to dredge up a specific answer to the question at hand."[3] Eisenhower's principles formed the bedrock of his presidency and shaped how he guided America's space endeavors.

Eisenhower's Secrecy

A common complaint after Sputnik concerned the dearth of public information. The *Washington Post* wrote that the president "should keep the country informed at frequent intervals of the steps that are being taken to close the defense gap and of deficiencies that demand more concentrated effort." "Perhaps there has been too much secrecy," Lyndon Johnson said, adding that "there is such a thing as keeping a project so secret that the people who have to work on it can't find out anything themselves."[4]

PSAC member Caryl Haskins believed that "Eisenhower had a full appreciation of the grave importance of Sputnik, and of its historical significance," although that cognizance "tended to be muted by frequent reluctance to share his closest views with the general public." In that respect, Eisenhower had unwittingly contributed to the post-Sputnik uproar. By keeping America's defense secrets too tight, Eisenhower had left Americans unaware of Soviet as well as U.S. rocket technology, and his sphinx-like silence failed to tout the Pentagon's progress in ICBMs and IRBMs. "It is certainly true," Haskins recalled, "that Eisenhower had an exaggerated view of military secrecy."[5] Indeed, covert operations abroad (such as Eisenhower's use of the CIA to install pro-American regimes in Iran and Guatemala in

1953 and 1954, respectively) and nuclear weapons development were central elements in Eisenhower's strategy to fight a long Cold War without running up debt, but they made Eisenhower touchy about secrecy. The veil covering Eisenhower's activities made the media and Congress psychologically prone to the Sputnik surprise and quick to claim U.S. defense deficiencies.

The secrecy reflected Ike's military background. An army's success depended on concealing information and Eisenhower acquired this idea from his warfare experiences. During World War II, many plans—especially the D-Day invasion—rested on the utmost secrecy, which he carefully guarded, issuing firm orders not to let word slip. When one general carelessly let out operation details while drunk, the punishment was swift. Eisenhower demoted him and shipped him back to the United States, remarking to George Marshall that he wished he could shoot loose-lipped security risks.[6]

As president, Eisenhower received intelligence on Soviet rocketry. When the Russians built their massive Kazakhstan launch pad to test the R-7 rocket, U-2 spy planes monitored site work. As the editor of *Aviation Week and Space Technology* wrote after Sputnik, a superb American intelligence network "explains why President Eisenhower and his top defense officials could shrug their shoulders and blandly announce to the public: 'This is no surprise; we knew about it all the time.'" After administration members denied that Sputnik changed their estimates of the Soviet Union's technological capabilities, one ex-CIA official remarked, "The tragic thing is that they are telling the truth." His regret was that although the White House had kept abreast of Soviet rocketry, it failed to apprise the public. Secretary of State Dulles admitted that the administration had vigilantly watched Soviet technology, saying it respected its rival and knew the Soviets bested the United States in some technology fields. But as *Fortune* magazine complained, "It failed to convey this respect, and the information on which this respect was founded, to the American people."[7]

Even administration members rued the tight clampdown on news of U.S. missile development, which hurt both the White House and Americans. James Killian ascribed the Sputnik cacophony in part to "the excessive secrecy that enveloped our ballistic missile technology. People were woefully ignorant of how much qualitatively advanced and forehanded technology had been under development by the Department of Defense. . . . This ignorance—the result of excessive secrecy—undoubtedly contributed to the American people's frantic reactions to Soviet pronouncements and achievements."[8]

To administration insiders, Eisenhower's passion for secrecy was infamous, and his anger over leaks was far greater than his memoirs revealed. Aides reported that he exploded in wrath over security leaks, which he took strong measures to prevent or protest. Three weeks after Sputnik, he instructed an aide to fly to Manhattan to meet with Donald McGraw, president of the McGraw-Hill Publishing Company, to discuss a just-published issue of *Aviation Week and Space Technology* containing information that he believed compromised national security.[9]

Eisenhower "used to get furious about the leaks to the press," Attorney General Herbert Brownell recalled. Officials divulged information partly for profit, the president thought, and their disclosures threatened the nation. In November 1959, he called Secretary of State Christian Herter to say that he was "sick and tired" about leaks he suspected came from the State Department, expressing his desire to catch the culprit. During a February 1960 flight to Cape Canaveral, Eisenhower fumed about security leaks by Senator Stuart Symington and other members of Congress, even questioning their patriotism.[10]

Eisenhower followed precedents that became well defined during World War II, when Franklin Roosevelt kept the Manhattan Project an airtight secret. Robert Sherwood, the FDR speechwriter who coined the wartime phrase "arsenal of democracy," remarked that his boss had a mind with a "heavily forested interior" and failed to inform even Vice President Harry Truman about the atom bomb. Eisenhower "didn't make the secrecy," physicist Hans Bethe observed. "Roosevelt made the secrecy. The atomic bomb project was completely secret and even its existence was completely secret, more secret than was useful," noting that even with all the precautions, the Soviet Union still acquired both atomic and hydrogen bomb technology.[11]

Cold War suspicions reinforced the confidentiality. Haskins recalled "the intensity and pervasiveness of the Soviet espionage effort" and noted that "Eisenhower had this threat continually at the front of his mind." The Soviet Union was far more cloaked than America, with even Moscow's phone book confidential. Eisenhower complained that "in the Soviet Union there is a fetish of secrecy and concealment. This is a major cause of international tension and uneasiness today." "[The Soviets] were extremely secretive right up to the [Sputnik launch]," Herbert York recalled. "They never showed any pictures of Sputnik even after it was launched. . . . So it wasn't Eisenhower who kept the [satellite] program a secret. It was the Soviets."[12] The Soviets kept Sputnik's details out of public view, and only in 1967 did they display the R-7 rocket. They also concealed the name of the Soviet space program's architect, Sergei Korolev, treating him as a security risk and insisting that the government, rather than any individual, bathe in the glory of Soviet achievements. "Chief designer" was Korolev's official appellation, and only after his death in 1966 did the world learn his identity.[13]

Ironically, the trump card that Eisenhower held in his hand—the object that could have quelled concerns over Soviet satellites and missiles—was too secret to reveal: the U-2 spy plane and the intelligence information it reaped. "I would say that Eisenhower's failure—and it's an understandable one—was that he could not use this key piece of information," said William Ewald, who believed that "there is no way that Eisenhower really could have allayed public opinion short of revealing the U-2." U-2 intelligence would have been the coup de grâce to charges that America trailed Russia in rockets. But U-2 flights over the Soviet Union were diplomatic dynamite; Eisenhower conceded that if the Russians had done the same to the United States, he would have considered it an act of war. Moreover, blowing the program's cover would have ended it, depriving the United States of further valuable intelligence. By staying silent, Ewald argued, Eisenhower bought "two more years of flying over the key Russian installations. He wanted to be sure that he knew everything . . . about the strength of their military system." Senator Barry Goldwater observed that "Ike took the heat, grinned, and kept his mouth shut."[14]

Yet democracies are built on openness and transparency, while it is authoritarian regimes that rest on a cloak-and-dagger mentality and covert operations. When secrecy has become a presidential preoccupation, it has sometimes bred rogue operations, such as Nixon's White House plumbers or Ronald Reagan's Iran-Contra cabal. Moreover, presidential secrecy begets more press probing and a retributive attitude among reporters. Ewald observed that "a wise president is as open as possible, taking into his confidence the public, not just his advisers: Sputniks, like Vietnams, cannot be hidden." In the end, it did Ike little good to fulminate over press leaks. Donald Regan, who served as Ronald Reagan's treasury secretary and later chief of staff, wrote, "As a practical matter it is impossible to control the leakage of information in a large democratic society in which many people in the government have access to its innermost deliberations." Rather than provoking his wrath, leaks "never failed to amaze" Reagan, who accepted them with more equanimity than Eisenhower did.[15]

Ironically, Eisenhower knew that disseminating information helped to keep Americans secure. He stressed that all Americans needed to grasp public issues and their import. "Public opinion is the only motivating force there is in a republic or in a democracy," he said, "and that public opinion must be an informed one if it is going to be effective in solving the problems that face this poor world internationally and in many instances domestically." During the 1952 campaign, when President Truman told candidate Eisenhower that he would provide weekly CIA information for him, Eisenhower replied that because Americans should be apprised of all important world facts (except for sensitive national security information), "I would want it understood that the possession of these reports will in no other way limit my freedom to discuss or analyze foreign programs as my judgment dictates." Eisenhower's response angered Truman, but it indicated that he placed a high premium on the dialogue with Americans that open information generated.[16]

After Sputnik, Eisenhower's security clampdown hobbled rather than helped; an ignorant press became an agitated press. Privy to information to which reporters were not, the president felt stunned at the media uproar. One effect of Sputnik, the *Wall Street Journal* hoped, was to question "the usefulness of our wrapping military-scientific research in the protective mantle of secrecy."[17]

Yet Eisenhower never learned the lesson, and to the end, he deflected criticism of his secrecy. At his last presidential press conference, a reporter told him that "some of your critics contend that one liberty, the people's right to know, has suffered under your administration because you have tolerated the abuse of executive privilege in the Defense Department and other departments and agencies." Eisenhower brusquely brushed off the idea, retorting, "Well, they are critics and they have the right to criticize." He then moved on to the next question.[18]

Surveillance

Among Eisenhower's principles, peace stood first. His chief goal as president was "the job of keeping this world at peace," he once said. During the 1952 campaign, he spoke before a group of World War II veterans, some of whom bore war wounds. Ewald recalled that Eisenhower was so moved that "it was all he could do to hold on to the lectern. He said, 'I just want to assure you that I'm running for president for just one reason, that is to ensure that nothing like that war will ever occur again.'" One of Eisenhower's aims was "the avoidance of useless, needless expenditures of human life or human bodies, making casualties," said Roemer McPhee, a special counsel to the president. Eisenhower once declared, "War is the ultimate failure of everything you try to do as a country. It's the ultimate failure of diplomacy. It's the ultimate failure of civil behavior."[19]

Eisenhower belonged to a generation of Americans who never forgot the day the Japanese struck at Pearl Harbor. More than anything else, he feared another surprise attack, which nuclear weapons would make more devastating. He remarked, "Actually, the only thing we fear is an atomic attack delivered by air on our cities." Eisenhower once defended his use of espionage by saying, "No one wants another Pearl Harbor. This means we must have knowledge of military forces and preparations around the world, especially those capable of massive surprise attacks." As insurance against a surprise attack, Eisenhower agreed to hold simulation drills in which he and top officials fled to a secret bunker in the North Carolina mountains to continue the federal government's operations. He also approved the construction of the Greenbrier bunker, buried in West Virginia's hills, where congressional leaders were to evacuate in a nuclear attack. But even the CIA could give no reassurances to allay his fears of a surprise attack. During Eisenhower's first months in office, CIA Director Allen Dulles said that his agency could provide no advance warning of a Soviet first strike.[20] Thus, to keep tabs on Soviet plans and guard against a sudden attack, Eisenhower made full use of espionage.

Surveillance over the Soviet Union was vital to Eisenhower. In the late 1940s, the government even resorted to devices such as balloons with cameras, which floated over the USSR taking pictures. Eisenhower approved the balloon surveillance but was disturbed when Russians shot them down. In July 1958, when a balloon went down over Poland, he ordered an end to the missions and their funding.[21] He still needed to check Soviet arms development, though, especially if he achieved an achieve arms control breakthrough, so his administration monitored Soviet missile work through two principal means. One was a CIA radar station in Turkey that allowed U.S. intelligence to eavesdrop on Soviet airwaves, giving valuable information on Soviet progress in rocket boosters.[22]

The other tool, vastly more important, was the U-2. The aircraft was a technological marvel. Its fuel supply could last more than 5,000 miles, enabling it to cover a country as sprawling as Russia. From altitudes of more than 70,000 feet, it took pictures so clear that Eisenhower said he could see parking lot lines between cars and individual cows on his Gettysburg farm. The official government story was that the spy plane was a high-altitude weather jet, and security leaks about the U-2 naturally angered Eisenhower.[23]

The president hated sending the spy planes over the Soviet Union. But as Andrew Goodpaster recalled, he ordered the overflights out of the "ugly necessity" of gaining information on Soviet defenses. He also acted out of his own frustration that Soviet secrecy created, causing Americans to feel anxious about Soviet military power and to support defense spending that Eisenhower wanted to reduce.[24]

The U-2 kept Eisenhower current on Soviet satellite and rocketry work, bracing him for Sputnik and allowing him to remain unfazed in the teeth of media and congressional criticism. In June 1957, a U-2 pilot flying over Russia photographed an advanced Soviet rocket test site, and the CIA informed Eisenhower that the Russians were prepared to launch satellites. But the U-2 gave evidence that the Soviet Union was no paragon of rocket progress. Eisenhower monitored Soviet ICBM tests in August 1957, and he knew that Russian ICBM development proceeded slowly and ran only a few months ahead of America's, and the USSR had no operational ICBMs to deploy. In fact, delays and setbacks plagued the Soviet ICBM program, keeping it far behind Khrushchev's boasts. In many areas of rocket technology (such as guidance and solid-fuel technology), the United States led. After Sputnik, CIA Director Allen Dulles and his brother John Foster urged the president to share this information with Americans to help them remain calm. But to do so, Eisenhower thought he would have to reveal the U-2 (although he might have been able to make the information public while attributing it to more routine intelligence). He was likely referring to the U-2 when he wrote to childhood friend Swede Hazlett that "there are many things that I don't dare to allude to publicly, yet some of them would do much to allay the fears of our own people."[25] "Reluctantly," Eisenhower recalled, "I decided I could not make such a revelation," even though he knew the U-2's secrets "would have reassured our people." Historian Robert Divine has written, "This may well have been one of the wisest as well as most courageous decisions of his entire presidency."[26]

Beyond the U-2, satellites were to provide the ultimate surveillance tool. The October 4, 1950, RAND report recommended that the United States use satellites for reconnaissance, which would push back the veil shrouding the Soviet Union. In May 1955, Eisenhower's NSC endorsed the building of a small satellite, which would test the "freedom of space" principle, and it looked forward to orbiting a larger satellite that could conduct surveillance in passing over the Soviet Union.[27]

Sputnik embodied ironies. By cloaking it in mystery and springing it on the world, the Soviets violated the IGY's open, cooperative spirit. At the same time, the enigmatic Soviet vehicle also helped the United States by establishing the international principle that space is free, similar to the 1955 Geneva summit's "Open Skies" proposal to allow mutual aerial inspection of military installations, an idea that the Soviets rejected. An internal press release that the Eisenhower administration drafted for possible media circulation ended with the hopeful note, "Perhaps now the Soviets will recast their thinking and cease their opposition to our Open Skies proposal which we believe could mean so much in advancing world peace."[28] No country objected that Sputnik violated its territorial rights. Thus the Soviets themselves proved that space knew no international boundaries; a satellite over another country's atmospheric space was no provocation or act of war.

Eisenhower hoped that satellites would relieve him of the need to use the riskier U-2. He also wanted to beat the Soviets at their own game, for he thought that superior U.S. technology would allow American intelligence to gather even more information from space than the Soviets could.[29] Ultimately, satellite surveillance could prevent the surprise atomic attack that Eisenhower feared, and satellites interested him especially for this reason, even more than for their scientific value.

Mutual Aid

Eisenhower worried that aid from Russia and China would tempt Third World countries, especially those just tasting independence, to follow communism's banner. But he believed he knew how best to influence less developed countries, a question that nettled politicians and presidential aspirants. In 1952, when Congressman John Kennedy first ran for the U.S. Senate seat from Massachusetts—ironically, against incumbent Henry Cabot Lodge, a key organizer of Eisenhower's presidential campaign—he sought to beef up his foreign policy credentials. As he viewed the Cold War, he found something unsettling. Although capitalism provided free markets, consumer choices, and economic opportunities, it failed to grab imaginations in undeveloped nations. There, people sought a larger purpose to inspire and convince them of capitalism's benefits. This shortcoming helped to explain why communism gained ground in lesser developed Asian countries such as China, North Korea, and Vietnam.[30]

To Eisenhower, the Cold War was as much a political and economic struggle as a military one. Through a strong economy, America could offset propaganda gains the Soviets made with Sputnik. And using mutual aid, the United States could win over uncommitted nations. (Eisenhower preferred using the term "mutual aid" to "foreign aid" because it conveyed reciprocity. In discussing foreign aid, he once noted, "The trouble with this whole problem is its name. Fundamentally, this is a program to help ourselves.")[31]

Money spent on mutual aid ranked even higher on Eisenhower's list of priorities than military aid. In his 1958 State of the Union address, he said, "Our problem is to make sure that we use [America's] vast economic forces confidently and creatively, not only in direct military defense efforts, but likewise in our foreign policy, through such activities as mutual economic aid and foreign trade." Through mutual aid Americans could foster international cooperation and help other nations grow stronger, not to mention boost American prestige. Eisenhower called such aid America's "best investment." It kept foreign economies stable and enriched standards of living, which would ultimately translate to less American military protection and lower Pentagon costs, in addition to increased demand for U.S. exports.[32]

Mutual aid bestowed other benefits. U.S. aid strengthened less developed nations, turning them into bulwarks against communism. Almost half of the world's population lived in uncommitted nations, many endowed with natural resources, which Eisenhower wanted to keep out of the communist orbit. The media warned of a "Sputnik diplomacy," whereby the Soviets might use their achievement to woo uncommitted Third World nations into their grasp, and Vice President Nixon believed that the Soviet Union would try to pull Africa to its side.[33] But as Andrew Goodpaster recalled, Eisenhower "felt that the kind of country we were would speak for itself, and that if we gave support and assistance to these countries, that would weigh more than trying to propagandize these [space] achievements." Foreign nations would gauge an economic system's worth not on satellites but on progress, consumer comforts, and economic strength. The space race was a small element in this contest, which would be, in Eisenhower's view, not just a race but a marathon.[34]

London's *Economist* magazine shared Eisenhower's perspective. Noting that the Soviet newspaper *Pravda* had boasted that Sputnik showed communism's superiority, the magazine wrote, "This claim would be more convincing if some of Russia's older satellites were in better shape." Daily life in the Soviet Union's East European satellite countries was bleak, with consumer goods shortages and inefficient transportation systems. If material standards represented the litmus test of a system's superiority, the *Economist* concluded, then the West was beating communism. Moreover, Sputnik represented no military threat but rather just "a unique prestige and propaganda victory." Thus the United States "must not be drawn into a sputnik-for-sputnik race with the Russians. It should use its economic power in ways that will be of more value."[35]

Military aid to the Third World was critical, for it obviated the need to deploy American troops, saving lives and money. A fine example was the Truman Doctrine, which pledged aid to countries fending off a communist threat. "That policy saved [Greece and Turkey]," Eisenhower said. "And it did so without the cost of American lives." Economic aid was vital, too. Whereas military aid was more fleeting, the United States could sustain economic aid over the long term. One form of economic assistance was free trade, and Eisenhower strongly advocated reduced tariff barriers. Liberal-ized trade not only promoted peace and understanding with the United States but also bolstered the domestic economy. Eisenhower estimated that world trade provided jobs for 4.5 million Americans, and it delivered more raw materials to the country. Conversely, trade barriers acted as an eco-nomic drag and diplomatic irritant. For example, in 1955 the United States increased a tariff on imported bicycles, and the Dutch—proud of their bi-cycle industry and celebrated worldwide for their bicycling passion—reacted angrily. Because reducing tariff barriers encouraged trade and soothed world tensions, Eisenhower induced Congress to approve more liberalized trade agreements with other nations. In fact, the concept of "trade not aid" em-bodied his hope that trade with foreign countries would enrich them enough to obviate the need for government assistance.[36]

Humanitarian help and exchanges also bridged international gaps of understanding. Eisenhower supported a worldwide five-year campaign to eradicate malaria, and after Sputnik, he suggested a "Science for Peace" program to disseminate worldwide the results of scientific research. At one White House meeting, Eisenhower vigorously defended the idea of student exchanges, banging the table and exclaiming that while B-36 bombers had a price tag measured in the billions, student exchanges cost only millions and represented American friendship. Eisenhower wrote to Soviet prime minister Nikolai Bulganin proposing to admit three or four thousand Rus-sian students to the United States for study, although the idea suffocated, partly because John Foster Dulles opposed it.[37]

Dulles was not alone in his skepticism and resistance. Capitol Hill had been a redoubt of protectionist or isolationist sentiment, and many mem-bers of Congress fought foreign aid as a wasteful giveaway. Opponents of Truman's Marshall Plan groused that it was a boondoggle and a "European TVA"—implying that it lavished money as some New Deal programs had—and they wanted no more such schemes. Democratic congressman Otto Passman of Louisiana once cracked to a State Department official, "Son, I don't smoke and I don't drink. My only pleasure in life is kicking the shit out of the foreign aid program of the United States of America." Senator Styles Bridges called foreign aid "a do-gooder giveaway." At the White House, Eisenhower gave Bridges a tongue-lashing and declared, "Frankly, I would rather see the Congress cut a billion off . . . defense [than off foreign aid]. . . . If we depend exclusively on our own arms, we are headed for a war; there is going to be no other answer." When Congress cut appropriations for mutual aid, Eisenhower pledged that he would "never cease striving" for it. He proposed a Development Loan Fund to lend money and capital to young nations so they could invest in transportation networks and power grids. Congress approved a scaled-back version of this initiative later in 1957, and although Capitol Hill's intransigence irritated Eisenhower, his mutual aid program—although far less than he wanted—emerged as one of his presidential legacies. As Ewald reflected, "He figured it's much better for the United States to be cooperative with other countries, help them along, and be a good citizen of the world. I think that those were the things that motivated him."[38]

➤● Defense

"Good defense is not cheap defense," Eisenhower said. Weapons grew more expensive constantly, and "we do not want, because of this cost, more military force than is necessary." He proudly said, "I am the only army general to have disassociated myself from Army thinking, and I have been called a traitor for this more than once." He often repeated the idea that he wanted "the most defense we can get for the least money."[39]

Eisenhower promised that "nothing—and I mean *nothing*—is going to come ahead of assuring the safety of the United States," but he also made exhaustive attempts to check military spending. It was the fulcrum on which everything else balanced, including entitlement programs, tax cuts, and peace itself. Eisenhower capped defense spending at $38 billion and tried hard to enforce this limit, even signing a written pledge to hold it there. He demanded cooperation from the Pentagon, once ordering Defense Secretary Wilson not to exceed his budget: "Not one penny over, do you understand? Not under any circumstances!" "Yes, sir," Wilson meekly replied, looking "like a schoolboy getting a scolding," Arthur Larson recalled. Ewald recalled that Eisenhower used to "go over the budgets for the Marine Corps, the Army, [and] the Navy with a pen and strike out things." He insisted that "we're going to get an adequate defense budget, and we're not going to spend one more dime than is necessary." Eisenhower's "New Look" defense policy relied on nuclear supremacy and retaliatory power to deter Soviet aggression while lowering military spending. Thus Eisenhower hoped to cushion the U.S. economy from the Cold War's grind.[40]

Eisenhower believed that "a weak economy was a weak defense," said Larson. He said that the Soviets searched for "one great victory," the collapse of the American economy, which could happen if the United States accumulated too much debt, and they were "laughing at us for spending so much money on pointless armaments." The president "was firmly convinced that the country's economic prosperity was as important to its security as planes and weapons," Sherman Adams recalled.[41]

A key to economic strength was a balanced federal budget, which in turn meant limiting military expenditures. Eisenhower remarked, "I'm just tired even of talking about the idea of a balanced budget against national security. . . . I say that a balanced budget in the long run is a vital part of national security." Truman's defense spending appalled Eisenhower. After the Korean War started and Truman approved NSC-68, which recommended a massive arms buildup to fight the Cold War, the defense budget tripled, while the overall federal budget doubled. Eisenhower disagreed with NSC-68's findings, pointing out that unchecked federal spending posed a threat tantamount to any danger communism posed. Inheriting a $50 billion defense budget, Eisenhower "immediately cut it to $40 billion and it stayed at $40 billion throughout his administration," Larson recalled. As a share of the federal budget, Eisenhower reduced defense spending from 69.2 to 59.1 percent.[42]

As Eisenhower dilated on the dangers of military spending, he often concluded with the caveat that if the Pentagon's checkbook were unlimited, inflation would result, after which the government would impose price controls. At that point, Americans would lose the very freedoms they strove to protect by using the military. Ultimately, a dictatorship could take hold of the country, he feared. To illustrate his point, Eisenhower recalled telling Columbia University freshmen that if they wanted complete security, they could commit a crime and be sent to prison. There they would have complete security, but they would lose freedom and independence.[43]

Eisenhower believed that absent an emergency, defense spending should never exceed 10 percent of GNP. The United States could afford to spend less of its GNP on defense than Russia did. While the Soviet economy grew faster than America's during the 1950s, its GNP was still less than half that of America's, and the U.S. economy was more diverse. Had the United States devoted the same proportion of its GNP to defense that the Soviet Union did, its military spending would have been $120 billion, rather than $40 billion.[44] Treasury Secretary Humphrey echoed these views. Along with Dulles, Humphrey was the cabinet officer to whom Eisenhower felt closest, often going to his Georgia plantation on hunting trips. (The two men hit it off from the beginning. Upon first meeting him and seeing his balding pate, Eisenhower cracked, "Well, George, I see you part your hair the same way I do.") A notorious fiscal tightwad, Humphrey lambasted excessive defense spending, and, talented at invoking metaphors, he referred to money going to the Pentagon as headed for the "dump heap." Eisenhower,

likewise, complained that military spending produced jobs that were nuga-
tory; it yielded "sterile, negative things, silent policemen standing around our
house all the time." Peace would save lives and avoid bloodshed, but Eisenhower also strived for it for another reason, so that "the products of our toil
may be used for our schools and our roads and our churches and not for
guns and planes and tanks and ships of war."[45]

The military's waste of resources horrified Eisenhower, especially defense boondoggles. If a country squandered money on defense, its collective
intellect, culture, and well-being would stagnate. Eisenhower believed in
"sufficiency"—having just enough weapons to meet defense needs—and he
had no patience for redundant weapons systems. "Goddamn it to hell, how
many times can you kill a man?" he exploded at one meeting. On another
occasion, when told of a plan to make four hundred Minuteman missiles
yearly, he exclaimed, "Why don't we go completely crazy and plan on a force
of 10,000?"[46]

But even Eisenhower wasted money on defense, try as he did to avoid it,
partly because presidents had to throw out red meat to sate supporters, and
also because the political pressure to maintain a formidable defense—especially
after Sputnik—was intense. Even a normally loyal Eisenhower backer, Republican senator Clifford Case of New Jersey, said that Sputnik sent a warning that it was a "dangerous gamble" to sacrifice defense spending just to
balance the federal budget.

The 1950s was the golden age for the atom, and "nuclear" defense projects had a talismanic attraction. Designers envisioned all sorts of atom-
powered devices (even an atomic car), and politicians and the military
"were just obsessed [that] nuclear was going to solve all the problems," recalled Spurgeon Keeny. "There was one head of the Bureau of the Budget
who said to me at a meeting, 'Those guys, anything that has the word
'nucleus' in it, they want to spend money on.'" Nelson Rockefeller, for
example, mentioned to Eisenhower the idea of using nuclear explosives to
propel a satellite to the moon.[47] The Air Force pushed for nuclear-powered
aircraft with its Nuclear Energy for the Propulsion of Aircraft (NEPA) project, and it lumbered toward reality. Eisenhower objected to its $200 million
development cost, and the project teemed with problems. A nuclear reactor
aboard a plane needed heavy shielding—absurd for an aircraft, which was
supposed to be light—and the prospect of a crash was horrifying. Beckler
recalled that "the whole idea was cockamamie." Still, the AEC argued that
a nuclear airplane would bolster U.S. scientific prestige after Sputnik. Hearing a report that the Soviet Union was developing a similar aircraft, mem-

bers of Congress railed against "yet another blow to the prestige and security of our nation and the world," as Senator Richard Russell charged.[48] Under such pressure, a reluctant Eisenhower approved research for the program, even though he wanted to cancel it, illustrating the post-Sputnik clamor for technologically advanced weapons that advocates believed could buy security. Eventually, President Kennedy scrapped NEPA, but the government wasted $900 million on it. Similarly, during the 1950s the Air Force received millions of dollars for its "Dyna-Soar" space glider, which rockets would boost into space, after which it would return to the earth's atmosphere and then fly—a "dynamic soaring"—above ground. The Air Force envisioned the Dyna-Soar conducting reconnaissance, inspecting satellites, even carrying weapons. By the time Lyndon Johnson canceled this brainchild of rocket science, it had squandered $400 million in federal money and was more dinosaur than Dyna-Soar.[49]

In weighing defense projects, Eisenhower wanted to brace the American economy for what he called the "long pull." He believed the Cold War would be protracted, perhaps a half-century effort. The panicked political cries after Sputnik focused on a perceived emergency with no perspective on later needs. To shape national security policy, Eisenhower believed, a president had first to consider spending levels America could afford over the long haul. Eisenhower wrote that "our plans must be based upon the probability of their lengthy prolongation. We face, not a temporary emergency, such as a war, but a long term responsibility." The country might have to continue some national security programs "for years, even decades." At the October 9 press conference, in describing rockets and other new methods of weapons delivery, he said, "It is going to be a long term. It is not a revolutionary process that will take place in the reequipping of defense forces, it will be an evolutionary."[50] On another occasion, he predicted that America would have to endure heavy defense costs "for the next 40–50 years," which proved an accurate prediction for the Cold War's duration. He stressed to Republican congressional leaders that the answer to critics' charges was not just to "give the military another ten billion dollars," because defense was a long-term problem. It was possible to do almost anything you wanted to do for one year, he said, but not over thirty or forty years.[51]

Eisenhower was not prescient enough to see the Soviet Union's eventual collapse. "The Soviet system was too strong at the time," said Raymond Saulnier. But he looked warily at defense profligacy, knowing that it could doom a country, warning that "the Communist objective is to make us spend ourselves into bankruptcy."[52]

Balanced Budgets

During the two decades prior to Eisenhower's presidency, the federal budget had mushroomed from $4 billion in 1932 to $85.5 billion in 1952. Saulnier recalled, "The intellectual drift at the time was in an entirely different direction [from Eisenhower's]. It was toward more centralized control of the economy, and that is just exactly the opposite of what Eisenhower was thinking of." He felt a prime duty to save public money, and he set the tone immediately. During his first State of the Union address, he pledged that "the first order of business is the elimination of the annual deficit."[53]

Eisenhower had various parables and metaphors to warn of the dangers of excess. He likened too much spending to giving too much water to a plant. He told of a man who died and found himself indulging in treats and pleasures galore in the hereafter. It was all too much, and the man asked to be taken to hell instead. He learned he was already there. In explaining his approach toward federal spending, Eisenhower mentioned a story about Abraham Lincoln. Someone asked him how long a person's legs should be. "Well," Lincoln responded, "they ought to be long enough to reach the ground." Figuratively speaking, Eisenhower explained, the federal budget "ought to reach the ground," he said, or be just adequate for national purposes.[54]

Eisenhower had no desire to tear down the panoply of New Deal social programs. During his first term, he allowed for increased federal spending during emergencies. At one cabinet meeting, Treasury Secretary Humphrey compared the federal government to a household, insisting that neither could spend beyond means. Eisenhower interrupted. What if a child in the home developed infantile paralysis, he asked. "You'll go into debt then, won't you," he challenged his treasury secretary.[55]

But Eisenhower wanted to stop deficit spending, an addiction whereby "each dose increases the need for the next one," he said. Perhaps the worst result of Franklin Roosevelt's presidency, Eisenhower believed, was a drastic change in expectations and entitlements and a weakened personal resolve. Americans had come to expect that the federal government would provide for them, and they thought themselves entitled to such succor. Only during national emergencies, he believed, should the government engage in deficit spending. He viewed the New Deal and Fair Deal's spending and governmental expansion as a "national disgrace." Government spending stifled the self-reliance that nurtured American exceptionalism and the country's best institutions. Eisenhower was appalled when one university president threw up his hands and confessed that without federal aid, "Why, we'd have to close our doors. We'd be virtually broke." Where agriculture—a profession that Eisenhower once felt himself destined for—had been a pillar of American economic strength, he found that farmers now planned crops based on federal subsidies and acreage allotments rather than their own calculus. "Thrift," he once said, "is one of the characteristics that have made this nation great. Why should we abandon it now?" He exhorted his cabinet at one meeting, "We must remember: frugality, economy, simplicity with efficiency, I cannot tell you how deeply I believe this." Eisenhower wrote that he was especially concerned "for our children. If we irresponsibly keep on passing them our bills, they will inherit, not a free country with bright opportunities, but a vast wasteland of debt and financial chaos." During retirement, he wrote eloquently about bequeathing a fiscally sound nation to younger Americans, worrying that "we are stealing from our grandchildren in order to satisfy our desires of today." He urged Americans to "think a bit about our young people, and the young people to come, instead of concentrating all our compassion on the indigent and the elderly."[56]

Eisenhower's fiscal conservatism was a deeply embedded personal philosophy. He described his parents as "frugal," and his hometown of Abilene, Kansas, epitomized small-town values, even lacking a police force. There he saw the hardscrabble lives of working Americans, including his father, who raised six boys while employed at a local creamery. Eisenhower believed that the federal government was "subject to the same time-tested rules as those followed by any farsighted householder or businessmen," and he warned, "No family, no business, no nation can spend itself into prosperity." Throughout his career, Eisenhower scrimped and saved on an Army officer's salary, even rolling his own cigarettes rather than buying brand-name packs. Such traits surfaced repeatedly, sometimes annoying colleagues. William Ewald recalled taking a salary cut to help Eisenhower write his memoirs, while the former president earned a princely sum. "And it didn't help to send him regularly Christmas and birthday presents and receive a letter in return," Ewald confessed.[57]

Once president, Eisenhower translated his personal economy into policy. Saving public money became a constant concern, and he took various austerity measures. He mothballed the presidential yacht *Williamsburg* and then swung his axe at the federal workforce, cutting it from 2.6 million to 2.3 million.[58] One reason Eisenhower personally opposed Alaska's admission as a state while favoring Hawaii's was that Hawaii, with its modern economy, would cost the country less in development and federal aid. (He compromised and agreed to admit both.)

A cardinal means to save money was the veto, and Eisenhower wielded it forcefully. He was the last one-hundred-plus veto president: over eight years, he vetoed 181 bills; no president since has come close to rejecting one hundred bills (during two terms, for example, Ronald Reagan issued 78 vetoes; Bill Clinton, thirty-seven; and George W. Bush, just twelve). Although many of Eisenhower's vetoes blocked payments to individuals, some involved major projects. In 1958, for instance, he vetoed a bill to construct a $60 million Coast Guard nuclear-powered icebreaking vessel and another, more substantial bill authorizing appropriations for rivers, harbors, and flood control projects, which would have set aside more than $800 million for previously approved projects and another $900 million for new ones. "I cannot overstate my opposition to this kind of waste of public funds," his veto statement read.[59]

Democrats charged that the vetoes hurt Americans. Former president Harry Truman said that the veto "ought to be used to protect the people from special interest legislation—not to block all forms of progress. That is what the Republicans use it for. No Eisenhower veto . . . built a dam—or helped a farmer—or put a power line on a Texas farm."[60] Yet as president, Truman called the veto "one of the most important instruments" a president had, and he vetoed more bills than Eisenhower—250 in total—and had an opposition Congress for only two years, compared with Eisenhower's six years. Eisenhower regarded the veto as an almost solemn measure and said he took no pleasure in vetoing legislation. "I don't enjoy having to say that these things are bad and to explain the reasons why I think they are bad," he commented. "What I'm trying to do is to get legislation passed that will benefit the United States and keep us solvent at the same time." Moreover, the president had a responsibility to use the veto because he was less vulnerable to the special interests and lobbying that bent Congress's will, especially in the House, whose members faced the electorate every two years. In the end, with more than one hundred vetoes and just two overrides during eight years, Eisenhower had a "remarkable record," Ewald wrote.[61]

But Eisenhower's fiscal conservatism seemed questionable after Sputnik. For a president, espousing cost cutting and balanced budgets meant suffering political and public relations setbacks. Presidents such as Eisenhower and later Gerald Ford (who vetoed sixty-six bills during just two and a half years as president) seemed negative and passionless, sacrificing large national goals on the altar of budgetary restraint, and both lost congressional and media support. The media pressured Eisenhower; one newspaper writer lamented that "the emphasis under the Eisenhower Administration has been primarily on dollar economy not on [Civil War Confederate General]

Nathan Bedford Forrest's goal of 'gitting there fustest with the mostest.'"
Yale economist James Tobin, who later served on Kennedy's CEA, said,
"Sputnik will be well worth the blow it dealt our national pride if it frees
national policy from the shackles of fiscal orthodoxy." Keynesian economists like Tobin saw Eisenhower restrained within a rigid corset of old-
fashioned economic principles that placed balanced budgets above grand
programs and prestige.[62]

Eisenhower's domestic priorities were inherently hard to tout—a balanced budget, spending restraint, and low inflation. Critics assailed presidents who embraced these goals as lacking vision or being do-nothing leaders
who wasted the magnificent powers brimming in the White House. Moreover, by the 1950s, Eisenhower's views seemed old-fashioned. His philosophy
of cost cutting and budget balancing was hard to make attractive, for it promised no great spending initiatives as the New Deal or Fair Deal did. Even
political semantics proved challenging, Saulnier observed, as Eisenhower's
program was sensible, "but nothing tested the talents of Eisenhower's
speechwriters more than the task of devising a felicitous phrasing of it."[63]

During his last years in office, the president's struggle to hold down
the budget became a battle. Sputnik came just after a critical juncture in his
administration. Around Easter 1957, a few months before Sputnik, Eisenhower began to espouse even more rigid conservatism than previously. The
transformation began in January, when Democrats pounded his proposed
fiscal 1958 budget as excessive, and they came back from the Easter recess
convinced that the country wanted greater fiscal economy. Eisenhower
complained about congressional Democrats who became Johnnies-come-
lately to fiscal conservatism during 1957. In a supreme irony, he found
Democrats labeling him as fiscally reckless, and Larson noted that "Eisenhower's preoccupation with holding down the budget increased visibly
from that point on." Political scientist John Sloan has argued that beginning
in 1957, a "New Eisenhower" emerged, more rigidly conservative and combative with Congress. Cries for crash programs after Sputnik disgusted the
new Eisenhower, who grew more determined to resist them.[64]

Economic Strength

A month after Sputnik, Republican senator Barry Goldwater of Arizona
declared, "I am more concerned about the strength of the economy than
I am about Sputnik." With ominous signs portending a recession, Goldwater's remark was understandable. It also echoed the president's position.[65]

Eisenhower feared that high spending and inflation would lead to price controls and warp the free enterprise system. He viewed inflation as a great bane to the nation, and when confronted with demands for increased defense or space spending, he reiterated his philosophy that excessive spending created a vicious cycle, fueling inflation, which in turn eroded the dollar and weakened the country. Fear of deficits was one reason that Eisenhower emphasized state and local government instead of Washington. Whereas many state governments required balanced budgets, he explained that the federal government ran chronic deficits and could print money. In resisting spending, Eisenhower believed he defended principles more profound than a balanced budget. He wrote that "we are defending a way of life. . . . That way of life, over the long term, requires the observance of sound fiscal policies and the use of the fruits of our productivity so that the system may continue to work primarily under the impulse of private effort than by the fiat of centralised government."[66]

A fierce free-market exponent, Eisenhower believed that freedoms were intertwined, as if bundled together in a package. Political and social freedoms depended on economic freedom. A government might be tempted to infringe on the free market with price controls or large federal programs that displaced private concerns. But if a government invaded economic freedom, Eisenhower believed, it would soon violate political and personal freedom. "Each is an indispensable part of a single whole. Destruction of any inevitably leads to the destruction of all," he said.[67]

Economic concerns goaded Eisenhower to run for president in 1952, when he wrote that the GOP faced a crossroads. It could win the election and counter federal spending trends, or it could "abjectly accept the conclusion that a 'centralized' power philosophy was permanently supplanting our once-proud tradition of depending for national progress upon individual initiative, self-reliance, and private, competitive enterprise."[68] Once he became president, Eisenhower delved into economic issues. Like a general sketching battlefield plans, he reviewed economic data carefully and was "sort of a statistics bug," recalled Saulnier. "I'd go in with charts, and he'd reach in and pull out his pencil and he'd start taking charts and making marks of where he thought those figures would be next month. He was a forecaster. He loved to do that."

Eisenhower also saved the Council of Economic Advisors from being scrapped. Created in 1947 as an advisory organ to the president, the CEA "had lost its support in the Congress on both sides of the aisle," Saulnier remembered. Acting on advice from Arthur Burns, who criticized the divided authority among the three CEA members, Eisenhower made the CEA chair exclusively responsible for reporting to the president. His relations with both CEA chairs, Burns and Saulnier, "could not have been better," the latter recalled, adding that his contact with Eisenhower "was very frequent and very direct."[69]

Balance

After leaving office, Eisenhower penned an essay in which he outlined his political tenets. One was balance. "The need for balance in governmental programs," he wrote, "is always present—a balance between current pressures and future good . . . between creature comforts provided by the state and the maintenance of a national creative capacity depending upon individual initiative." He referred to his policies as "the middle way," straddling liberalism and extreme conservatism and keeping both at bay while pursuing what he called "a practicable middle course between too little and too much government."[70]

William Ewald remarked that balance "reverberates like a pedal point through Eisenhower's conduct of his country's defense." In fact, it applied to his entire presidency. Whereas his 1961 farewell address was best known for warning of a "military-industrial complex," he used that term only once. The speech rang another theme more loudly—balance—a word he invoked nine times. Eisenhower stressed the "need to maintain balance in and among national programs—balance between the private and the public economy; balance between cost and hoped-for advantages; balance between the clearly necessary and the comfortably desirable; balance between our essential requirements as a nation and the duties imposed by the nation upon the individual; balance between actions of the moment and the national welfare of the future."[71] (In a fetching coincidence, Eisenhower, born on October 14, had the astrological sign of Libra, whose scales signified balance.)

The Soviet Union lacked a balanced economy. In the spring following the launch, Khrushchev gave a speech on the Soviet chemical industry in which he conceded that it failed to provide vital materials, such as plastics and synthetic fibers, and needed help from the West. Yet the same chemical industry, directed by the government, had provided rocket fuel for satellites. The drive to achieve a propaganda coup, supported by the state as a national goal, twisted the Soviet economy and drove resources away from consumers. Eisenhower was far prouder of an economy that provided a wide array of choices to consumers than one that only furnished fuel for a government mission and little else. Moreover, every economy had limited means, and

Eisenhower believed that the private sector allocated scarce resources better than the government could.[72]

Eisenhower felt that the most prudent reaction to Sputnik was to steer a steady, balanced course and avoid splurging on emergency programs. A month after Sputnik, *Fortune* wrote, "To its credit the Eisenhower Administration . . . refused to be stampeded into any crash program of spending." The magazine commented that America's strength lay "in its free institutions, and in its marvelously adaptive and creative economy based on individual initiative and effort," rather than in "creeping socialism and the ceaseless extension of government activities into additional economic fields. If the advent of man-made satellites serves to reaffirm that truth it will have accomplished a purpose as important in the long run as the conquest of outer space." The ability to resist spending set Eisenhower apart from pandering politicians, as he believed that "the demagogue tries to develop a saleable list of items to hold before the public."[73]

After leaving office, Eisenhower continued to warn about unbalanced budgets and unchecked federal spending. Complaining about a speech by President Kennedy that implied deficits were beneficial, Eisenhower stated that Americans "cannot continue to prove to the world that we cannot and will not pay our debts as we go along—that we are building up a situation that is certainly going to be difficult for us, and is going to be a hundred times worse for our children and our grandchildren, unless we stop it. This, I think, is a very serious matter . . . whether [Americans] want to pile up these extraordinary debts."

On another occasion, he wrote to Larson and complained that Kennedy took nearly all Eisenhower administration programs and "expanded them very greatly in the theory that public spending is, per se, the cure-all for all economic weaknesses in the nation."[74] That principle proved a dramatic distinction between Eisenhower and Kennedy, and the space race put it on display.

 # PART TWO

Setbacks

CHAPTER 5

Cheerleader-in-Chief

Eisenhower had always been an optimist. West Point classmates called him "Sunny Jim" (after a popular cartoon character of the era), and at the military academy he showed his ability to rebound from a devastating setback. The center of his college life was football, and he played with decent ability and fanatical energy. But in the fall of 1912, during his first year on Army's varsity squad, he twisted his knee in a game. His football career was finished, and for a time, Ike found no consolation. His grades slipped, and he racked up demerit points. He wrote, "Seems like I'm never cheerful anymore. The fellows that used to call me 'Sunny Jim' call me 'Gloomy Face' now." Yet he found ways to keep his classmates'—and his own—spirits high. He became a cheerleader, appearing at rallies and bonfires, and he coached the freshman football team. Both roles gave him his first taste of speaking before a group, plus practice at giving rousing pep talks and inspiring optimism.[1]

World War II reinforced these lessons. While leading the Allied forces, Eisenhower always gave optimistic appraisals to the media. He wrote to Mamie that when "pressure mounts and strain increases everyone begins to show the weaknesses in his makeup. It is up to the Commander to conceal his; above all to conceal doubt, fear and distrust." In 1950, when he assumed his position as NATO's supreme commander, he toured the European capitals of member countries, meeting with leaders and giving them pep talks, trying to instill confidence and boost morale. In his diary, he complained that civilian leaders acted as if they could do nothing about morale. That supine attitude, Eisenhower noted, contrasted with that of a military leader, who "looks on morale as . . . the greatest of all his problems, but also as one about which he can and must do something."[2] In the fall of 1957, Eisenhower's charge was to raise the nation's morale.

"Barbarism Armed with Sputniks"

Eisenhower "was determined to counteract this groundswell [of American self-criticism]" after Sputnik, Arthur Larson recalled. Yet he barely had the time to get over the first satellite when a second one rose. On November 3, 1957, the Soviet Union launched Sputnik II, a craft far more sophisticated than its predecessor. This one weighed 1,100 pounds, contained instruments to measure solar radiation, and, most impressive of all, carried the world's first living space traveler, an eleven-pound dog named Laika (Russian for "barker"). Sputnik II's technical embellishments were astonishing. A temperature control system sustained Laika; air conditioning kept her cool; a television camera monitored her. Although the dog died just a few hours after takeoff, the satellite stayed in orbit 162 days. (In April 1958, when Sputnik II broke up and blazed in the night sky upon reentering the earth's atmosphere, some residents along America's East Coast thought they were witnessing a pack of UFOs.)[3]

Khrushchev was perennially jousting with the United States, engaging in a game of one-upmanship in everything imaginable. When he visited the United States in 1959, he swore that Soviet cows would yield more milk than American ones and that Russian telephones would be superior and more plentiful. When the Soviet Union shot down an American U-2 spy plane in 1960, he praised its reconnaissance photos but said that his country's cameras produced better ones. He could not resist space competition, and for the second Sputnik, Khrushchev wanted to pull off another stunt to outdo the United States and also commemorate the Bolshevik Revolution's fortieth anniversary. When he broached his brainchild to Sergei Korolev, the rocket engineer suggested putting "a living being" aboard a satellite. The idea grabbed Khrushchev, who cried out, "With a dog in it!" More than Eisenhower, Khrushchev was a risk taker, and although this tendency later brought the world to the precipice of nuclear slaughter when he installed IRBMs in Cuba, this time it paid off. He scored another space triumph.[4]

It was no surprise, the White House insisted. On October 11, Andrew Goodpaster telephoned Eisenhower and told him that the Soviets might launch a second satellite "any time in the next few days." To avert a new media and political frenzy, a State Department spokesman had announced in advance that the United States would not be surprised if the Soviets launched a second Sputnik soon. The day after the launch, assistant White House press secretary Anne Wheaton claimed that the president had received information about it beforehand and maintained his normal daily schedule.[5]

Eisenhower sensed more calm across the land. "This time there was no hysteria," he wrote. "By a strange and compassionate turn, public opinion seemed to resent the sending of a dog to certain death." It was a fatal mission, because the Soviet Union lacked the technology to return the dog alive. The American Society for the Prevention of Cruelty to Animals and humane societies worldwide protested the animal sacrifice. Rather than augur doom, much of the U.S. media made light of the second Sputnik. Calling the new space episode "the shaggiest saga of all time," *Time* noted the "Muttnik jokes and doggerel" that became a press indulgence: "Headlines yelped such barbaric new words as pupnik and poochnik, sputpup and woofnik." Entrepreneurs celebrated the satellite. In Philadelphia, a grocer called his potatoes "spudniks," while an Atlanta restaurant created the Sputnik Burger, complete with a sausage "dog" topped by "Czarist Russian dressing." Comedian Stan Laurel noted that his home television reception was "awful" in early November and he could not "figure why this happened, as there has been no change in the weather conditions—maybe 'Sputty' and 'Mutty' had something to do with it!"[6]

Yet at a November 8 NSC meeting, Eisenhower reported receiving information that fear gripped Americans. Media and congressional reactions remained agitated. Technologically, Sputnik II was more impressive than the first and six times heavier. Some scientists speculated that the Soviet Union might have discovered a special new chemical fuel to propel such mass, even nuclear propulsion units. The CIA wondered whether Sputnik II really carried a dog. "Available evidence does not permit a positive determination," the agency noted, surmising that the satellite probably did have a dog aboard and concluding, "Placing animals into space and studying the effects thereof is a necessary step to a manned space flight program as well as providing very valuable scientific data on the composition of outer space." The CIA and the Defense Department ginned up their estimate of the rocket power the Soviets produced. Now they guessed it was around 1.5 million pounds of thrust.[7]

The satellite's weight concerned the president. After the launch, he encountered Herbert York at the White House and asked the physicist to estimate the craft's weight. It was more than a thousand pounds, York replied.

Although Eisenhower showed no alarm, York sensed that the feat left him at a loss.[8]

The second launch confirmed one fact: the Soviet Union was the world's premier space-exploring nation, and it was taking tentative steps toward sending a human into space. Whereas the satellite implied that the Soviet Union could launch one spacecraft per month, the United States still had nothing. Abroad, allies lost confidence in America. The *New York Times* reported that Sputnik II "astounded" the Japanese. "There was no doubt that the United States had taken a body blow in prestige," the paper said. "Temporarily at least, in Japanese eyes, the United States is the second military power in the world, and not the first." Taken together, the two Sputniks had an incalculable global impact. Jokes and doggerel aside, *Time* wrote, "In 1957, under the orbits of a horned sphere and a half-ton tomb for a dead dog, the world's balance of power lurched and swung toward the free world's enemies."[9]

The Soviet success also kept the political cauldron boiling. Senator Henry Jackson implored, "It is time for the President of the United States to act. He is the only person who can give us the leadership our people want and need." Jackson urged Eisenhower to "go all out in getting operational missiles as soon as possible." Senator Hubert Humphrey added tinder to the fire by asking the president to brief a special congressional session on America's defenses. The day after Sputnik II was launched, the Senate authorized Lyndon Johnson to begin hearings before his Preparedness Subcommittee to investigate Eisenhower's space and defense policies.[10]

The media continued their rumbles of warning. NBC commentator Merrill Muller said, "Behind the scientific success lies a grim military warning. . . . [T]he rocket that launched Sputnik number two is capable of carrying a ton-and-a-half hydrogen bomb warhead more than five thousand miles to a target." That distance would put the United States well within Russia's nuclear crosshairs. The *New York Times* demanded increased money for missiles, saying that Americans "are ready for sacrifices if the President will provide the needed leadership by enunciating policies and initiating actions appropriate to the crisis posed by barbarism armed with sputniks." The *Washington Post* warned, "The Soviet State is playing with no mere 'baubles.' It is playing with the destiny of mankind and at the moment it seems to have the upper hand." An unusual appeal came from American Aviation Publications, which addressed an open letter to Eisenhower covering almost an entire newspaper page, declaring, "You Needn't Be a Scientist To Understand Sputnick [*sic*], Mr. President[,] But You Must Be a Leader." The group argued that the United States was indeed involved in a space race and "a battle of the minds," and only a titanic effort could overtake the Soviet Union, which already demonstrated "the ability to smash the Western World by missile bombardment." Urging a cabinet-level secretary of science and a manned moon landing, the publishers told Eisenhower that the Sputnik launches were "much, much more than 'neat scientific tricks.' You know it, and the American people know it. And the American people expect you to do something about it."[11]

It was a fierce drumbeat. Yet it was far too early in the space race to counter Sputnik with American one-upmanship. In 1957, had Eisenhower thrown presidential backing behind an ambitious space goal such as a manned lunar mission, it would have been a response disproportionate to the stimuli. Eisenhower wanted another way to respond, one more balanced and restrained.

Television Talks

In the television age, presidents have addressed the nation to plump for programs, sometimes trying to create a sense of crisis to generate momentum for their legislation. Positive results have been no guarantee. In February 1993, President Bill Clinton gave his first State of the Union message and tried to describe a health care system in shambles, saying, "Our families will never be secure, our businesses will never be strong, and our Government will never again be fully solvent until we tackle the health care crisis. We must do it this year. The [crisis is] endangering the security and the very lives of millions of our people." He followed his address a year later by presenting Congress with a gargantuan, 1,342-page health care bill, which never came to a vote. It sapped Clinton's presidency of momentum and became his greatest legislative fiasco.

In essence, Eisenhower did the opposite. After Sputnik, he used television to illustrate that there was no crisis, that no rash action or legislative program was needed. "One of Eisenhower's major tasks was to calm people down," noted biographer Stephen Ambrose. This was true throughout his presidency but especially after Sputnik. In the White House, the staff believed that the president had to involve himself personally in the national space policy discussion. "There was enough public excitement and misunderstanding about [Sputnik] that it would take Eisenhower himself" to calm the country, Goodpaster said.[12]

Eisenhower feared frenzied calls for wild programs that emanated from Congress. "Act now before it is too late" became an apocalyptic theme to many Capitol Hill cries, and four days after the first Sputnik launch, Stuart Symington sent the president a stinging three-page letter urging him to call a special session of Congress. Americans, the Missouri senator wrote, "expect their own missile and aircraft and satellite programs to be pressed to the maximum by your Administration." Henry Jackson began pulling together a new defense plan that would hike military spending by up to $2 billion. Both the Defense Department and Congress exerted pressure on Eisenhower to support development of a nuclear-powered aircraft, fearing that the Soviet Union would build one first. (U.S. intelligence predicted that Russia would have one sometime in 1961–62; the United States expected to complete its own in 1963–64.[13])

Eisenhower was doubly determined to resist these demands. He worried that in the hot skillet of political charges, emotions could spill over and inflame the public. For this reason, Goodpaster recalled, one of Eisenhower's chief concerns "was the idea of steadying down the American people." Goodpaster remembered that Eisenhower "was concerned that if public confidence were not reestablished that there could be these crash programs that would be unnecessary, that would be very wasteful and misdirected."[14]

To suppress such cries and allay anxiety, Arthur Larson thought about a television correlate to Franklin Roosevelt's radio "fireside chats" during the Great Depression. Thus began the most serious presidential effort to reach the public in two decades, as Eisenhower decided to give a series of nationally televised speeches on science and national security, which the White House dubbed Operation Confidence.[15]

Although television was new, Eisenhower recognized its importance as a political appurtenance. During the 1952 presidential race, he donned horn-rim instead of steel-frame glasses to improve his appearance and starred in the first-ever campaign commercials, in which he answered canned questions from average-looking Americans. The scenes were manufactured and the spots simple—especially by later standards—but they were effective. Eisenhower came across as decent yet decisive—a true leader, although he felt uncomfortable in a television studio. (In particular, he resented the fuss about his bald pate being too shiny under the lights.) By contrast, Democratic nominee Adlai Stevenson's refusal to tape television commercials hurt him and likely widened his margin of defeat.[16]

Eisenhower, in fact, was the first chief executive of the television age. The television became a White House fixture during Truman's administration, but Harry and Bess never took to the new device. Ike and Mamie did. Together, they ate dinner on TV trays while they watched the evening news, and during the daytime Mamie grew hooked on the soap opera *As the World Turns*. More important was how Eisenhower used TV to function as president. He held 193 televised press conferences, and he hired actor Robert Montgomery to polish his performances, as he felt ill at ease before the camera. Press conferences gave him good practice, and by 1956, *New York Times* chief congressional correspondent William White wrote admiringly of Eisenhower's improved TV style, which he called "one of the best." Eisenhower became the only president to win an Emmy Award for his pioneering use of television as a White House political instrument.[17]

Ike learned to use television to his advantage, and he addressed the nation at seminal moments. By setting the proper tone and invoking the right words, he hoped he could generate interest in an issue or banish it from the news. In 1957, before Sputnik, Eisenhower used television on two notable occasions. In May, he made two addresses to the nation, one to explain the controversial $71.8 billion federal budget and a second to expound on mutual security's virtues. During the Little Rock crisis, on September 24, he turned to television again, rushing from his Newport vacation to speak from the Oval Office and denounce the "mob rule" that threatened to block the integration of Central High School.[18]

After Sputnik, although Eisenhower wanted to speak directly to Americans via television, an immediate speech might have only fueled the media frenzy and made the satellite's launch seem an emergency. Thus, unlike with Little Rock, Eisenhower waited a month. He hoped to expatiate on U.S. achievements in science and rocketry, putting Sputnik in perspective. Goodpaster remembered that Eisenhower thought that Americans needed "a better appreciation of what was involved" with the satellite. Larson noted that in preparing for the speech, the president "stressed over and over again that what people needed is *understanding* of facts and *understanding* of what we are trying to do." As Eisenhower remarked, "The price of liberty is understanding."[19]

The president also wanted to lift morale. That objective was a constant during his military career, and he stressed it when he assumed command of World War II's European theater of operations. When he arrived in London, he sensed gloom among the staff. "Pessimism and defeatism will not be tolerated," he told them. Later, as he prepared for the D-Day invasion, Eisenhower told his staff, "This operation is being planned as a success. There can be no thought of failure. For I assure you there is no possibility of failure."[20]

During Eisenhower's presidency, "from start to finish, he valued morale—strength of heart, strength of spirit," said William Ewald, who recalled that while he worked with the former president on his memoirs, Eisenhower once exclaimed, "I want to be positive!" In pep talks to White House colleagues, Eisenhower often managed to find the right words or an epigram to generate a good mood. Edward McCabe remembered that the president once said to his staff, "I want you to take your work seriously; don't take yourself too seriously," advice that originally came from Ike's Army mentor, General Fox Conner, to which Eisenhower gave his own embellishment, adding, "And don't forget to pray."[21]

In October 1957, Eisenhower needed these skills. One of Ike's great strengths, Nixon believed, was a "determined optimism." Like a coach rallying his team, the president was "constantly waging a battle for high spirits on his staff," and Nixon remembered that Eisenhower used phrases like "long faces don't win battles" to keep his White House upbeat (a curious contrast with Nixon himself, whose dour behavior led law school classmates to dub him "Gloomy Gus"). The president knew better than most politicians, Nixon wrote, "how to move people, how to rally the nation to his support, and how to inspire their faith and win their trust—and these are the essence of politics." Calling himself a "born optimist," Eisenhower explained that "most soldiers are, because no soldier ever won a battle if he went into it pessimistically." Two weeks after Sputnik, while speaking in New York City, Eisenhower used a variation of that phrase, remarking that no man had ever won a battle with his chin on his chest. "You have to get it up!" he exhorted. The media dubbed his subsequent televised speeches the "chin-up" talks.[22]

A National Pep Talk

After Sputnik, Eisenhower heard suggestions that he create a cabinet-level Department of Science to give advice on scientific matters and direct the nation's science efforts. Democratic senators John McClellan of Arkansas and Hubert Humphrey of Minnesota sponsored legislation to create such a department. The plan would have involved an ambitious reorganization of government, with the new department consolidating the Atomic Energy Commission, the National Science Foundation, and other agencies under its aegis.[23]

The constitutional separation of powers reserves to the president the power to create cabinet departments, making the suggestions from the congressmen unusual. That alone generated opposition to them within the executive branch. Eisenhower also believed that these ideas would expand government and create entrenched programs with vocal constituencies. Sputnik was a short-term issue, he insisted, and scientific endeavor was "so kaleidoscopic and so widely dispersed" that no single department could capture it all.[24]

This perspective was wise. Often an event or issue exploded on the national consciousness and dominated political discussions, with proposals to establish a cabinet department to address the problem. During the Great Depression, for example, some New Deal thinkers promoted consumer spending as the key to economic recovery, and some advocates of this belief wanted a cabinet-level Department of the Consumer.[25] By the 1950s, though, this idea was forgotten. Yet had such a department been created, it would have been a lingering Great Depression relic that demanded federal money and resources, the kind of bureaucratic leftover that Eisenhower disliked. His resistance to a Department of Science illustrated the principle that presidents should weigh cautiously the impulse to found new departments representing transitory concerns; it is better to take the long view to judge whether such concerns might still merit an institutional response in another generation.

Although he opposed a science department, Eisenhower needed to explain scientific matters to Americans, especially so that they could support informed choices on science policy. Thus he made a personnel change. The television speeches meant moving a top aide to a new post. USIA Director Larson had attracted Eisenhower's attention with his 1956 book, *A Republican Looks at His Party*, which eloquently expressed the tenets of moderate Republicanism while attacking the New Deal. Larson had a gift for smooth prose, and the president asked him to become his new speechwriter, giving him the title of special assistant to the president. "My position is desperate," Eisenhower said. He "explained to me that he had this idea of a series of speeches that would patiently and unemotionally explain [science and national security]," Larson remembered. "But at the time he didn't have anybody to do it. So this is why I moved over from USIA to do this." The events after Sputnik "changed the whole direction of my career," Larson later recalled. He began work on the first speech immediately, acting on a "forced-draft" basis, meaning an all-out, hurried effort.[26]

The speech illustrated salient Eisenhower traits. He had a fantastic ability to concentrate on a single task. Shifting his focus from foreign policy and Little Rock to space and national security, he devoted maximum attention to the new charge at hand. Close Eisenhower friend Ellis Slater commented, "I don't believe I've ever known a person with such concentration. When doing anything . . . he has an ability to completely lose himself." During his post-presidential years, he once returned early from a party and found

William Ewald's young son alone, weaving a gimlet out of stringlike material. Eisenhower observed for a moment, then asked to try. The young boy, Ewald said, never forgot "the intensity of the attention Eisenhower put into that lariat . . . and his interest in finding out how you weave these pieces together." That ability to focus allowed Eisenhower to move easily from one pursuit to another. Edward McCabe recalled once coming to the Cabinet Room with a speech. Eisenhower "was out hitting some golf balls on the back lawn. He came in with his golf shoes on and sat, looked this thing over. All business—we jumped right to it." Moreover, in preparing for his first chin-up speech, Eisenhower wanted to zero in on just one topic. When Larson presented an outline covering multiple topics, the president turned it down. Instead, at the president's behest, they agreed to focus on "science and economy" in the first speech.[27]

The televised talks also illustrated Eisenhower's attention to prose. He liked to write, and during the early 1930s newspaper magnate William Randolph Hearst had even offered him a generous salary—triple his Army pay—to serve as a correspondent, which he turned down to continue serving as General Douglas MacArthur's aide. He was amused that MacArthur's speeches had won praise as fine oratory. "Do you know who wrote General MacArthur's speeches? I did," he said. Larson observed, "He reworked and revised his manuscripts endlessly." He had no patience for poor oratory, once complaining that Robert Cutler's writing was "pedantic and dull," adding that the national security advisor took an hour to tell a three-minute story. When Eisenhower drafted a message declaring his interest in the 1952 Republican nomination, he and General Edwin Clark tried to get the wording just right, fussing over phrases for five hours, with Eisenhower objecting to words like "aggressive." ("That's Hitler's word," he protested.) Eisenhower's editing resulted in a better product. McCabe said that when the president "tinkered with the language, he wasn't doing it for some peculiar editorial inclination that he had. He was doing it because he thought the text needed it. And he was just real good at that kind of thing."[28]

Eisenhower took speeches seriously. When he was in London after World War II, Winston Churchill asked him to give a keynote address in the city's historic Guildhall. Eisenhower memorized his speech and reviewed it every night for three weeks, and he delivered it with such panache that London media compared it to the Gettysburg Address. He spent considerable time preparing for the "Science in National Security" speech as well. In giving instructions to Larson, he said it "could emphasize the fact that a purely materialistic dictatorship has concentrated in particular areas and has accomplished a very significant scientific achievement." By contrast, he maintained, "we are not merely racing in the materialistic way; we are defending priceless spiritual values." Eisenhower said he wanted the talk to conclude "on a note of determination and earnest purpose," for he believed that "the American people can meet every one of these problems and these threats if we turn our minds to it." He also derived comfort from the mere knowledge of strength without having to demonstrate it. "He knew it great to have a giant's strength," observed Ewald, but he wisely "knew it tyrannous to use it as a giant."[29]

Eisenhower had planned to give the first of his science and national security talks during a visit to Oklahoma City. But at the conclusion of a November 4th NSC meeting, where he received the disturbing findings of the Gaither Committee, a panel member suggested to Eisenhower that the first speech would be more effective if delivered from the White House. The next day, the president surprised the news media by announcing he would give the first speech from the Oval Office on November 7, six days earlier than originally planned.

It was one of Eisenhower's most important addresses. Forty-eight million Americans watched. The talk, he later wrote, "was no exercise in positive thinking based on hopes alone. We had much about which to be confident." In it, Eisenhower acknowledged Sputnik's scientific importance, dispelling his aides' awkward attempts to dismiss it, saying, "The Soviet launching of earth satellites is an achievement of the first importance, and the scientists who brought it about deserve full credit and recognition." While he assured Americans that satellites "have no direct present effect upon the nation's security," he acknowledged their military implications because they used rockets and other technology that could be used in weaponry.[30]

The main goal was to quell anxiety about national security and dampen temptations for costly military projects. He gave specifics about defense accomplishments and outlined actions to strengthen defense and technology. Admitting the picture was hardly rosy, he said, "I am going to lay the facts before you—the rough with the smooth. Some of these security facts are reassuring; others are not—they are sternly demanding."

Larson wanted to inject drama into the speech. He recalled that one of his tasks was "to go around and dig up every kind of promising scientific project that I could find in town." In particular, he was "looking about for graphic items to brighten up the speech and to give it visual interest for the television audience." He wanted also "to point out that we weren't doing too badly ourselves on the science front." Larson learned of tangible success in space rocketry: the August 1957 recovery of the Jupiter C nose cone. To enable Eisenhower to show it on television, he inserted the line: "The object here in my hand is a nose cone that has been to outer space and back." After asking the Defense Department to bring it to the White House, Larson was surprised to arrive there and find a crew of men wrestling a massive object into the Oval Office. It was the nose cone, and Eisenhower jokingly read the line Larson had prepared.[31]

FIGURE 3.   Eisenhower inspects the Jupiter C nose cone before his November 7, 1957, "Science in National Security" speech. The nose cone's size surprised Eisenhower and speechwriter Arthur Larson, who expected something the president could hold in his hand. (Library of Congress, Prints & Photos Division, *U.S. News and World Report* collection)

They amended the line, and in a dramatic moment, Eisenhower showed the nose cone. Having survived atmospheric reentry, it now sat in the Oval Office next to his desk. "Here it is," the president beamed, "completely intact." While Eisenhower conceded that the Soviets were ahead in some missile areas, and certainly in satellite development, he assured Americans that "the over-all military strength of the free world is distinctly greater than that of the communist countries."

He gave more examples. The Navy had an atomic depth bomb. The Air Force's B-52, the backbone of its bomber fleet, "can carry as much destructive capacity as was delivered by all the bombers in all the years of World War II combined." The air-breathing Snark missile had recently hit a target from a range of 5,000 miles. The United States had a stock of nuclear weapons and planned a nuclear-powered aircraft carrier and a supersonic bomber. "Our scientists assure me that we are well ahead of the Soviets in the nuclear field, both in quantity and quality. We intend to stay ahead," he promised. A favorite Eisenhower adjective was "spiritual," which he invoked by saying that "the spiritual powers of a nation—its underlying religious faith, its self-reliance, its capacity for intelligent sacrifice—these are the most important stones in any defense structure."

But the president warned that without determined effort, the United States "could fall behind" the Soviet Union. He proposed actions to meet the Sputnik challenge. He promised to introduce legislation to remove legal barriers impeding exchange of technological information with friendly countries. To promote missile development, he endowed the Pentagon's guided missile director with greater authority. Most important, Eisenhower announced he would now have a science advisor. He was creating the Office of Special Assistant for the President for Science and Technology, and he tapped James Killian to fill the post, an appointment that both the scientific and political communities applauded. The president of MIT, Killian had helped the school secure numerous federal research grants, and his leadership of the Technological Capabilities Panel enhanced his Washington connections. The appointment also allowed Eisenhower to avoid creating a Department of Science and the creeping bureaucracy that would accompany it.

Eisenhower liked to have his speeches stress a central point, which he called a "QED" (from the Latin phrase *quod erat demonstrandum*, meaning "which was to be demonstrated"), and he concluded by emphasizing two cherished principles, economy and peace. "Certainly, we need to feel a high sense of urgency," he admitted. "But this does not mean that we should mount our charger and try to ride off in all directions at once." He reminded

Americans, "Defense today is expensive, and growing more so. We cannot afford waste." The country would have to exercise "selectivity in national expenditures of all kinds. We cannot, on an unlimited scale, have both what we must have and what we would like to have." Above all, the military was devoted to preserving peace. The world needed "a giant step toward peace" even more than "a giant leap into outer space," and he looked forward to the day "when the scientist can give his full attention, not to human destruction, but to human happiness and fulfillment."[32]

Not all reaction to the speech was favorable. Paul Butler, the Democratic national chairman, dismissed the president's data as "warmed over" material that the administration had released two years earlier. These leftovers raised "grave questions as to whether this Administration is giving the public the real facts to which it is entitled." The *New York Post* complained, "Two Sputniks cannot sway Eisenhower. The President's answer in each instance is the same: we can't do very much." In Oslo, Norway, the newspaper *Dagbladet* blasted the speech as failing to give "a single word" of inspired leadership, while London's *Daily Telegraph* said that Killian's appointment "is not a very exciting answer." Indeed, the president's appeal to "spiritual" abstractions was arcane, and the Jupiter C nose cone was less impressive than the two Sputniks orbiting the earth.[33]

Some media offered cautious praise. While criticizing Eisenhower because he "offered very little specific information" and "was not as candid as he might have been in acknowledging the tardiness of his own Administration" in responding to Sputnik, the *Washington Post* commented, "The specific steps he has taken are constructive and seem to hold a good deal of promise of forward action." The *Wall Street Journal* found that the "merit of the President's assessment is that it rejects both complacency and hysteria." Eisenhower's projection of a positive tone was important. He had come to Washington hoping to avoid partisan rancor, reaching across the aisle to work well with Democrats. As foreign policy remained a realm of bipartisanship, he hoped to cooperate with Congress in space policy, too, while avoiding an upsurge in political polarization.[34]

The day after the president's speech, the administration took even more decisive action. Defense Secretary McElroy announced that the Army would use the Jupiter C rocket to "supplement" the Navy's Vanguard to launch at least six satellites during the IGY. McElroy emphasized that the satellite program would still be geared toward the Vanguard, emphasizing, "All test firings of Vanguard have met with success, and there is every reason to believe Vanguard will meet its schedule to launch later this year a fully instrumented scientific satellite." Although the policy change represented a vindication for the ABMA, Medaris said that he "blew up" after hearing the announcement, furious that his team was relegated to just a backup status rather than receiving outright permission to launch a satellite. Bitterly, he interpreted the decision as saying, "We are going to give Vanguard every possible chance, right up to the last minute, and if by some miracle they do get something up, you can put your toys back on the shelf." Although Medaris was miffed, the move represented a major administration shift. After denying a race and the need for attention-grabbing accomplishments, Eisenhower wanted substantive achievements in space—and soon. As Larson commented, Eisenhower "knew that he had to do something to show that we weren't totally idle."[35]

"Money Cannot Do Everything"

On November 13, the president delivered his second science address from Oklahoma City, where he was celebrating the fiftieth anniversary of Oklahoma's statehood. He and Larson worked feverishly on the speech, entitled "Our Future Security," even as they flew to Oklahoma.[36] The speech conveyed the relationship between his national security concerns and economic principles. Eisenhower worried about the economic security that enabled Americans to defend themselves and enjoy better standards of living than the Soviets did. Yet some Americans seemed inclined to spend lavishly on defense. "The sputniks," he noted, "have inspired a wide variety of suggestions," ranging from accelerated missile programs to a moon rocket to increases in all military and scientific outlays. He catalogued the weapon prices: "A single B-52 bomber costs $8 million. The B-52 wing costs four times as much as the B-36 wing it replaces. . . . A new submarine costs $47½ million—ten times the cost of a World War II submarine. And so on, for our entire arsenal of equipment." The government's duty was to review military expenditures "with redoubled determination to save every possible dime." For scientific ventures, "we must adopt a sensible formula to guide us in deciding what satellite and outer-space activity to undertake."

Much more than the first, this speech resonated with the idea of fiscal austerity. Eisenhower pointed out that tripling a researcher's salary would not generate three times as many breakthroughs. He impressed upon Americans that "there is much more to the matter of security than the mere spending of money." Although the American people "will not sacrifice security to worship a balanced budget," he said, "do not forget, either, that over the long term a balanced budget is one indispensable aid in keeping our economy and therefore our total security, strong and sound." The fact was that "money cannot do everything."

Eisenhower assured Americans that "the quality of our life, and the vigor of our ideals" would triumph over those of the Soviet Union. "Now once again," he said, "we hear an expansionist regime declaring, 'We will bury you.' In a bit of American vernacular, 'Oh Yeah?'" Eisenhower said that the nation needed people to "keep their heads" during crisis and meet human as well as scientific problems: "In short, we will need not only Einsteins and Steinmetzes, but Washingtons, and Emersons." He stressed that the government would meet the Soviet challenge by prudently beefing up defenses, undertaking an increased space effort, encouraging education, and stepping up research programs. Although Americans faced hard work and sacrifice, Eisenhower concluded that the "eventual triumph of decency and freedom and right in this world is inevitable."[37]

The speech lacked the gravitas of the previous week's White House talk; no setting could match the Oval Office's majesty. Yet Eisenhower had taken steps toward confronting the challenges that the post-Sputnik uproar had posed, demonstrating that he worked best in crises, as he had during World War II and other key moments in his life. He kept a steady hand on the national tiller, refusing to allow the Soviet satellites to goad him into hasty, costly space initiatives. The speech's homage to humanistic thinkers elicited praise from educators in the liberal arts as well as sciences. Tulsa University's president remarked, "The President's speech means that not only will we offer more science training but improve our courses in the arts and humanities which are the basis for scientific thinking." Eisenhower also stressed that technological triumphs posed no threat to U.S. security, and his approval of Jupiter C as a Vanguard backup showed solid action.[38]

Eisenhower himself was at the vanguard, showing innovation in using television to reassure Americans. The new medium became his tool to neutralize a problem and replenish his public support when it threatened to crater. By acting in this way, he followed a cardinal rule of presidential crises: a leader should stay ahead of the public opinion curve, shaping rather than reacting to it. Moreover, Eisenhower was a shrewd judge of timing. By waiting a month, he had allowed the media and political panic to dissipate. Standing outside the White House, he stared at the sky and reflected that any decision made during a panic would be "a bad one." He bided time, avoided knee-jerk reactions, and used television to convey the facts. NASA deputy administrator Robert Seamans said, "Eisenhower did exactly the right thing."[39]

But for some Americans, a crisis continued. Journalist Walter Lippmann scoffed at Eisenhower's assertion that America "could fall behind" the Soviet Union. The country was lagging, he insisted, "and the President will never restore the confidence of the people until he gives them the confidence that he is telling them the full truth."[40]

 **CHAPTER 6**

"Gloom, Gloom, Gloom"

On September 24, 1955, while vacationing in Colorado, Eisenhower suffered a heart attack. For the next two months, he remained in Denver, recuperating at an Army hospital, before he finally returned to Washington to resume his presidential duties.

Eisenhower was susceptible to stress-related illnesses, and worse, he held the world's most difficult position. "No man on earth knows what this job is all about," he said. "It's pound, pound, pound. Not only is your intellectual capacity taxed to the utmost, but your physical stamina." After the heart attack, doctors ordered the president to modify his diet, avoid fats, and take more breaks during the day. They also told him to avoid situations that might elicit emotions such as anxiety, frustration, or anger. Upon hearing this, Eisenhower replied, "Just what do you think the Presidency is?"[1]

Eisenhower recovered enough that in February 1956, he announced that he would run for reelection. But in June came another health scare. Complaining of severe stomach pain, Eisenhower was rushed to Walter Reed Army Hospital. White House staff assumed he had another heart attack, but instead doctors diagnosed the problem as ileitis, or inflammation of the ileum, the small intestine's lining, complicated by an intestinal blockage. They performed an emergency operation to clear Eisenhower's intestinal tract.[2]

Two scares within two years raised questions about the sixty-six-year-old president's health. Yet in 1956 he won reelection handily, beating

Democratic challenger Adlai Stevenson, and he was determined to serve a second term. But in the fall of 1957, just eleven months into that term, Eisenhower experienced yet another health crisis.

The Gaither Report

The crush of events after Sputnik II's launch showed the merciless "pound, pound, pound" that Eisenhower faced. Just hours before he gave his November 7 television address, he held an NSC meeting at which he received the report of the Gaither Committee, a special panel that illustrated the almost fraternal relationship between the federal government and outside specialists, a bond that had grown closer during World War II. Eisenhower later called the Gaither panel's findings "useful" and a "gadfly" to spur action. But they also magnified political pressure after the two Sputniks.[3]

Throughout his presidency, Eisenhower parried criticism from Capitol Hill that he was remiss on national security. These charges came from Democrats and Republicans, and they intensified during his second term. In January 1957, GOP senator Jacob Javits described Congress's mood as "deeply mortified that the United States . . . is in a position where it must catch up with the Soviet Union in the missiles race at the price of our very survival." Javits added, "We do not think we have too much time to catch up and we do not think that catching up is enough." Nothing angered Eisenhower more than the accusation that he allowed American defenses to slip. At one press conference, he raged, "I want to tell you this: I've spent my life in this [defense], and I know more about it than almost anybody . . . because I have given my life to it." But now he faced greater recriminations about his leadership in national security.[4]

In early 1957, the Civilian Defense Administration conducted a study on bomb shelters that raised troubling questions about America's ability to defend its population during an attack. The report recommended building $40 billion worth of blast shelters. On April 4, 1957, Eisenhower appointed a special commission to investigate whether this move was justified. Its chair was H. Rowan Gaither, Jr., a San Francisco lawyer who headed the Ford Foundation, the private establishment that drew on the Henry Ford family fortune to award grants in various fields. The panel became known as the Gaither Committee (its official title was the unwieldy "Security Resources Panel of the Office of Defense Mobilization Science Advisory Committee"). During the summer, arterial thrombosis forced Gaither to withdraw from the committee, which continued to operate under his name, and Robert

Sprague of Sprague Electric Company and William Foster of Olin Mathieson Chemical Corporation replaced him. A blue-ribbon panel comprising experts from science, government, business, and other fields, the committee was a motley assemblage, including some names with star power, such as General James Doolittle and CBS president Frank Stanton. Its original task was to determine whether America should create a program to construct fallout shelters, and Eisenhower specifically advised the group to stick to that task. Against his instructions, the committee expanded its charge to conduct a massive review of the country's defense posture. A key question was whether the United States could survive a nuclear first strike from the Soviet Union and retaliate. The result was what committee member Spurgeon Keeny called "a dreadful study, sort of a hysterical reaction" to the panel's original mission.[5]

On November 4, 1957—the day after Sputnik II went up—Sprague, Foster, and two other committee members presented an oral distillation of the Gaither Report's findings to Eisenhower. At the November 7 NSC meeting, all Gaither Committee members crammed themselves into the White House broadcast room to present a written report to the president, the NSC, and the Joint Chiefs. The committee had expanded enormously, recalled Keeny, "so I don't think any of the large group of working people in various working committees and study groups had even seen the report until it came out." Most Gaither Committee members, Keeny said, "had almost nothing to do with [the final report]. They were just conferred with or met with."[6]

The "intellectual engine in the [report] was Paul Nitze, who was extremely hawkish," Keeny recalled. A former State Department official, Nitze had been the principal author of NSC-68, and the Gaither Report struck a similar tone. It was a no-holds-barred comparison of America's military strength with that of the Soviet Union, and it gave no solace, presenting a sobering picture of America's defenses and arguing that a Soviet first strike could cripple Strategic Air Command bombers. (SAC was the Air Force operation that, among many functions, maintained a fleet of B-52 bombers carrying atomic weapons.) Not only was America's military vulnerable; its civilians were, too, and the Gaither Report predicted that a Soviet first strike would destroy up to 50 percent of the American population. The stunning figures reinforced what Eisenhower already believed, that nuclear war was unwinnable. He once commented, "You can't have that war. There aren't enough bulldozers to scrape the bodies off the streets."[7]

The Gaither Committee's first priority was to enhance America's offensive missile capabilities. It recommended that the military keep five hundred

SAC bombers flying at all times and scatter the entire bomber fleet around the country. The need for missile development was urgent, the committee said, and it supported a crash program to increase IRBMs and ICBMs. To pay for beefed-up defenses, the president would have to boost military spending from $38 billion to $46 billion.[8]

The Gaither Committee's second priority was a network of fallout shelters—not merely bomb shelters to shield citizens from blasts, as the Civilian Defense Administration had urged—to protect Americans from radioactivity after a nuclear attack. The committee recommended a $5 billion-a-year shelter construction program that would stretch out over five years. The total would be $25 billion, but it would save lives and form the linchpin of America's passive defenses (as opposed to the active defenses, the SAC bombers) against a Soviet attack.[9]

With classic understatement, Eisenhower described the report as "far from optimistic." William Ewald was closer to the mark when he said it was "gloom, gloom, gloom." Moreover, it was urgent. The committee exhorted the president to enact its recommendations immediately. "The next two years seem to be critical. If we fail to act at once, the risk . . . will be unacceptable," the report implored. For three committee members, the report's alarmist stance did not go far enough. They thought the United States should attack the Soviet Union first as a preemptive measure. Keeny said, "the Gaither study almost called for initiating a garrison state. It was very alarmist, very extreme."[10]

The report and its ominous conclusions caught Eisenhower in a quandary that highlighted issues intensifying after Sputnik. First was the question of secrecy, involving not only the media but members of Congress. After the Gaither Committee concluded its work, a tug-of-war ensued between the president and Senate majority leader Johnson, who wrote to Eisenhower on December 4 to demand release of the Gaither Report and Killian's TCP report. Citing executive privilege, the sensitive nature of the documents, and the confidential relationship he had with the committees, Eisenhower declined.[11] Still, Johnson could use the report's disquieting assessments to his political advantage as he conducted a special congressional investigation. And soon the Gaither Report became public knowledge.

On December 20, 1957, the *Washington Post* broke the story with a page-one headline that declared, "Secret Report Sees U.S. in Grave Peril." The top-secret Gaither Report, the paper wrote, described America "moving in frightening course to the status of a second-class power" and "exposed to an almost immediate threat from the missile-bristling Soviet Union." The *Post* described a "current missile gap" and disclosed that the Gaither Report estimated that—at the earliest—America could close the gap only by 1960–61.

The breach in confidentiality incensed Eisenhower. Killian recalled, "The leaks and the consequent demands for publication of the report angered the president. . . . General Cutler once said to me that the most difficult experience he had with the president during his long service as special assistant for national security affairs arose out of the leaking of the Gaither report."[12] The incident so bothered Eisenhower that he considered dispensing with outside study groups, even though he valued their independent thought. But the Gaither Report's timing made it especially sensitive. Coming just after the Sputniks, it had the potential of further exciting the media and making the president vulnerable to congressional attack. Critics now had more proof that Eisenhower sacrificed security for parsimony, and he worried that Congress would endorse the report's costliest recommendations.

How much Eisenhower supported the committee's findings was a key question. He backed the concept of having more B-52s in the air at all times and spreading them more widely. He believed that for the next few years, bombers would be the main delivery vehicles for atomic weapons, but he also recognized that missiles would supersede aircraft, so he agreed with deploying more IRBMs and ICBMs. Still, he opposed unnecessary money for them, and he also spurned an idea to burrow SAC airstrips into mountains for protection. Sometimes the differences between Eisenhower and the Gaither Committee were in degree. For example, Eisenhower supported the idea of deploying more IRBMs; he felt 120 missiles would be adequate, while the Gaither panel supported twice that amount. Eisenhower compromised by agreeing to 180, the number that McElroy and Quarles recommended. Thanks to U-2 photos that Gaither Committee members could not view, Eisenhower had a better understanding of Soviet military capabilities and could keep U.S. defense spending in check on the basis of his privileged information. In his memoirs, Eisenhower noted that he "did not agree with all of the panel's hypothetical figures" and explained his differences by observing, "The President, unlike a panel which concentrates on a single problem, must always strive to see the totality of the national and international situation. He must take into account conflicting purposes, responding to legitimate needs but assigning priorities and keeping plans and costs within bounds."[13]

Cost was indeed a problem. The money that the Gaither Report envisioned appalled Eisenhower, and he discounted the panel's notion that the economy could easily shoulder vastly increased defense spending, or even benefit from it. At a luncheon with committee members, he expressed shock that the figure of a billion dollars seemed so casual. "Why, it's a stack of ten-dollar bills as high as the Washington Monument," he exclaimed. The committee predicted the greater military spending would produce only moderate deficits, but that assumed a steady revenue stream and no economic disruptions, which were factors beyond anyone's control. At the November 4 meeting, Eisenhower complained of "hysteria" and said, "We must neither panic nor become complacent. We should decide what needs to be done, and do it—avoiding extremes." One extreme that Eisenhower struck down was the fallout shelter program. In rejecting it, he saved billions of taxpayer dollars and avoided offending allies, who would see a "Fortress America" mentality in such a program and an indifference to the plight of the European and Asian populace during a nuclear attack. Keeny later commented that if Eisenhower "had reacted to all the recommendations in the Gaither study, he would have gone into really crash ballistic missile programs across the board. He would have started a major ABM system immediately. He would have gone to national fallout and blast shelter programs and all sorts of other things."[14]

Eisenhower resisted these and, in truth, doubted a Soviet first strike. He once complained to Robert Cutler that NSC staffers worried too much about it. "Well, I don't believe for a second they will ever attack," he said. He had disagreed with NSC-68's labeling the year 1954 as a "year of maximum danger," when the Soviet Union's nuclear arsenal would gain such strength that Moscow would be tempted to strike. In Eisenhower's calculus, the Soviet leaders' foremost priority was to retain power—not even to spread communism—and they dared not risk any move, especially nuclear holocaust, that would destabilize their regime and drive them from their positions.[15]

Despite Eisenhower's logic, the Gaither Report forced his hand. The fallout after Sputnik, Goodpaster recalled, "led [Eisenhower] to take actions to try to put it in some perspective and to give a degree of reassurance that we had programs where it counted, that is, military programs, that were appropriate for the security of the country." To Eisenhower's chagrin, that meant spending more money on defense. In December 1957, he asked Congress for a $1.3 billion supplemental defense appropriation. The money, he believed, would assuage the public, especially by accelerating the Jupiter, Thor, and Polaris IRBM programs. For the FY 1959 budget, he proposed $40.3 billion for defense, an increase of $2.7 billion over his FY 1958 request, which reflected the pressures facing him.[16]

The unfortunate fact was that considerable money ended up in the defense "dump heap." "What became of all the new ideas born out of the reactions to Sputnik? Where did they lead us? What did they contribute to our security in general and to closing the missile gap in particular?" asked Herbert York. "The surprising, perhaps unbelievable, yet most significant answers to these three questions are: Nothing, nowhere, nothing." The programs almost all ended eventually, York explained, and had few technological derivatives, yet cost taxpayers billions.[17]

Although Eisenhower wisely fought many Gaither Committee recommendations, the report influenced his national security policy for the rest of his presidency. The Gaither Report and the charged post-Sputnik political atmosphere painted him into a corner. Eisenhower agreed to higher defense expenditures that he found distasteful and wasteful. As popular as he was, Eisenhower's power to fight Congress on these issues had limits, especially in the wake of Soviet space successes.[18]

⟩⟩● A "Drastic Personal Test"

The events of the autumn of 1957 severely tested Eisenhower's physical stamina: Little Rock, two Sputniks, the Gaither Report. In rapid succession, his administration also lost three of its most prominent members: George Humphrey left in July, Charles Wilson in October, and Attorney General Herbert Brownell in November. All three men had faults, but they also were vital cogs in Eisenhower's administrative machine. They had wisdom, and they deflected criticism from the president and often absorbed it themselves. After their departures, Eisenhower felt more lonely. He complained to Swede Hazlett that since the Suez Crisis of July 1956, "I cannot remember a day that has not brought its major or minor crisis."[19] At an October 30 press conference, CBS reporter Charles von Fremd mentioned all the crises that had struck and asked, "Do all of these great problems sap your strength physically or mentally in any way, sir?" The president conceded that troubles had rained down on him for more than a year and added, "I find it a bit wearing, but I find it endurable, if you have got the faith in America that I have." Writing to Eisenhower in early November 1957, Arthur Burns expressed concern about the president's hectic work pace. "I felt quite unhappy to read that you may not be getting any vacation this month," Burns said. "In view of the kind of summer you had, and the rough time that the Democrats are planning to give you in the next session of Congress, you really should regard a vacation as a must."[20]

On November 15, Eisenhower left for a vacation in Augusta. But the time away failed to relax him. Upon returning, he looked tired, and he complained of trouble sleeping because he had been "so wrought up thinking about things."[21] He scheduled a third speech in the science and national security series, to be delivered from Cleveland, on the topic of international cooperation and America's security.

He never gave it. On November 25, 1957, Eisenhower went by motorcade to National Airport to receive the king of Morocco for an official state visit. It was a raw autumn day in Washington, with temperatures in the forties, yet the presidential limousine motored through the city without its bubble top, blasting Ike with cold air, and the airport reception ceremony chilled him further. In the afternoon, while working in the Oval Office, Eisenhower had trouble. Papers slipped from his grasp, and his fingers fumbled for his pen. Glancing at the document before him, he saw the words tumble off the page. Trying to get up, he lost balance, and when he called for help, the words came out garbled.[22]

The president had suffered a stroke. The incident "was classified as a TIA: temporary ischemic attack, a mini-stroke," said Dr. W. North Sterrett, who later served as Eisenhower's physician during his retirement in Gettysburg. Sterrett explained that "one of the blood vessels in the brain develops a spasm, and it just shuts off. But it's only temporary. Within 24 to 36 hours, it lets up, and then the symptoms are all gone."[23] But Eisenhower called it "a drastic personal test," and after spending the rest of the day in bed, he showed classic determination. In the evening, he prepared to attend a state dinner for the Moroccan king. Mamie and his physician were "appalled" to see him up, he recalled, and forced him back to bed. Vice President and Pat Nixon hosted the event along with Mamie, who looked pale and preoccupied, leaving right after dinner to be with her husband.[24]

Close aides worried that Eisenhower's third major illness would permanently disable him. "The atmosphere of gloom and despair and grief around [the White House] was beyond description," Larson recalled. "We all really thought the President this time was finished." Sherman Adams warned Nixon to prepare to assume the presidency within twenty-four hours. At a December 6 meeting, top aides discussed ways to lighten the president's workload, agreeing that they should limit meetings with him and bring only the greatest problems to his attention. Rumors circulated in the White House that the rest of his term would be a protectorate presidency, similar to Woodrow Wilson's after a stroke had incapacitated him. Larson recorded in his private diary that "I began to accept the idea of a sort of protectorate, an idea I have resisted until now." Democratic senator Wayne Morse of Oregon said that Eisenhower should resign.[25]

After his 1955 heart attack, Eisenhower felt depressed—a common reaction among heart patients—and he sunk into a funk after the stroke, too. As in 1955, he repaired to Gettysburg to recuperate, but he seemed emotionally as well as physically frail. Even the optimistic Eisenhower felt disheartened. "This is the end," he said gloomily. "Mamie and I are farmers from now on." She feared even worse, confessing, "I'm not so sure we're ever going to be able to live in Gettysburg."[26]

The television talks on science and national security were finished. After the stroke, "the idea of a heavy speaking schedule was pretty much out of the question," Larson said. "We managed to get through the State of the Union message [in January 1958] but kept the speaking schedule fairly light after that." During each of the last three years of his presidency, Eisenhower gave fewer major addresses than during any of the previous five years. During his last quarter year as president, he gave almost no press conferences. In a way, the president had become a victim of the Sputnik fallout.[27]

Eisenhower recovered rapidly, but two months after the stroke, he found that his speaking skills still suffered, noting "a tendency to use the wrong word—for example, I may say 'desk' when I mean chair.'" At a 1959 meeting, scientist George Kistiakowsky remarked, "His difficulty in expressing his thoughts was far greater than I have ever encountered before." For the rest of his life, Eisenhower complained of aphasia. "Even today, occasionally, I reverse syllables in a long word and at times am compelled to speak slowly and cautiously if I am to enunciate correctly," he wrote during retirement. Although observers might not have detected this difficulty, he found it frustrating.[28]

Eisenhower had to prove he was still up to the job. On December 2, he held a cabinet meeting, and *New York Times* columnist Arthur Krock wrote that one cabinet officer "in whose integrity I have every confidence" (it might have been Attorney General William Rogers, with whom Krock had friendly relations) reported, "I have never seen the President more alert or giving more of an impression of perfect health. This was especially conveyed by his eyes, his color and physical coordination, including the way he walked. There was not the slightest impairment of speech or trace of fumbling for a word the President needed." More important, Eisenhower had a December 13 summit scheduled in Paris, a meeting of NATO leaders designed to secure agreements to place IRBMs in Europe to counter Soviet missiles. Top administration members—Nixon, John Foster Dulles, Sherman Adams, James Hagerty—urged Eisenhower not to go, and Nixon planned to attend as the president's substitute. Fearing more ministrokes, doctors instructed Eisenhower to forgo the summit, telling him that he needed a minimum of sixty days of rest.[29]

Larson recalled that with "icy determination" the president announced, "I'm going to take this trip if it kills me. This is my job. I *am* going to run this damn show." Eisenhower saw it as a self-imposed personal test. If he fared poorly, he would resign. After Thanksgiving, he showed the same resolve, going to Gettysburg but returning to Washington on Monday, brushing aside entreaties to stay away longer.[30]

On December 13, Eisenhower left for Europe. As he neared Paris, he rode in an open car, braving the frigid air to acknowledge the greetings of French citizens. His schedule was grueling. He met foreign heads of state, gave a presentation, and visited his former NATO headquarters office. Importantly, Eisenhower got what he wanted, an agreement from NATO allies that the United States would base IRBMs in their countries as a bulwark against Soviet threats to Europe, especially as Russia developed the ICBM. England and later Turkey and Italy provided bases for the missiles; the actions made the United States and NATO look formidable against any Soviet threat. The IRBMs gave NATO allies reassurance, and their presence "was significant in holding the alliance together and reducing the possibility of Soviet intimidation," recalled Harold Brown, the director of defense research and engineering during the 1960s who later served as President Jimmy Carter's defense secretary. By making Europeans fear Soviet missiles, Sputnik had the effect of knitting NATO allies closer together, especially important for Anglo-American relations that had been strained in 1956 when the United States protested the joint British, French, and Israeli invasion of Egypt during the Suez crisis.[31]

The NATO journey also confirmed to Eisenhower that he still measured up to the presidency's rigors. He missed one late-night dinner to go to sleep early, instructing Press Secretary Hagerty, "Tell those [reporters] I'm a 9:30 or 10 o'clock boy tonight and I am going to bed at that time." Other than that concession to conserve energy, he attended all functions and showed an élan vital. Larson later observed that "I have never in my life witnessed such a towering act of personal will as Eisenhower's grim determination to go through with the NATO conference."[32]

Eisenhower bounced back after illness, usually with good cheer. As he lay in bed after his heart attack, with four doctors at his bedside smoking cigarettes, he smiled and asked why he—who had given up smoking six years earlier—suffered a heart attack while they had not. As he recovered from ileitis and had to be fed rectally, he told a nurse that his troubles were now "behind" him. In the difficult days after the stroke, the vice president tried to brace up Eisenhower's wavering spirits. "The trouble with most politicians is that their mouths move faster than their brains," Nixon told the president. "With you it is the other way around." Eisenhower "laughed more heartily than I had heard him laugh for weeks," Nixon remembered. Ironically, at a press conference earlier in 1957, Eisenhower was discussing presidential disability and said hypothetically, "There could be a case where a man has a stroke that was slight, from which he would recover. We have great statesmen in the world today that recovered from a couple of them and carried on for years." Now Eisenhower had become one of those statesmen.[33]

In light of Eisenhower's recovery, abandoning the televised talks was a mistake. He showed grit and determination on high-priority issues, such as the NATO alliance. When he plugged for a plan to reorganize the Department of Defense, he vowed to appeal to Americans on television and "get onto the air as often as the television companies would let me get on." Hughes regretted that Eisenhower "never employed such resources [to command national attention] in any coherent and sustained campaign. Rather did he restrict the use of each device almost to the minimum that his advisers would tolerate." Eisenhower disliked doing the television talks, and typically self-effacing, he added, "I can think of nothing more boring, for the American public, than to have to sit in their living rooms for a whole half hour looking at my face on their television screens." Yet a more sustained public relations effort from the White House might have corrected the false impression that the United States lagged behind the Soviet Union in science and space. That correction would have inoculated the president from considerable criticism and made his recovery—indeed, his whole second term—easier.[34]

➤● "Sputternik"

In space racing against the Soviet Union, America had to play catch-up, and Project Vanguard's team felt the pressure. John Neilon recalled that "the heat turned on and this slow and easy scientific project got the fire put under it to go launch a satellite as soon as [we] could." One week after Sputnik, the White House released a statement announcing that the Vanguard satellite would be launched in December 1957, four months ahead of schedule. This publicity from the White House forced a reluctant Vanguard director John P. Hagen to attempt to launch the satellite rather than just test it. The administration's new timetable was to have the Navy launch a test vehicle in December 1957 and an instrumented satellite in March 1958.[35]

By announcing the Vanguard launch so early, the White House took the kind of action that the president had scrupulously avoided, generating intense media attention. Although Eisenhower wanted the Vanguard program to be open, he "was against what he thought of as stupid publicity," recalled Herbert York. "And so he did very much try to keep the generals and admirals and scientists from boasting about what they wanted to do in the future because he'd seen too many instances in which somebody said, 'We're going to launch a rocket next Tuesday,' and Tuesday would come and it didn't work."[36]

That was a concern, because Vanguard was not fully operational. Although engineers had tested some of the stages, the December launch would be the first time that all three stages would be assembled to launch the actual satellite. The upper stages, in particular, used new technology, and experts pegged the chances of success at just 50 percent. It was more a test vehicle than a real rocket.[37]

During the 1950s, new rockets were lubberly beasts that often collapsed. Neilon liked to explain the contrast between twenty-first-century satellite launches and those of the 1950s: "The difference between now and then was now, you expect them to work. Then, you hoped they would work." Success rates in the 1950s, he estimated, were as low as 30–35 percent. Lyndon Johnson recalled that the first tests on the Atlas ICBM and the Jupiter and Thor IRBMs resulted in eight failures in eleven attempts. In World War II Germany, the original V-2 rockets fared even worse: in eighteen attempts, only one flew successfully. The Soviet Union, too, suffered numerous rocket mishaps but kept them secret, only publicizing successes. Sergei Khrushchev recounted the series of R-7 tests and attempted satellite launches, writing, "Successes alternated with whole sequences of explosions, 263 crashes, and breakdowns. . . . [I]t would take a large book to [describe them]."[38]

In the United States, some mishaps were spectacular. Rockets fishtailed in the air, as if in a death spiral, before exploding. Yet even disasters reaped benefits. As engineers sought to understand why rockets failed, each incident became a learning experience and reduced the chance of future problems. They shrugged off setbacks, joking that spectacular failures provided local entertainment. The Air Force's Snark, a top-secret, air-breathing cruise missile first launched in 1952, exploded so frequently that engineers kidded about "Snark-infested waters" near Cape Canaveral. Although the outside world expected Vanguard to function smoothly, Neilon recalled, many engineers had doubts. Its tentative state, combined with intense media attention, brewed ingredients for disaster.[39]

More than one hundred members of the media converged on Cape Canaveral to record the launch of Test Vehicle 3, the new Vanguard satellite. It was to be the first mass broadcast of a launch, and after a two-day postponement that agonized news-hungry reporters, liftoff was set for December 6, 1957. Then came national humiliation. The seconds counted down, and ignition followed. Vanguard rose two feet into the air, exploded in a fireball, and crumpled to the launch pad. America's first satellite lay in a burning heap. As Vanguard engineer Kurt Stehling described the spectacle, "[The rocket] toppled slowly, breaking apart, hitting part of the test stand and ground with a tremendous roar that could be felt and heard even behind the two foot concrete walls of the blockhouse and the six-inch bullet-proof glass. For a moment or two there was complete disbelief. I could see it in the faces, I could feel it in myself. This couldn't be." The first two stages of the satellite were destroyed, but in the grass near the launch pad lay the satellite portion of the rocket, beeping uselessly. (Al Nagy, an Army officer working on Project Vanguard, later recalled that "the crushed and burned satellite from that launch sat in a cardboard box in my office for a number of years before I finally relinquished it to the Smithsonian.") The culprit, engineers later surmised, was likely a fuel line leak (although the official cause was "indeterminate").[40]

A media editor observed that nobody could muster humor about the event; only sadness prevailed. "It wasn't the first time a missile had blown up on the stand at Cape Canaveral," he noted. "But this rocket, Vanguard, seemed much more important than the other rockets. Here American scientific prestige was at stake—and the whole world was watching." Lyndon Johnson exclaimed, "How long, how long, O God, how long will it take us to catch up with the Russians?" America's entire space program seemed smothered in its cradle. Eisenhower failed even to mention the fiasco in his memoirs.[41]

The simple explanation was that Vanguard was untested and too new. "It would have been a near miracle if it had worked," former defense secretary Wilson commented. Asked if the Navy tried to test the satellite too soon, Wilson replied, "Well, I think they got crowded by the publicity point of view—the press and everybody, and perhaps some of the politicians—into an over-early try. You have to go through these experimental stages, and you ought to be able to do it quietly without doing it all publicly." The United States had tried hurriedly to transform a modest IGY scientific vehicle into a symbol of national prestige, and the result was calamitous.[42]

As 1957 came to a close, the Soviets had two successful satellites, whereas America's one had failed spectacularly. World media mocked the fallen satellite with monikers like "sputternik," "stallnik," "dudnik" and "kaputnik." Warsaw's *Zolnierz Wolnosci* sneered, "Who else could manage to spend millions of dollars gathering correspondents from the whole world only to show them wonderful fireworks?" Soviet UN diplomats suggested the United States apply for Soviet aid as a backward nation.[43] American prestige had hit rock bottom.

 **CHAPTER 7**

Space Highs, Economic Lows

During Eisenhower's first term, the worst economic news was a recession that struck in 1953, as the economy adjusted to the Korean War's end. The downturn was mild, with unemployment peaking at 5.5 percent, yet some voices urged dramatic action. David McDonald, head of the U.S. Steel Workers, recommended a $4 billion tax cut and a massive infusion of federal spending, including a $5 billion public works program.[1]

Eisenhower gave a restrained response. At first, he declined to propose tax cuts, finally doing so in August 1954, once the economy was already recovering. Raymond Saulnier recalled, "He was always very informed about this [idea of a tax cut] and always ready to do what could be expected to be constructive. But he was not prepared to do something just because newspapers were pushing him on it or his political opposition was pushing him on it." Instead, his administration sped up fiscal programs already in place for fiscal year 1955, such as public works and defense, and, more important, relied on the Federal Reserve to ease money and credit. To help workers, he approved unemployment benefits and an increase in the minimum wage from seventy-five cents to one dollar. By the summer of 1954, the economy was in recovery, and Eisenhower had helped to erase Republicans' image as the party of Herbert Hoover and the Great Depression.[2]

In a pattern plaguing his presidency, Eisenhower received little credit for his measures to ameliorate the downturn. One reason for the oversight,

Saulnier believed, was "his style of working with little publicity, and his habit of keeping his own efforts in the background. . . . Eisenhower's was not a media-oriented presidency." Reflecting this handicap, Republicans lost control of both houses of Congress in the 1954 midterm elections, even though the economy was in recovery. In late 1957, Eisenhower confronted a new recession, this one far deeper than the 1953–54 slump. Moreover, its timing was worse. During Eisenhower's second term, his administration was no longer fresh and felt trammeled by its lame-duck status; the economic slump reinforced a sense of paralysis. Coming after Sputnik, it added to an image of a president unable to control events whirling around him.[3]

America Enters Space

Although Eisenhower hesitated "racing" the Soviet Union in space, he had to accept the facts. The Vanguard failure intensified pressure to launch a satellite. The president looked to his old service for help.

Before Sputnik, in mid-1957, General John Medaris hewed to the official line that the ABMA was working on only the Jupiter C missile, not satellites. He reminded von Braun that he had authorized no work on a fourth stage to the missile, which would be a satellite. In his journal, Medaris wrote that he "cautioned Dr. von Braun that there must be no public claims or discussion by employees of this agency which would falsely give the impression that we are in the satellite business." Medaris and von Braun persisted until they persevered, but they did so largely in secret. Clinging to his satellite dream even after Vanguard beat out Project Orbiter, von Braun continued to communicate with William Pickering and James Van Allen, two scientists designing the satellite's instrument package. In 1958, von Braun dramatically said, "I'll let you in on a secret. We bootlegged work on the satellite." On the sly earlier in 1957, Medaris had ordered von Braun to keep two Jupiter C rockets ready in case they got the official go-ahead. They could, Medaris guessed, have a satellite ready within four months if approval came. He later wrote that "I stuck my neck out." Indeed he did. In 1966, when a surprised former President Eisenhower learned that the Huntsville team had prepared for a satellite launch without authorization, he declared that the actions "would have been a court martial offense!"[4]

Within thirty-six to forty-eight hours after Sputnik's launch, Goodpaster estimated, Eisenhower found himself swept by events and took "quite a different tack" in his approach, finally granting von Braun his wish. On October 8, Donald Quarles signaled that the Army could prepare its rocket for an imminent launch but estimated it would cost an additional $13 million, a figure that made Eisenhower bristle (Vanguard's escalating costs irritated him enough).[5] Eisenhower met with aides and stressed that "a sudden shift in our approach would be to belie the attitude we had all along." Yet he agreed to a redoubled space effort. At a meeting several hours later, outgoing defense secretary Wilson advised that the United States should have a backup to Vanguard, in case that program failed or encountered delays. Eisenhower concurred and ordered director of guided missiles William Holaday to "keep track of the program day by day, and do what is necessary to have the Redstone ready as a back-up [to Vanguard]." Eisenhower never fully elucidated the reasons for his shift, and his memoirs were strangely silent on the decision. But the policy reversal implied that he acknowledged a connection between space and world prestige, even if he were unwilling publicly to proclaim it as others had.[6]

The November 8 Defense Department press release announcing the Jupiter C as a "supplement" to Vanguard, coupled with Vanguard's disastrous December failure, meant that the ABMA would have the chance to launch a satellite using Jupiter C, and it scheduled January 29, 1958, as a launch date. Caltech's Jet Propulsion Laboratory built the satellite, and on November 18, 1957, the JPL's Pickering asked Medaris to rename Jupiter C "Juno," a name that went back to mythology: Juno was the sister of the god Jupiter, and Juno would, in effect, be the sister of the original Jupiter C. The name also was consonant with Eisenhower's wish to keep the military and scientific rocket work separate, even if in name only.[7]

Juno was sixty-eight-feet tall, but its scientific instrumentation was crammed within the satellite's six-inch shell, which weighed just 30.8 pounds, prompting the Communist Party newspaper to call it "markedly inferior" to its Soviet counterparts. But as the *Huntsville Times* wrote, "Somewhere in there, too, rode the prestige of the United States." The rocket flew aboard a cargo plane from Huntsville to Patrick Air Force Base, twenty miles south of Cape Canaveral, where ABMA officials secretly prepped and then trucked it, covered in canvas, to Cape Canaveral.[8]

Then the elements interfered. High winds in the upper atmosphere postponed the launch for two straight days, and by January 31, the Cape Canaveral crew was waiting with nervous intensity. Men gulped coffee "by the bucket," Medaris recalled. But that night the weather cooperated, and at 10:48 p.m., as its plume of flame turned night into day, Juno rose from the launchpad. For more than an hour, the crew waited, hoping to receive word that a California tracking station had picked up the satellite's signal, indicating that it had made one complete trip around the earth and was officially in orbit. After one hundred minutes, on February 1, the message came. Shortly after it achieved orbit, it was dubbed Explorer I, a name Eisenhower had chosen.[9]

It was a late but historic night. Vacationing in Augusta, Eisenhower stayed up until the early morning hours to get confirmation of an orbit. When the news came, the buoyant president repeated the word "wonderful" three times and added, "I sure feel a lot better now." But wishing to avoid boasts of bigger projects, he warned James Hagerty, "Let's not make too great a hullabaloo over this." The official White House statement made no mention of the Army, instead declaring that the launch was part of the IGY and the satellite's data would be disseminated to the scientific world, a subtle dig at the Soviet Union, which had not yet provided the IGY with scientific information from the two Sputniks. Explorer was not just good news; it showed that the president's original fear had been unfounded. The military could contribute to a civilian project without detracting from the IRBM or ICBM efforts. The Explorer launch pointed out the folly of Eisenhower's original insistence on separating military and civilian rocket efforts, and after it went up, there were no objections that the satellite used an Army rocket.[10]

Here was an important distinction: where Sputnik had been a technological triumph, Explorer was a scientific success, marking the single most significant contribution of any nation to the IGY. The craft carried a Geiger counter that detected a magnetic field encircling the earth, which was eponymously named the Van Allen Belts after the University of Iowa physicist who designed the experiment. Explorer I made other scientific discoveries. It found that the dangers of cosmic rays in space were far less than previously thought, removing a concern for human space travel. Congressman Gerald Ford later reported that one witness testifying before the House Select Committee on Astronautics and Space Exploration said that Explorer "brought back data in two weeks equivalent to a century of work with sounding rockets of the type he had been using for the previous ten years." Eisenhower, too, was proud. Writing ten years after Explorer's launch, he reflected that the scientists' feat could be "ranked as one of our brightest" achievements.[11]

Soon the United States experienced another space success. By the spring of 1958, the Vanguard rocket had endured so many problems and fallen so far behind schedule that wags dubbed it the "Navy's anchor." But on March 17, at Cape Canaveral, members of the Vanguard team joyously sang "Anchors Aweigh" as they launched Vanguard I (technically TV-4, the fourth test vehicle in the Vanguard series). Although it weighed just 3.25 pounds, its lightness allowed its orbit to reach a higher apogee and perigee than any satellite previously launched (2,513 and 407 miles, respectively; its high orbit will allow Vanguard to remain in space for centuries). Eisenhower was elated, so much so that he sent Admiral Arleigh Burke, the chief of naval operations, a bottle of Chivas Regal, Burke's favorite scotch. Burke, the president's old friend, concluded an otherwise serious letter to Eisenhower with the line, "Mush quitnow and fine anodder bodel odish delicious boos." Ike loved it and carried the letter with him for weeks.[12]

Vanguard represented a high point of America's scientific satellite program under Eisenhower. During his administration, the United States launched two more Vanguard rockets. Despite the program's problems, John Hagen wrote, "Vanguard started with virtually nothing in 1955, completed vehicle design in March 1956, and had a fully successful flight two years later. One can challenge any other new rocket program in the United States to demonstrate a completely successful launching within such a short time." Vanguard rocket design and technology provided a foundation for America's space effort, influencing designs and technology for decades and pioneering electronics miniaturization and the use of solar cells for power. Laden with scientific instruments and utilizing cutting-edge technology, Vanguard set the stage for important American space discoveries.[13]

Meanwhile, the Explorer program continued to make the case for American preeminence in space. On March 26, the Army used another Jupiter C rocket to launch the thirty-one-pound Explorer III (Explorer II had failed earlier that month). By launching a third satellite, America sprung ahead of the Soviet Union—which had orbited only two—and for the rest of Eisenhower's presidency, it never again trailed. Although the good news took the sting out of the two Sputniks, the Soviets soon scored another coup. On May 15, the USSR launched Sputnik III, a 2,925-pound satellite carrying advanced scientific instrumentation, hoisted aloft by rockets with more than 500,000 pounds of thrust—far more than any American engine. Even Eisenhower was concerned. Before Sputnik III, he wrote to John Foster Dulles expressing his determination to remain unshaken by Soviet achievements and counteract their propaganda. Sputnik III tested that resolve. Moreover, he had earthly concerns to address.[14]

"Eisenhower Breadlines"

After Eisenhower's ministroke, rumors circulated that he might resign. In January 1958, Sherman Adams finally scotched such talk by declaring that the president would "run out his string" and finish his term. Ominously,

though, he added, "This man is not what he was." The pressure took a toll
on Eisenhower. Customarily beginning cabinet meetings with silent prayer,
he remarked after the first one in 1958, "One nice thing about the silent
prayer—for at least a minute I can't make any mistake." Once, when Killian
and Goodpaster met with the president, he put his head in his hands and
said that his "poor brain" might not be able to endure the stress.[15]

By mid-March, the *Wall Street Journal* noted that Eisenhower's popularity
was "at its lowest ebb. Not only is his party battered but the President himself
is now the target of open criticism." The *Journal* continued, "His Democratic opponents no longer hesitate, from a fear of public opinion, to attack
him personally. There have even been demands for his resignation." The *Journal* saw a sense "that there has been nobody in Washington really running
the show." *Newsweek* reported that the president had lost considerable public
confidence. A Des Moines, Iowa, insurance company worker said, "I was for
Ike and still am for him as a person. But I think he has gone past his real worth
to the country." A furniture store dealer in Cleveland commented, "I'm disgusted with government by remote control. Everyone knows Sherman
Adams and James Hagerty are running the government." The editor of
Harper's magazine called on Eisenhower to resign, likening him to a ship's
"crippled captain" issuing orders from the sick bay. By April 1958, Eisenhower had a 49 percent approval rating, his lowest point in public opinion
polls.[16]

The mainspring behind Eisenhower's popularity plunge was not Sputnik
but the economy. In July 1957, a recession had begun, and by late October,
signs of the downturn were palpable enough that Eisenhower commented,
"there is no question that the economy is, in effect, taking a breather." On
November 1, CEA chair Arthur Burns wrote to Eisenhower and noted that
"fear is beginning to spread about unemployment. There has been, as you
know, a deterioration of business sentiment since the middle of the year."
Burns added, "I have reached the conclusion that not a little of today's business pessimism is caused by uncertainty over our national security that the
Russian missile and Sputnik have stirred up. My business friends these days,
worried as they are about profits and sales, seem to be worried still more by
the Russian threat."[17]

The 1957–58 downturn cast a darker shadow than the 1953–54 recession
had. GDP fell 2.6 percent during 1953–54; in 1957–58, it fell 3.2 percent.
Unemployment hit 7.5 percent; five million Americans were out of work.
And the recovery was sluggish: unemployment remained "sticky" for the
next two years, never dropping easily, averaging 5.3 percent during 1959–
60. A jobless Maryland steel worker dubbed unemployment queues "the

Eisenhower breadlines." In the 1950s, memories of the Great Depression were still raw, and this downturn was a haunting reminder of that event. By March 1958, a poll showed that recession topped Americans' list of national concerns, with 40 percent of those surveyed saying that unemployment was the country's number one problem. Only 7 percent cited space problems.[18]

Sputnik's impact, though, made this recession hurt far more. It magnified a central Cold War question—whether capitalism or communism was superior. As the American economy tried to shake off the recession, Russian planners set ambitious industrial output goals. The *New Republic* predicted, "If present tendencies persist, the Soviet economy will soon be as large as our own, and the consequences of that throughout the world are awesome." Truman's CEA chair, Leon Keyserling, called for higher U.S. growth rates, pointing out that between 1953 and 1957 the economy grew at just more than 2.5 percent. That rate should be more like 4.5 percent, Keyserling advised.[19]

Here again Eisenhower's image hurt, and his apparent inactivity undermined public confidence. On February 13, he scooted off for a ten-day stay at George Humphrey's Georgia plantation. The sojourn reinforced the appearance of an out-of-touch president who preferred to escape rather than confront the nation's problems. Led by Lyndon Johnson, congressional Democrats appeared more active, calling for unemployment relief and increased spending on public works, housing, highways, and other projects to combat the recession. Eisenhower opposed such projects, believing they dwelt on the short term and would "cause more acute trouble later on." They represented the same political expediency he resisted after Sputnik because they threatened the objectives of a balanced budget and low inflation. In April, when Congress passed a $1.7 billion River and Harbor and Flood Control Works Bill, Eisenhower vetoed it, calling it a "stupid" measure with aspects that "made no economic sense whatever." (He signed a scaled-down version of the bill that Congress submitted to him in July, after economic recovery had begun.)[20]

Calls for more spending strengthened Eisenhower's resolve to resist them. He complained to Burns that pursuing conservative policies during a recession "can well get me tagged as an unsympathetic, reactionary fossil. But my honest conviction is that the greatest public service we can do for our country is to oppose wild-eyed schemes of every kind." Sputnik, recession, political attacks, and the threat of recrudescent inflation all converged to make Eisenhower veer more sharply toward conservatism. He won some accolades for holding steady; *Time* noted that he "refused to panic when recession came." But Democrats, the media, and even some Republicans, *Time* noted, "demanded that he 'do' something. He was in fact doing quite a bit: by fighting effectively against irresponsible tax cuts and wild pump-priming he was proving that a sound free-enterprise economy could right itself without massive Government interference. He also was holding down the inflation that would have been the inevitable result of a big Government spending spree."[21]

But staying true to his principles created political trouble for Eisenhower. He was unable to make his crusade for reducing deficits and restraining inflation popular, just as he failed to advertise his administration's space achievements. And adhering to his principles looked difficult. In January 1958, the *New York Times* proclaimed "Space Age Upsets Balanced Budget" and predicted that after presiding over two consecutive budgets in surplus, Eisenhower "had seen the last balanced budget of his tenure." The recession robbed the government of tax revenue, and the result was the largest peacetime deficit in history, $12.4 billion. Funding for space exploration was at stake, and along with it the modest international prestige that Eisenhower reestablished with Vanguard and Explorer. Moreover, with the economy mired in its worst downturn since the Great Depression and midterm elections approaching, 1958 promised to be a tough year. And an arch rival made sure of it.[22]

 CHAPTER 8

Eisenhower's Rival

 Space and the Making of a President

In 1950s Washington, Lyndon Johnson's political star rose like a rocket. As Senate majority leader, he had welded together two bickering factions of the Democratic Party, the Northern liberals and Southern conservatives, and in 1957, he kept the two wings from splitting over the hotly debated Civil Rights Act. It was good policy and, for Johnson, good politics, as the act allowed him to gain more heft as a presidential aspirant.[1]

Eisenhower had reservations. In private, he heaped harsh words on Johnson, calling him "superficial and opportunistic," "the most tricky and unreliable politician in Congress," a man who "was not to be trusted in any sense of the word." When Johnson was later president, Eisenhower criticized him for being "too poll-conscious," commenting, "The difficulty with Johnson is that he is only interested in what people will approve, and that makes it difficult to get people to believe him." In a rare display of scorn, Eisenhower mocked President Johnson's delivery of the 1964 State of the Union address, mimicking his mannerisms and pronunciation. Privately, Johnson reciprocated the scorn. When Eisenhower told Attorney General William Rogers that Senator Richard Russell called the president a "hydra-headed monster," Rogers replied that Senator Johnson uttered even worse epithets about Eisenhower.[2]

Despite the backbiting, the two leaders, both born on Texas soil, seemed to get along well, sharing rural Southern values and interests such as raising steer on their respective farms. At photo opportunities, they grinned broadly, and at private meetings they engaged in easy banter. They shared a bond of medical malady, too; in 1955, both longtime smokers suffered heart attacks.

Yet Eisenhower and Johnson had contrasting personal styles and in many ways were polar opposites. Johnson stood six foot three inches and liked to apply the "Johnson treatment," in which he physically badgered politicians for support. He cornered a victim, towered over him and invaded his space, and then showered him with cajolery or veiled threats. George Reedy described it as "like standing under Niagara Falls. . . . It was just unbelievably potent."[3]

At five feet ten and a half inches tall, Eisenhower was relatively small for a president (among postwar presidents, only Truman, Eisenhower, Nixon, and Carter stood below six feet), and Johnson's physical contact repulsed him. Once, Johnson poked his finger in Eisenhower's chest. Edward McCabe recalled that he and other aides "wondered if the president was ready to haul off and belt him one." He did not, but he learned to take precautions. Before one Johnson visit to the White House, Eisenhower asked an aide to try to stand between him and the senator, explaining that Johnson's constant grabbing of his left arm aggravated its painful bursitis. But the "Johnson treatment" reflected his utter absorption in his trade: Johnson lived, breathed, and ate politics, and Eisenhower remarked that the senator had no hobbies to escape from the job's daily grind. By contrast, Eisenhower had a wealth of pastimes that allowed him to relax and ruminate outside of work, and he indulged in them while president.[4]

Johnson also delighted in crude behavior and humor. As president, he urinated openly in front of reporters while outside at his ranch. He expected aides to follow him into the bathroom to continue meetings. Vulgar put-downs of colleagues tumbled out of his mouth. He called Adlai Stevenson "the kind of man who squats when he pees." During the mid-1960s, irritated by House minority leader Gerald Ford's political criticism and haunted by the foreboding that Ford would someday be a formidable presidential prospect, Johnson tried to cut him down with the wisecrack that Ford "can't walk and fart at the same time." By contrast, Eisenhower found scatology appalling. While grilling a trout outdoors at a Colorado retreat, he heard a Secret Service agent make an earthy remark about the genitals of a bull wandering in a nearby field. Disgusted, Eisenhower pulled off his apron and chef's hat and stalked back into his cabin. The agent felt so humiliated that he broke down and cried.[5]

Eisenhower had an "almost exaggerated" respect for the presidency, Arthur Larson observed. But it had a functional purpose; for example, recognizing the commander-in-chief's need for round-the-clock vigilance, he drank only in moderation while president. As a young Army officer, he had to help a drunken Franklin Roosevelt to bed and, appalled by the memory of the president's condition, Eisenhower swore, "I like a highball or two myself, but I'll tell you one thing: nobody's ever going to have to put me into bed." By contrast, aides often observed President Johnson inebriated, a condition that worsened his temper and bullying of staff. Aboard Air Force One, he once berated a steward for the mixed drink he prepared and flung the glass to the floor.[6]

Even more significant than their contrasting behavior, the two men clashed politically and ideologically. Eisenhower sought to limit federal spending and government's role, while the Senate majority leader pushed for more New Deal–style public works legislation. When Johnson became president, he pursued a stunning array of programs with his Great Society legislation. Eisenhower told him that he objected to "many of the things that he had succeeded in having enacted into law" and was "philosophically opposed to the level of expenditures we now have."[7]

The two men's antithetical views on space were apparent in 1958, a moment when *Time* characterized the senator as being "second in power only to the President of the U.S." and having "Washington's keenest political eye." Sputnik opened that eye wide and allowed Johnson, like a magnet drawing metal fillings, to attract power and attention. Whereas power seemed almost to pursue Eisenhower, Johnson craved it, and he exemplified the Southern senators who accumulated seniority and power and ruled over the Senate during the 1950s. Johnson's quest for power led Eisenhower to comment, "That fellow's such a phony."[8]

Sputnik became a piece of putty that Johnson could mold to fill out his grand ambitions. Ewald observed that there was "a cacophony of American Democrats seeing the next election heading their way and wanting to get on board, thinking they've got a winner" with a new political issue. Johnson believed that space would win him recognition beyond Texas and Washington, garnering a national following to land him in the White House.[9]

On October 4, 1957, Johnson was at his home, the LBJ Ranch near Austin, Texas. It was a sprawling compound along the Pedernales River where, like Eisenhower at Gettysburg, Johnson loved to retreat from Washington, relaxing, raising steer, and entertaining friends. Later, as president, Johnson held barbecues there for world leaders, and he had even planned to host John Kennedy in a special guest house on the evening of November 22, 1963,

FIGURE 4. Eisenhower with Senator Lyndon Johnson at a 1955 White House bipartisan luncheon. Although they cooperated publicly, Eisenhower considered Johnson a "phony." To Eisenhower's right is William Knowland, the Senate GOP leader. (Library of Congress, Prints & Photos Division, *U.S. News and World Report* collection)

after the president was to have left Dallas. But in 1957, Johnson's radio crackled with news of Sputnik. He later claimed that he felt "uneasy and apprehensive," upset by "the profound shock of realizing that it might be possible for another nation to achieve technological superiority over this great country of ours."[10]

Johnson moved at a feverish pace. That evening, he called two fellow senators, Richard Russell and Styles Bridges, to lay the groundwork for an investigation. On Monday, October 7, Johnson talked to Eileen Galloway, a defense analyst who had worked for Russell's Armed Services Committee and whose advice the senator recommended Johnson seek. He barked out a command: "I want to make a record in outer space for me," he told her, "and I want you to help me." The big Texan was ready to reach for the next political rung.[11]

Johnson aide George Reedy stirred the senator's consciousness about the politics of space. Less than two weeks after Sputnik, Charles Brewton, an administrative assistant to Democratic senator J. Lister Hill of Alabama, drove with Reedy to a desolate spot in the hills around Austin. Staring out at the landscape, the two men spoke candidly. Brewton "didn't know very much about outer space," Reedy remembered, "but he had grasped immediately the fact that this was something that could change the whole way that we lived, change our nation. He convinced me." Brewton told Reedy that the issue of space could "first of all clobber the Republicans, secondly lead to tremendous advances, and, third, elect Lyndon Johnson as president." Reedy told his friend that Johnson had no interest in the presidency. Brewton replied that he would settle for clobbering the Republicans.

The talk had a huge impact on Reedy. He stayed up during the night, reading about space, obsessed with the idea. The next day, he wrote Johnson a long memorandum outlining the importance of space. Using dramatic language, he wrote of "our lost lead in technology" and stated, "The Russians are ahead of us." Comparing Sputnik to the Japanese attack at Pearl Harbor, he maintained that the "present situation differs only in degree. We do not have as much time as we had after Pearl Harbor." Reedy told his boss about Brewton's views, reporting, "Eye [*sic*] told him that you weren't interested in the Presidency and he said he would settle for knocking the Republicans and unifying the Democratic Party." Reedy advised Johnson, "Eye [*sic*] think you should plan to plunge heavily into this one."[12]

Democrats had been grasping for a winning issue. During the 1950s, the Republicans manipulated politics at Democrats' expense. The string of five consecutive Democratic presidential victories beginning in 1932 had exasperated Republicans, and they cast about for an effective issue to retake the White House. Some Republicans capitalized on the Red Scare, including, notably, Joseph McCarthy, who used anticommunism to win reelection in 1952—when Republicans took control of the Senate—and catapult himself into the national limelight. Eisenhower's 1952 and 1956 victories further pounded the Democrats, and when the Little Rock desegregation fights erupted, they felt anxious about the party's identification with civil rights. Reedy wrote Johnson that "in the integration issue [Republicans] have a potent weapon which chews the Democratic Party to pieces so efficiently that it cannot be an effective opposition." He warned, "The integration issue is not going to go away. . . . The only possibility is to find another issue which is even more potent. Otherwise the Democratic future is bleak."[13]

Space provided what Democrats had been searching for, and Johnson crowded the opportunity, making exaggerated statements. Whoever dominates space, he said, "would have the power to control the earth's weather, to cause drought and flood, to change the tides and raise the levels of the sea, to divert the Gulf Stream and change temperature climates to frigid." He claimed that space exploration "will dominate the affairs of mankind just as the exploration of the Western Hemisphere dominated the affairs of mankind in the sixteenth and seventeenth centuries." Johnson wanted to get on equal footing with the Soviets regardless of cost. "If more money is needed, let's spend it," he said. "If more resources are needed, let's use them. If more hours are needed, let's work them. Let us do whatever it takes."[14]

To exploit the issue fully, Reedy told Johnson, Congress should conduct an inquiry into space. Such a move was tailor-made to benefit Johnson, Reedy argued, because the inquiry's leader "must be a Senator who has a reputation for statesmanlike, non-partisan investigations of defense and who is not involved too heavily in the emotional issues surrounding segregation." Senator John Stennis also told Johnson that he was the right man for the job, saying, "This is so vital a matter that nothing short of your own guidance will give it the necessary prestige and force." Reedy also advised, "If a Congressional Inquiry into the satellite situation is to have any effect, there are two points which must be drummed into the public consciousness with the same monotonous technique used in soap commercials. . . . They are: a) The extreme importance of the satellite. b) The fact that his country could have had the satellite but did not do so *because of a leadership decision.*"[15]

On October 17, 1957, Johnson appeared in Tyler, Texas, for the town's twentieth annual Texas Rose Festival. Actor Ronald Reagan, functioning as master of ceremonies, introduced the senator to the crowd. Johnson promised that the Senate Armed Services Committee would investigate the American space effort, trying to answer questions such as "Could we have matched the Soviet achievement?" and "Does the Soviet satellite indicate that this country has slipped behind in the development of its defenses?" Johnson chaired the Armed Services Committee's Preparedness Investigating Subcommittee, which committee chair Richard Russell had originally formed to allow his Texas protégé to investigate Korean War activities and gain a reputation. With his supplicating mien and persuasive powers, Johnson convinced Russell to allow him to chair hearings into the state of the nation's defenses, which the Texan promised to carry out in a spirit of bipartisanship and concern for the country.[16]

➤● "Mr. Space"

Johnson wasted no time. Although Ed Weisl, a subcommittee staff member, recommended that the hearings begin in 1958, Johnson wanted an earlier start to monopolize headlines and gain momentum on space. On Monday, November 25—the same day that Eisenhower suffered a stroke—the hearings began. Johnson opened them with the foreboding line "We meet today in the atmosphere of another Pearl Harbor." "The timing was just perfect," recalled Glen Wilson, another subcommittee staffer, "because it grabbed all the attention in the newspapers and television." Moreover, the hearings began before the Christmas holidays could distract Americans' attention from politics.[17]

Over the next month and a half, the subcommittee investigated the state of America's space program and defenses, calling hundreds of witnesses, including scientific luminaries like Edward Teller and Vannevar Bush, and military brass like Army secretary and former Michigan governor Wilbur Brucker and generals James Doolittle, James Gavin, and Maxwell Taylor. Rebuffed ABMA men Medaris and von Braun appeared before the committee, the general urging a rocket engine with a million-pound thrust by 1961, the scientist proposing a national space agency with an annual budget of $1.5 billion.[18]

The hearings gave a platform to precisely those voices who Eisenhower worried could push the nation in the wrong direction. Later, when privately pressed about whom he meant when he criticized a "scientific-technological elite" that exerted a baneful influence on government policy, Eisenhower instantly replied, "von Braun and Teller." Yet to Johnson the hearings were a boon. With the national spotlight shining, he questioned witnesses, projected an authoritative air, and established himself as the premier politician on space. Although far from eloquent, he made up for his unpolished speaking style with a clever mix of Southern drawl and, at times, steady cadence, as when he questioned Medaris, telling him, "You are getting down now to where you are telling us now what we want to hear, what we want to know, what we have to do, what we have to face up to." He arranged for scientists to testify in the first weeks of the hearings, when public attention was greatest. Johnson let his witnesses criticize the Eisenhower administration, which allowed him to escape partisan mudslinging and appear dignified. Rather than plunge a sword into a bleeding target, Johnson took grazing swipes at the administration, coming across as a statesman concerned for the nation's safety. Witnesses' rhetoric played perfectly into his hands, stressing the Cold War themes of a race, survival, and the need to act immediately.[19]

Journalists Rowland Evans and Robert Novak called Johnson's performance "a minor masterpiece." The Eisenhower administration emerged with egg on its face, yet Johnson personally threw no eggs, letting the hearings do it for him. They revealed no coherent space policy, insufficient funding, and no clear government organ to direct space initiatives. Space policy seemed in disarray, and witnesses gave dire warnings of a backward

American space performance, while army generals criticized the Eisen-hower administration's stingy defense allotments.[20]

Johnson made sure the media could rely on him for a headline-grabbing quote. He adopted what aides referred to as "government by press release," a style that maximized publicity. His higher profile and newfound com-mand of space issues gave him the chance to deliver a Democratic state of the union address on January 7, 1958, in which he presented his subcommit-tee's preliminary findings. "Control of space means control of the world," he stated. Johnson asserted that the Democrats had to take a lead on space issues, which would give them "an incomparable opportunity to save the nation and the world." In a competition for the most spectacular quotes on Sputnik and the space race, the palm went to Johnson. And as he hoped, his apoca-lyptic language gained wide press play and focused more attention on him.[21]

When the hearings concluded in January 1958, seventy-three witnesses had testified, and the proceedings resulted in three volumes totaling more than two thousand pages. The subcommittee unleashed a small fusillade of recommendations, seventeen in all, including a rocket with a million-pound thrust for space exploration, which Eisenhower favored, and crash programs for ICBM and IRBM development, which he opposed. On January 23, Johnson read a statement to the Senate. "We are in a race for survival, and we intend to win that race," he declared. The space race, he said, "much more at stake than the prestige of being 'first.'". Sputnik demonstrated that the "Soviet Union leads the United States in the development of ballistic missiles." Such remarks infuriated Eisenhower, and they added to his politi-cal wounds and the swoon in public opinion polls.[22]

On February 6, 1958, the Senate voted to create a Special Committee on Space Aeronautics to plan space policy. LBJ pushed the resolution through the Senate and prevailed with a 78–1 vote (the lone dissenter, Allen Ellender of Louisiana, fought all new committees on principle). Unsurprisingly, John-son chaired this committee. The House established the Select Committee on Astronautics and Space Exploration. Both committees were poised not only to flex political muscle but also to promote civilian space interests against those of the military.[23]

Even Eisenhower conceded Johnson's new preeminence in space policy, and he also needed the senator's cooperation. Historically, the Senate was the legislative chamber mostly likely to frustrate presidents. Senators wielded more power and media attention than House members, harbored greater presidential ambitions, and were more inclined to have maverick streaks; among senators, Johnson had unusual clout in riding herd and delivering votes. Eisenhower also knew that any space program would need bipartisan support; indeed, the nation's most impressive legislation, such as the Civil Rights Act of 1957, gained heft because both parties backed it.

So Eisenhower massaged Johnson's ego. In November 1958, just after the midterm elections, some senators were meeting the president in the White House Cabinet Room, and Eisenhower gestured toward his chair, inviting Johnson to sit there. With obligatory false modesty, Johnson declined, but Eisenhower urged, "It'll be yours someday." Johnson said, "No, I will never sit in that chair." Later that month, Eisenhower surprised Johnson by asking him to be the American spokesman to address the Political Committee of the UN General Assembly, even sending a plane to San Antonio to fly the senator to New York. Johnson used the opportunity to press the Soviet Union to cooperate with other nations in space rather than "proceed unilaterally." The speech gave him increased international exposure, allowing him to speak for the nation, and it marked one of his first ventures into diplomacy, an area where his political résumé was slim. As the *Dallas Morning News* commented, the appearance "will certainly do him no harm if he decides to become an active candidate for the 1960 Democratic nomination."[24]

Johnson grasped the importance of space and its relationship to world prestige where the president did not. Bryce Harlow said, "LBJ was eager to get out front in space because it was the new national toy. He was trying to get to become President of the United States . . . so LBJ wanted to get in front of the space rush so that everybody would say, 'Oh, that's our leader.'" He also wanted to land space activities—including a space center—in his home state. Edward McCabe contrasted this posture with that of Eisenhower, who asked about America's interests when ruminating about policy. "Now, Lyndon Johnson had a lot to do with it in locating [a space center] in Houston. Like every good political operator, he wanted to bring it home. And he did," McCabe said.[25]

It was vintage Johnson. Observers who watched him up close noted that every aspect of the Texan was oversized, including his ego, ambition, and physicality. (Upon becoming president, Nixon had to rein in some of Johnson's excesses. He eliminated LBJ's three Oval Office television sets and asked that Johnson's multiple bathroom showerheads be replaced—their big, powerful water blasts had almost bowled him over.) Johnson inflated the importance of policy issues, too. Science advisor James Killian recalled, "Senator [Lyndon] Johnson had a view of space that was Olympian. Space was going to be the greatest thing in our time and we must get organized adequately to deal with it. But I think he overestimated its total significance in the scheme of things." Eisenhower had no patience for LBJ's exaggerations. He once scoffed, "Lyndon Johnson can keep his head in the stars if he wants. I'm going to keep my feet on the ground."[26]

Some of Johnson's constituents thought more like Eisenhower. A Fort Worth man wrote to Johnson, "We Texans believe in defending ourselves at all times, and will leave no stone unturned to ferrit [sic] out our foes, but we are not pleased to see billions on top of billions of good hard cash being tossed aside in a 'stunt race' into outer space." A Houston man observed that Americans "will give freely of their tax dollars for space exploration so long as they are scared, but the time will come when people won't scare so easily and then they will question the expenditures of billions for space research." He warned that "Russia has set out to bankrupt us" and predicted "that around the year 2000 or better the historians will refer to the mid 1950's as the 'decade of moon-shooters.' "[27]

Regardless of any criticism, Johnson had become "Mr. Space," the politician whom the public identified as a champion of U.S. space policy, the man who could fix the "space gap" between America and Russia.[28] Space, Johnson found, made easy politics. Compared with the Pentagon budget or large entitlement programs, it involved relatively little federal money, yet it returned great dividends, creating attention-grabbing achievements, bringing aerospace jobs to constituents, and casting politicians as bold leaders. A politician who resisted space seemed too meek to challenge the Soviet Union in the newest competitive arena. Thus Johnson attacked where Eisenhower was vulnerable, and his strong stand brightened his political future.

But there was a latent problem with Johnson's approach. As subcommittee chair, he showed an expansive, overweening view of America's capabilities worldwide, leading Washington insiders to call his subcommittee the "Johnson Earth Control Clinic." It was the same vantage point that later contributed to his disastrous descent into Vietnam. By contrast, already after the Korean War, Eisenhower recognized that the United States "cannot be strong enough to go to every spot in the world, where our enemies may use force or the threat of force, and defend those nations."[29] This moderate, limited view of U.S. military entanglements overseas mirrored Eisenhower's space policy. Curiously, where Eisenhower preferred to approach space incrementally, Johnson wanted an unstinted effort; during the 1960s, when U.S. ground forces were in Vietnam, it was Eisenhower who wanted maximum force, where Johnson proceeded incrementally, allowing the Viet Cong to match U.S. moves at every step. The approach struck a fatal blow to Johnson's presidency and retrospectively helped Eisenhower by making him look wise for avoiding a quagmire.

But it took another decade for those tables to turn. In the late 1950s, the blow was to Eisenhower in space, a policy arena that hurt him and helped Johnson. At the same time, though, because of their oddly symbiotic political relationship, Johnson helped Eisenhower in formulating a legislative response to Sputnik.

CHAPTER 9

"Radical Moves"

Sputnik riveted attention on the importance of brains to a nation, and with that the federal government's role in promoting education. On that score, Eisenhower's contribution was unanticipated, for he believed that education was outside the federal government's purview. But as he once observed, when he detected a need for change, he made "radical moves."[1]

As a rule, Eisenhower favored only gradual change, once remarking that facts did not change rapidly, and thus neither did strategies or plans. But he was open to new approaches to policy, even if not truly radical. HEW secretary Arthur Flemming recalled, "He was the kind of person who kept turning over in his mind new ideas and trying out new ideas." During 1958, as he responded to media and political pressure following Sputnik, Eisenhower signed legislation that indeed appeared radical to him, for they involved changes in his thinking. They also enhanced his presidential legacy.[2]

"My Scientists"

Whereas politicians like Lyndon Johnson irritated Eisenhower, he came to regard scientists differently. After appointing James Killian as his science advisor, Eisenhower grew closer to PSAC, and he developed such a fondness for its members that he called them "my scientists." Goodpaster recalled, "He had a personal liking for these people and I think he was impressed that those of the finest minds, the ones that he was in touch with, had a clarity of thinking that commended itself to him very strongly—a sense of the relationship of action and purpose."[3]

Killian was the right man for the job. Although not a Ph.D. graduate, he had amassed enough honorary doctorates to be called "Dr. Killian." Although uncharismatic, he displayed passion for science and administration, and he also had experience in both areas, having chaired the TCP and served on PSAC. As MIT president, he built bridges between academia and government, and his administrative talents were numerous. "He was an ultimate chairman of the board," said Spurgeon Keeny, because "he didn't come at [an issue] from any particular science discipline or point of view," but rather as someone who managed diverse interests. Keeny noted that Killian "had very good insights in picking people, both the best and brightest scientists, but also people who were in the real world. . . . And he picked a very strong team, and people all accepted him as someone who would pull all the information together and make a decision." David Beckler recalled, "He was just a born leader, and scientists had the greatest affection for him and loyalty to him. He could take the views of the group and put them together in a way that really fit into the policy making structure. He was a remarkable person."[4]

Importantly, Killian's public policy dovetailed with Eisenhower's. Like the president, he believed in melding science and humanities, and he exemplified that ideal himself; in college, he had majored in English, and one of his pastimes was collecting original works from George Meredith, a nineteenth-century British writer. He also wanted to put the Sputnik launch in proper perspective and feared the media had exaggerated its importance.[5]

Eisenhower placed his science advisor in an independent position, not charged with any particular program and less vulnerable to special interests. Ideally, he was beholden only to the president and could speak freely with him. This arrangement, Eisenhower felt, allowed Killian and other scientists to give impartial advice, divorced especially from military interests. Because he was uncomfortable accepting Pentagon opinions at face value, Eisenhower esteemed scientists' advice. He "knew the military well, so he knew he couldn't trust what the military said," Eugene Skolnikoff said. "They didn't lie, but they wouldn't necessarily tell the whole story. So you get the military recommending a new weapon system and they would say all the right things about it, but they wouldn't say what was wrong with it. And Eisenhower got increasingly frustrated, and he knew he didn't have people he could trust."[6]

FIGURE 5. The Presidential Science Advisory Committee (PSAC). Eisenhower grew so fond of this group that he called them "my scientists." To Eisenhower's left is James Killian, the first special assistant to the president for science and technology. (Dwight D. Eisenhower Library)

But he trusted scientists and viewed them as above politics. When told that many PSAC scientists were Democrats, Eisenhower was unfazed. After they joined PSAC, Ewald noted, "they didn't go through any kind of political clearance," and the president even assumed that the scientists were likely all Democrats. "But he didn't care," Ewald said. What he wanted was "the best scientific advice he could get in his office . . . so that we continued our forward motion." The last time that Killian saw Eisenhower, gravely ill at Walter Reed Army Hospital, the former president commented, "You know, Jim, this bunch of scientists was one of the few groups that I encountered in Washington who seemed to be there to help the country and not help themselves."[7]

Through his meetings with scientists and the palpable affection he had for them, Eisenhower brought the presidency closer to the scientific community. That relationship had not always been warm. In April 1951, Truman had established the Science Advisory Committee as part of the Office of Defense Mobilization, an executive branch agency set up the year before to help in coordinating defense-related employment, procurements, transportation, and other war activities. (It was called the ODM Science Advisory Committee.) For several reasons, policy makers and administration members resisted giving scientists direct presidential access and instead put them under the ODM's aegis. They feared that scientists could push for their projects, infringe on the Pentagon's turf, and even pose a risk if they accessed national security information. Having an image as eggheads, they also seemed likely to waste a president's time on arcane matters and, almost like mendicants needing alms, demand money for science. "You know those scientists," George Humphrey commented months before the Sputnik launch, as the president rejected the idea of accelerating the U.S. satellite program to beat the Soviets into space. "When they've put up one satellite, first thing you know, they'll want to put up another."[8]

Initially, Eisenhower failed to warm to scientists. According to Robert Cutler, Eisenhower remarked that "every time the scientists looked into a matter their exact minds required them to come to a very finite conclusion which inevitably added up to a great expenditure of money." In 1954, his relations with them underwent severe strain when J. Robert Oppenheimer, the director of the Manhattan Project and so-called father of the atomic bomb, lost his security clearance because of his previous Communist Party ties and opposition to the arms race. With scientists' self-esteem already battered, former president Truman charged after Sputnik, "Morale of our scientists is at the lowest ebb."[9]

Yet auspicious signs appeared. In 1954, Eisenhower formed the TCP and embraced its recommendations, including the U-2 spy plane idea. Beckler commented, "Eisenhower's readiness to receive a proposal of this kind and act upon it on the recommendation of a group of scientists external to the government was an omen of great importance for the future relationship of the scientific community to him. It was also an illustration of his responsiveness to innovative ideas." The TCP, Beckler believed, was a milestone in history because it affected policy and created stronger ties between scientists and the White House. In June 1957, a reporter asked Eisenhower whether he had considered adding a science advisor to his staff. "It hadn't occurred to me to have one right in my office," he replied, "but now that you have mentioned it I will think about it."[10]

Sputnik provided opportunity for change. After Eisenhower appointed Killian, the ODM SAC became the president's own eighteen-member committee of scientists—a "new," revitalized PSAC, with Killian as its chair, formally beginning operations on November 20, 1957. Now the committee was a White House organ, in closer contact with the president. Beckler wrote that Sputnik had the "salutary effect of elevating the Science Advisory Committee to report directly to the president." Killian observed, "Not since World War II had there been such a stellar congregation of scientists available to government policy makers." They helped to guide and coordinate the government's burgeoning involvement in scientific research and development, and they reduced the president's reliance on ad hoc outside groups such as the earlier Killian Panel and Gaither Committee. PSAC assembled the era's most scintillant scientific minds, including Nobel laureate Isador Rabi of Columbia and future Nobel laureate Hans Bethe of Cornell, and brought them into the president's inner circle. Beckler wrote that Eisenhower commented that "the strength of government lies in its ability to mobilize the best abilities that exist throughout the country," and PSAC exemplified it. The high caliber of presidential science advisors "was characteristic of Eisenhower. . . . When there was a problem, he would want to have the most capable, competent persons in that area and have the benefit of their knowledge of what was happening and their help in shaping policy with respect to it," Beckler said.[11]

Killian's appointment and the PSAC reformulation improved scientists' morale and allowed insights into an area where presidents traditionally had limited knowledge. In the past, some presidents had dabbled in science and engineering. Thomas Jefferson showed strong mechanical inclinations; his Monticello home bore testimony to his forays into nail manufacturing, farming, and inventing. Fascinated by technology, Abraham Lincoln enjoyed new military inventions and before becoming president earned a patent for a mechanism to lift boats out of shoals, making him the only chief executive to hold a U.S. patent.

But in the twentieth century, many presidents came from legal backgrounds. Both Roosevelts, William Howard Taft, Richard Nixon, Gerald Ford, and Bill Clinton all had attended law school. With the exception of engineers Herbert Hoover and Jimmy Carter, none had formal science training. Likewise, most presidential advisors came from political, military, or economic backgrounds rather than in science. Keeny noted that "among the top department people [in the executive branch] there was very little scientific knowledge." Thus science was an arcane field to the president and most of his advisors. National Security Advisor Robert Cutler once said jocularly to PSAC scientists, "Gentlemen, I'm appearing before this committee [and] I want you to know I don't even know how to operate my television set."[12]

But in the modern world, poor scientific knowledge was no joking matter. World War II had stimulated tremendous technological advances and brought government and scientists closer. Government depended on science and engineering to provide tools and weapons to win the war while giving science, in return, the funding it badly needed; the symbiotic relationship continued during the Cold War. During the 1950s, science's rapid pace impressed Eisenhower and those around him. He marveled at the progress of airplanes since the Wright Brothers and noted that while he was in office the presidential aircraft had changed from a piston-driven plane to a Boeing 707 jet. White House usher J. B. West noted that jet airplanes increased presidential travel as well as the volume of guests at the mansion, while another technological wonder, air conditioning, allowed the Eisenhowers to spend more time in Washington during the summer. These changes were so vast that by the 1950s no president could hope to master the intricacies of technology and science.[13]

Eisenhower was ready to nurture the relationship following Sputnik. Guyford Stever, who later served as White House science advisor for Gerald Ford, wrote that "the tremendous influence that Dr. Killian had because of the nature of the crisis—the country reaching out almost in desperation to him—has, in my mind, never been equaled since, although all presidents since Eisenhower have had a science advisor in some form." Eisenhower became close to Killian and to George Kistiakowsky, who succeeded Killian in 1959, and both men found easy access to the president, with meetings informal and friendly.[14]

The appointment of a science advisor added a new layer to the federal bureaucracy, and critics noted that the president now had three dozen special advisors to dole out counsel on various topics. But Eisenhower knew he had no monopoly on knowledge. "Now look," he remarked, "this idea that all wisdom is in the president . . . that's baloney. . . . I don't believe this government was set up to be operated by any one acting alone; no one has a monopoly on the truth and on the facts that affect this country." Before making a decision, he solicited expert opinion. "In any discussion of policy, Eisenhower encouraged everyone to speak out," Ewald observed. "Challenging, and urging the others to challenge, he wanted to hear all sides." Moreover, scientists provided an important angle of thought that lawyers, generals, and economists could not, which the analytically minded Eisenhower valued. "The really important process was being able to relate the scientific information to the political choices the president makes," Eugene Skolnikoff observed. "And that couldn't be done by the typical NSC staff. It had to be done by the science advisors."[15]

The new science advisor and reformulated PSAC also represented shrewd politics for Eisenhower, showing Congress and the media that he was reacting energetically to Sputnik. The media made Killian a celebrity, dubbing him the president's "missile czar." "I avoided the appellation like the plague,"

Killian recalled, because he claimed no dictatorial powers nor did he control America's missile program. Yet to some critics, that was precisely the problem. At a White House meeting with congressional leaders, Democratic representative John McCormack of Massachusetts, the House majority leader, worried that Killian lacked power. Eisenhower disagreed, pointing to Killian's long list of responsibilities. Science now had a seat at the White House and became an influence in shaping presidential policy. As Killian later wrote, "For the first time in the history of the Republic, science and engineering were in peacetime formally related directly to the president and his policy-making councils."[16]

 ## PSAC and Presidential Policy

Among PSAC's duties was space policy. In March 1958, Eisenhower ordered the release of a sixteen-page document, "Introduction to Outer Space," compiled by a PSAC panel that Harvard physicist and 1952 Nobel laureate Edward Purcell chaired. "I have found this statement so informative and interesting," Eisenhower explained in a press release, "that I wish to share it with all the people of America, and indeed with all the people of the earth." The report listed four principal reasons motivating space exploration: man's urge to explore, national defense applications, prestige, and science experimentation. The scientists touched on space exploration's practical applications, such as reconnaissance and meteorology, and they even forecast that satellites would facilitate worldwide television viewing. They envisioned sending probes to Venus and Mars, and they discussed "The Moon as a Goal," accurately predicting, "To land a man on the moon and get him home safely again will require a very big rocket engine indeed—one with a thrust in the neighborhood of one or two million pounds." But the scientists also knew that, compared with humans, machines and instruments could explore the heavens on the cheap. In distinguishing between automated and manned space probes, they set a scale of priorities, preferring feasible, financially practical missions, such as first gathering scientific data, then attempting a robotic moon shot, and later landing men on the moon.[17]

"Introduction to Outer Space" represented the administration's first coherent space policy, distilling PSAC members' opinions into unifying themes. Perhaps the document's most singular aspect was that its realistic nature reflected Eisenhower's posture. While outlining ambitious goals, it stressed that they should be "part of a balanced national effort in all science and technology." The scientists acknowledged that the nation might face failures and delays in its space program and concluded, "It therefore appears wise to be cautious and modest in our predictions and pronouncements about future space activities—and quietly bold in our execution." "Quietly bold" was an apposite way to describe the history of U.S. space endeavors under Eisenhower; he preferred a program that was substantial yet subdued and devoted to scientific inquiry, relying primarily on exploring space with robotic instruments.[18]

PSAC welcomed competition with the Soviet Union but cautioned that the United States should pick certain areas to enter the lists. The views of both Eisenhower science advisors, Killian and Kistiakowsky, reinforced the president's balanced approach to science and technology endeavors. Killian warned about "copying" the Soviet Union in scientific endeavors and emphasized science and "basic understanding" over "expedited" programs designed only to get fast results. When Killian resigned, Eisenhower thanked him by recalling the atmosphere "when millions, startled by sputniks, wanted to plunge headfirst and almost blindly into the space age." Killian, he continued, developed programs that "were not dictated or designed in an atmosphere of panic." Likewise, Kistiakowsky wrote that he and Eisenhower supported "a sensible space program, and not just a silly attempt to overtake the Soviets without the means to do so." Later, when John Kennedy challenged Americans to land men on the moon, Eisenhower recalled his scientists' advice as he tried to warn against what he considered Kennedy's folly, writing, "Most of the scientists who advised me on space matters—all men of great knowledge and integrity—believed in this step-by-step program as the most effective for the long pull. . . . [T]his racing to the moon, unavoidably wasting vast sums and deepening our debt, is the wrong way to go about it."[19]

Scientists also acted as an intellectual prism through which the president could view innovations and new projects. Once, Killian and a group of scientists sought Eisenhower's approval for a new linear accelerator. They were uncertain whether he would like the project; it was expensive—more than a $100 million—and had no military applications. Yet Eisenhower showed interest, asked probing questions, and gave his approval.[20]

Eisenhower relied on PSAC to help him to formulate thoughts on his forte, defense issues. At a May 1960 NSC meeting, Eisenhower said that he wanted to hear the report from "my scientists" about reconnaissance satellites before receiving the Pentagon's recommendations, implying that he regarded the scientists' views as more impartial than the military's. Acting on PSAC's recommendations, he also decided to rely more on solid-fuel missiles such as the Polaris IRBM and Minuteman ICBM, based on the view that liquid-fuel rockets were just interim vehicles until the former became operational.

Eisenhower's emphasis on solid fuels led to a more advanced nuclear arsenal in the 1960s.[21]

Scientists also pressed the president toward arms control. Haunted by fears of a Soviet surprise assault, Eisenhower asked Kistiakowsky about "the capability of the Russians to launch a great salvo-like attack with their missiles, so as to destroy all of our SAC bases within minutes of each other," as the scientist recalled. Kistiakowsky believed the Soviets were years away from any ability to do so. Still, scientists urged Eisenhower to limit arms. A nuclear test-ban treaty interested him, but critics argued that Soviet compliance was impossible to verify and a treaty would allow the Soviets to surpass the United States in nuclear weapons. Despite these risks, PSAC recommended that the president proceed with test ban talks. Although the U-2 incident destroyed Eisenhower's last chance for an arms control agreement, the impetus for a treaty continued after he left office. When John Kennedy was president, he asked his science advisor, Jerome Wiesner of MIT, what happened to radioactive elements after an atmospheric atomic bomb test. The scientist replied that they would get washed down to earth with the rain. At that moment, it was raining in Washington, and Kennedy looked outside the White House window and silently observed the downpour, as if deep in thought. This conversation might have given Kennedy more fillip to achieve the 1963 Nuclear Test Ban Treaty, the Cold War's first major arms control agreement, in which the United States, Soviet Union, and eventually more than one hundred other nations agreed to stop atmospheric and underwater atomic weapons tests.[22]

PSAC members gave Eisenhower high marks for his relationship with scientists. Donald Hornig, who later served as Lyndon Johnson's presidential science advisor, believed that "under Eisenhower, I'd say that the relationship, in some ways, to science and scientists was the closest of any president." Hornig felt that Killian and Kistiakowsky gave Eisenhower "great years" for science and its relationship with the White House. By the time of the Vietnam War, which most scientists opposed, "the whole science advisors apparatus was thought to be of increasingly dubious loyalty," and Johnson asked for fewer PSAC meetings.[23]

Decades later, Caryl Haskins believed that "Eisenhower listened to his science advisors with a care, seriousness, and deep attention that has not been duplicated" since then. Indeed, some presidents have fared badly in relations with scientists. Suspicious of scientists and believing they opposed his policies, Richard Nixon disbanded PSAC. George W. Bush had a notoriously poor rapport with scientists, who charged that his administration blocked stem cell research, suppressed the publication of scientific findings it disagreed with, and dismissed global climate change as liberal pabulum. The contrast makes Eisenhower's record stand out. Haskins recalled, "Dr. Killian's role in making scientific matters clear to [the president] and aiding him . . . in making scientific judgments must rank, I think, as one of the preeminent intellectual practical contributions from the civilian sector in the whole history [after] World War II."[24]

The Education Race

Sputnik and the space race affected American science in another way; it revealed the limitations of science education. Many science teachers were World War II veterans and had earned their college degrees courtesy of the 1944 GI Bill. They were patriotic, had received science training through government largesse, and believed in America's values. Sputnik shook their beliefs. One Brooklyn native remembered that his high school chemistry teacher, a war veteran, appeared grouchy the Monday after Sputnik was launched and began class by announcing, "The Russians beat us into space."[25] The science teacher's grumpiness was understandable, for rocket science was a cerebral endeavor, and a country's preeminence in this discipline reflected its world stature. If a nation led in rocket science, it likely enjoyed leads in other critical areas.

Science enabled countries to make quantum leaps in prestige, and America was a case in point. Before World War I, the United States trailed Western Europe in science. The first-rate physicists were European—Albert Einstein, Max Planck, Niels Bohr, and Pierre and Marie Curie. But during World War II, reacting to wartime demands and aided by great universities, American science jumped ahead of Europe's. Between 1901 and 1930, the United States claimed just five Nobel science prizes. But between 1931 and Sputnik's launch, it garnered thirty, which added luster to America's world image.[26]

But Sputnik sprung open like a jackknife, slicing into the confidence that had grown around American education and opening a wound of worries. It also linked learning and national security as never before in history, and the picture appeared somber. In 1955, as baby boomers crowded schools, America needed an estimated 300,000 more classrooms. Millions of high school students graduated with little grasp of science, appreciation of the world around them, or the skills to become cosmopolitan world citizens. Just one out of every three high school students took chemistry. For physics, the percentages were worse: one out of every four. Only half of all high schools offered foreign language courses. Former president Herbert Hoover, an engineer, blamed high schools for giving students too much academic freedom, allowing them to take "soft classes" instead of science and math. He said that teachers were too few, underpaid, and inadequately supplied with essential laboratories.[27]

The Great Depression had winnowed the ranks of teachers, and World War II swept like a scythe through a generation of young Americans, mowing down many future teachers. After the war, as the consumer economy grew, industry lured prospective teachers away from the classroom. Science teachers were in especially short supply. In 1955, only 125 new physics teachers were available to join high school faculty nationwide. There was little financial incentive to become a teacher because the average salary was equivalent to a construction worker's pay. Those who entered education were often unqualified; in 1956, one-third of school teachers lacked a bachelor's degree.[28]

The poor quality and paucity of science instruction bred a dearth of trained specialists. A 1954 survey reported that the country suffered a shortage of 35,000 to 40,000 engineers. Some experts predicted that within another decade, America would lack at least 100,000 scientists and engineers. Basic research languished, which threatened to stifle future technological breakthroughs.[29]

Critics charged that the Eisenhower administration made matters worse by scorning books and brains. Frederic Collins of the *Providence Journal* wrote, "In its tenure, to be sure, the Eisenhower administration permitted, even if it did not deliberately initiate, an upsurge of brutal anti-intellectualism." The *New York Times* characterized the administration as one "that is not distinguished for intellectual excellence." In an almost comical confirmation of such charges, although Eisenhower created the cabinet-level Department of Health, Education, and Welfare, he had trouble remembering its name, calling it "Health, Welfare, and Whatever." Walter Lippmann warned, "What we have to worry about is that with the declining level of education, with the vulgarization of the cultural standards in our mass society, we shall become a big but second-rate people, fat, Philistine, and self-indulgent."[30]

What hurt even more were contrasts with the Soviet Union. Sputnik validated a suspected Soviet lead in science, and Americans believed it. NASA deputy administrator Robert Seamans recalled meeting with high school students after the Sputnik launch, and their views surprised him. He said that "they all felt that the Russians were ahead of us scientifically and that we might never catch up." Sputnik seemed proof positive that Russia was an educational titan, turning out smarter students. Soviet teachers enjoyed greater prestige than their American counterparts and higher salaries, too—commensurate with those of physicians. Harvard president Nathan Pusey claimed that U.S. college professors earned an average $5,400, whereas Russian professors received $18,000. The director of the Smithsonian Astrophysical Observatory predicted, "Until the time comes when the Phi Beta Kappa has the same social standing as the football player, we are going to fall behind in our technological race with the USSR."[31]

Americans who observed the Soviet system up close confirmed these observations. In 1955, William Benton, publisher of *Encyclopedia Britannica* and a former U.S. senator, visited Russia and concluded that its schools, libraries, and laboratories posed a threat more dangerous than weapons. No observer attracted more attention than Admiral Hyman Rickover. Known as the father of the nuclear navy and for his lacerating verbal slashes (television news anchor Diane Sawyer later named him the toughest interviewee of her career, recalling that he began their conversation by calling her "dumb"), Rickover accompanied Richard Nixon during a 1959 trip to the Soviet Union. Upon returning, Rickover said that the principal race between the two countries was in education. "They are currently graduating more qualified scientists and engineers from their universities than we are," he warned, and he predicted that the "nation that wins this race will be the potentially dominant power." To ensure American victory, Rickover urged Americans to break away from the tradition of local control over education and accept national standards and federal aid. But the Soviets seemed poised to win the education race. After Sputnik, George Reedy observed that in 1955, "Soviet schools graduated nearly three engineers for every one of ours. It is not difficult to forecast the future if we permit that trend to continue."[32]

Yet just as with the space race, the American system had many merits. Its university engineering programs were the cynosure of world attention, and although the Soviet system might have shown an edge in numbers, the quality of each scientist and engineer in the United States was sturdy, and many persons whom the Soviets called "engineers" might have qualified only as "technicians" in the United States. Whereas the typical U.S. doctoral student in the sciences earned his or her degree while under thirty years of age, the average Soviet scientist earned a Ph.D. at a more advanced age—usually over fifty. The later completion of their education meant that Soviet scientists had shorter careers and less time to contribute to their fields, and they might also have been past their intellectual prime when they finished school. Americans achieved breakthroughs in medicine, such as the polio vaccine, and in technology, such as transistors. The American educational system offered opportunities to create and develop. By contrast, the Soviet system failed to encourage research and innovation as free countries did. It bred technicians and workers, rather than true scientists, while limiting education to society's upper crust. Attending a February 1958 White House cabinet meeting, U.S. ambassador to the Soviet Union Llewelyn Thompson reported that "the exaggerated stories appearing in our press" inflated the true quality of the Russian school system.[33]

Moreover, the Eisenhower administration was stocked with scholars bearing impressive credentials that belied the media criticism of it. For example, Gabriel Hauge, an architect of Eisenhower's economic policy, held a doctorate in economics from Harvard and was a Princeton professor. And many Ivy League alumni in the administration were impressed with the president's intellect and leadership talents. Staff secretary Andrew Goodpaster had one of the sharpest minds in Washington. Graduating second in his West Point class, Goodpaster went on to earn a doctorate in international relations from Princeton; one military colleague recalled that Goodpaster seemed like "just a quiet guy" until he spoke, after which anyone within earshot realized he had "a few brain cells to rub together." During the space race, Goodpaster lauded Eisenhower's knowledge of outer space, commenting that he used terms that Goodpaster himself did not know. William Ewald, a Harvard English Ph.D., marveled at Eisenhower's powers of concentration and attention to clear prose. Pundits and scholars often believed that Eisenhower was "not very bright," Ewald recalled. "But the truth to the matter is when it came to sorting out issues and asking questions and coming up with a decision, Eisenhower was always on top of it. And the people who worked with him at the time saw that."[34]

Still, despite the administration's academic pedigree, even level-headed observers expressed concern to the president about American education. When Eisenhower met with his science advisory committee on October 15, 1957, he asked whether American science was really being outdistanced. Isador Rabi responded that given the quality and scope of science education in the Soviet Union, that country could surpass America in science, just as the United States had outpaced Europe. Moreover, the outcry after Sputnik for improving America's schools was one that Eisenhower had to acknowledge. Some schools took matters into their own hands, offering Russian language courses, lengthening the school day, or holding Saturday classes in science and mathematics.[35] Education became a hot-button issue, and politicians cried for more federal support. One week after Sputnik's launch, Senator Jacob Javits urged "a strong new effort to team up public and private research and development in a common, coordinated purpose to keep our country abreast in science and technology; and this must include broadening the opportunity for young men and women to study science by increased scholorships [*sic*] and student loan funds." When Senators Humphrey and McClellan proposed a cabinet-level Department of Science and Technology, their plan included establishing a $580 million, eight-year program of federal scholarship loans for students taking college science, math, and engineering courses.[36]

Science educators looked to the federal government with ample precedent to support them, because Washington had aided education in wartime crises. During the Civil War, the Morrill Act of 1862 enabled states to receive enormous tracts of land to establish land grant colleges. During World War I, the Smith-Hughes Act of 1917 encouraged vocational training among high school students. The seminal Serviceman's Readjustment Act of 1944—better known as the GI Bill—enabled millions of World War II veterans to receive college degrees,[37] and Eisenhower had personal exposure to its impact: the year before he became its president, Columbia University established a special School of General Studies for nontraditional students to accommodate the influx of veterans. After Sputnik, the federal government appeared primed to enact education legislation to fight the Cold War. The question was whether Eisenhower—normally averse to federal intervention—would approve.

 ## A Historic Education Bill

The Constitution, which Eisenhower normally looked to for guidance, made no mention of education, leaving the issue to the states. Thus, for most of the nation's history, education was the province of local communities, which resisted federal intervention, and that situation meshed with Eisenhower's principles. He felt the federal government should stay out of curricula and instruction. At an April 1957 press conference, he said, "I have tried to make clear time and again that I think the Federal Government has not any proper role in the operations and in the general maintenance of our public school system. It belongs to the localities and the States." He allowed that during national emergencies, Washington could step in with temporary aid, "and then turn the whole thing back to the States, and have nothing more to do with it." This thinking led Eisenhower to deprecate the 1954 Supreme Court *Brown v. Board of Education* decision, viewing it as a federal intrusion onto state jurisdiction and at times making him just a passive observer in the historic civil rights movement.[38]

But the president was willing to modify his stance and make one of his "radical moves." He acknowledged that schools lacked funds and facilities, and during his first term he supported a four-year, $325-million-a-year program for federal aid to construct new schools, although it failed to pass Congress. Still, the issue of federal assistance to education reverberated in Washington. In the summer of 1957, HEW formed a Task Force on Higher Education to begin crafting a federal program to boost education. Sputnik acted as a catalyst by reducing opposition to federal education aid and tying the issue to national security, which won the president's approbation. In November, Eisenhower instructed HEW secretary Marion Folsom to shift his department's focus away from school construction and toward new federal education measures. He emphasized that the new program should stress science and must be only temporary, ending when the national emergency abated.[39]

Just two and half weeks after the Sputnik launch, Eisenhower wrote that "my scientific friends" believed that the greatest challenge the United States faced was inducing more Americans to study science. He urged, "We must start recruiting and educating scientists *now*." At an October 30 press conference, he put it a different way, saying that when he met with scientists, "I was a bit astonished to find this: their chief concern is not the relative position of ourselves today in scientific advancement with any other nation, but where we are going to be in ten years."[40]

In his second speech on science and national security, Eisenhower stressed scientific education and basic research. He suggested more laboratories and fellowships as well as nationwide tests for high schoolers and incentives for studying and teaching mathematics and science. At a December 2, 1957, cabinet meeting, Folsom outlined the HEW's skeletal plan. The $300 million initiative would last five years, with the states having most responsibility. Eisenhower liked the plan's relatively small price tag, limited nature, and emphasis on state jurisdiction. Its features included scholarships and matching grants for improved science, math, and foreign language instruction. Just after Christmas, on December 30, Folsom visited Eisenhower in Gettysburg to review a revised version of the program, which had grown to $1 billion and stressed the relationship between education and national security. The president approved it with the understanding that it would be temporary in nature.[41]

Eisenhower called an education bill "a top priority objective." On January 27, 1958, he sent a special message on education to Congress outlining a $1 billion program that would last four years. It proposed 10,000 federal scholarships, 5,500 fellowships, matching grants to encourage universities to start or expand graduate programs, and more grants to promote foreign language, science, and mathematics instruction. For the next several months,

Congress worked on a bill. (Meanwhile, in late July 1958, Folsom resigned as HEW secretary, and Arthur Flemming, the former president of Ohio Wesleyan University, took his place.) In August, as legislators itched to leave Washington for summer recess, they worked feverishly to complete the legislation. The bill that emerged more closely resembled the House's scaled-down $1 billion bill rather than the Senate's more ambitious $1.5 billion version. Lawmakers in both chambers took special care to ensure that state and local governments would retain control over education despite a massive infusion of federal aid. In the end, lawmakers passed the bill by large margins, 66 to 15 in the Senate and 212 to 85 in the House. In September, Eisenhower signed the National Defense Education Act. All told, the legislation set aside $1 billion in aid for the next seven years. At a time when the nation's defense budget stood at $41 billion, $1 billion in educational aid ostensibly designed to buttress national security seemed a reasonable expenditure.[42]

The loan program accounted for about one-third of the NDEA's expenses, $295 million. The federal government was to provide loans to graduate and undergraduate students, which colleges would administer, matching one dollar for every nine the government provided. As Eisenhower preferred, these loans would be based primarily on financial need rather than scholarly talent or merit, and students could borrow up to $1,000 per year for a total of $5,000. For a year after the student graduated, no interest would be charged on the loan, after which the student would have ten years to repay it at 3 percent interest. Future teachers would receive special consideration for the loans, with half the amount erased if they taught for five years after graduating from college. Students who specialized in science, engineering, math, or a foreign language were to receive similar opportunities.[43]

State grants made up another third of the NDEA's cost. The federal government offered matching grants to states for science, mathematics, and foreign languages to allow schools to buy modern laboratory equipment. The matching grants encouraged states to fund new programs while allowing them to retain control over education.[44]

A large slice of NDEA money, $59.4 million, went to "national defense fellowships," designed to encourage graduate students to become teachers and universities to develop graduate programs. Those graduate students attending universities that were either establishing or expanding graduate programs could receive fellowships of $2,000 for their first year of study and increasing amounts in subsequent years ($2,200 for a second year, $2,400 for a third, terminal year). Thus, over three years, graduate students might receive $6,600 for their studies—a princely sum in the 1950s—and could get even more money if they had children. Just as with the student loans, the government gave special consideration to students who planned to teach.

The NDEA also contained an Eisenhower administration proposal to bolster foreign language instruction, granting federal money to colleges and universities to establish special institutes for high school teachers of commonly taught languages (French, German, Italian, and Spanish), where enrollees would receive weekly stipends for attending classes. For more uncommon languages, such as Arabic, Chinese, Hindi, Japanese, and Russian, the federal government provided matching grants to establish instruction centers, where students would also get stipends.[45]

The bill inspired controversy. Some critics argued that linking the bill to national defense was disingenuous; the provisions had nothing to do with security, they said, and the bill's supporters employed casuistic arguments and a sense of "crisis" to get it passed. Others worried about its expense. It would fatten the deficit and encourage local schools to run up red ink because they would grow to depend on the federal government to bail them out. Opponents such as Senator Barry Goldwater also warned that federal aid implied federal control, and local educational institutions now would have to answer to Washington. Democratic senator Strom Thurmond of South Carolina argued that Washington would eventually discriminate against the South by denying aid to segregated schools.[46]

The NDEA's most controversial change from the administration's original proposal was a loyalty oath. It was "misguided, discriminatory, superfluous, ineffective, futile," raged Harvard president Nathan Pusey. Students who received federal aid would have to pledge allegiance to America's government and sign a so-called negative affidavit, saying that they did not belong to or support any organization aiming to overthrow the U.S. government through violent or coercive means.[47]

The American Council on Education, the National Education Association, and the American Association of University Professors all protested the oath. Students would have to swear their loyalty to receive federal aid, yet other groups receiving government help—businessmen, laborers, farmers, and more—faced no such hurdle. Carleton College's president pointed out, "We give $6 billion to the farmers but don't expect any loyalty oath." Critics also questioned the disclaimer's efficacy: those students with communist ties who wished to gain government aid could swear by the affidavit, with no real way to determine their sincerity. Since the Bill of Rights protected freedom of belief, the oath pushed the limits of constitutionality, singling out individuals for beliefs rather than for actions.[48]

Immediately, six institutions refused NDEA aid to protest the oath: Bryn Mawr, Haverford, Mills, Princeton, the University of Richmond, and Swarthmore. Fourteen more soon joined them, including Harvard and Yale, as well as liberal arts colleges such as Amherst, Grinnell, and Wellesley. Top administration officials, such as Arthur Flemming and new NASA administrator Keith Glennan, spoke out against the oath, as did the president. Eisenhower said that he could "well understand the resentful feelings of a citizen who believes himself singled out to make a special affirmation of his loyalty to his country."[49] At the same time, though, he objected to institutions' refusal of NDEA loans because of the oath. "I rather deplore," he said, "that universities have found it necessary to . . . keep a number of citizens out of taking advantage of the loan provisions that the Federal Government set up." In 1959, Senator John Kennedy cosponsored a bill to repeal the loyalty oath, which he said "seriously handicaps our colleges and universities and unnecessarily slanders the students who apply for loans so that they can complete their education." But by a 49–42 vote, the Senate turned it down. (In 1962, Congress finally rescinded the oath.)[50]

Despite the boycott by some colleges, by June 1962, 1,450 educational institutions had participated in the NDEA's student loan program, and 350,000 undergraduate and graduate students had borrowed $225,000 in aid.[51] By the mid-1960s, 5,500 students had received graduate fellowships to become college teachers, and more than 11,000 participated in the special counseling institutes the NDEA helped to establish. Results were palpable: the NDEA led to nineteen foreign-language centers and brought badly needed focus on languages of Asia and the Middle East. Worldwide, billions of people spoke these tongues, yet they rarely received attention inside U.S. schools. As a result of NDEA attention and funding, for example, the number of colleges offering Russian more than doubled.[52]

As with space, Eisenhower's wariness of deficits and espousal of low federal spending kept him from becoming an enthusiastic education advocate. When President Kennedy proposed extending the NDEA, Eisenhower spoke out publicly against the move, saying it would "not only become permanent but also, by natural progression, it would result in Federal control of education." Yet in 1961, Congress extended the NDEA for two years, and it received another extension in 1962 and still another in 1964.[53]

A parallel marked the space race and the state of American Cold War education: no great crisis existed. As Eisenhower's presidency concluded, the Soviet Academy of Sciences' vice president even complained that Russian schools and universities failed to train skilled scientists, and the American media grew aware of the Soviet educational system's flaws. By the early

1960s, most experts recognized that the dire warnings of Soviet superiority in education were misplaced. In plugging for his Elementary and Secondary Education Act of 1965, Lyndon Johnson used no arguments of national security. Instead, he framed the act as another weapon in his legislative arsenal against poverty, which he tried to make the new decade's overarching concern. Yet Johnson's HEW secretary, Wilbur Cohen, conceded that the national security argument was a critical hook on which to hang the NDEA. The act "could not have passed at that time without the 'defense' label," Cohen said.[54]

Despite the limits to Eisenhower's support, he left a notable legacy in aid to education. Federal spending on education reached $14 billion in 1960, up from $2.34 billion twenty years earlier. Moreover, the expenditure aligned with public opinion. A 1959 survey showed that Americans' top spending priority for federal money was education. Importantly, investing in education was investing in America's long-term future. In Eisenhower's day, CEA chair Raymond Saulnier had said half-facetiously that he liked to count automobile-transport trucks on the highway as a measure of U.S. economic activity. But as the economy matured, the strength of its manufacturing sector was bound to fade, and America had to lay foundations in other areas, such as science, technology, communications, and foreign languages, the disciplines that the NDEA stimulated. Science and technology boosted innovation, which in turn created new jobs and economic growth. Education also bolstered productivity growth, the linchpin to a nation's economic health. In these facets, the NDEA fit well with Eisenhower's perspective that federal action should aim to help America over the long term, and he buttressed the growing "knowledge economy," joining the ranks of presidents—dating back to the country's founding—who recognized that education benefited the nation and needed federal support. One of George Washington's pet projects was a national university, and he even mapped out an area in the new District of Columbia where one could be built. Even John Tyler, a states' rights advocate who opposed federal aggrandizement, supported national scientific inquiry and pushed for a naval observatory, seeing knowledge as a means to enhance America's greatness.[55]

After the NDEA's passage, one of its principal authors, Democratic congressman Carl Elliott of Alabama, boldly stated, "I really think the bill is a landmark and will take its place alongside the Northwest Ordinances, and the acts creating our land grant colleges." It was an audacious statement coming from a not-so-disinterested source. Yet the NDEA further broke down the long-standing taboo against federal involvement in education, making Washington an active player in the field. In an era when education

assumed national importance, it was a logical extension of federal authority, and like the Interstate Highway System, Eisenhower could support it
on the grounds of national security. He was justified, during his final State
of the Union address, in calling the NDEA "a milestone in the history of
American education." His aides felt similarly. Killian called it "a profoundly
important breakthrough" in federal education aid to the states that brought
Washington "into a whole new relationship to the educational system."
Almost thirty years later, Arthur Flemming recalled that Eisenhower "took
the lead in recommending the adoption of the National Defense Education
Act which was the first piece of legislation at the federal level involving
post-secondary education since the passage of the Land Grant Act. He did
that with a considerable degree of enthusiasm." Again, one of his "radical
moves" had the right touch. (His commitment to education was later em-
bodied in the eponymous Eisenhower College in Seneca Falls, New York,
which was founded in 1968 but struggled with low enrollments before
finally folding in 1982.)[56]

At the same time, though, Eisenhower's concern that federal help for education be only temporary proved well founded. To monitor compliance
with the act, the HEW received a deluge of paperwork from schools nationwide, and it needed more manpower almost immediately. The department
added 150 new staffers in 1958, 279 more in 1959, and another 314 in 1960.
HEW continued to grow during the next two decades, and in 1977, President Jimmy Carter created a separate Department of Education.

Just as with space, Eisenhower was right to support more structured, substantive aid to education. He was also right to worry about schools depending on federal support. Unwittingly, he presided over the growth of federal
money for both space and education. It was a trend that, try as he did, he
could not stop.

# CHAPTER 10

Order from Chaos

Eisenhower demanded punctuality, ran the White House with military precision, and told staff to work in clearly defined channels, bristling if anyone threw him a policy curveball. "I don't want people springing things on me!" he exclaimed whenever it happened. William Ewald called Eisenhower "an organization man." He could structure an organization, Ewald said, "whether it was a squad, army, set of invading armies or the executive branch of government. . . . This was always his concern: How do you hold this crowd of people together, whatever the size of the crowd, and get them rolling forward toward some kind of a worthwhile goal." The president ordered his White House staff in a tight arrangement with clearly delineated duties but gave them wide latitude to act. "It was almost scary how much power he delegated to you," commented Attorney General Herbert Brownell.

The special White House organs and their meeting schedules reflected Eisenhower's desire for order. His cabinet met every Friday, with Eisenhower beginning each meeting by observing a silent prayer. (Once, when he forgot the ritual and cabinet secretary Maxwell Rabb slipped a note to remind him, Eisenhower blurted out, "Goddammit! We forgot the silent prayer!") A special National Security Council Planning Board met at least twice weekly to debate and draft policy papers, and the NSC itself and Operations Coordinating Board, the latter designed to implement NSC decisions, met weekly. Eisenhower regarded the NSC conclaves the most important of the entire government.

Eisenhower's insistence on a rigid command structure reflected his military background and differed from other presidents' approaches. Roosevelt and Truman saw no need for a chief of staff, but Eisenhower's wartime experiences taught him that he needed an adjutant like Sherman Adams to handle the flow of people and information into the Oval Office. Although Eisenhower appreciated the new organs that Truman established, such as the NSC and CIA, he believed that Truman's overall organization was haphazard. Privately, he let his scorn show, writing, "[P]oor HST, a fine man who in the middle of a stormy lake knows nothing of swimming. Yet a lot of drowning people are forced to look to him as a lifeguard. If his wisdom could only equal his good intent." Later, John Kennedy eliminated the Operations Coordinating Board, and the cabinet and NSC met irregularly under both him and Lyndon Johnson because both men favored speedy decisions that they believed the NSC, a seemingly sluggish body, prevented. Eisenhower disdained Kennedy's thin rationale that disorder reflected genius. During retirement, he advised Nixon that the secret to his well-run White House was "adequate and skillful organization." As he wrote, "Organization makes more efficient the gathering and analysis of facts, and the arranging of the findings of experts in logical fashion." Although he believed that "disorganization can scarcely fail to result in inefficiency and can easily lead to disaster," he explained that organization "is effective in minimizing the chances of failure and in insuring that the right hand does, indeed, know what the left hand is doing."[1] Eisenhower's quest for order guided him in space policy, as he realized that he needed a well-defined organization to bring coherence to the government's welter of competing space efforts.

 ## A Civilian Space Agency

Arthur Larson recalled an incident that, in retrospect, pointed like a pennant, foretelling the direction Eisenhower would take in establishing a government space agency after some initial hesitation. It was November 5, 1957, and the president was discussing the nation's missile program with Defense Secretary McElroy on the phone. Eisenhower broached the prospect of a special Director of Missile Development, but the idea cut no ice with McElroy, who hemmed, hawed, and offered reasons against it. Eisenhower grew exasperated. Slamming down the telephone, he cursed, "Goddamn it, I'll do it through Killian then and give him all the power he needs.

At least that way I won't have to worry about restrictions on his power." The conversation bore out Eisenhower's worst fears—that service rivalries hamstrung the Pentagon, preventing progress on missile development. By extension, the military might retard space gains, too, perhaps even using space for selfish purposes. Andrew Goodpaster recalled that as space became a national issue, Eisenhower worried about exclusive military control over space policy because defense officials "would use it for the purpose of building their own programs [and] exciting public opinion in order to enlarge their own programs." These concerns prompted a sea change in Eisenhower's thinking about a civilian space agency, helping to give birth to the National Aeronautics and Space Administration.[2]

Until 1958, America's space program resided almost entirely in one place: the Pentagon. Initially, the post-Sputnik uproar only fortified the military's role in space. On November 27, 1958, responding to cries for accelerated space and missile activity, McElroy announced the formation of the Pentagon's new Advanced Research Projects Agency, to coordinate and direct all research on space projects. Its first director, Roy Johnson, a vice president of General Electric's appliance division, had no training in science but had proved an effective manager at GE, setting records for appliance sales. Historian Paul Dickson has noted that "in a sense ARPA was the first U.S. space agency," keeping the country in the race with the Soviet Union while America tried to find its space legs.[3]

Sadly, the Defense Department's administration of space projects gave it a disjointed, ad hoc feel, yet Eisenhower still opposed locating space activities outside the Pentagon. The most important space endeavors impinged on national defense, he thought, and military activities should take priority over science projects. Thus, he felt that the Pentagon should control any space agency.[4]

Waste and expense were additional concerns. Placing space projects in an outside agency would lead to duplication. Ever fearful of prodigal spending and more layers of bureaucracy, Eisenhower worried that a separate space agency would invest talent and capital in boondoggles. At one meeting, he said he could agree to a "great Department of Space" but warned against rushing into a costly government expansion. Instead, he thought the Defense Department's new ARPA a logical place to house America's space program.[5]

The military liked that talk and exerted fierce pressure to retain space activities. John Medaris argued that a civilian space agency would cost more money and create another government bureau, and he vigorously defended the military's prerogative in space exploration. While touring California factories that produced missile parts, he told reporters, "No organization except the military has the experience [to explore space]. You have no civilian agency to substitute for the services. If you take time out to organize one, you'll be further behind in competition with the Russians."[6]

The Air Force appeared the logical service to guide space activities, and it popularized the term "aerospace" to link air with space as its bailiwick. The Air Force had other claims to rockets and space: it was developing the Atlas and Titan ICBMs; it flew the X-15 aircraft, which broke the sound barrier in 1947; it broached ideas such as a nuclear rocket to ferry materials to a moon base.[7] But other agencies, both military and civilian, wanted to direct space policy. The Army, which already had the ABMA and had launched Explorer I, fought to stay active in the nation's space program. At least one civilian agency tried to jump into the fray: the Atomic Energy Commission believed that because nuclear propulsion would eventually power space vehicles, it should direct the U.S. space program. Senator Clinton Anderson even introduced legislation to let the AEC lead the U.S. space program, and supporters included Democratic senator Albert Gore, Sr., of Tennessee, who argued that the AEC was "uniquely qualified to perform the technical work required for the development of manned nuclear rockets, capable of space travel. There is no necessity for creating an additional agency to undertake the task—at least, I see none now." But the measure failed to gain broad support in Congress, whose members knew space would involve issues far larger than nuclear power or the still-speculative concept of nuclear-powered rockets.[8]

As government agencies battled over turf, the nation's space program grew fitfully. ARPA failed to develop an effective relationship with the services. The Air Force resented ARPA's very existence, insisting that it should gain sole control over space research. Arguments even broke out among the services over which name should appear on the sides of rockets. In the end, the confusing patchwork of government agencies engaged in space projects hindered America's ability to develop policy and goals.[9]

James Killian believed that the Pentagon could capably control the nation's space efforts, but many PSAC members felt otherwise. Jerome Wiesner, George Kistiakowsky, Lloyd Berkner, and Isidor Rabi all wanted a civilian agency, and other prominent scientists agreed. Military control over space might suffice, James Van Allen said, "but the bulk of the scientific community feels as I do," that the country needed a separate civilian organization to direct space projects, and his assertion appeared accurate. Ten days after Sputnik, the American Rocket Society proposed an Astronautical

Research and Development Agency to direct non-defense space projects. In February 1958, the National Society of Professional Engineers floated the idea of a civilian Federal Space Exploration Commission that would control all space projects, even those related to the military.[10]

As he had immediately after Sputnik, Vice President Nixon walked a step ahead of Eisenhower on space policy. He supported a civilian agency, warning that the Pentagon might limit scientists' creativity or ignore projects that lacked military import. Military control of peaceful space projects would look bad, and Nixon feared that America's image might suffer without a civilian space agency, which could encourage international cooperation in ways a military agency could not. He argued, "The best way to insure that the scientist in this field [of space] makes the greatest contribution to the national welfare, including our missile program, is to keep him free from the requirements of immediate military necessity."[11] Other politicians pressed for a civilian space agency. Killian told the president that Congress exerted "great pressure" to place some of America's space efforts outside the Pentagon. Lyndon Johnson even declared, "Congress will ultimately determine what agency should handle space development," and one recommendation of his subcommittee hearings was to establish an independent agency devoted to space exploration.[12]

Eisenhower sought the advice of "my scientists." On February 4, 1958, he asked PSAC to tackle the issue of civilian versus military control over space, with Killian heading the study. Later that month, a PSAC panel under Killian's direction recommended establishing a civilian agency. Although Killian recalled that Eisenhower "arrived at the conclusion independently of us" to support a nonmilitary space program, his scientists' recommendations reinforced his thinking. He might have even supported a civilian agency as a way to cement his close relationship with scientists, who felt more comfortable working for a civilian agency than for the military. Goodpaster explained that Eisenhower "knew that the scientists would be happier having [space] in a civilian organization than having it given to the military. He wanted, in a way, to placate the scientists. He wanted to draw them closer to his operation."[13]

Eisenhower had reversed himself on important issues before. Before becoming president, he looked askance at Social Security, throwing out his old chestnut that if someone wanted complete security, he could find it in jail; as president, though, he expanded Social Security coverage. He reversed gears on Alaskan statehood, at first opposing the idea because the territory seemed a remote, frozen tundra. Although he never got over his skepticism, he ultimately deferred to Interior Secretary Fred Seaton's judgment to make Alaska the nation's forty-ninth state. Eisenhower changed his mind on a civilian space agency, too, softening and then reversing his opposition. Goodpaster recalled that "as we looked into this and as the matter was reviewed, the idea of an established, recognized space agency" began to have great appeal. Administration members acknowledged that the country could not plan space and satellite projects "on an ad hoc basis as the Vanguard program had attempted to do," Goodpaster said, adding, "I think it came across quite well that you can't extemporize this kind of thing. . . . It had to be organized, planned for, and developed."[14]

A civilian agency appealed to Eisenhower's desire for order, and he began to see the drawbacks of Pentagon control over space projects. The military's schemes to establish space weapons systems troubled him. They would militarize space—precisely what he wanted to avoid. He knew that Pentagon spending took on a life of its own, with wasteful results. Eisenhower "just did not wish to see the military getting into [space projects]," remembered Goodpaster. Knowing the military's tendency to grab new turf, Eisenhower thought that a civilian agency would fence off space and keep the military out. He also liked the idea of a civilian agency to emphasize the peaceful nature of America's efforts. It would be a propaganda coup for the United States, offsetting the rich harvest that the Soviet Union cultivated from its own space efforts. "That was part of the whole strategy that the Soviet Union's program, because it was a covert program, would appear to threaten people all around the world," said Arnold Frutkin. "And our program, being an open program, would reassure them as to our purposes, and we would look a hell of a lot better than the Soviet Union did in the eyes of the rest of the world."[15]

Eisenhower articulated another reason for a civilian agency: "I cannot, for the life of me, see any reason why we should be using or misusing military talent to explore the moon," he said. "This is something that deals in the scientific field, and to give this to the Air Force or Army or Navy, it just seems to me is denying what really is a sort of a doctrine in America. You have given to the military only what is their problem and not anything else; the rest of it stays under civilian control." Meanwhile, the Pentagon provided no cogent reasoning to retain control of the space program. "There really was not any major argument for putting it in the Defense Department," recalled David Beckler.[16]

On December 30, 1957, Killian had already drafted a key memorandum that expressed scientists' opposition to exclusive military control of America's space program. They argued that Pentagon management "might improperly limit the program to narrowly concerned military objectives" and also "tag our basic space research as military and place the United States in the unfortunate position before the world of apparently tailoring all space research to military ends." Killian suggested limiting the Pentagon to military space efforts while granting another agency jurisdiction over nonmilitary ones. "One obvious way of doing this," Killian wrote, "would be to encourage [the National Advisory Committee on Aeronautics] to extend its space research and to provide it with the necessary funds to do so."[17]

Indeed, the National Advisory Committee on Aeronautics seemed a logical nucleus for a new space agency. On March 5, a special President's Advisory Committee on Government Organization, chaired by Nelson Rockefeller, recommended a civilian space agency designed around a reconstituted NACA. The new organization, the committee recommended, should be called the "National Aeronautics and Space Agency." PSAC supported the proposal, as did the Bureau of the Budget, and even some military officials liked the idea, fearing that a defense-based space agency would become spider-webbed and paralyzed in the Pentagon's vast bureaucracy. "I wouldn't squeal very loudly if they gave the job to the N.A.C.A," admitted one Air Force officer. Support also came from science writers; *Aviation Week* commented, "If N.A.C.A. gets the job, our jump into space will be catapulted from a solid launching pad."[18]

The Speedy Birth of NASA

Created in 1915 during Woodrow Wilson's presidency, the NACA was a throwback to aviation's earliest days and even used a picture of the Wright Brothers' historic 1903 flight as its symbol. For more than four decades, the NACA had worked on aircraft and missiles, developing experience in both military and scientific space projects. By 1958, the NACA employed almost eight thousand staff members, and the agency had five research laboratories, in addition to its Washington headquarters: Ames Aeronautical Laboratory and Edwards Air Force Base in California; Langley Field and Wallops Island in Virginia; and Lewis Flight Propulsion in Ohio.[19]

Yet by federal standards, the NACA's budget was meager, just $100 million annually, and its Washington headquarters were small. By the 1950s, it attracted less attention and funding as the military played a larger role in rockets and missile development. Lacking money and political heft, the NACA's best days appeared to be over; developing into a full-blown space agency represented an opportunity to grow. NACA chair James Doolittle supported the organization's conversion to a space agency, and some NACA members, who earned the nickname "Young Turks," began to push from within for a mutation into a space agency.[20]

NACA's wealth of engineering knowledge helped to make its case. Goodpaster pointed out that "in the NACA you had a core there of proven integrity and ability that could be built upon." Conducting numerous launches from Wallops Island, it researched high-speed, high-altitude rockets and the shapes of missiles—including the use of blunt noses, which proved better than pointed ones for dissipating the heat of atmospheric re-entry. The NACA developed the legendary X-15 aircraft, which flew at eight times the speed of sound at altitudes of up to 350,000 feet, and it was even planning manned spaceflight. And although it worked closely with the military, the NACA remained a civilian agency, making it attractive as the core for a new space organization. On April 2, 1958, Eisenhower's endorsement of a civilian agency became official when he sent a message to Congress recommending that a National Aeronautics and Space Agency be established around the NACA, along with proposed legislation. He wanted the new outfit to lead America's space activities, except for those involving military missions.[21]

But insiders wanted a name change. Administration members felt uncertain about the word "agency" and discussed alternatives such as "institute." Meeting with House majority leader John McCormack, Eileen Galloway mentioned that "agency" sounded too weak for such an important organ; the government already had many "agencies" floating about. She suggested "administration," with an "administrator" to lead it. The name change would not affect the existing acronym, NASA, she added. She recalled that—to her surprise—McCormack simply pressed a button on his desk, summoning an aide to implement the change in the bill.[22]

In June, the House and Senate passed versions of a bill creating NASA, and the next month conferees smoothed over differences in the two pieces of legislation. The Senate version proposed a "Space Council" to advise the president on space policy, which Eisenhower disliked. He feared it would add more bureaucracy, slow down policy formulation, and wrongfully assume powers that should remain with the president, perhaps becoming a rogue organ, just as detractors feared the National Security Council was becoming. Preferring only a NASA chief administrator who would report directly to him, Eisenhower had no need for a "council" to coordinate space policy. The Space Council, observed Eugene Skolnikoff, seemed "just one more impediment to doing something sensibly and with alacrity." Killian visited Lyndon

Johnson to express the president's dissatisfaction. But the senator refused to budge, arguing that the Space Council would help to resolve conflicts and coordinate between NASA and the military. Subjected to the "Johnson treatment," Killian realized that the senator "was going to be part of this picture, period. So I think [Killian] just accepted [it]," Skolnikoff said.[23]

On Sunday, July 7, 1958, at Johnson's request, Eisenhower met with him at the White House and reached a compromise. Later that day, Eisenhower asked Killian to accompany him to the airport as he prepared to leave Washington. Inside the presidential limousine, Killian recalled, Eisenhower "almost apologetically" said that he had invited Johnson to the White House. "I agreed with Lyndon to support the Space Council to hasten passage of the bill," he told Killian. The president and the senator had lubricated their differences over drinks, and Johnson allayed some of Eisenhower's concerns by promising that the president would chair the nine-member Space Council. Its other members included the NASA administrator, the secretaries of state and defense, the AEC chair, plus four more members, at least one of whom would come from outside government. The two men also agreed to model the Council after the NSC.[24]

The controversy over the Space Council was the only major obstacle to the bill's passage. Overall, Congress had acted with stunning speed. The congressional conference committee met in only one session, on July 15, and the next day both houses received its report. The House and Senate approved the bill by unanimous voice vote. On July 29, Eisenhower signed the bill into law. On August 8, after hearing favorable reports about Case Western Reserve University president T. Keith Glennan, Eisenhower appointed him as NASA's first administrator. Hugh Dryden, who had served for nine years as NACA director, became NASA deputy administrator.[25]

Although no expert in space policy, Glennan had been Atomic Energy Commissioner from 1950 to 1952, a stint that gave him experience in running a new government agency. Just as with his appointment of Killian as science advisor, Eisenhower had picked an administrator whose views on limited government reflected his own. Glennan expressed concerns that the United States was "drifting further and further and faster and faster down the socialist stream," and he protested the notion that "the federal government is a 365-day Santa Claus and that the national Treasury is an inexhaustible storehouse of largesse." Under Glennan, NASA rejected von Braun's arguments that America had to use space exploration for psychological gains and instead concentrated on science, preferring constructive satellite launches rather than propaganda stunts.[26]

For both Eisenhower and Congress, the NASA legislation was significant. Johnson remarked that history might record that the most important act of the entire congressional session "was to establish an agency to guide America's effort in the exploration of outer space." Representative Gerald Ford, a member of the House Select Committee on Astronautics and Space Exploration, commented that congressmen worked on the NASA legislation with unusually strong bipartisan cooperation. Democratic House majority leader McCormack chaired the committee, with Republican Joseph Martin, Jr., the former speaker, as vice chair, an anomalous structure that stressed bipartisanship by departing from the tradition of one-party committee control. Invoking one of the sports metaphors that he was fond of using, Ford—a former star University of Michigan football player—praised the "complete team play" that committee members showed in forging the legislation. Although they "debated the issues vigorously in our closed sessions," he said, "when it came time for decision, there was such a meeting of the minds that there was never a dissenting vote within the committee." Eileen Galloway pointed to the NASA legislation as an example of a Republican president working with a Democratic Congress for the country's good. "We had the President and the Majority Leader of the Senate in harmony on what we wanted. We did not have a lot of partisanship," she recalled. As a new political issue, space lacked a long pedigree of cemented opinions and political positions, making consensus easier. Moreover, members of Congress acted in a patriotic sense of helping their country to race Russia.[27]

The speed was impressive. Although Eisenhower had caused a delay by initially resisting a civilian space agency, NASA was still founded quickly. The creation of a new federal agency often takes years; NASA's birth took just months. Galloway said that she was "awed by the speed of the legislative process." Given Eisenhower's early opposition, his acceptance of NASA was another "radical move" for him, but it took political pressure off the White House and gave him another legislative achievement with the Democratic Congress. In the end, Eisenhower got what he wanted without provoking political wrangling in Congress or politicizing the issue of space.[28]

More Consolidation at NASA

On October 1, 1958, NASA officially began operation, absorbing the NACA, which ended its existence on September 30. The Pentagon gave NASA jurisdiction over a number of projects, including scientific satellites and lunar probes. One year later, NASA acquired Project Vanguard and Cal

Tech's Jet Propulsion Laboratory. On October 21, 1959, Eisenhower interrupted a vacation to announce that he would transfer the ABMA to NASA. NASA absorbed the ABMA in its entirety, keeping the Huntsville group of more than five thousand intact. By 1960, NASA had sixteen thousand employees, up from its nucleus of eight thousand NACA workers.[29]

NASA's absorption of the ABMA was controversial, and ABMA personnel bitterly resisted it. "I rose up in wrath," Medaris later wrote, at the thought of surrendering the von Braun team. Von Braun once pounded a table with his fist and said he would fight to keep all five thousand ABMA jobs, down to the last floor sweeper. But by moving ABMA, Eisenhower ended confusion over control of the new civilian Saturn super-booster project, which was civilian in nature, and made clear that NASA would control long-term space projects. In effect, he erected fences to confine the military's space activities. The Air Force remained in charge of military space rockets, and the Army controlled only short-range missiles for military use.[30]

NASA enhanced Eisenhower's desire for order by consolidating the mishmash of space-related projects and organs. His satisfaction with NASA led him to write that it compiled "a splendid record" in space exploration. Its creation gave direction to a confusing welter of competing programs and solved the American space program's great flaw: that it was a fragmented, blurry government effort lacking resources and goals. For example, NASA consolidated moon projects. Before NASA, the ABMA had planned to use a Jupiter C rocket to circumnavigate the moon in the fall of 1958, while the Air Force had its own plan, hoping to hit the moon with a payload in mid-1959. By initiating Project Apollo in 1960, NASA set a clearer moon goal, aiming at a manned lunar orbit and later a manned lunar landing.[31]

Within the government, NASA won the space race, while the Defense Department lost. Although the Pentagon still had a space program for military uses, NASA's creation ended the military's aspirations to lead America's space efforts and made the entire program more transparent.[32] A civilian agency, open to media scrutiny and committed to publicizing its activities, provided a propaganda coup for America by its contrast with the Soviet Union's secretive space program, which was closely intertwined with its military. NASA's civilian flavor embodied the tenets of a democratic society. In the years to come, NASA launches—failures and successes both—attracted searching reappraisals and candid media coverage and disclosures. Blastoffs became tourist attractions along Florida's "Space Coast" near Cape Canaveral, and crowds gathered on beaches to watch spacecraft begin their journeys. These events represented more than a government agency engaged in scientific endeavor; in a real sense, they symbolized a people's way of life.

 CHAPTER 11

Defeat and a SCORE

The year 1958 proved an active one for legislation. In August, the president signed the Defense Reorganization Act, legislation that he believed would lead to a more efficient Pentagon and reduce interservice rivalries. The new law increased the defense secretary's and Joint Chiefs of Staff's authority while preserving the individual services' independence. It also created a new post, the director of defense research and engineering, who would oversee all Defense Department research and engineering; Herbert York of the ARPA filled the post. Although Eisenhower invested much personal time and effort in overcoming congressional resistance to his proposed reorganization, the end result was disappointing, for the act failed to reduce interservice bickering and military lobbying on Capitol Hill, as he hoped it would.[1]

The summer of 1958 was active for other reasons as well. It marked the only time in Eisenhower's presidency that he sent troops abroad with the possibility of engaging them in combat. In July, he ordered American marines to Lebanon to maintain order, after pro-Western president Camille Chamoun appealed for U.S. help when he feared political opponents might topple his government. Eisenhower wanted to protect Persian Gulf oil and maintain America's image, but he also wished to avoid war. Still, he liked to say, "Every once in a while, though, in the history of a country, you do have the misfortune of getting into a war. And if that misfortune ever befalls you, there's only one thing you must never do. That is to lose. You cannot lose." To ensure military success, he employed overwhelming force. He sent more than fourteen thousand troops to Lebanon, a swift and convincing exertion of power. To reach a political settlement, Eisenhower sent deputy undersecretary of state Robert Murphy, who forged an agreement that helped to stabilize Lebanon, allowing Eisenhower to withdraw the troops after three months. Although only one U.S. soldier was killed during the intervention, the crisis convinced the Eisenhower administration that it could not confuse communism—which the president mistakenly labeled as the source of instability in Lebanon—with Arab nationalism. Thereafter, it attempted to cooperate more through foreign aid, for example, sending Egypt $153 million in food assistance.[2]

For Eisenhower, the most nettlesome problem of 1958—because it took the greatest personal toll on him—involved Sherman Adams. A House subcommittee began to investigate the president's chief of staff for accepting gifts from New England industrialist Bernard Goldfine, checking whether Adams made inquiries with federal agencies on Goldfine's behalf. The gifts formed a motley assortment: a vicuna coat, a Persian rug, and hotel accommodations. Adams seldom wore the odd-looking coat, and Arthur Larson suspected that Democrats only sought a political controversy to weaken the president. Perhaps, too, they wanted revenge for Republican charges of corruption during Truman's presidency, which included incidents where administration members—including First Lady Bess Truman—accepted mink coats from a Reconstruction Finance Corporation officer who sought special White House consideration.[3]

But Adams's brusque behavior had earned him a bevy of enemies from both parties. A hard-bitten, rugged man who had worked eighteen years for a New Hampshire lumber company, Adams dispensed with courtesies and came across as rude. Larson recalled receiving a phone call from him in which Adams said neither hello nor goodbye. "Where's Jim?" he asked, meaning secretary of labor James Mitchell. When Larson replied that he was in San Francisco, Adams simply hung up. Larson described him as a "human-relations version of a completely stripped-down racing car, from which every non-functional ornament had been ruthlessly torn." Even Eisenhower felt the frigid blast of Adams's behavior. When he presented his chief of staff with a portrait that he had painted of him, Adams simply remarked, "Mr. President, thank you, but I think you flattered me," and then walked away. In recalling Adams's gruff telephone behavior, Eisenhower said, "You know, he hung up on me once."[4]

After years of tactlessness, Adams found few friends in Washington willing to pull him back from the fire, and politicians and the media preferred to see him burn. When they called for his resignation, Eisenhower protested, "I need him," but the anti-Adams groundswell proved too much. In August, he quit. The scandal marked one of many weaknesses Eisenhower suffered heading into the 1958 midterm elections. Space was an additional worry.[5]

"Sputnik Syndrome" and Midterm Disaster

Even though Explorer, Vanguard, and NASA's founding had established the Eisenhower administration's momentum on space in 1958, politicians continued to capitalize on what they decried as the U.S. lag behind the Soviet Union. In August, House majority leader John McCormack said, "I don't want to catch up with the Russians. I want to get ahead of 'em. We have the facilities and the brains. What we need now is leadership." For Democrats, space provided a welcome distraction from the divisive issue of civil rights, which began to split the party in the South. One Democratic senator joked, "Little Rock is now just a place that Sputnik flies over."[6]

But in truth, as months passed, space lost its grip on the public imagination. By September 1958, a Gallup poll found that less than 1 percent of Americans believed that space issues and Sputnik constituted the nation's "most important problem." (Peace, communism, relations with Russia, integration and segregation, and the economy all registered higher numbers.)[7] *Time* sarcastically described a "Sputnik Syndrome" that "afflicted many who should know better" and was "characterized by whirling satellites before the eyes, by alternating periods of deepest gloom and wildest premonitions of impending doom, and by the steadfast conviction that the U.S., helplessly and hopelessly, is falling behind the U.S.S.R. in military technology." The phenomenon afflicted politicians more than the public. Indeed, a salient show of Sputnik Syndrome, *Time* wrote, came from Senator John Kennedy of Massachusetts, who warned that "soon we will be the underdog." In August, he charged that the Eisenhower administration "tailored our strategy and military requirements to fit our budget—instead of fitting our budget to our military requirements and strategy." Kennedy rejected Eisenhower's stress on the economy as a country's true measure of strength, charging that "during the period when emphasis was laid upon our economic strength instead of our military strength, we were losing the decisive years when we could have maintained a lead against the Soviet Union in our missile capacity." The U.S. "missile-lag," which was "another symptom of our national complacency," he warned, would shift the balance of world power toward the Soviet Union.[8]

The Sputnik Syndrome afflicted media outlets, too, which made Cassandra-like charges. "Today the Russians have achieved substantial superiority in the field of intercontinental missiles," *Commonweal* wrote. "Although U.S. scientists are trying hard to narrow this gap between U.S. and Soviet capabilities, the five-year period from 1960 on will be one of maximum peril for the free world." Sputnik's first-year anniversary also provided an occasion for the Soviets to chortle at American space efforts. One Russian scientist called U.S. satellites small, "unripe lemons."[9]

But one year made a big difference. In numbers, the United States had pulled ahead of the Soviet Union in the space race. America had launched four satellites, three of which were still in orbit. The Soviet Union had put three satellites in orbit, only one of which remained aloft. Although the Soviet satellites were heavier, America's had more advanced instruments and collected valuable scientific data. Even failures were successful. An example was the Pioneer satellite, which the United States launched on October 11, 1958. It shot for the moon, literally, aiming to make a lunar flyby, but it fell far short, traveling only 71,300 miles out (the moon is 240,000 miles from the earth). Yet the Air Force, which guided the Pioneer project, put a positive spin on the failure. Pioneer flew farther than any Soviet vehicle, and it gave scientists the first readings of magnetic fields among planets and a better idea of the shape of the earth's magnetic field. Campaigning for Republicans in San Francisco, Vice President Nixon said that Pioneer made the Democrats "deader than poor little Laika" for the midterm elections because they were "fresh out" of issues.[10]

But Nixon was wrong, and even though Eisenhower admitted that he did not "care too much about the congressional elections," by mid-October he had to hit the campaign trail for Republicans. In Baltimore, he railed against "extremists" who "wanted to indulge in wholesale reckless Federal spending." Their effort, he said, "was blocked both by sturdy Republican opposition and by my vetoes." He declared, "In satellites, sputniks have been matched by Explorers, Vanguards, and Pioneers." More important to Eisenhower, the "sputnik issue" led Democrats to charge that "our technology and our missile programs lagged woefully behind [those of] the Soviets." False, Eisenhower countered, saying, "Today . . . hundreds of millions [of dollars] go into missile programs annually."[11]

But Eisenhower's meager appearances betrayed how little he cared for the midterms. He campaigned only in six states, and belatedly; meanwhile, critics lambasted him. In late October, speaking in New Castle, Pennsylvania, former president Harry Truman said that the administration "is now claiming that the recession is over. It does not look like it is over in Pennsylvania, with . . . over 400,000 unemployed. It does not look like it is over in the rest of the country, with farm prices down and business failures up and some 5 million people unemployed."[12]

Eisenhower had been lucky enough after the 1952 elections to have a Republican Congress storm into Washington on his coattails, albeit with precarious margins—just 221–214 in the House and 48–47 in the Senate (with one independent). It did not last long. The Democrats regained control of Congress after the 1954 midterms, and at a cabinet meeting after the elections, the mood was gloomy. In an odd move, Vice President Nixon pulled out a toy drummer boy, wound it up, and let it march on the cabinet table, as he urged, "We've got to keep beating the drum about our achievements."[13] Yet midterm elections historically meant bad news for the party holding the White House, especially in a weak economy, and 1958 proved no exception. The Republicans endured a terrible thrashing, as Democrats picked up forty-nine seats in the House and seventeen in the Senate. The Democratic lead in the Senate grew to 64–34. In the House, the Democrats' advantage leapt from 234–201 to 282–154. Eisenhower worried that he might lack the votes to sustain vetoes. Democrats also picked up five new governorships. In a stinging rebuke, even Kansas, Eisenhower's home state and a perennial GOP stronghold, now had a Democratic governor.[14]

Republican losses in the Senate were especially seismic because northern and western senators gained more leverage at the expense of southern Democrats, whom Eisenhower liked personally and relied on to cut deals and reach compromises. Northern and Midwestern Democrats like John Kennedy and Hubert Humphrey, both of whom wanted the 1960 presidential nomination, were more liberal than their southern counterparts and feisty about challenging Eisenhower. And Republican Senate giants tumbled to defeat. John Bricker, the deeply conservative 1944 GOP vice presidential nominee, lost his reelection bid in Ohio and retired from politics. Former majority leader William Knowland of California, who gave up his seat to run for California governor, lost his race to Edmund "Pat" Brown.[15]

Gerald Ford acknowledged that the GOP "took a terrible licking" in the 1958 midterms. In addition to the recession, Ford believed that "the old and tired image that the party was projecting" caused the disaster at the polls. For the last two years of his presidency, Eisenhower would face an energetic Congress and the greatest opposition on Capitol Hill that any president had yet faced in the twentieth century. Democrats in the new Congress wanted to spend money—precisely what Ike disliked. Congress was also to have two new committees, the Senate Committee on Aeronautical and Space

Sciences and the House Committee on Science and Astronautics, both ready to monitor the administration's support for space.[16]

Eisenhower learned an important truth in politics: even presidents who won landslides (like FDR in 1938, and later, Lyndon Johnson in 1964 and Ronald Reagan in 1984) could endure scalding midterm losses during their second terms. The results put Eisenhower in a grumpy mood. The day after the disaster, he walked into the Oval Office and muttered, "Pretty bad, wasn't it?" Angrily, he vowed, "I'm going to go on the attack . . . [and] relate every bit of legislation from now on to the pocketbook of the individual Americans. I'm going to put a price tag on everything." As usual, he contained his anger when he faced the press later that day. Still, he appeared defiant, inveighing against "the spender-wing of the Democratic Party" and labeling them "a radical group," warning, "I believe that that kind of spending must stop or the United States is in the most serious trouble that we can think of." He pledged that "for the next 2 years, the Lord sparing me, I am going to fight this as hard as I know how."[17]

 A SCORE

Late in November, the bad news continued for Eisenhower when Khrushchev, acting more aggressively since Sputnik, issued his famous ultimatum on Berlin. If the West failed to reach a solution on the city within six months, he declared, the Soviet Union would sign a peace treaty with East Germany, thus leaving West Berlin—embedded 110 miles within that country—even more isolated and hard to defend.[18]

Things were going so badly that Eisenhower later called the year 1958 the worst of his life. Ironically, it was space—so hurtful to his image in 1957—that ended the year on a high note. After Pioneer I, the United States tried twice more during the fall of 1958 to reach the moon with a rocket. Both efforts failed. Pioneer II, launched November 8, reached only 7,500 miles. On December 8, Pioneer III rose to 66,654 miles. But the U.S. space program had touted its contributions to science rather than propaganda, and Pioneer III stayed true to this theme. Although it fell ignominiously to earth, it made the significant discovery that the Van Allen belt actually comprised two belts, making the rocket another successful failure.[19]

Then came a top-secret project that achieved unqualified success. Every one of the eighty-eight persons involved in it had to keep silent, including the president. Just a few weeks before Christmas 1958, a small group of

Army Signal Corps technicians entered the Oval Office to tape-record a greeting from Eisenhower that he had personally composed, a message of peace to the world. He then waited until he learned whether the project succeeded or failed.

The project was called SCORE (Signal Communication by Orbiting Relay), and it was born after the Soviet Union's May 1958 launch of Sputnik III. At the time, ARPA director Roy Johnson was worried. Sensitive to public relations from his work at General Electric, he wanted an American space feat to bolster the country's image. "We've got to get something big up," he urged. Jim Dempsey, who directed the Atlas ICBM program, suggested a novel idea: instead of putting just a satellite into orbit, the United States could place the entire Atlas rocket in orbit.[20]

Now more attuned to prestige projects, Eisenhower liked this concept and approved it in August. But he insisted on secrecy. America could not risk the embarrassment of the Atlas rocket-satellite combination failing with the world as an audience. If anyone leaked word of the project, Eisenhower warned, he would cancel it. He wanted to reveal the master stroke only after it was successfully in orbit. At Cape Canaveral, as NASA prepared the vehicle for launch, only ten people of the hundreds working on it knew the vehicle's true nature.[21]

On December 18, 1958, NASA launched the Atlas, which became the largest object man had ever put into orbit, at 85 feet long, 10 feet in diameter, and 8,600 pounds, with 200 pounds of instruments; it was akin to lofting two buses into orbit. While hosting a White House state dinner, Eisenhower received word that SCORE achieved orbit, and he dramatically asked for the guests' attention. Beaming, he said, "Ladies and gentleman, I have something interesting to announce. I have just been advised that a satellite is in orbit and that its weight is nearly 9,000 pounds."[22]

On December 20, SCORE sent out the president's tape-recorded Christmas greeting, marking the first time that a human voice emanated via radio transmission from space. "My message is a simple one," Ike's voice said. "Through this unique means I convey to you and to all mankind America's wish for peace on earth and good will toward men everywhere." By modern standards, it was a crude communication. The sound quality was poor, static crackled over Ike's voice, and most Americans heard it through radio rebroadcasts rather than directly from the satellite.[23]

But Eisenhower was pleased. Listening to the recording with White House reporters, he remarked, "That's one of the astounding things again in this age of invention. Maybe the next thing they'll do is televise pictures down here." Moreover, as he had wished, every person involved with SCORE's progress kept it secret, and the president had frozen out all those he wished to exclude—the media, Congress, ABMA, the Pentagon, and all the services.[24]

SCORE also showcased a high-priority Eisenhower project, the Atlas ICBM, demonstrating its strength and use as a satellite booster. Up to this time, the Soviet Union had far outdone the United States in instrument payload weight. Its heaviest payload to date, within Sputnik III, was 2,925 pounds, while America's heaviest had barely exceeded the thirty-pound range. But SCORE's total weight was 8,750 pounds, even greater than Sputnik III's total 7,000 pounds.[25] The feat demonstrated what the United States could do using an ICBM rocket—as the Soviet Union had been doing all along—instead of an IRBM rocket. The launch inaugurated Atlas's service as a space booster, which lasted until its retirement in 2005. Over the years, the rocket sent countless military and civilian missions into space and received notable publicity in 1962 when it propelled astronaut John Glenn into orbit.[26]

Atlas also gave the United States some space race heft. With Pioneer launches and SCORE's success, by December 1958, *U.S. News and World Report* wrote, "The U.S. has rocketed far out in front in the space-missile competition."[27] For Eisenhower, the triumphs helped to wash away some of the bitter aftertaste of the midterm elections. They marked a precursor to his bolder space projects. They also showed his belated but incremental awakening to the link between space and world prestige.

 CHAPTER 12

Priorities and Prestige

Throughout his life, Eisenhower seemed to command respect, and he realized that respect translated into power. He learned this lesson early. As a small boy, when he tried to enter a barn on his uncle's farm, a goose chased him away. Only by brandishing a broomstick could he make the animal back down. The incident taught him that adversaries respected strength, and an episode at school reinforced the idea. A bully attached a bolt to a rope and, threatening to swing the weapon, challenged other children to defy him. Young Eisenhower jumped out and disarmed the bully. Thereafter, classmates regarded Ike as a kind of police officer, and if a playground problem arose, they ran to him, crying "Ike! Ike!"

Eisenhower enjoyed similar respect as an adult. In 1940, while serving as the commanding officer at Fort Lewis in Washington State, he learned that two privates had bickered and brawled, and he conjured up a unique punishment. The two men had to wash windows together, one on the outside of the building, the other inside. At first, the privates glared balefully at each other through the glass, but by day's end, cooperation and familiarity had softened their anger, and they were laughing and making playful faces through the windows. Word of the incident spread around the camp, and it deepened respect for Eisenhower; the men there knew they had a shrewd yet humane commander. (The men's fascination with Eisenhower grew greater after they learned that, while inspecting the camp's kitchen, he grabbed some raw beef and a slice of uncooked onion and wolfed them down.)[1]

As a war hero and president, Eisenhower enjoyed enormous respect and goodwill worldwide, and he wanted to deploy those assets to promote world peace and enhance America's reputation. "Such prestige and standing as I have on the earth, I want to use it," he vowed. Throughout his presidency, he also faced a question of how best to enhance his country's image. A pressing issue was whether space exploits could do so.[2]

"Muted Enthusiasm"

Eisenhower faced heavy demands to increase spending on space. The new House Select Committee on Astronautics and Space Exploration said that "failure to take account of [space capabilities] would virtually be to choose the path of national extinction." The pressure even came from Ike's inner circle. In 1959, new science advisor George Kistiakowsky warned Eisenhower that if NASA administrator Glennan failed to advance space activities aggressively enough, the Pentagon would take up the slack.[3]

Caryl Haskins remembered that "Eisenhower's interest in the space program was high." But Haskins observed that the president's enthusiasm for space "was muted by at least two factors—Eisenhower's chronic fear and suspicion of the 'military-industrial complex' . . . and his habitual underplaying of his own knowledge and interests in many fields." Haskins added, "Certainly, my recollection of long sessions with him on behalf of the President's Science Advisory Committee left me in little doubt of either his comprehension or his will in the field, or of his (muted) enthusiasm." A third factor tended to suppress the president's interest: the limited military applications for space. Eisenhower "did not see that there was all that much in the way of a military promise for the space program," David Beckler recalled, and maintaining sufficient defenses was his prime pursuit.[4]

Certainly, Eisenhower showed curiosity about space and satellites and asked perceptive questions. At a 1958 NSC meeting, after listening to a presentation from Edward Purcell on space exploration, Eisenhower asked the scientist whether other planets rotated on their axes as earth did. In discussing reconnaissance satellites with Alan Waterman, he asked whether one side of the vessel had to face the earth; it did, the scientist confirmed. Certain space projects piqued the president's interest. In December 1960, when the carrier *Valley Forge* retrieved a space capsule from the ocean, Glennan reported the news to Eisenhower. "He seemed quite excited about it," Glennan wrote.[5] Eisenhower wanted projects—such as sending men into space—that would "encourage and hearten" Americans while making scientific advances, especially those benefiting the military. Goodpaster recalled that after Sputnik and his talks with scientists, Eisenhower "was prepared to see an orderly, substantial space program."[6]

Eisenhower also showed more interest in space than his Soviet counterpart. Although technology fascinated Khrushchev, who visited factories to watch machines at work, he had opposed a rocket research center, explaining, "Rockets are the weapons of imperialist aggressors, not the weapons of the peace-loving U.S.S.R." Before Sputnik, Khrushchev had seen satellites as boondoggles. Although he came to value them for propaganda, he never appreciated their scientific contributions or attended launches. He isolated rocket engineer Sergei Kovolev from contact with foreign scientists, a move that stifled the program's growth. Sporadic, spectacular space shots pleased Khrushchev enough, even if their scientific harvest proved minor.[7]

Khrushchev also saw space as a race, as did some American officials. In 1959, when asked about America's space program, John Medaris leaned forward over his desk and said intently, "The first thing this country has to do is to make up its mind whether it is in a space race with Russia or not. It is my personal opinion that we are stupid if we don't make a race out of it." That was a critical point. Glennan said that the administration had to decide whether to regard the space endeavor as a "race" with the Soviets or as just a scientific venture. If space was solely a scientific affair, then it needed only half the budget of a race. Kistiakowsky argued that it should be a scientific endeavor, because a race would drain resources and stifle achievement in other technological areas. Eisenhower, too, believed that the chief reason for space exploration was to advance science. Rather than try to match each Soviet achievement, he preferred to develop America's own space objectives and emphasize scientific inquiry.[8]

According to Goodpaster, Eisenhower "supported an ongoing, serious scientific program at a reasonable rate and did not want to be drawn into having that characterized as a race," and he backed space projects bearing reasonable price tags. At one White House meeting, Eisenhower said that he was amenable to a lunar probe if it could be done with missiles already developed or nearly ready, so as to minimize costs. Even during an election year, when political motives were heightened, Eisenhower concentrated on space's scientific importance. At a February 1960 press conference, he explained, "The reason for going into space, except for those activities that are carried on by the Defense Department as having some value to the security of the country, is purely scientific. Therefore, you are not talking about racing [the Soviets or] . . . naming the particular course you are going to run in this race; you work out a proper and an appropriate plan of scientific exploration and you follow it positively."[9]

Ultimately, Eisenhower "was not convinced that space would become all that important," Killian recalled. He complained about Americans who were "obsessed with space" instead of fixing problems on earth. Serving his final term as president, Eisenhower was also insulated from political pressures to see space as a political instrument for reelection. By contrast, Vice President Nixon, gearing up for a 1960 White House run, argued for space's political impact, even though he was uncertain whether space offered great scientific benefits.[10]

An administration adviser who recognized the political and international implications of space, Special Assistant to the President Karl G. Harr, called it "a welcome escape" from Cold War crises. "I believe that the whole world feels the dramatic implications of our arrival into the space age," Harr opined. "It is not just American kids who go around in space helmets, counting down, blasting off and talking of orbit, moon shots, etc." Writing in October 1958, Harr wanted "firmly to commit the U.S. and the personal prestige of the President to the basic principles involved in this world's entry into outer space." No one but the president "can speak with the same conviction on a fundamental question of this kind." Warning against "anything that appears to be niggardly or haggling," Harr called on the president to make a specific proposal, accompanied by "a ringing title or slogan," that would establish America's space leadership. Harr urged the president, "I feel strongly that the question of outer space is of such importance to all the peoples of the world that we cannot afford to lose the initiative in this field." Harr tried again the next month, proposing that Eisenhower address the UN General Assembly to propose that all nations reserve space for peaceful purposes and renounce any propriety ambitions for space, moons, and planets. Harr also wanted the president to invite other nations to explore space jointly with the United States.[11]

Eisenhower never pursued Harr's suggestions, reflecting his muted enthusiasm for space and his conservative views generally, which led him to eschew the flamboyant. By taking this perspective, he failed to give attention to the psychological and political aspects of space and its impact on world prestige. That shortcoming reflected his undramatic sense of leadership. During World War II, he had only a flaccid definition of leadership, calling it "pulling a piece of spaghetti across a plate instead of trying to push it." It showed his preference for solid results and the best return on government money. Nixon said of Eisenhower that "when it came to making a final decision, he was the coldest, most unemotional and analytical man in the world." He had little use for gimmicks or showmanship, which evoked visceral, emotional responses that defied analysis. Eisenhower's perspective also reflected his scale of priorities, which differed from those of Nixon, Harr, Larson, and other advisors who urged more positive publicity on space.[12]

Priorities

Nine months before Sputnik, while delivering his 1957 State of the Union address, Eisenhower spoke of America's willingness to enter into an agreement to "control the outerspace missile and satellite development." Goodpaster recalled that Eisenhower "gave close attention, going back quite a number of years, to space in the sense of the passage through space of some of the more advanced weapons, and specifically the long-range ballistic missiles." But Goodpaster emphasized that "he wanted to keep these two things [scientific space exploration and space for military purposes] separate."[13]

That distinction spoke volumes about Eisenhower's priorities. He discriminated between missiles for defense and rockets for space, and the former took priority. As he explained to reporters after Sputnik, the ICBM and IRBM programs were "the top priority within the Government . . . a priority which was never accorded to the satellite program." Although science sparked his interest, it remained subordinate to national security. In early 1958, when PSAC presented its landmark "Introduction to Outer Space" report elucidating four reasons for a space program, Eisenhower nodded his head when he heard the first reason, military and defense. For missiles, by early 1958, he approved the following priorities, in order, for research and development: first, the Atlas ICBM weapon system, followed by the Titan ICBM, the Thor–Jupiter IRBM, the Polaris missile, a missile defense system, and early warning defense; next, the Vanguard and Jupiter C programs for the IGY; and then other satellite programs. At an October 1959 meeting with McElroy, Glennan, and Kistiakowsky, he voiced his top three priorities for space: military needs, then superbooster development, and then science.[14]

For a president, priorities are critical. No president can do everything, so he must exercise judgment as to what Americans need, what the nation can afford, and what the federal government can accomplish. For more self-aggrandizing reasons, he must also set his sights on his legacy and focus on fulfilling it within at most eight years. Eisenhower concentrated first on foreign policy and military affairs, and he "gave lowest priority to and was least liberal in the realm of domestic affairs," Larson recalled. Even during the post-Sputnik clamor, Eisenhower viewed the problem more from a military rather than space angle, writing that the concerns that "seem to be disturbing the country so much" related to "our relative position with Russian in arms development," failing to mention space or satellites.[15] Space never topped Eisenhower's priority list, and sometimes, it failed to make the list at all. In June 1958, he wrote of "the things that seem constantly on my mind," enumerating ten items. He cited Lebanon, Cyprus, France, Indonesia, defense reorganization, mutual trade renewal, mutual aid appropriations, economic recovery, Governor Adams, and racial relations. Space failed to appear. He devoted more time to national security than to space: whereas his chairing of Space Council meetings was erratic, he attended more than 90 percent of National Security Council sessions.[16]

Eisenhower "was not at all enamored of going ahead in a major way in space. . . . [H]e was, I would say, very conservative when it came to what we did in space," recalled Robert Seamans. On occasion, the president minimized space endeavors when compared with other pursuits. He told a group of five hundred exchange teachers, "We shall not be serving mankind well if we become obsessed with just the business of putting new satellites into orbit—so obsessed that we overlook the fact that we have some real problems left right here on earth."[17]

Repeatedly, Eisenhower stressed that the United States could not beat the Soviet Union at everything, nor should it try. Instead, it had to select areas where it wanted to compete and prevail in them. "We should not try to excel in everything," he urged. He advised concentrating on one or two space projects representing the best use of federal money and having the most scientific impact. Worried that the United States might "scatter our effort across the board," he favored a gradual curve of space project growth, even if that meant no attention-grabbing feats. For attracting world attention, he favored safer projects that promoted peace, such as a nuclear-powered peace vehicle, which he proposed but Congress rejected. If it were a race, Eisenhower wanted America to take the role of the tortoise and let the Soviet Union be the hare.[18]

On the president's scale of priorities, federal projects that built infrastructure and generated economic activity ranked high, which reflected his preference for investment rather than "spending for spending's sake." He urged, "It must always be borne in mind that we grow only by investing more and producing more, not simply by spending more." Like a building's foundation, such projects would allow further growth and promote prosperity. Thus, he supported initiatives like urban renewal, school and hospital construction, and road and highway improvement, where government spending was a more productive investment, he believed. Over time, they brought more benefits, and millions of citizens reaped the rewards—unlike the relatively small number of Americans who might travel in space, let alone go to the moon.[19]

Eisenhower's Interstate Highway System project, which he unveiled in February 1955, fit his concept of using federal money effectively. For decades he had yearned for better roads. In 1919, he had joined an army team that traveled from the West Coast to Washington, surveying America's highways. The journey, which lasted a month, convinced Eisenhower that the nation's roads were in sad shape, and during World War II, he looked enviously at Germany's autobahn. "The Interstate Highway System was dear to his heart," Roemer McPhee recalled. He hoped that such a massive public works project would stimulate the economy and stave off recessions. Improving the nation's roads brought other benefits, from promoting tourism to improving safety to saving on vehicle wear. Better roads also bolstered national defense by allowing quick emergency evacuation of cities and permitting military vehicles to move. The hidden costs of inadequate roads included higher insurance premiums, greater fuel use, and lost time. Thus, the president declared that "the interstate system must be given top priority in construction planning."[20]

Other infrastructure projects ranked as Eisenhower's priorities. In January 1958, he approved a site in Virginia to construct an international airport to service the Washington, D.C., area; in 1962, he attended the ceremony at which President Kennedy dedicated the new Dulles International Airport, named after Eisenhower's secretary of state. Eisenhower also wanted to expand the St. Lawrence Seaway to give large, oceangoing ships access to America's heartland. It would boost economic activity and strengthen national security, he noted, since Canadian iron ore—critical for weapons and wartime vehicle production—made its way to American steel mills via the St. Lawrence Seaway. In 1954 Congress approved the project, which was completed five years later, enabling ships more than seven hundred feet in length to gain access to inland port cities along the Great Lakes.[21]

As ever, the budget and economy influenced Eisenhower's concerns. Goodpaster recorded, "The President stressed that we must think of the maintenance of a sound economy as well as the desirability of all these projects. He thought perhaps NASA sights are being set too high, including too many speculative projects." When Hugh Dryden raised the idea of accelerating a moon shot to achieve it in 1960 instead of 1961 or 1962, Eisenhower—desiring balance—asked whether other, less important projects might be slowed down in exchange for the acceleration. Eisenhower concluded the meeting by repeating his favorite maxim. He wanted to consider, as the meeting notes recorded, "what is best for the United States from an over-all standpoint—that we must balance measures of fiscal soundness against extra measures in [space]. In the present circumstances, he felt we must lay more stress on not going into debt by spending beyond our receipts. At the same time, the relationship of the program to the Soviet rate of advance must be clearly recognized."[22]

Eisenhower said he wanted to avoid the danger of space spending "growing and growing with no foreseeable limit. Instead, we should try to find a level that seems about right." Once Eisenhower stated that he wanted NASA's budget to stay under half a billion a year. At a December 1960 cabinet meeting at which Glennan and Kistiakowsky discussed NASA's budget, Eisenhower wrapped up the discussion by asking, "Can anybody tell me what is the best space program for $1 billion?" Such an amount was too parsimonious, and he soon reconsidered. But he kept NASA's budget below 1 percent of all federal expenditures, in contrast to Kennedy and Johnson; by 1965, at a time when Eisenhower believed NASA's budget should be $2 billion per year, it already exceeded $5 billion and represented more than 5 percent of all federal expenditures.[23]

Senator Richard Russell charged that the United States trailed the Soviet Union in space because Eisenhower neglected to give space "the priority it should have." Yet Eisenhower refused to relent, and fellow budget hawks endorsed his approach. Congressman Gerald Ford praised Eisenhower "for his fight against inflation and his realization that deficit spending inevitably reduces the value of the dollar." Ford continued, "I am particularly impressed that the budget has not been balanced at the expense of essentials. It recommends a sound program for improving our defense posture and for moving ahead with our space and research activities." More money would not accelerate developments. Glennan stressed that the United States would bridge the gap in rocket thrust in two to four years, but a crash program would not help, "even if we spend $100 million a year," he said.[24]

Some media favored Eisenhower's low enthusiasm for moon shots and other space spectaculars. While the *Wall Street Journal* conceded that the United States could be trailing the Soviet Union in rocket propulsion, it reminded readers that the government had to make wise financial choices, reasoning, "It is a question of allocation, not of blind spending for the sake of performing stunts in space." The *Journal* also drew a distinction between "space science and space stunts." Cautioning that "the resources of this rich country are not unlimited, abroad or at home," the *Journal* urged fitting space projects to the country's resources and needs rather than "aping the enemy." The *Journal* agreed with Eisenhower's perspective that "a thriving American economy" would create "far more prestige in the world than any particular space exploit."[25]

Writing in *U.S. News and World Report*, conservative David Lawrence editorialized that a space race against Russia "makes little sense." Although the Sputniks "threw us off our course and started a wave of spending in Congress," Lawrence hoped that new Soviet satellites would not "open the floodgates to more indiscriminate expenditures for the spinning of metal balls in orbit around the sun or the moon." Criticizing members of Congress for viewing the space race "as a gripping matter deserving priority above all else," he said instead, "The most important task for our legislators today is to conserve the economic strength of the United States of America."[26]

Eisenhower espoused such beliefs into his retirement. In 1962, he castigated the Kennedy administration's challenge to land men on the moon. Eisenhower warned against trying "to win a stunt race" and added, "If we must compete with Soviet Russia for world 'prestige,' why not channel the struggle more along the lines in which we excel?" He asked to measure "some other items in this 'prestige' race: our unique industrial accomplishments, our cars for almost everybody instead of just the favored few, our remarkable agricultural productivity, our supermarkets loaded with a profusion of appetizing foods. Let's ask the world: 'What has Soviet Russia or Red China got to compare with these achievements?' "[27]

Only an American like Eisenhower, who had lived overseas as much as he had—including in France, England, and the Philippines—could have written such words, appreciating the diversity and abundance of consumer riches available in the United States compared with foreign nations. Yet on the international stage, the problem with such "soft power" displays was that they lacked drama and the ability to captivate. Far from evoking emotional responses, statistics on goods and services had a soporific effect. Reliable roads and sound seaways, resplendent grocery stores, vaccinations for polio and other diseases, and foreign student exchange programs—all of which Eisenhower advocated—bore eloquent testimony to the American system, but they seldom splashed onto headlines or won instant international admiration. Even America's impressive scientific space discoveries, such as the Van Allen radiation belts, failed to burn brightly in world opinion. During the 1960 presidential campaign, the Democratic Advisory Council acknowledged America's scientific achievements in space. But it noted, "Unfortunately, from the standpoint of U.S. prestige, these accomplishments are not readily appreciated by the layman nor is it easy to translate them into readily understood form."[28]

As president, Kennedy argued this point to science advisor Jerome Wiesner when he considered whether to support a manned lunar landing to bolster U.S. prestige. "Well, it's your fault," Kennedy said. "If you had a scientific spectacular on this earth that would be more useful—say desalting the ocean—or something that is just as dramatic and convincing as space, then we would do it." The two men discussed options to demonstrate American power, such as nation building, but their conversation returned to the space race because of its drama and hard power overtones. "I think he became convinced that space was the symbol of the twentieth century," Wiesner said. "It was a decision he made cold bloodedly. He thought it was right for the country." Much of the rationale for this objective was to bolster America's world standing.[29]

The Prestige Race

Prestige has been a factor motivating nations to explore, expand, and send citizens to the earth's far reaches. Prestige was a form of power. During the fifteenth and sixteenth centuries, Portugal and Spain competed with each other to explore and colonize the world, their intrepid voyages helping them to reign as global superpowers. In the United States, the nineteenth-century "Manifest Destiny" ideal saw continental expansion as a means to vault the country into the upper echelons of world nations. By the late 1800s, Britain, France, Russia, and the United States raced to grab colonies worldwide. The drive for prestige even accrued some tangible benefits for the powers of the era, as new colonies expanded trade and opened opportunities for business (while also inciting the nightmare of colonial oppression). Heroic exploits enhanced national standing, too. The Wright brothers' flight coincided with America's emergence as a world economic and military power. Four years before Sputnik, New Zealand treated Edmund Hillary as a national hero when he and Sherpa guide Tenzing Norgay became the first men to scale Mount Everest.

As a military man, Eisenhower knew about prestige. Winning war bestowed honor on an army and a nation, and image also played a part in wartime strategy. During World War II's closing days, Eisenhower argued against dropping the atomic bomb on Japan because the weapon would slaughter the Japanese when they appeared ready to surrender and would also scar

America's image. In 1954, Eisenhower refused to send U.S. troops to help the French in Indochina because, as Secretary of State Dulles said, the country could "not afford to send its flag and its own military establishment and thus to engage the prestige of the United States" if it could not win.[30]

Eisenhower preferred stature based on economic strength, and he admired major industries such as automobile manufacturing that became twentieth-century sources of world attention, national pride, and jobs. The Bretton Woods System, established in 1944, enshrined the dollar as the world's standard currency, lending the United States enormous prestige. After World War II, America stood as the world's peacekeeper but also became the guarantor of the international economic system, a role no nation had played after World War I, dooming the planet to suffer another world war.

Prestige involved a grand form of psychological warfare, and Eisenhower recognized its Cold War importance, closely tracking surveys measuring foreign opinion of him. He once remarked that psychology was as important as technology, adding that "at times appearances are as significant as the reality, if not more so." He wanted to counter Soviet propaganda, especially through agencies such as the USIA and the Operations Coordinating Board, which he created early in his administration to wage psychological warfare. He also approved projects to influence world opinion, such as offering communist pilots $100,000 if they defected in a Soviet MIG jet and surrendered it to American authorities.[31]

Racial segregation demonstrated both Eisenhower's cognizance of prestige and his blind spot to it. He regretted how much incidents such as the Little Rock crisis besmirched America's stature worldwide. When he addressed the nation to explain his deployment of the National Guard to the city, he noted, "At a time when we face grave situations abroad because of the hatred that Communism bears toward a system of government based on human rights, it would be difficult to exaggerate the harm that is being done to the prestige and influence, and indeed to the safety, of our nation and the world." He continued, "Our enemies are gloating over this incident and using it everywhere to misrepresent our whole nation." Yet even while conceding these ill effects, by not supporting desegregation more fully Eisenhower failed to exert the moral leadership needed to position America as a crusading country in civil rights, and racism hurt America's standing especially in Africa, amid decolonization and the collapse of Western empires there.[32]

The Cold War intensified the race for prestige and opened new avenues for enhancing it. During the 1950s, the Soviet Union began pouring resources into its sports machine, hoping to show up capitalist nations during the Olympics. In the 1952 Helsinki Summer Games, the United States edged the USSR in the total medal count, seventy-six to seventy-one. Four years later, in Sydney, the Soviet Union soundly beat the United States, ninety-eight to seventy-four. (Already during the 1950s, though, the stench of rumors involving Soviet athletes using performance-enhancing drugs hung heavily in the air.) By participating in the IGY and launching Sputnik, the Soviet Union tried to demonstrate its primacy in science. So skillfully did the Soviets milk their space "firsts" for agitprop that in early 1958, when the United States and the Soviet Union both had launched two satellites, one *New York Times* correspondent joked, "The score is now 2 to 2 in favor of the Russians." Even more impressive was a technological triumph with military implications, such as the announcement that a country had developed the atomic bomb. During the 1950s, both England and France proudly announced that they had joined the nuclear club.[33]

But a project geared toward global attention failed to sway Eisenhower. It had to have substantive benefits, such as bolstering economic strength or military security. The notion that "the United States should be number one in prestige and should seek that position in the world: I think it left him absolutely cold," William Ewald believed. "He did not see that as a worthy goal. . . . I think he was much more interested in what the United States is doing in cooperation with other countries to help them along, help ourselves along and be a good ally in peace as in war. That was the kind of thing that really turned him on, rather than 'America should be number one.'"[34]

Eisenhower "cared about the country incredibly and wanted it to succeed in every imaginable way," Roemer McPhee recalled. But attention-grabbing projects were "fluff" to him. "It was the substance that mattered," McPhee said. "And he thought, you know, if you do a good job, credit will be given for having done so and for having enhanced U.S. prestige with honor." Eisenhower preferred, for example, to enhance America's stature by improving the dollar's strength and bolstering foreign trade. Throughout his career, he had focused more on results than publicity-generating moves. While working under Douglas MacArthur, he wrote in his diary that war had taught him that "the flashy, publicity-seeking type of adventurer can grab the headlines and be a hero in the eyes of the public, but he simply can't deliver the goods." Once the space race heated up, he complained that he had grown "a little weary of Von Braun's publicity seeking."[35]

Doubts about U.S. stature provoked flashes of the famous Eisenhower temper. At a January 1960 press conference, William McGaffin of the *Chicago*

Daily News asked, "Mr. President, in view of the international prestige at stake, why are we not moving with a greater sense of urgency to catch up with Russia in the field of space exploration?"

"Just start at that again," the president snapped. "How did you start it, how did you start that question?"

McGaffin replied, "I said, in view of the international prestige at stake."

"Is it?" Eisenhower asked.

McGaffin pressed him: "Well, sir, do you not feel that it is?"

"Not particularly, no," Eisenhower said. He acknowledged the Soviets' "very spectacular achievements," but he said that Americans should not "begin to bow our heads in shame, because in a few years we have gotten up and gone past them in many fields of this work, when they have been working on it ever since 1945." He went on to explain, "Now, I don't deny that this spectacular achievement more excites the public imagination than does the good, hard, steady work of the scientists that are keeping satellites in the air and getting from them information all the time. It is more spectacular, and it has more effect on the casual reader. But in the actual examination of these two programs, I think we've got a pretty good record."[36]

To the end of his presidency, Eisenhower bristled at any mention of a lost or diminished U.S. reputation. After the 1960 U-2 incident, the USIA deputy director mentioned the need for America to "regain our leadership." That triggered the temper. The United States had lost none of its leadership, Eisenhower retorted, adding that he did not want to hear that phrase again. In particular, he warned against using it before congressional committees.[37]

But the evidence contradicted Eisenhower's views. The Cold War was not just a contest between Russia and America; it was a global event, with people the world over watching. The USIA showed that the space race had influenced Third World countries into thinking that the Soviet Union, though trailing the United States in science, was catching up. "Achievements in space programs will continue to serve as an index, or symbol, in judging national achievement in all fields," the agency reported in 1959. "Unless the United States can achieve a sensational 'first' in some space project, the world probably will continue to believe that the Soviet Union is ahead and can maintain its lead." In 1960, USIA director George Allen testified before the House Science and Astronautic Committee and reported "a great loss of prestige" to the United States because of the Soviets' space successes. The space competition was a race "we can't avoid," and Soviet achievements bred a dangerous confidence. Allen said, "If this new-found Soviet cockiness (arrogance is not too strong a word) translates itself into adventuresomeness in foreign affairs, the world is in for a good deal of trouble."[38]

Even before Sputnik, Cold War pressures intensified concerns about prestige. Behind closed doors, policymakers debated the concept, sometimes arguing that the United States should protect its reputation. At a 1953 NSC meeting, when AEC chair Admiral Lewis Strauss outlined plans to cut research and development money, Secretary of State Dulles objected, saying that America's research and development lead over the USSR bolstered its image. Losing this edge, Dulles warned, would be a "grave blow" to the country's world leadership. These concerns intensified after Soviet space successes. In 1958 the OCB worried over how America could "minimize the adverse psychological and political repercussions overseas which would arise" if the Soviet Union launched a moon vehicle before the United States did.[39]

Some public image projects, Eisenhower believed, could boost the country's standing. He wanted an "atomic peace ship" that would exhibit American culture, arts, and industry. "On top of that," he explained, "I would hope that it would actually carry cargo as it went around the world on unscheduled runs, be ready to pick up such cargoes it could, so that everybody could see it performing a useful service in the world." In 1960, when Kistiakowsky suggested that establishing the first observatory aboard a satellite would enhance America's image, the president expressed interest—although he quickly added his standard caution that he would not support a crash program for it since it was a scientific venture and not "something like missiles" for national security.[40]

Eisenhower never pursued the idea, but administration members broached others. Arthur Larson suggested using a "clean" nuclear bomb, with minimal radioactivity, to create an artificial harbor. R. V. Mrozinski thought the United States could tout its Boeing 707 jet airliner, showing it off at fairs in Brussels and flying international dignitaries. The CIA developed numerous suggestions to improve world prestige, such as organizing an "International Medical Year" aimed to eradicate diseases such as malaria or sponsoring events to demonstrate U.S. superiority over the Soviet Union in synthetic food research, the conversion of plankton into food, and other areas. The CIA wanted to block Soviet influence in Africa, especially after the Little Rock crisis, and suggested an "Africa Center" in the United States to display African cultural items. The agency also proposed having "a competent Negro scientist read a paper during the 1958 Geneva Conference on the Peaceful Uses of Atomic Energy. A photograph of the Negro reading this paper at the Conference should be widely circulated in Afro-Asian countries" and in the Soviet Union and its satellites.[41]

The ideas might have been controversial, but on one point there was no debate: America's global image suffered after Sputnik. The USIA's confidential report on world opinion noted that "American prestige is viewed as having sustained a severe blow." As one example, the report noted that in Tehran, Iranian government officials "considered the satellite such a blow to U.S. prestige that they displayed uneasy embarrassment in discussing it with Americans." Arnold Frutkin recalled visiting science laboratories around the world after Sputnik, where he made an unsettling discovery: "American instruments in the labs were on the decline," he said. "Clearly, instruments from other countries were coming in. The foreign labs were buying foreign instruments rather than American instruments presumably because our scientific prestige had dropped off." USIA director Allen warned that space had become "the primary symbol of world leadership in all areas of science and technology." Polls from Europe revealed improved Soviet stature—and concomitant damage to America's—resulting from the space race. A February 1960 poll showed that most Europeans felt that in a decade, the Soviet Union would be the world's preeminent country for science. In France, 59 percent thought the USSR would lead the world in science by 1970, while only 18 percent thought America would. In Great Britain, 48 percent thought the Soviet Union would lead, and just 17 percent thought the United States would.[42]

Soviet space achievements gave that country something it craved: credibility. *Newsday* concluded that the Sputnik launch was "an impressive display of both power and know-how that will not be lost on the many peoples who want to be on the stronger side. In the eyes of the world, Russia has become not only a military giant, but a scientific giant—a title previously reserved for the United States." One 1959 NASA Space Council meeting featured a frank discussion in which members conceded that even though America had launched more satellites than the USSR, the latter's achievements "have resulted in substantial and enduring gains in Soviet prestige." In drafting the 1959 document "U.S. Policy on Outer Space," the Space Council set as one goal the need to have American space programs that would "counter overseas the psychological impact of Soviet outer space activities" and showcase America's space progress "in the most favorable light."[43]

Keith Glennan could no longer ignore the intensity of Soviet propaganda. By September 1959, he viewed space as a superpower race in which America needed to counter Soviet successes. Their impact, he said, "is too great to neglect." Glennan told Eisenhower what the president disliked hearing: "Personally, I do not believe we can avoid competition with the Soviets in this field." He added with feistiness, "I do not believe we should want to avoid that competition. But I do believe that we can and should establish the terms on which we are competing." Eisenhower wanted to keep those terms focused on scientific achievement, and in this arena, he had much to tout.[44]

The Science Race

Although first in psychology, the Soviets raced second in science. That pleased Eisenhower, who preferred science over grandstanding because it measured a nation's progress and could be most easily translated into benefits in other fields, such as economics, medicine, and national security. Although Sputnik made history, it was too crude to make notable contributions to the IGY or to science, and the Soviets' intense focus on propaganda irritated him, even dampening his interest in joint U.S.–Soviet space activity.[45]

Here Eisenhower owed a debt to those he called "my scientists." His PSAC advisors consistently emphasized the scientific purpose behind space exploration, acting as a corrective to cries for space stunts. In a sense, Eisenhower's concentration on science also reflected his background in military strategy, which influenced him in defining a conflict's terms rather than allowing an adversary to do so. In various discussions, he liked to mention the example of Robert E. Lee during the Civil War, who fared well on his home turf, Virginia, but did poorly when he took his troops onto Union soil. Likewise, by rebuffing a race and emphasizing science, Eisenhower could govern the character of space exploration and dictate the terms of the contest to the adversary.[46]

The U.S. space program indeed paid great science dividends. Vanguard I recorded the effects of light pressure—the tiny physical force exerted by light—as its delicate instruments showed that sunlight slightly altered the satellite's course. U.S. satellites made discoveries that shattered long-held ideas. Until the late 1950s, for example, scientists assumed that the earth was a flattened sphere. But satellites found the planet's shape uneven, appearing more like a pear: the Arctic region was tapered, while the Antarctic bulged. Satellites revealed that the earth was slimmer at the equator than expected, indicating a harder core than scientists had thought, and the planet's electromagnetic field extended twice as far into space as conventional thinking had held. Vanguard also used solar cells to generate electricity, so that when its conventional batteries gave out after just three months, it operated on solar power for an additional six years. The United States used its sophisticated satellites for practical purposes. Photographs from high-altitude planes never completely compensated for the earth's curvature, resulting in cartography mistakes. Vanguard's orbit was regular and high, capturing the planet's gentle bend, so that mapmakers could determine the exact location of islands by tracking the satellite's orbit, a technique that corrected previous inaccuracies and allowed scientists to measure the position of Guam and Wake Island with an accuracy of less than 50 feet.[47]

In May 1960, the *New York Times* made the assessment, "From a standing start we have forged into a clear-cut scientific lead in the race for space." At that time, the United States had launched eighteen earth satellites plus two deep-space probes; the Soviet Union had launched only six in total. "Despite the far greater weight of the Soviet space vehicles the United States has gathered far more scientific information from space," the *Times* reported. "In instrumentation, communications, electronics, reliability and guidance United States space vehicles have made giant steps; in these aspects of space exploration, we need fear no comparisons with Russia or any other nation." Only in using powerful rocket boosters and reaping political and psychological rewards did the United States trail the Soviets.[48]

Eisenhower appeared sensitive to the impact of science on global reputation. He recognized that world opinion on space was too important to ignore—"even if it is not too well informed," he added. The United States had to perform well in this field, he said. When told that the Vanguard satellite would have a lower orbit than Sputnik, he asked whether the difference might hurt U.S. prestige. Just after Sputnik, he pondered a way to recover lost U.S. stature, saying that a U.S. IRBM had to hit a target soon.[49] But that was Eisenhower's problem. In ruminating over image, he usually repaired to his strong suits, national security and economic strength, diverting the discussion from space. As the concept of world prestige grew during the Cold War, his own outlook changed only incrementally. To critics, that showed his passivity. Yet Eisenhower still had space projects to support.

PART THREE

Space

 **CHAPTER 13**

Satellites, Saturn, Spacemen

In July 1959, Eisenhower conferred with Richard Nixon before the vice president left for the Soviet Union to open an American exhibition at Moscow's Sokolniki Park. The president gave careful instructions not to negotiate a summit meeting between himself and Nikita Khrushchev. Nixon should be "positive" and speak "plainly" in his dialogue with the Soviet leader, Eisenhower counseled, but his visit should be mostly symbolic.

What ensued became a classic Cold War confrontation. On July 24, after verbally sparring with Khrushchev at the Kremlin, Nixon and his host headed to Sokolniki Park. As workers milled about constructing sets, the two politicians argued over the merits of capitalism and communism. Noting that the Soviet Union had existed for just forty-two years while the United States was more than 150 years old, Khrushchev boasted that "in another seven years we will be on the same level as America. When we catch you up, in passing you by, we will wave to you."

Nixon hewed to Eisenhower's stance of emphasizing America's economic strength and consumer products. "There are some instances where you may be ahead of us," he conceded, "for example in the development of the thrust of your rockets for the investigation of outer space; there may be some instances in which we are ahead of you—in color television, for instance." The clash between the two men gained visual force when they stood before a display of a model U.S. kitchen, the room that usually forms the heart of a house. This kitchen, Nixon told Khrushchev, was typical of those in America. Pointing out its modern conveniences, he asserted that capitalism offered citizens an array of options. "We hope to show our diversity and our right to choose," he said. "We do not wish to have decisions made at the top by government officials who say that all homes should be built in the same way. Would it not be better to compete in the relative merits of washing machines than in the strength of rockets. Is this the kind of competition you want?" Khrushchev scoffed at the consumer contraptions. "Do you have a machine that puts food into the mouth and pushes it down?" he asked sarcastically. "Many things you've shown us are interesting but they are not needed in life. They have no useful purpose. They are merely gadgets."

As the Kitchen Debate heated up, Nixon stood toe-to-toe with a super-power leader who sometimes jabbed a finger at him. Nixon "met him point by point and in my opinion came out considerably better than even," Eisenhower wrote. Broadcast on U.S. television, the exchange burnished the vice president's reputation and enhanced his prospects for the 1960 GOP nomination. It also hardened Nixon's determination to vie with the Soviets in any venue. Biographer Christopher Aitken has written that Nixon recognized that "the US should demonstrate in its national relations with the Soviet Union the same resolve he had shown in his personal dealings with Khrushchev. Only when the Soviets knew that the US was prepared to match them blow for blow in competition, would they recognise that their true interests lay in conciliation." The heat of racing against the United States later forced the Soviet Union to the bargaining table and paved the way for the détente and Strategic Arms Limitation Treaty that Nixon achieved as president during the early 1970s.[1]

The Kitchen Debate came at a time when the United States was developing impressive projects to match the Soviet Union in the space race. Some were for science, others for surveillance, still others for showmanship. In approving them, Eisenhower quietly built a prepossessing space record.

Transitions

During a president's second term, fatigue sets in—both political and physical—and aides feel like spent rockets, depleted by the rough grind and long hours of White House service. One symptom of the exhaustion is their departures from public life, and in 1958 and 1959, notable Eisenhower aides left, some prompted by considerations that went beyond fatigue. In September 1958, Arthur Larson resigned. As Eisenhower fought to hold down spending, his administration's increasingly conservative tone marginalized the moderate Larson, who found himself at odds with presidential policy; moreover, his combativeness during speech writing sessions exasperated Eisenhower. Once, Sherman Adams conveyed word to Larson that the president wished Larson "wouldn't argue so much with him." In a way, Eisenhower was outmatched—Larson had been a standout on his college debate team—but the president wanted to have the last word. During one editing session lasting three and a half hours, in which he argued strenuously with Larson, he blurted out, "Dammit, Arthur, if you don't let me write this in, I'll extemporize it in anyway." Malcolm Moos, who took up speech writing duties afterward, commented that a speechwriter should not "push a President in the direction of the way he does not want to move. Now, this was a problem with Arthur Larson. Arthur would argue, and argue to the point where he had to go."[2]

On May 24, 1959, Eisenhower lost another trusted colleague when John Foster Dulles died. Ill with cancer, Dulles had resigned as secretary of state the month before; former Massachusetts governor Christian Herter replaced him. The president openly professed how much he missed Dulles, whom he deeply respected and whose views on the Soviet Union coincided with his own. Then, five days after Dulles's death, James Killian told Eisenhower that he wished to return to MIT. The *New York Times* praised Killian for his eighteen-month tenure as the president's science advisor, saying he worked "quietly but effectively to improve . . . [America's] progress in science and technology. He deserves the nation's thanks."[3]

Since Killian was an administrator by training, he believed that now a true scientist should advise Eisenhower, and he recommended one of the nation's premier chemists, George Kistiakowsky. Born in Kiev, Ukraine's largest city, "Kisty" immigrated to the United States in 1926 and eventually taught at Harvard. An expert in explosives and a Manhattan Project alumnus, he joined PSAC in 1957. He gave vital advice on defense and space projects during Eisenhower's last year and a half in office, allowing the president to take a multilayered approach to space, stressing ambitious missile development for national defense while permitting an array of projects for both military and civilian purposes. Eisenhower cherished balance, and in space, he achieved a middle ground among various priorities.

 The ICBM Race

Atlas, the workhorse of America's ICBM program, marched steadily toward development during Eisenhower's second term. On June 11, 1957, the first Atlas ICBM was fired at Cape Canaveral, and in September 1959, the Air Force declared the Atlas operational. The Titan, although lagging behind the Atlas in development, was a better rocket. Whereas the Atlas was a single-stage rocket stationed aboveground, the Titan had two stages that burned separately in sequence and was nestled in underground silos. On February 6, 1959, the first Titan ICBM was launched at Cape Canaveral. Thus, by 1959, Eisenhower was satisfied that the United States led in the race that really mattered to him, for ICBMs and national security.[4]

On July 20, 1960, rocket development took another leap when the nuclear submarine USS *George Washington* launched the first Polaris IRBM, whose mobility and solid fuel made it a more versatile weapon than the Atlas and Titan. In September 1957, Eisenhower had approved a third ICBM, the Minuteman, which would use solid fuel and be ready at a moment's notice, unlike liquid-fueled ICBMs; on February 1, 1961, the first Minuteman was launched at Cape Canaveral. With a range of 6,300 miles, it was the deadliest weapon known to mankind. The go-ahead for Minuteman development meant that Eisenhower presided over six missile systems for national security—three ICBMs and three IRBMs.[5]

As weapons systems, the Atlas and Titan had short lives. Once the Minuteman missile became operational in 1962, it rendered the Atlas's and Titan's liquid-fuel systems obsolete. Again, Eisenhower could thank his ties to scientists for the advance. Drawing on his knowledge of chemistry, Kistiakowsky criticized liquid propellants for rockets and argued for a better way. He was "the principal mover in the direction of solid propellants," recalled Spurgeon Keeny. "Of course, he was probably the world's expert in kinetics and explosives. So when he talked about what you could do, it carried some weight. And everything he said turned out to be correct."[6]

In less than a decade, Eisenhower advanced the country's missile weaponry by quantum leaps. All he wanted was sufficiency, so that even when PSAC told him that the Soviet Union led the United States in ICBM propulsion, he was unfazed. Superiority was unnecessary, he explained, saying, "What you want is enough, a thing that is adequate . . . for compelling the respect for your deterrent." Yet America's balanced mix of missiles, in fact, gave it clear superiority over the Soviet Union.[7]

That edge became critical during the 1962 Cuban Missile Crisis, when the Soviet Union backed down against a country with a decisive advantage.

Three main factors allowed John Kennedy to prevail over Khrushchev during this crisis: the U-2 spy plane, which detected the Soviet missiles in Cuba; the Polaris missile, which protected European allies (although America agreed to pull its Jupiter IRBMs from Turkey to assuage Khrushchev); and finally, overwhelming superiority in ICBMs. "Where did Kennedy get those? He got them from Ike, all three," William Ewald said. "[T]hey were the underpinning for the Cuban Missile Crisis success." Although critics assailed Eisenhower for retarding rocket development and lapsing in national security, a year and a half after he left office, the United States scored a diplomatic victory that relied on technologies he had fostered.[8]

 ## The Satellite Race

The United States achieved similar progress in the satellite race. Heady from SCORE's success, the U.S. space program brimmed with confidence as 1959 began. Then came Lunik. On January 2, 1959, the Soviet Union fired a satellite that passed by the moon and then hurtled itself into an orbit around the sun. Moscow radio crowed that Lunik, which carried a 796.5-pound payload of scientific instruments and weighed 3,245 pounds in total, "again demonstrates to the world the outstanding achievements of leading Soviet science and technology." The *New York Times* headline read, "Russia Again Ahead in Race into Space."[9]

But the United States rattled off a series of successful satellite shots, some achieving notable space "firsts" as SCORE had. In February, NASA launched Vanguard II, America's first weather satellite, which took the first photo of earth from space. After the disappointments of the first three Pioneer shots, on March 3, the Army launched Pioneer IV, which missed the moon but entered into an orbit around the sun. It was a small vehicle, just 13.4 pounds, but Keith Glennan felt "overjoyed" about it and the other Pioneer probes because American tracking stations communicated with them while they were two hundred thousand miles in space. He noted that "the Soviets could never talk to their birds more than ten thousand miles up. So we were beginning to get a little sense that we were doing things right, that we were getting better all the time." In May, NASA experimented with life in space by sending two monkeys, named Able and Baker, into a suborbital flight aboard a Jupiter rocket. Unlike Laika the dog, both monkeys came back alive.[10]

Despite the successes, America felt the space contest intensify. On September 13, 1959, the Soviet Lunik II became the first manmade object to land on the moon, a trick that required technical precision. When it settled on the moon, the probe released pennants reading, "U.S.S.R. September 1959." *Time* said that Lunik II gave Khrushchev "perhaps the greatest prestige blast-off of all time." That achievement, cried Senator Stuart Symington, showed "how far the Russians are ahead of us in the conquest of outer space." In the Kremlin, Khrushchev's satellites allowed him to consolidate power, and his new confidence found expression in diplomacy. In May 1959, Khrushchev expressed a wish to visit the United States and summit with Eisenhower. In a sense, space exploits bolstered Khrushchev on the world stage and helped him to enunciate this objective. He later confessed, "Of course, we tried to derive the maximum political advantage from the fact that we were the first to launch our rockets into space. We wanted to exert pressure on the American militarists—and also influence the minds of more reasonable politicians—so that the United States would start treating us better."[11]

And he got his wish. In July 1959, while enjoying a break at his Moscow River dacha, he received a phone call telling him that Eisenhower was inviting him to the United States. Immediately, Khrushchev accepted, although Eisenhower was hardly as happy. He disliked the idea of hosting Khrushchev, fearing that their meeting might raise undue expectations and generate ambiguous results. He loathed what he felt the Soviet leader represented—a repressive system of government—and he had little fondness for Khrushchev. Privately calling him "Crook-chef," Eisenhower described him as "shrewd, but not wise" and speculated whether his erratic behavior stemmed from diabetes and insulin fluctuations. But a State Department official jumped the gun and issued an invitation before the president could approve the move, forcing Eisenhower to agree. The momentum of events that began with Sputnik's launch forced Eisenhower into another Procrustean position.[12]

Khrushchev milked maximum benefit from the trip, putting the best of Russia on display. He arranged for the big, new Tupolov 114 passenger plane to fly him to the United States because, even though new and largely untested, it could get make the flight without refueling stops and its airspeed was one of the world's fastest for a propeller-driven aircraft. Khrushchev also insisted on getting there on time because he believed that "if we were late it would be a blow to our prestige" (he was still an hour late).[13]

Khrushchev still smarted from his Kitchen Debate with Nixon, and on September 15, 1959, when he arrived at Andrews Air Force Base, it was time for payback. He spoke to reporters and sprinkled saccharine encouragement on America's space program while lauding Lunik II. He said, "We have no doubt that the excellent scientists, engineers and workers of the U.S.A. will also carry the pennant to the moon. The Soviet pennant, as an old resident, will then welcome your pennant." Later that day, in the Oval Office, Khrushchev offered Eisenhower a model of Lunik II. Eisenhower tried to play the gracious host, as he outwardly glowed. Inside, he glowered. The gift irked him, although he gave the Russian the benefit of the doubt, surmising that "the fellow might have been sincere."[14]

Khrushchev made a whirlwind thirteen-day tour of the United States, starting in Washington at the White House and stretching to New York, California, Iowa, and Pennsylvania, his outrageous behavior grabbing headlines along the way. At an Iowa farm, he flung ears of corn at reporters; he fulminated against scantily clad women on a Hollywood movie set; he threw a tantrum over being barred from Disneyland because of security concerns, demanding, "I ask, why not? What is it? You have rocket launching pads there?" These exploits culminated in a Camp David summit with Eisenhower, which yielded only a few substantive agreements, notably Khrushchev easing his demand that the West surrender Berlin, the city that obsessed him and that he variously called "a thorn," "a cancer," and a "bone in my throat." Rescinding the threat eased tensions, and the summit produced another spell of "Eisenhower Weather," the more congenial Cold War atmosphere that U.S.–Soviet summit meetings engendered. Two months later, at an NSC meeting, when National Security Advisor Gordon Gray described the growing Soviet threat, Kistiakowsky recalled that Eisenhower "suddenly stopped his usual doodling, raised a hand, and said: 'Please enter a minority report of one.' The clear implication was that he considered the threat decreasing."

The first-ever visit to the United States by a Soviet leader, Khrushchev's sojourn had the long-term effect of setting a precedent for meetings between American and Soviet leaders in their respective countries, exchanges that continued throughout the Cold War, without making the U.S. president look weak or making him vulnerable to charges of appeasing the Soviets or abandoning allies.[15]

Space formed a backdrop to the diplomatic dance at Camp David. With a new Vanguard satellite scheduled for launching during Khrushchev's visit, Eisenhower's advisors worried that a failure would embarrass him. When Goodpaster, Kistiakowsky, and Hagerty warned Eisenhower about possible humiliation, he replied, "You all are wrong. We will go ahead with Vanguard and that fellow [Khrushchev] is not going to scare me out of anything I plan to do." On September 18, the United States successfully launched Vanguard III, which carried fifty pounds of instruments.[16]

The USSR answered on October 7 with Lunik III, an 860-pound satellite that jokesters dubbed "cownik," because, like the cow of fairy tale lore,

FIGURE 6. Eisenhower and Soviet premier Nikita Khrushchev greet each other in Washington. Eisenhower viewed his Russian counterpart dimly, but space success gave Khrushchev diplomatic leverage, which he parlayed into a 1959 visit to the United States. (Library of Congress, Prints & Photos Division, *U.S. News and World Report* collection)

it jumped over the moon. But it was no funny matter: Lunik III pulled off one of the most impressive feats of the early space age. Showing pinpoint precision, the craft landed on the moon, took pictures of its dark side, and radioed images back to earth, giving the world its first glimpses of that side of the moon. The triumph was another notch in the Russian belt, and the Soviet Union printed a postage stamp to commemorate Lunik.[17]

Lunik III aroused renewed cries for more space spending. House majority leader John McCormack said that Americans "want this country to overtake and surpass Russia in the exploration of space regardless of the cost." Lyndon Johnson charged, "We should be going farther faster in our military preparations and in our space program," adding that the Eisenhower administration acted "as if we were living in a static world rather than an exploding and developing world."[18]

The media painted dark streaks across the sky. In October, *Time* reported that "the U.S. is still running a poor second in the two-entry space race. And in high-level Washington last week," the magazine maintained, "there still were no detectable signs of urgency about the U.S.'s space lag. The President, his advisers reported, was convinced that the U.S. space effort must be kept 'within reason.'" *Time* asked, "Why has the U.S. failed to make an adequate national response to the challenge of space? The failure traces not to a lack of technological skill but to a lack of vision. In the confusion of U.S. space programs, the bulk of the blame can be laid upon no single person—except perhaps the man whose responsibility it is to boss the whole show, President Eisenhower." *Business Week* featured a story headlined "What Keeps the U.S. in Second Place," in which it predicted "for the next two years at least, the U.S. record in space exploration research will probably look dismal indeed." *U.S. News and World Report* ran a feature article, "The Space Race: How U.S. Became No. 2," which began with the arresting sentence, "The U.S. has lost—and Soviet Russia has won—the race into space for years to come."[19]

Yet in reality, the United States was doing well in space. By October 1959, America had twelve scientific satellites orbiting earth, plus three probes that went deeper into space. The Soviet Union had launched just three satellites and three deep space probes. Moreover, U.S. technology gave the country supremacy, and Khrushchev witnessed evidence of this almost at the same time as he boasted over Lunik II. When Eisenhower proposed giving him a helicopter tour of Washington, Khrushchev saw the chopper as a death trap, and he hesitated to climb into it, suspecting an assassination plot. But when Eisenhower boarded, his worries subsided. He marveled at the vehicle and saw it as a symbol of American excellence. The Soviet Union, he said to his country's aviation experts, needed to build one, too—and make it better than America's.[20]

Far from trailing the Soviet Union, the United States had more and better satellites in space, and 1960 brought impressive milestones. Especially remarkable were satellites' applications, which went far beyond acquiring scientific knowledge. On April 1, 1960, NASA launched the 270-pound Tiros, the Television Infrared Observation Satellite, with two television cameras. Tiros took the first pictures of earth clouds and storm patterns from space, a meteorological breakthrough, and the United States made the pictures and data available to other countries. Operating for almost two and a half months, Tiros took nearly nineteen thousand photographs and transmitted them to earth. Glennan rushed the first photos to the White House to show them to the president, who called them "a marvelous development." Tiros also had defense applications, monitoring missile launches and atomic bomb blasts to keep the United States abreast of other countries' arms developments. Later that year, on November 23, NASA launched Tiros II, a 280-pound weather satellite. In keeping with the open, internationalist spirit that NASA fostered, it invited twenty-one nations—including the Soviet Union—to participate in sharing meteorological data from Tiros II.[21]

On April 13, 1960, the United States launched Transit I-B, which became the first navigation-test satellite, designed to help ships, planes, and submarines travel the earth. On August 12, the United States launched Echo I, a metallic balloon satellite, dubbed a "satelloon." It was enormous. Measuring a hundred feet in diameter, it was the largest object any country had hurled into space, although for the launch it was compressed into a tight, 136-pound package that unfurled once in orbit. Visible to the naked eye, it appeared as a tiny light in the night sky, its shiny aluminum exterior—as thin as paper—reflecting the sun's rays. This launch showed the accuracy American guidance systems could achieve; a three-stage Thor-Delta rocket put the satellite in the precise orbit that NASA engineers wanted, one thousand miles above the earth, the highest altitude of any manmade satellite up to that time.[22]

The satellite's name was fitting. Echo was the world's first "passive communications" satellite, generating no radio signals of its own but rather bouncing them from space back down to another point on land, which

FIGURE 7. August 12, 1960. Eisenhower with NASA's first administrator, Keith Glennan (to the president's right), listening to a tape recording of Eisenhower's voice that the Echo satellite broadcasted. (Dwight D. Eisenhower Library)

represented a communications breakthrough. It broadcast a tape recording of Eisenhower's voice that went from a station in California to one in New Jersey. His message said, "The satellite balloon which has reflected these words may be used freely by any nation for similar experiments in its own interest. . . . The United States will continue to make freely available to the world the scientific information acquired from this and other experiments in its program of space exploration." Newspapers carried photos of Eisenhower and Glennan, both grinning broadly, as they listened to the presidential message. Echo stayed in orbit almost eight years.[23]

Corona

Since national security was Eisenhower's top priority, he was especially anxious to use satellites for reconnaissance. Robert Seamans recalled that Eisenhower was "very well aware of the reconnaissance side and the difficulty that we were having in finding out what the Soviets were really doing. And he saw [Sputnik] as somewhat of a bonanza from that standpoint, that if we already had somebody else put up an orbit, then we could push something in orbit. And then from orbit, we could gather information that would be very valuable in determining really how many ICBM terminals that the Soviets had." Prestige provided another motive for spy satellites. Four days after Sputnik's launch, David Beckler wrote to acting Office of Defense Mobilization director Victor Cooley urging, "The early attainment of a reconnaissance satellite capability should be recognized as an important national security objective, as a possible psychological as well as physical breakthrough of the Iron Curtain and a means for regaining the prestige lost with the Soviet satellite."[24]

Beginning in 1955, Eisenhower authorized funding for military satellites, and no single space project received more federal money during his presidency. These space vehicles included satellites with cameras that would take pictures of the earth and others that would watch missile launches by using infrared sensors, with the ultimate goal of using them instead of the U-2 to monitor weapons development behind the Iron Curtain. On June 22, 1960, the United States launched its first reconnaissance satellite as part of the GRAB (Galactic Radiation and Background) program to sweep over the Soviet Union and collect data from the country's radar signals. (Like U-2 missions, Eisenhower approved each of the satellite's overhead flights, and the National Security Agency divulged GRAB's existence almost forty years later, in 1998.)[25]

GRAB's successor, Corona, was even more important. In February 1958, Eisenhower designated the CIA to head a top-secret spy satellite program code-named "Corona" (after the Smith-Corona typewriter used by CIA officer Richard Bissell, who spearheaded U.S. surveillance projects such as the U-2 spy plane). Secrecy was a concern, because thunderous rocket launches generated media curiosity. Thus, the CIA developed a cover story that the Air Force was canceling an earlier publicly known reconnaissance satellite, Weapons System-117L (or WS-117L), and instead was developing a new project, Discoverer, which would be devoted to biomedical experiments, including the effects of space travel on mice, to pave the way for manned spaceflight.[26]

Together, the CIA, ARPA, and the Air Force developed and ran Corona, which involved physically retrieving data from satellites that released capsules with photographic film that the military recovered. (To facilitate the film pickups, Corona made great advances in using heat shields and parachutes, and NASA later benefited from this technology in its manned space program.) But success was not easy. Corona's first twelve attempts failed, and Eisenhower deserved credit for keeping faith and funding in the program, which showed how vital he regarded it. As Andrew Goodpaster recalled, "It is important to note that despite CORONA's initial failures, Eisenhower always said, 'Let's not worry about it. Let's stay with it. It's so important, and we need it. We need to just keep going with it.'"[27]

Finally, on August 11, 1960, a breakthrough came. While orbiting at two hundred miles above the earth, the Discoverer XIII satellite dropped an instrumented capsule that survived atmospheric reentry and landed in the Pacific Ocean, where a Navy ship retrieved it. This marked the first time an object from a satellite had been recovered, a feat not even the Soviet Union had achieved. Lockheed's missile chief, Herschel Brown, exulted, "The U.S. has accomplished an unprecedented first. The Russians have attempted a recovery orbit and failed. We have succeeded—and we feel pretty darned good." Later, at the White House, Eisenhower received Discoverer XIII's capsule and an American flag carried within it. Although Discoverer XIII took no photographs, it was significant simply because the retrieval system worked.[28]

The next Corona satellite, Discoverer XIV, produced a surveillance bonanza. Launched on August 18, 1960, it made seven orbital sweeps over the Soviet Union, then reentered the earth's atmosphere. A parachute deployed, and as the capsule floated downward, a U.S. Air Force plane recovered it at 8,500 feet. Its photographs, which CIA director Allen Dulles showed to Eisenhower in the Oval Office, provided detailed information on Soviet military installations. Ever circumspect, Eisenhower left no written record of his reaction to the massive lode of information that the satellite's twenty pounds of film revealed. Yet the harvest was stunning: this one satellite mission provided more reconnaissance data than all previous U-2 overflights combined. The revelations, which destroyed the myth of massive Soviet ICBM production, were so earth-shattering that Albert Wheelon, the CIA deputy director for science and technology, later commented, "It was as if an enormous floodlight had been turned on in a darkened warehouse." Discoverer XIV gave convincing testimony to the efficacy of Eisenhower's new surveillance.[29]

But building America's satellite reconnaissance program must have frustrated Eisenhower. To him, it was the most substantive part of the country's space efforts, and it would have silenced media and political critics who complained of America's space stagnation. Yet Eisenhower was in the awkward position of muzzling himself, refusing to divulge classified information. It was the same stifling silence he had to endure after Sputnik's launch; only now he had even more information to tout. (Even Senator John Kennedy, as the 1960 Democratic presidential nominee, had no knowledge of Corona. In September 1960, he asked Trevor Gardner, an advisor to his campaign and a former assistant secretary of the U.S. Air Force for research and development, "Will the Soviet Union have a reconnaissance satellite before we do, and what will it mean?" The United States had already beaten the Soviets in this race, although Kennedy was unaware of it.)[30]

Indeed, Corona became one of Eisenhower's greatest legacies. For more than a decade, it was the sine qua non of U.S. intelligence. He intended it to be just a stopgap measure until the Air Force developed more permanent reconnaissance satellites. Instead, Corona lasted until May 1972 and encompassed 145 launches, costing just $850 million yet yielding invaluable insights into Soviet defenses, especially their ICBM and IRBM complexes and submarine bases. It changed the whole outlook of U.S. intelligence. Rather than rely on conjecture or human informants, American officials used hard data from eyes in the sky. Oddly, Lyndon Johnson, who as a senator had trumpeted the importance of space, showed little interest in the intelligence bonanza from spy satellites once he became president. Not so Richard Nixon, who saw the link between reconnaissance and an arms control agreement, the achievement that had eluded Eisenhower. Corona's information gave U.S. negotiators the confidence to bargain with Soviet diplomats, which paved the way for the 1972 Strategic Arms Limitation Treaty, a crowning triumph for Nixon, who visited Moscow to sign the accord.

Although Eisenhower could not brandish Corona as a public relations or diplomatic instrument, it aided in his chief goals of reducing the risk of a Soviet surprise attack and tamping down Cold War tensions. Reconnaissance satellites gave presidents the knowledge they needed to keep current of America's military needs vis-à-vis the Soviet Union, monitoring Russian technological advances and military activities and verifying compliance with arms agreements. Wheelon called the spy satellite initiative "every bit as impressive as the Apollo Moon landings. One program proceeded in utmost secrecy, the other on national television. One steadied the resolve of the American public; the other steadied the resolve of American presidents."[31]

The Super-Booster

Despite America's satellite achievements, it trailed the Soviets in developing large rocket boosters. Von Braun's ABMA team wanted to redress that gap, and in December 1957, it gave the Defense Department a plan to build a super-booster generating 1.5 million pounds of thrust. This rocket would put the United States on equal footing with the Soviets and their powerful boosters. In August 1958, the Defense Department's ARPA ordered the ABMA to begin developing the "Saturn" super-booster, which would cluster eight Jupiter-Thor engines (it was called Saturn to signify the next solar system planet after Jupiter). Von Braun urged putting the Saturn program on a crash basis and warned that without increased spending on space, "we will have to pass Russian customs when we finally reach the moon." Although unwilling to give the program unstinting emergency funding, Eisenhower wanted Saturn "vigorously pressed forward," and ABMA devoted more than 90 percent of its time to it. During discussions, Eisenhower often repeated his principle of focusing on one big objective at a time, and he expressed his desire to concentrate on developing a super-booster. That, he maintained, would allow the United States to achieve indisputable leadership in space endeavors.[32]

Saturn was impressive. More powerful than any Soviet rocket and four times stronger than Atlas, it could throw twenty-ton objects into space. When completed, the entire rocket stood two hundred feet tall, fifty feet taller than the Statue of Liberty.[33] Although the administration anticipated that by 1964 Saturn could place advanced satellites into high orbit, it was really geared toward sending men into space. Thus, Eisenhower supported a super-booster rocket partly to bolster U.S. pride. As Glennan wrote, "The political, scientific, psychological, and perhaps military, ramifications of the projects made possible by SATURN will greatly affect and strengthen the nation's role as the leader of the free world." Saturn was Eisenhower's visible effort to fend off critics, and he gave it high priority even though he knew that it would cost, by 1959 estimates, at least a half-billion dollars and that it had no use as an ICBM. His support, in effect, was his concession that rocket power boosted U.S. prestige worldwide.[34]

In January 1960, Eisenhower asked Glennan to conduct a study to determine the need for more funding to accelerate the super-booster program. He wrote to Glennan, "As we have agreed, it is essential to press forward vigorously to increase our capability in high-thrust space vehicles." Eisenhower said he wanted to build the super-booster fast, and in early 1960 he even asked for a $113 million supplemental appropriation for it. By October 1961, Saturn had undergone ten successful tests, and it later gave rise to the Saturn V rocket that lifted men to the moon.[35]

Manned Spaceflight

From the start, most observers assumed the data and information that Sputnik and other satellites gathered would pave the way for manned spaceflight. But that project had no direct applications for national defense, so it neither grabbed Eisenhower's enthusiasm nor ranked high on his priorities. In speaking of space, he once indicated that he preferred to talk of "capabilities" rather than committing the nation to specific projects. Manned spaceflight was an area where Eisenhower preferred that NASA demonstrate capability rather than effect expensive reality.[36]

But manned spaceflight had many advocates, for machines alone could not slake man's thirst to explore. Harold Urey, a 1934 Nobel laureate in chemistry, said that one man with a pickax on the moon could do more than any machine. Other scientists envisioned colonizing the moon or traveling to planets. *Fortune* magazine argued, "To put a man in space, or on the moon, or on Mars may not be a military or a scientific goal in any rigid sense. But it is not a circus stunt, either; it is an adventure comparable to Columbus' non-military, non-scientific maritime probe—which turned out to have more military consequences than all the work ever done by staff planners and more scientific consequences than all the work ever done in laboratories."[37]

Manned spaceflight also involved complicated, even disturbing issues. It was inherently risky; during launch, astronauts would sit aboard what was essentially a fuel-laden bomb. Once in orbit, they faced an environment hostile to life, with neither air nor liquid, and atmospheric reentry put them at risk of incineration. Preserving the heavens as a peaceful frontier was another concern. The *New York Times* predicted that once man penetrated space, he would fight there. Another problem was expense. Kistiakowsky called the cost "staggering." By one estimate, a manned spaceflight cost one hundred times more than an unmanned mission, and scientists doubted its worth. Killian could point to no scientific value to support its cost and argued it could be justified only to compete with the Soviets "for world prestige." He maintained that instruments could make space discoveries more efficiently than humans could. Glennan agreed; he worried about overemphasizing the importance of sending a man in orbit around the moon, even telling Eisenhower that he was ready to say publicly that the United States should not attempt it.[38]

Yet Eisenhower faced pressure to approve manned spaceflight. In January 1960, U.S. intelligence estimated that the Soviet Union would launch a manned earth satellite later that year or in early 1961 and believed that it would achieve a lunar landing "about 1970." The Army, Navy, and especially the Air Force all developed plans for sending men into space, as did NASA. NASA wanted the project to have the "highest priority," arguing it was critical "to the national prestige in the eyes of the world." The media concurred. Addressing the question of why the United States and USSR raced to put a man in space, *U.S. News and World Report* explained, "For both the U.S. and Russia there is vast prestige involved—and important propaganda victories around the globe."[39]

In August 1958, Eisenhower designated the new NASA as the agency controlling manned spaceflight. This important action staved off turf wars among the services for manned space projects (even so, the Air Force continued to lobby for military manned spaceflights throughout 1959 and 1960). On October 5, just four days after NASA began operating, it announced Project Mercury, a manned satellite program. "Mercury was part of an orderly exploration . . . it wasn't thought as highly competitive," Don Hornig recalled. It aimed not to explore space in any depth but rather to allow man to follow a quick, inexpensive course into orbit. Still, Mercury was the most ambitious NASA program during Eisenhower's presidency, and the competition to fly was fierce. Initially, 110 specially selected Air Force, Navy, and Marine officers endured a battery of physical and psychological tests that included having their feet plunged into ice water, sizzling inside a 130-degree Fahrenheit chamber, and enduring isolation in a box cut off from light, sound, and other stimuli for three hours. NASA then winnowed the group down to seven finalists. One Air Force general explained, "What we're looking for is a group of ordinary Supermen." Before

Eisenhower left office, Project Mercury had achieved many of the preliminary steps to prepare for sending humans into space. NASA developed a worldwide tracking and communications system to monitor the orbiting Mercury capsule, and in December 1960, an unmanned Mercury was launched to an altitude of 135 miles and recovered by an aircraft carrier.[40]

The Democratic Advisory Committee on Science and Technology, an arm of the Democratic Advisory Council, charged that the Eisenhower administration approved Project Mercury only because "it was a 'quick and cheap' way to recapture international prestige." In a sense, that was true. Project Mercury illustrated how Eisenhower deferred to pressure to compete with the Soviet Union and bolster America's stature in space. Although costly and inconsonant with his principles for spaceflight, he still approved it. Glennan admitted that "we didn't know very much about what we were doing" in Project Mercury. But it was good public relations, and it resonated politically because it generated more media and public attention than satellites. In a 1960 report prepared for Democratic presidential nominee John F. Kennedy, Trevor Gardner and physicists Ralph Lapp and Frank McGuire admitted what insiders knew, that Mercury "will contribute relatively little to science" but would be a major publicity project. (In apparent recognition of this, Eisenhower even included a photo of the Mercury Seven in his presidential memoirs.)[41]

Seamans believed that "the great success of Mercury in the Kennedy years was due to the planning and product development in Eisenhower's administration." On January 26, 1960, Eisenhower approved a new "U.S. Policy on Outer Space" that stated, "To the layman, manned space flight and exploration will represent the true conquest of outer space and hence the ultimate goal of space activities. No unmanned experiment can substitute for manned space exploration in its psychological effect on the peoples of the world." But a long-term worry lurked behind the exhilaration surrounding the Mercury Seven. Glennan voiced Eisenhower's deeper concerns when he fretted that manned spaceflight would open up a can of worms. After a successful Mercury flight, he said, the nation would want longer, more difficult follow-ups.[42]

In December 1960, as the administration wound down, a six-man ad hoc panel chaired by Don Hornig issued recommendations on manned spaceflight. Its findings were negative. It believed that Project Mercury lacked "a high probability of a successful flight while also providing adequate safety for the Astronaut." The real motivations behind such a flight were "emotional compulsions and national aspirations. These are not subjects which can be discussed on technical grounds." Machines and instruments could just as well achieve scientific findings that humans in space could, the panel believed, concluding, "It seems, therefore, to us at the present time that man-in-space cannot be justified on purely scientific grounds." The expense included an estimate that a manned lunar orbit would cost $8 billion and a manned lunar landing would fall in the $26–$38 billion range. The report reinforced Eisenhower's thinking that the endeavor was a poor use of public money.[43]

Before leaving office, Eisenhower wanted to close the issue of manned space exploration by saying that he would not approve its continuation beyond Project Mercury. In mulling over NASA's funding with budget director Maurice Stans, he swore that if he had dictatorial powers, he would have decreed "no manned space program, period." But he decided against such an adamant stance, cracking the door open for manned spaceflight, partly because of pressure from Congress, the media, NASA, and other quarters. In a January 1961 meeting three weeks before he left office, Eisenhower approved wording for his last budget message that read, "Further testing and experimentation will be necessary to establish whether there are any valid scientific reasons for extending manned space flight beyond the Mercury program." Eisenhower, caught between the political imperative of continuing manned spaceflight and the economic imperative of limiting spending, still managed to get his views across. He approved a NASA budget that was $300,000 less than the agency requested. Among the items the Eisenhower budget targeted for curtailment was the Apollo capsule, designated as the vehicle for a manned moon mission.[44]

Manned Moon Mission

But once rockets hoisted men into space, the next logical step seemed a lunar voyage. The leap appeared inevitable, and the media clamored for it. Already in November 1957, a *New York Times* reporter wrote, "Planting a flag on the moon, like planting one on Everest, is a supreme human goal." In February 1958, after the United States exulted in the Explorer I launch, the *Economist* threw cold water on the feat by revisiting the embarrassment left from Sputnik. It predicted that redemption "will come only if the Americans are the first to reach the moon—the achievement on which the public imagination and also, it seems, much of the country's scientific effort is now concentrating." Manned lunar landings were the touchstone of all prestige-oriented space endeavors. After the United States launched its first satellite, von Braun formulated ambitious plans for a lunar landing, predicting that America could achieve it in 1967, with a fifty-man lunar expedition possible by 1971.[45]

Such schemes raised Eisenhower's hackles. At a meeting with congressional leaders, he complained about hearing a scientist on television who spoke about a moon shot. Such talk was premature, Eisenhower believed, and showed a scientist who got carried away when thrust in the limelight. But von Braun's exuberance had company. In April 1959, NASA established a Research Steering Committee on Manned Space Flight, more commonly called the Goett Committee after its chair, Henry Goett, an aeronautical engineer. The committee concluded that NASA's manned spaceflight program should set the objective of a lunar landing. In November 1959, *Time* predicted, "Prestige for unnumbered years will go automatically to the nation that is successful in reaching the moon and making it a steppingstone to further space exploration. And the nation that first lands men and instruments on the moon will be the one whose political and economic outlook becomes the dominant force on earth, whether it tells its story through a horde of propagandists or lets its accomplishments speak for themselves." The House Committee on Science and Astronautics also issued a 1960 report recommending that the United States send a manned flight to the moon during the 1960s.[46]

Resisting another "race," Eisenhower believed that concentrating resources on the moon would cause the country to fall behind in other space projects. In sarcastic moods, he poked fun at the idea, once asking NSC members, "Any of you fellows want to go to the moon? I don't. I'm happier right here." At a December 1960 cabinet meeting where Glennan mentioned the cost of landing a man on the moon, he recalled, "The president was prompt in his response: he couldn't care less whether a man ever reached the moon."[47]

Saying he was "not much of a man on spectaculars," Eisenhower thought that sending a man around the moon was an indulgence. He once remarked that the "moon's been there a long time. It's going to be there a great many eons yet. And we'll get there one day. But it isn't necessary to break our necks and break the budget to get there now." He expressed more interest in reaching Mars or another planet rather than the moon because of the chance of finding life on planets. "It was a big question with him about Sputnik, and putting a man on the moon was not a high priority with him," recalled Raymond Saulnier. "He had other priorities."[48]

Again, Glennan's thinking paralleled the president's. He wrote, "I am convinced that [a moon landing] will be done one day, but I am not at all certain that it is a matter of prime importance. When one starts to talk about the prestige of the United States resting on the question, 'When do we get a man on the moon?,' it seems clear that all sense of perspective has gone out the window." Even if the United States put no men on the moon within the next two decades, Glennan maintained, "there is nothing lost." Administration members worried about opening up a Pandora's box of spending. At the cabinet meeting where Kistiakowsky tossed around possible price tags for a lunar landing—from $26 to $38 billion—Robert Seamans recalled, "The room filled with sighs, and someone volunteered, "If we let scientists explore the Moon, then before you know it they'll want funds to explore the planets."[49]

Yet Democrats exerted political pressure on Eisenhower. While admitting that a manned moon mission had no scientific urgency, the Democratic Advisory Council stressed that "in the psycho-political space race the rewards for being first are exceedingly great; there is little pay-off for second place." The DAC predicted, "Given the profile of the first three years of Soviet space efforts and their advantage in propulsion, it is reasonable to project a Soviet manned mission to the moon as a Russian 'first'. The question is therefore: Can the United States accept this further erosion of its prestige?"[50]

In 1960, NASA began to answer that question. Early that year, deputy administrator Hugh Dryden appeared before the House Science and Astronautics Committee to unveil a ten-year plan for its space activities, beginning with more satellite launches in 1960 and a manned spaceflight in 1961, culminating in a manned lunar landing sometime after 1970. In July, NASA announced plans to initiate a Project Apollo to carry three men around the moon sometime "after 1970." Eisenhower resisted these plans, and for the rest of his presidency, he preferred other initiatives, in space and at home. But the juggernaut of media and political pressure was difficult to oppose. By approving Project Mercury and allowing manned spaceflight, Eisenhower presided over the genesis of a government program for which he cared little.[51]

CHAPTER 14

Voyages, Mirages, Images

During 1957 and 1958, Eisenhower had taken a political pounding. Sputnik, the recession, and the erosion of American prestige combined to drag him down in the polls. By April 1959, one British newspaper described him as "a man who can hardly perform his day-to-day tasks." But later that year, the media talked about a "new Eisenhower." Gone was the calcified leader, replaced by a dynamic one. In August, *New York Times* reporter Cabell Phillips wrote that the president's stature "is growing rather than shrinking—his heroic image has almost as much luster in the public eye as it had six and one-half years ago, and in the techniques of the Presidency his hand is steadier than it ever has been." In December, *Time* declared Eisenhower its 1959 "Man of the Year," noting that he seemed to have recovered from his illnesses, even surprising onlookers during overseas trips by taking two-step strides up stairs.[1]

Foreign and domestic observers praised the presidential resurgence. "For years the present Eisenhower has been quiescent, as [if] it were submerged," Walter Lippmann wrote, noting that he now showed the energy and initiative of his early administration. The *New York Times* observed that in 1958 congressional Democrats salivated over the prospect of wrenching governmental control from the hands of "a tired, ineffectual old man." But by 1960 Eisenhower was "more confident of his power and more zestful to use it than at any time since 1953." London's *Daily Mail* reported, "The sick man leaning away from leadership has become the keen-eyed, confident head of state ready to cope with anything." Eisenhower again ranked as the "most admired" man in America, heading the list as he had for his entire presidency.[2]

He showed more zest for his job, traveled extensively, and reveled in budgetary scraps with Congress. Speechwriter Bryce Harlow recalled, "The only time he was relaxedly happy in the presidency was 1958 to 1960. . . . He liked the last two years because he just threw bombs at will, he was himself. He was not going to run again, he was getting out of the troublesome business. . . . He stood for what he thought he should stand for; he didn't shade it. He whaled away."[3] A grueling travel schedule symbolized Eisenhower's new energy. He believed that he could use his personality and reputation as diplomatic assets, going abroad to improve America's relations and world image. In December 1959, Eisenhower voyaged to South Asia and southern Europe, visiting Afghanistan, India, Iran, Pakistan, Greece, Tunisia, France, Spain, and Morocco. Later, in March 1960, Eisenhower took a ten-day trek through four Latin American countries, Argentina, Brazil, Chile, and Uruguay. In New Delhi, the crowd seemed endless, stretching to a distant horizon. Prime Minister Jawaharlal Nehru remarked that the crowds exceeded those that Mahatma Gandhi attracted, and police had to use truncheons to beat back people who crowded the presidential motorcade.[4]

Roemer McPhee recalled a journalist writing that after the U-2 incident and the failed Paris summit, Eisenhower was a broken man for the remainder of his presidency. "Well, that just wasn't true," McPhee said. "He was ebullient, as usual." When administration members returned from the India trip, most were exhausted. But McPhee recalled, "The president was buoyant and feeling terrific. The huge crowds that turned out energized him." Moreover, through his diplomatic outreach, he moved the Republican Party beyond the shadow of its isolationist fringes, which had led some Europeans to distrust it and doubt its ability to lead American foreign policy.[5]

Eisenhower had staged a comeback, reviving his presidency from the doldrums of the post-Sputnik, recession-plagued months. As 1960 began, most Americans felt good about the future. Fifty-six percent of those polled thought the year would be a better one than 1959, and Eisenhower enjoyed a 71 percent approval rating. With the Twenty-Second Amendment now in effect, Eisenhower became the first president to labor under true lame-duck status, yet he experienced a resurgence in popularity and political will.[6]

Significantly, the United States now led in an important area where it had trailed the Soviet Union after Sputnik: public perceptions regarding rocketry and science. A 1958 survey showed that a plurality of Americans—40 per-

FIGURE 8.   In March 1960, Eisenhower received rousing welcomes during a visit to Latin American countries, a trip he undertook partly to bolster U.S. prestige. Here crowds in Rio de Janeiro, Brazil, line his motorcade. (Library of Congress, Prints & Photos Division, *U.S. News and World Report* collection)

cent compared with 37 percent who thought otherwise—believed that Russia led the United States in long-range missiles and rockets. But in a December 1960 Gallup poll, when asked whether the United States or Russia was ahead in long-range missiles and rockets, 51 percent thought the United States was, while only 24 percent considered Russia the leader. By a 70-to-16 percent majority, most Americans believed that their country, not the Soviet Union, would be the champion in science by 1970.[7]

 The Media Mirage

Despite the polls and impressive American space achievements, the image persisted that the United States trailed the Soviet Union in the space race. Respected, authoritative sources in the scientific community and media propounded the idea. The statements were neither responsible nor accurate, but following Sputnik's backwash, they were believable.

Some scientists exaggerated the allegedly backward status of America's space program. "Acutely embarrassing," Herbert York said. Donald Wenzel, the director of the Harvard College Observatory, denied that the United

States was catching up to the Soviets. "The gap is widening, if anything," he insisted.[8] The media reinforced these assessments. In October 1959, *Time* described government assurances about America's space superiority as "fatuous," adding that officials "sound as if they think that U.S. and Soviet rockets are engaged in a beauty contest instead of a race for national prestige, power, and perhaps survival." A January 1960 *Chicago Sun-Times* editorial complained that "Russia is widening the gap in a space race played before a worldwide audience that accepts space progress as an important index of scientific and technological progress." In February 1960, *Newsweek* columnist and veteran Washington observer Ernest Lindley lamented, "Nearly two and one-half years have passed, and we are still behind. The result has been a cumulative gain in prestige for the U.S.S.R. and a cumulative loss for us." Even the *New York Times*, which prided itself on accuracy, qualified its assessment of a vibrant American space program. Despite recognizing that the United States had launched more than three times the number of satellites the Soviets had and far outdistanced them in scientific space work, the *Times* printed an odd headline implying that the United States trailed the Soviet Union: "U.S. Moves Steadily to Close Gap in Space Race." And a January 1960 CBS television special took the title "The Space Lag: Can Democracy Compete?"[9]

It was a media mirage. The nature of news itself explained the slant toward reporting a "second-place" status. Gloom-and-doom stories sold; they stoked public anxieties, and media outlets found ominous messages more eye-catching than routine events. The situation brought to mind English novelist Thomas Hardy's observation that "War makes rattling good history; but Peace is poor reading." News reports of the 1957–58 recession grabbed more attention than those on a stable, low-inflation economy; bulletins on Eisenhower's stroke made more headlines than his healthy days. Reporters succumbed to the temptation to play up the space race's pessimistic side, with scientists and politicians furnishing obliging quotes. Even into Kennedy's administration, the media continued to report on "the U.S. lag behind the USSR in space," as the *New York Daily News* termed it. After charging during the 1960 campaign that the United States trailed the Soviet Union in missiles and space rockets, John Kennedy took office and found himself impaled on his own sword. He complained to NASA officials that "we've been telling everybody we're preeminent in space for five years and nobody believes it because [the Soviets] have the booster and the satellite."[10]

That had been a perennial source of frustration to the Eisenhower administration. Keith Glennan felt confounded that the media failed to understand—or accurately report—the realities of America's space position. Into 1960, with wearying regularity, Glennan found reporters asking, "How far are we behind the Russians and when are we going to catch up?" Meeting with them, he tried to explain that while the Russians had powerful rockets that could be used accurately as missiles, the United States did, too, even if it had not matched the Soviet spectaculars feat for feat. "It took me quite a while to get this point across," he said. In August 1960, a *New York Journal-American* reporter called Glennan at 4 a.m. to ask about his comment that the United States had far outdistanced the Soviet Union in space research. "Actually, this is a fact," Glennan wrote. But the media "wanted to stretch this into a controversial statement" in light of highly publicized Soviet successes in space. (Even Glennan himself contributed to the media misrepresentations, although perhaps it was an effort to gain more funding for NASA. Speaking in Chicago, he said the United States was "at least a year behind" the Soviet Union in the space race, blaming an indifferent public for the lag.)[11]

Astrophysicist Harold Zirkin wrote persuasively of the space race's true status, pointing out that in scientific achievement, for example, American photographs of the sun far exceeded Soviet pictures of the moon's dark side. Yet the American breakthrough "has been drowned out by the cries of scientific doom that we have heard since the launching of various large Soviet rockets," Zirkin complained. "This is an illustration of what happens when science becomes an instrument of national propaganda." He blamed journalists: "A large part of the responsibility here lies with the newspapers and other media of mass communication. Undoubtedly it is easier to inform the public about a man flying in a satellite than about a shielded cosmic ray counter." Too much attention went toward "firsts" rather than "bests." He urged the media "to end the public hysteria over our space effort and make people realize that except for the gross size of our satellites we have done very well so far."[12]

Eisenhower's emphasis on fiscal stringency, which generated little excitement, left him even more handicapped. Glennan estimated that "90 percent of the top correspondents and columnists in [Washington]—and maybe the country—are solidly in the camp of spending more money, entering upon crash programs, and beating the Russians in space. They are not willing to recognize the fact that new technologies take time, which cannot be shortened merely by the application of money." Instead, most reporters likely agreed with a 1960 Herblock cartoon that showed Eisenhower wielding an ax labeled "Economy First." As George Washington looked on, Eisenhower chopped down a tree labeled "Space and Missile Development." To the end of his administration, Eisenhower was trapped within such caricatures.[13]

Poor PR

On Eisenhower's Oval Office desk lay a wooden block bearing the Latin inscription "Gentle in manner, strong in deed." It was an appropriate motto for his quietly effective leadership. But the presidency also demanded being strong in manner. Although sensational media coverage of America's space status hurt, Eisenhower's anemic public relations effort wounded him further.[14]

Eisenhower enjoyed smooth media relations during World War II, when he showed a keen cognizance of journalists' importance in the conflict. A media darling, he knew many reporters by name and regarded them as "quasi-members of my own staff." He invited them to home-cooked meals, golfed with them, and made them feel a vital part of the allied war effort. He held so many press conferences that British prime minister Winston Churchill grumbled about them. After witnessing the general massage the media, his aide Harry Butcher remarked, "Watching Ike deal with the press, I don't think he needs a public relations adviser. He is tops."[15]

Reporters responded in kind. When Eisenhower asked three journalists to suppress the disturbing story of General George Patton slapping and abusing two hospitalized soldiers, they assented, keeping the incident out of the news temporarily and saving Patton from a dismissal. Cosseted by warm relations with him, the media also began to buzz about General Eisenhower's possible future in the White House.[16]

When the general became president, he grew less sensitive to media relations. Defensive about leaks and thin-skinned about criticism, he allowed his White House to become the least media-savvy since Herbert Hoover's glum regime. Chummy relations with reporters were unheard of in the Eisenhower administration, and press secretary Jim Hagerty, whom some observers considered the most effective ever to hold the job, maintained tight control over interviews. Eisenhower himself "had very definite feelings about who were the good guys and who were the troublemakers in the media," William Ewald recalled. Eisenhower remarked, "The photographers are your friends. These guys are good guys and they take your picture. The pundits, they're the god-darndest." He let the sentence hang. When a colleague or even family member, such as his brother Edgar, criticized his presidency, Eisenhower often replied, "You've been reading these columnists too much. You're listening to the rantings of people who don't know what they're talking about."[17]

Eisenhower's deft handling of the media during World War II reflected sharp political instincts on a personal level, which Eisenhower took pride in, feeling no shame that he was more a political general who managed leaders and governments than one who created brilliant battlefield strategy. During a 1962 interview, when reporter Merriman Smith cast doubt on his taste for politics, Eisenhower shot back, "What the hell are you talking about? I have been in politics, the most active sort of politics, most of my adult life. There's no more active political organization in the world than the armed services of the U.S. As a matter of fact, I think I am a better politician than most so called politicians."[18]

That statement was stunning for its naïveté. True enough, during World War II, Eisenhower had soothed the prickly personalities of Franklin Roosevelt, Britain's Bernard Montgomery, France's Charles de Gaulle, the Soviet Union's Georgy Zhukov, and other allied leaders, and he reined in difficult subordinates like Patton. But managing personal politics and navigating the shoals of military bureaucracy were a far cry from national politics. Presidential politics involved mastering issues, campaigning relentlessly, raising money, leading a political party, handling reporters, and communicating and compromising with hundreds of independently minded Capitol Hill legislators. In the military, Eisenhower had scant exposure to these activities, and as president, he took little joy in them, dismissing the wearying political grind as "clackety-clack." He was like "the admiral who hated the sea," journalist William White wrote. He also never convincingly acknowledged the chasm between military and presidential politics or his dearth of political experience compared with the generals-turned-presidents who preceded him. Eisenhower was the nation's tenth general to win the presidency (the only one in the twentieth century) and one of only two who had never served as an appointed or elected political official before becoming president.[19]

When rumors circulated that General Eisenhower might run for president in 1948, House Speaker Sam Rayburn pithily dismissed it, "No, won't do. Good man, but wrong business." He had a point. Sherman Adams observed that Eisenhower never mastered politics. It grated on his nerves; he enjoyed the energy of crowds but complained about "the killing motorcades" and "another yowling mob." More seriously, he struggled to control issues at home that outpaced him—McCarthyism, civil rights, and the media response to Sputnik. The president tried to popularize his domestic programs with catchphrases, but they were wordy and opaque: "Modern

Republicanism," "dynamic conservatism," "progressive moderation," and "moderate progressivism." For Eisenhower, Larson recalled, "domestic political questions were an acquired taste." So, too, was public relations. Eugene Skolnikoff observed, "My impression was that he was always somewhat suspicious of public relations." The result was an image, riveted deeply into the public mind, of a passive president.[20]

Eisenhower's near-obsession with golf, so damaging to his image, underscored the problem with his public relations machinery. A fresh putting green on the White House South Lawn, a new miniature golf course at Camp David, and frequent trips to the links led to accusations that Eisenhower gave short shrift to White House duties—he was "golfing and goofing" instead of being president. (He even wore golf cleats inside the White House, leaving scruff marks that later led President Kennedy to complain, "Look at what that son of a bitch did to my floor.") Senator Wayne Morse of Oregon said Eisenhower should show "more interest in increasing employment and less interest in his golf game." After Sputnik, people joked about the administration sending a golf ball into orbit. A popular bumper sticker read, "Ben Hogan for President (If We've Got to Have a Golfer in the White House, Let's Have a Good One)." Detractors calculated that Eisenhower spent 150 days out of the year on vacation, much of that time devoted to golf. At a press conference, one reporter even asked whether the president had two special helicopters to whisk him to a golf course more quickly than a car could. Eisenhower curtly denied it. Privately, he fumed to aides that the question smacked of disrespect. But combined with his health problems, Eisenhower's passion for golf generated a picture of a president who focused on recreation while facing new world challenges flaccidly. An Idaho National Guard officer commented, "We need some administrative knocking of heads and fewer heart attacks and golf games." Ike was either golfing or, perhaps worse, cocooned inside the Oval Office, protected by aides who insulated him from tough realities.[21]

Eisenhower's clumsy public relations cost him multiple opportunities to play up America's space strength. In the days after Sputnik, the White House considered preparing a special train with exhibits on rockets and science to move around the country. It would be similar to the 1947–48 "Freedom Train," which traveled nationwide carrying key historical documents such as the Declaration of Independence and Gettysburg Address, reminders of the nation's principles amidst the growing specter of communism. But the president nixed the idea.[22] Eisenhower advisor and former Arizona governor Howard Pyle suggested that he visit a space center to illustrate "what is being done and why it is being done this way." Pyle explained that

FIGURE 9. Eisenhower golfing in Newport, Rhode Island, during a September 1957 vacation. Golfing was Ike's favorite pastime, but critics seized on it as evidence of presidential passivity. (Dwight D. Eisenhower Library)

a presidential trip would "do an excellent job of restoring a proper perspective to this whole business. No statement or press conference roundup can possibly do this like a Presidentially ordered look for everyone at what is actually going on. The people would eat it up and usefully."[23]

In February 1960, Eisenhower traveled to Cape Canaveral, but with underwhelming results. After touring the Missile Test Center, he gave a four-sentence statement to reporters, part of which said: "Obviously, it is the most highly instrumented place you can imagine, and certainly the personnel show every evidence of a high degree of competence. So from my viewpoint it was a very worthwhile trip, and I hope it has been for you fellows. Good luck to you." Although a better writer and speaker than critics claimed, Eisenhower was no Cicero, and these words were insipid. Worse, he allowed space events to pass with only a public relations footnote. Although the Tiros I satellite represented a major scientific success, Eisenhower issued only a two-sentence statement recognizing it. Roemer McPhee conceded that "we did not have good enough public relations throughout the whole Eisenhower presidency."[24]

Most presidents strive for an activist image, yet Eisenhower failed to crowd opportunities to communicate the space achievements occurring during his administration. Only the president, who commanded international attention and unequaled media access, could do such a task. Not even his science advisor enjoyed the president's "bully pulpit" on scientific matters, nor did scientists or NASA engineers, a famously reticent bunch. Indeed, poor press relations concerned top administration members, especially their inability to counteract unflattering depictions of the president. At a meeting the month after Eisenhower's stroke, Andrew Goodpaster raised the issue of how media portrayals might have contributed to the president's stress. Goodpaster wrote, "I suggested that, even though the President does not acknowledge reading or being affected by the press . . . it may well be that the press has 'gotten to him' and that he is troubled by the picture that they are attempting to create in the public mind, and is being drawn into a lot of specifics and details because of the charges of 'part-time' activity." Portrayals of Eisenhower as lackadaisical angered the fiercely loyal Goodpaster, who added, "There has been a complete misrepresentation of the matter to the public over many months, and I thought the question was a very serious one."[25]

FIGURE 10.   In February 1960, Eisenhower visited Cape Canaveral to tour NASA's launch facilities. The tall man with glasses, appearing above Eisenhower's left shoulder, is staff secretary Andrew Goodpaster, a close aide who, like Eisenhower, became NATO supreme commander. (Library of Congress, Prints & Photos Division, *U.S. News and World Report* collection)

More attuned to the public relations aspect of space than his boss, Glennan sought to enhance the White House's use of the press. He once met with the editors of the *Washington Evening Star* and *Washington Post* to seek their advice on improving NASA's media relations. He got the U.S. Postal Service to issue a commemorative stamp featuring Echo I, calling it "the world's first communication satellite." He also developed the stamp's slogan, "Communications for Peace."[26] Glennan believed a presidential statement would help to gain initiative against Congress and the media, and he repeatedly blandished Eisenhower to make a greater public relations effort. In late 1959, he urged a statement clarifying the nation's activities in space. Sensing "substantial and disturbing [public] confusion on these points," Glennan suggested that the White House demonstrate the Jupiter, Thor, and Atlas missiles, followed by a presidential address outlining national space objectives. At a subsequent meeting with Eisenhower, Glennan called a presidential statement "essential" for space policy. Eisenhower agreed but said it could be "very brief," adding that the space program and its budget should not grow "with no foreseeable limit. Instead we should try to find a level that seems about right." The next month, Glennan again recommended that the president issue "a strong public statement which will set our space program in the proper framework. . . . Such a move on your part would seem to me to avoid finding ourselves in the position of being on the defensive with respect to this program."[27]

On August 17, Eisenhower issued a statement on U.S. space achievements, citing "the impressive array of successful experiments" that the United States had conducted, including Pioneer V, Tiros I, Echo I, and Discoverer XIII. "While no one of them has been undertaken solely in an effort to achieve a 'spectacular first' in the eyes of the world," the statement said, "each has resulted in just such a 'spectacular first' in support of the desires of mankind for greater knowledge and understanding." The declaration concluded with the proud sentence, "The United States leads the world in the activities in the space field that promise real benefits to mankind." The statement, while a positive PR move, had little impact. Eisenhower's efforts fell short, and even he admitted his public relations savvy was wanting. After the U-2 fiasco, for example, White House Chief of Staff Jerry Persons told Eisenhower that if administration members including Persons himself, who were more skilled at politics and public relations, had known about the project, he could have smoothed over the incident and prevented it from spiraling into a disaster. Begrudgingly, Eisenhower agreed.[28]

Personal characteristics—both merits and defects—hindered the Eisenhower public relations effort. He was inherently modest, a trait that reflected his parents' instruction that he and his five brothers should show "ambition without arrogance." While serving in the Army, Eisenhower spurned the "glory-hoppers" who hogged the limelight, and when dogged by rumors of presidential ambitions, he exclaimed, "I am a soldier, and that's all I ever want to be. I'm no glory-hopper!" Facing reporters during the war, he responded to tough questions by saying, "That's just too complicated for a dumb bunny like me," a self-effacing answer that made him seem human and endearing. As president, he renamed the Catoctin Mountains presidential retreat "Camp David"—honoring his father and grandson—explaining that "Shangri-la," the name FDR had given it, was "just a little too fancy for a Kansas farm boy." (FDR acolytes hated the new name.) Edward McCabe said that Eisenhower "was a man of great ability. But he didn't flaunt that. He didn't fight the notion of some of the press, the editorial writers, [who said] he really wasn't polished and urbane and slick enough somehow to be the president. That was all right with him. He felt that probably added to his ability to get things done because if people don't expect much of you, you can outdo that in a hurry."[29] Time and again, Eisenhower wanted to repress publicity for his actions and efforts, an attitude that carried over into the administration's space achievements. When Glennan discussed a lunar probe at a 1958 cabinet meeting, Eisenhower expressed his desire to reduce public anticipation and expectations. Rather than seek publicity for Project Mercury, Eisenhower asked Glennan to downplay the astronaut superstars "to avoid generating a great deal of premature press build-up."[30]

Partly, Eisenhower wanted to avoid getting burned by the same inferno of embarrassment that accompanied the Vanguard explosion, but he failed to pursue other paths for publicity. He had a deep-seated belief in duty, and while it motivated him to devote his entire career to military and public service, it also led him to expect that everyone else should perform their duties as a matter of routine, needing no special acknowledgement or gratitude. His temper flared when he had to sign a private relief bill approving $175,000 for an Air Force officer who had developed a low-level strafing technique for bombers. When told the officer had devised the method "in his spare time," Eisenhower exploded, "My God, there's no such thing. Those people work twenty-four hours a day. We all do in the military for the country." As he signed the bill, he growled, "Goddamn it to hell. Jesus Christ! I hope the son-of-a-bitch dies." Speechwriter Malcolm Moos remembered that he spent all night working on an address and came to see Eisenhower at breakfast. No gratitude came from Eisenhower, just the comment, "Moos, I wish you wouldn't take your time with those speeches." Arthur Larson recalled a similar experience, pulling an all-nighter for the president, pounding away at his typewriter to produce a speech. Exhausted but beaming with pride, he showed up at the Oval Office at 8:00 a.m. and placed the manuscript before Eisenhower. "He did not even look up," Larson recalled. "Not the slightest flicker of expression to indicate that there was anything remarkable about this performance. I recall that the first time this happened my reaction was a little flush of resentment, as if perhaps he did not realize what a heroic piece of work had just been accomplished."[31]

Eisenhower was also remiss in acknowledging the work of government administrators and staffers, an unfortunate flaw for someone who valued morale and spoke of "spiritual" strength. This personal defect demoralized some government workers, and no one expressed bitterness more keenly than John Medaris. After watching the science and national security speech in which Eisenhower showed the Jupiter C nose cone, Medaris was disappointed that he made no mention of ABMA or the Army. After Explorer I was launched, Eisenhower failed to congratulate von Braun or Medaris, who felt slighted, even calling it "the most bitter disappointment of my entire life." Had the president thanked scientists and others more openly, America's space program would have received a needed boost, and the publicity would have enabled more scientists and administrators to act as spokespersons.[32]

As a rule, Americans like hope and optimism in their leaders, and personally, Eisenhower had these qualities in abundance. Yet he failed to project them enough to convince Americans of the country's lead in the space race. "Since the first part of President Eisenhower's first term there has been no one of much influence at a high level in the Government," observed New York Times military reporter Hanson Baldwin, "who spoke for public opinion, no one who has viewed governmental action or inaction in terms of their psychological effects upon the world conflict." Baldwin continued, "It is not good enough to say that we have counted more free electrons in the ionosphere than the Russians have, that we know more about cosmic rays. We must achieve the obvious and the spectacular, as well as the erudite and the obscure."[33]

In showcasing America's achievements, Eisenhower gravitated toward the commonplace. Before Khrushchev's 1959 visit, a reporter asked what Eisenhower would show the Soviet leader. The president replied that he wanted to take Khrushchev in a helicopter around the nation's capital "to see the uncountable homes that have been built all around, modest but decent, fine, comfortable homes—all around this country." He wanted the Soviet leader to "go into our great farmland and see our farmers, each one operating on his own, not regimented" and "see our great industrial plants and what we are doing." These features distilled the essence of what Eisenhower wished for Americans. In addition to securing them from military threat, he wanted them to enjoy abundant material comforts. He shied away from any great national crusade and instead wanted a strong economy with limited government interference and spending. They were the modest goals of a modest man.[34]

When Khrushchev visited, Eisenhower did these things, but mundane matters failed to impress the Russian. Aboard the presidential helicopter, Khrushchev stayed silent, even though he saw the sprawling highways and multitude of cars and homes that Eisenhower hoped would impress him. Later, Khrushchev scoffed that the cars were a waste, and Soviet citizens had no need for vast roadways since the population was more concentrated and the people less mobile. The houses were wasteful, too, he said, because they consumed so much energy.[35]

The incident showed Eisenhower's political shortcomings. Ironically, political inexperience was key to his persona, for it endowed him with a charm and innocence that Americans found endearing. They trusted Ike, because he seemed straightforward and uncomplicated, one of them. "I'm just folks. I come from the people, the ordinary people," he said. He often mentioned his Abilene roots, as if reminding audiences that had his life taken a different direction, he could have ended up a Kansas farmer. But inexperience also impaired Eisenhower's effectiveness as president, for he lacked the political savvy to parry criticism that dogged him after Sputnik. The political scientist, who could have helped him to counteract the attacks, deserved as much a place at Eisenhower's table as the space scientist.[36]

Eisenhower's shortcomings enabled critics to hit him hard. In their 1960 campaign position paper on space policy, John Kennedy's advisors wrote that the White House "fails to recognize that there are two distinct aspects to the Space Race. There is the purely scientific competition in which the United States has done very well and probably even exceeded Soviet performance." But they added, "There is also the psychological competition in which the U.S. and the U.S.S.R. attempt to impress the peoples of the world with spectacular and easily appreciated feats of technology. The Administration's initial attempts to go into space on a budgetary shoestring have made it difficult to compete in space spectaculars." That contrast gave Kennedy an advantage in the 1960 race, and he exploited it.[37]

Ultimately, Eisenhower's political blind spot hurt the GOP and detracted from his role as party leader. His testy relations with the Republican right wing had already hurt him in guiding the party. (In an ironic way, Eisenhower's first two years as president, when he had a Republican Congress, were more rocky in his Capitol Hill relations than the next six years, when Democrats ruled Congress.) He locked horns with conservatives in domestic and foreign policy, exacerbating party tensions. Some conservatives preferred isolationism to Eisenhower's internationalism. Others thought him too soft on the Soviet Union. Still others backed protectionist measures and opposed Eisenhower's attempts to lower trade barriers. They caused him immense grief in backing Senator John Bricker's proposed constitutional amendment to limit the president's power to make foreign treaties—a reaction to the Yalta agreements—provoking Eisenhower to complain, "I'm so sick of this I could scream. The whole damn thing is senseless and plain damaging to the prestige of the United States." On the domestic front, conservatives tried to block the 1957 Civil Rights Act and Eisenhower's move to expand Social Security coverage. Senator Barry Goldwater blasted an Eisenhower proposal for elderly medical care as a "dime store New Deal" and said he was "deeply disappointed" that the president chose to "continue the old New Deal, Fair Deal schemes, offering only a modification in scale and no change in direction." Eisenhower often relied more on congressional Democrats than Republicans to pass his domestic proposals, and that irony bothered him. He liked to tread along what he termed a "middle way" between Republican liberals and conservatives, but right-wing disaffection made that course difficult. "You don't have very many friends when you're walking a decent middle way," he complained.[38]

Yet space policy represented the middle way. It had little danger of backfiring or offending, as the anti-communism crusade or covert overseas action did. Rather than acting as a wedge issue that divided the GOP's wings—as civil rights had—space could have functioned as a bridge issue for Eisenhower. Republicans of diverse ilk coalesced around space; prominent liberals like Nelson Rockefeller and conservatives like Goldwater supported an active space policy, which even captured the imagination of Ronald Reagan, who as president later advocated manned space missions and celebrated NASA's space shuttle for symbolizing America's world leadership, despite his renowned aversion to government programs. (A science fiction buff, Reagan ruminated about space aliens descending on earth and forcing the United States and the Soviet Union to cooperate in repelling the invaders; he even mentioned the scenario to Soviet president Mikhail Gorbachev. Embarrassed by Reagan's attraction to the fantasy, National Security Advisor Colin Powell warned staffers about the "little green men" idea that the president liked to trot out.)

In 1959, Congressman Gerald Ford, a stringent fiscal conservative, noted that he had "a reputation with my colleagues for being pretty careful with the tax payers' money," but added that "it is in the light of this background that you must assess my plea for national support of the space program." As possible benefits of space research, Ford cited advances in weather prediction, communications, metallurgy, and even "freight and mail ballistic rockets [that] will give long distance delivery in a matter of minutes." Thus future presidents—Kennedy, Johnson, Nixon, and Ford—all had voiced their space convictions already in the late 1950s. More presidential support for a muscular space program would have especially helped Nixon, who acted as Eisenhower's link to Republican conservatives and needed winning issues for the 1960 presidential race.[39]

Ultimately, Eisenhower was left to nurse his political regrets. In retirement, he wrote that one of his goals was "to unify, and strengthen, the Republican party. My success was slight. Certainly I did not succeed in the hope of so increasing the party's appeal to the American electorate as to assure a few more years, after 1960, of Republican government." In part, the blame rested with him. Although space was not the defining issue in 1960, it was a pervasive one, and by failing to anticipate or capitalize on its importance, Eisenhower allowed opponents to confirm an image of him as a "reactionary fossil."[40] All of it hurt Eisenhower's party in the presidential race, as the nation stood poised at a new threshold.

 CHAPTER 15

Space, Prestige, and the 1960 Race

A top Eisenhower priority was achieving an arms control agreement and ameliorating tensions with the Soviet Union. On that front, he sighed late in his second term, "we haven't made a chip in the granite in seven years." But in 1960, he had hope. Khrushchev's 1959 visit to the United States had gone well, and the Russian leader invited Eisenhower and his family to the Soviet Union the next year, which was to be the first-ever state visit by a president to the USSR. Eisenhower had grown more amenable to meeting with the Soviets, and he, Khrushchev, British prime minister Harold Macmillan, and French president Charles de Gaulle had a four-power summit scheduled for Paris on May 16, to be followed by Ike's June visit to the Soviet Union. Perhaps he could achieve an arms control breakthrough and end his presidency on a high note.[1]

But two weeks before the Paris summit, Eisenhower made the fateful decision to approve a May 1st U-2 flight over the Soviet Union. The plane went missing, and he approved a cover story that used the new space agency, NASA, to hide the truth. A NASA weather research plane, the official line went, was lost over Turkey. But soon the truth came out. The Soviet Union had shot down the U-2 and caught CIA pilot Francis Gary Powers. Eisenhower had expressed concern that a U-2 failure would cause terrible damage to America's image worldwide, and the U-2 fiasco was his worst nightmare come true; the United States had been caught red-handed, spying on the Soviet Union. At the Paris summit, Khrushchev demanded an apology. When Eisenhower refused, saying he was safeguarding national security, Khrushchev stormed out. The two men never even shook hands, and the summit collapsed before it began. Reporter James Reston said he had never seen Eisenhower so shaken. Khrushchev angrily canceled Eisenhower's June visit to the USSR, and Ike never set foot on Russian soil as chief executive. Instead, the honor of being the first president to visit the Soviet Union during peacetime went to Richard Nixon, who went to Moscow in 1972 to sign the Strategic Arms Limitation Treaty.[2]

The U-2 incident had a sad irony. Had Eisenhower opted to use the Army's Orbiter satellite—instead of the Navy's Vanguard—the U.S. satellite program would have progressed more quickly, and reconnaissance satellites might have been in orbit by 1959, reducing or eliminating dependence on U-2 overflights, which flirted with disaster. Deputy CIA director Robert Amory, Jr., recalled that "everybody knew [the U-2] had a limited life. The Russian radar would improve, their fighters and intercepts and other things like their surface to air missiles would improve. And a precisely accurate prediction was made of about a four year life."[3]

Eisenhower had also been caught lying. For the first time in the television era, a president's mendacity was exposed and internationally disseminated, and Eisenhower's reassuring, grandfatherly image suffered damage. Democratic senator William Fulbright of Arkansas, who chaired the Foreign Relations Committee, blasted the administration for "bumbling and fumbling" the U-2 incident and bringing America's prestige to a "new low." People joked that the CIA, which operated the U-2, stood for "Caught In the Act." (A Gallup poll, though, showed a rally-around-the-president effect, as 58 percent of Americans thought the Eisenhower administration handled the incident well. Moreover, Democratic candidate John Kennedy hurt himself by suggesting that Eisenhower could apologize to the Kremlin, a reaction that even Democrats considered callow, highlighting his inexperience in foreign policy.)[4]

Just as health crises dragged Eisenhower momentarily into depression, the U-2 fiasco darkened his spirits. At one moment, he commented, "I would like to resign." The "stupid U-2 mess," he regretted, ruined the last year of his presidency, and in July he dolefully remarked that he had nothing to do but ride out his time in office. In reality, he had much to do, especially in space.[5]

Had the U-2 affair never happened, Eisenhower might have returned from Paris as he had after World War II, triumphantly touting success, this time in peace rather than war, brandishing not arms but arms control. With his administration's diplomacy vindicated, the beneficiary would have been Vice President Nixon, the Republican presidential nominee. Instead, during the 1960 campaign, Nixon had to defend the administration's handling of the U-2 incident. A trifecta of issues—space, the economy, and prestige—further hurt his chances of winning the White House.

Space and the 1960 Race

William Ewald believed that Sputnik represented the start of a downward arc in Eisenhower's presidency. He wrote that "one sees a single implacable sequence of events arching from the Soviet satellite shot to the final election of 1960. . . . It is a sequence driven by negativism and partisanship, ending in bitterness and defeat." The Soviet satellite provided a critical mass for "the multitude of petty political grievances that the Democratic party had against the lame-duck President," Ewald thought. The earth-rattling event of October 4, 1957 set the stage for the 1960 presidential race and GOP defeat.[6]

As the election year approached, a Democratic attack theme of a sluggish president and second-place America took shape. Harry Truman promised that Democrats would "restore [America] to its place of preeminence in the world," and they capitalized on space's political potential. They charged the Eisenhower administration with suffering a "space-myopia" that prevented it from seeing "the world impact of being the first in space," and the 1960 party platform slammed Eisenhower, stating, "The Republican Administration has remained incredibly blind to the prospects of space exploration. It has failed to pursue space programs with a sense of urgency at all close to their importance to the future of the world." The platform promised that Democrats would "press forward with our national space program in full realization of the importance of space accomplishments to our national security and our international prestige."[7]

More generally, Democrats accused Eisenhower of allowing America slip to second-rate status. Their party platform read, "When the Democratic Administration left office in 1953, the United States was the pre-eminent power in the world. Most free nations had confidence in our will and our ability to carry out our commitments to the common defense. The Republican Administration has lost that position of preeminence." At the Democratic National Convention in Los Angeles, speakers drove that theme home. Senator Frank Church of Idaho declared that the world's fate and freedom "all ultimately depend upon American principle, American prestige, and American power," charging that these had wilted under Eisenhower. In accepting his party's nomination, forty-three-year-old John Kennedy said that although Nixon was also young, "his approach is as old as McKinley. His party is the party of the past. His speeches are generalities from *Poor Richard's Almanac*. Their platform . . . has the courage of our old convictions. Their pledge is a pledge to the status quo—and today there can be no status quo." During the campaign, Kennedy hesitated to mention the popular president by name, but he established Eisenhower complacency as a theme. What he called "spectacular" Soviet gains in space and defense illustrated the problem with the current leadership, which he blamed for producing a "complacent, self-contented, easy-going" America.[8]

What Sputnik and space signified became a key point of the campaign. Kennedy speechwriter Theodore Sorenson acknowledged that by mid-1960, the senator viewed space "primarily in symbolic terms. . . . Our lagging space effort was symbolic, he thought, of everything of which he complained in the Eisenhower administration: the lack of effort, the lack of initiative, the lack of imagination, vitality, and vision." Sorenson said that Kennedy believed Soviet space achievements not only dramatized "the Eisenhower Administration's lag in this area" but also "damaged the prestige of the United States abroad."[9]

Sputnik themes of prestige, old versus new, and a race with the Soviets abounded during the presidential campaign, so much so that Republican congressman James Fulton of Pennsylvania commented that for the first time a campaign began in outer space rather than on earth. The candidates' space policies differed starkly. "The first vehicle in outer space was called Sputnik, not Vanguard," Kennedy reminded a Portland, Oregon, audience. "The first country to place its national emblem on the moon was the Soviet Union, not the United States. The first canine passengers in space who safely returned were named Strelka and Belka, not Rover or Fido, or even Checkers," he said. Kennedy promised a deeper commitment to space than Eisenhower had made. Saying that "we should err in [space] by spending a little too much rather than too little," he wanted to dispense more dollars to reduce the "disparity of quality and versatility in our space effort" compared with that of the USSR.[10] The name of Kennedy's proposed legislative program, the "New Frontier," invoked the idea of intrepidly exploring uncharted territory, and the ultimate frontier was space. A Harvard alumnus and winner of the 1956 Pulitzer Prize, Kennedy also created the impression of a cerebral politician who respected learning and had a greater interest in science than did Eisenhower. In one campaign speech, he ruminated on the moon, speculating, "It may be a perfect, fossilized record of everything that has happened in our universe since the beginning of time. It may tell the story of the origins of the solar system. With that knowledge we will know more about the origins of life. And with that knowledge we may come to understand fully the opposite of life—disease, and death itself." Space harmonized perfectly with a Kennedy need, fitting his self-created image of a doer, a thinker, and a visionary, none of which Eisenhower seemed to be.[11]

The importance of space and national security in 1960 might have been one factor that influenced Kennedy initially to select Missouri senator Stuart Symington as his running mate. Kennedy summoned Missourian Clark Clifford, Harry Truman's advisor and confidant, to his Democratic National Convention hotel suite to offer the number-two spot to Symington, who was a foremost Eisenhower critic on space and military matters. But the day after making the offer, Kennedy told Clifford, "Clark, I must do something I have never done before in my political career. I must renege on an offer made in good faith." He bowed to political reality and instead teamed with Lyndon Johnson, a bigger senator from a bigger state, who had formidable space credentials himself. (Jacqueline Kennedy, who also would have preferred to have Symington on the ticket, later wrote to the senator expressing her regrets and asked him to burn the letter, which he said he did.) Once on the ticket, Johnson went on the attack. He charged that most of America's space initiatives resulted from "Congressional prodding and reluctant acquiescence in Congressional programs by the Administration." He said the Eisenhower White House showed "drift, delay and dilution" in space, and he lambasted its alleged failure to pursue space projects more aggressively. In late October, Johnson released a report from the Senate Committee on Aeronautical and Space Sciences. It pummeled the administration for its space policy, charging that American efforts had been "hampered by the Republican administration's blind refusal to recognize that we have been engaged in a space and missile race with the Soviet Union and to act accordingly."[12]

Nixon denied it all and in doing so sounded like Eisenhower. Pointing to America's scientific breakthroughs in space, he said that the United States led the Soviets and cautioned against "hysterical" reactions to their space endeavors. "In science, sometimes we're ahead and sometimes they are ahead," he reasoned. Although the lead in space might shift, he said, overall "we are way ahead." He told a Peoria, Illinois, audience, "If they do launch a man into space, we're not going to get downhearted, because our program is coming along splendidly." Recognizing that Russia's only lead was in rocket strength, Nixon spoke against "a massive crash program" to go head-to-head against the Soviets.[13]

In truth, the news on space was good. By late August 1960, *U.S. News and World Report* headlined a story, "U.S. Moving Ahead in Space Race," detailing America's commanding lead in scientific achievements over the Soviet Union, and by late October, the numbers reflected the American advantage: the United States had launched twenty-eight satellites, while the Soviets had just eight. As if to add another notch in the scorecard, on November 3, NASA launched the ninety-pound Explorer VIII satellite, which made the most extensive exploration yet of the ionosphere (the area of the earth's atmosphere extending from 50 to 250 miles above the earth's surface, containing a concentration of ions, electrically charged particles).[14]

But Sputnik left enduring impressions of a space gap, and Democrats added a more damaging allegation: the "missile gap." Kennedy unveiled this charge during a 1958 Senate speech, alleging that Eisenhower's defense cutbacks had allowed the Soviet Union to overtake the United States in missile development. He doled out chilling statistics. With its missile arsenal, Russia could wipe out "85 percent of our industry, 43 of our 50 largest cities, and most of the Nation's population." The claims generated instant publicity, and Kennedy repeated them during the next two years, as he ginned up his campaign machinery. In just three words, the phrase "the missile gap" encapsulated all the setbacks and dire signs from the late 1950s—Sputnik, the Gaither Report, military vulnerability, ebbing prestige, and concerns over second-place status.[15]

In the summer of 1958, *Washington Post* columnist Joseph Alsop trumpeted the allegations in a three-part series of articles. He and Eisenhower held each other in mutual contempt. Alsop, who lived in the same Georgetown neighborhood as Kennedy and later wrote speeches for his 1960 campaign, compared the president to "a dead whale on a beach" or, more charitably, "a nice old gentleman in a golf cart," while Eisenhower called Alsop "the lowest form of animal life on earth." But Alsop's loathing of Eisenhower reflected the low regard that many pundits had for him, as he called Ike "the worst president of the United States with the possible exception of James Buchanan." That assessment lacked historical perspective, but Alsop also lost a journalist's premium for accuracy. He predicted that by 1963, the Soviet Union could have a crushing 1,500-to-130 lead over the United States in ballistic missiles. Echoing NSC-68's warning that 1954 would be a year of "maximum danger," he called the early 1960s a "time of deadly danger" and warned that the United States would be weak and disadvantaged in diplomacy with the Soviet Union. The fault, Alsop charged, lay with Eisenhower, who was "misinformed about the facts."[16]

This accusation touched a sensitive nerve in Eisenhower. It was he who had poured large amounts of federal money into building the nation's missile systems, after they had received little funding from Truman. As Herbert Brownell recalled, "The fact of the matter was that when he went into office there was a missile gap and the Russians were far ahead of us in planning for an intercontinental ballistic missile [program]. It was only by careful speeding up of that program over a period of three or four years that we caught up with the Russians." Eisenhower implemented steady yet dramatic advances in missiles, but now Kennedy and other Democrats made false charges that ramped up the hysteria Eisenhower had fought to quell. "By getting into this numbers racket and by scaring people, they are getting away with murder," he fumed. Although Eisenhower worried foremost about price inflation in the economy, another phenomenon vexed him—what historian and retired Army colonel Andrew Bacevich later called "threat inflation," the increase in perceived threats worldwide to justify greater military spending and hence more business for the defense industry. [17]

To help elect Kennedy, Alsop resorted to threat inflation. U-2 flights in early 1960 showed that the Soviet Union had just begun to deploy ICBMs; in 1961, they still had no more than thirty-five. The intelligence was proof positive that the United States led the Soviet Union in missile production, but Eisenhower could not reveal this information publicly because of the U-2's secretive nature. Killian recalled CIA director Allen Dulles briefing the president with reconnaissance pictures. "They showed clearly the state of Soviet missile technology," Killian remembered, and made Eisenhower confident that the missile gap was fiction. Killian knew that the president's missile program allowed him to resist cries for increased defense spending after Sputnik, having the inside knowledge that it was unnecessary. "The President had enough intelligence to be assured that there was no Missile Gap," Killian said. "The U-2 had a very important role in keeping down the Air Force budget as Ike was so anxious to do. There were billions of dollars that the U-2 saved."[18]

The U-2 incident forced Allen Dulles to come clean with Democratic congressional leaders about the overflights and the knowledge gleaned from them. In July 1960, Dulles briefed Senators Kennedy and Johnson, showing them classified information, to disabuse them of the "missile gap" notion. Yet even after seeing the evidence, Kennedy stuck to the charges. He pushed for stepped-up missile production, especially advocating the mobile Polaris and Minuteman, and came across as a true Cold Warrior. A frustrated Nixon vented, "I could explode that phony [missile gap charge] in ten minutes by displaying our high-altitude reconnaissance photographs. . . . I can't do that without destroying our source, and Kennedy, the bastard, knows I can't."[19]

Goodpaster observed that when Eisenhower obtained "estimates on what the Soviet missile program was, he went pretty carefully into what the data was that this [missile gap charge] was based upon, and he found that it was quite conjectural and speculative in many cases." But the missile gap charge helped Democrats in 1960, who inserted it into their 1960 platform by charging that "our military position today is measured in terms of gaps—missile gap, space gap, limited war gap." In addition to being political ammunition, the claims "reflected the parochial interests of the military services," Goodpaster said, because they gave the military a reason to demand more weapons spending.[20]

After the campaign, Alsop admitted that he had injected the issue into speeches even though it was a straw man. One of Kennedy's first moves as president was to ask the new defense secretary, Robert McNamara, to conduct a study on American and Soviet missile strength. The appraisal confirmed what Kennedy knew privately, that the United States was far ahead of the Soviet Union in missiles. Soon the public knew, too. On February 7, 1961, the *New York Times* reported, "Kennedy Defense Study Finds No Evidence of a 'Missile Gap.'" Privately, Kennedy scoffed, "Who ever believed in the missile gap anyway?" Science advisor Jerome Wiesner recalled that when he exploded the missile gap myth before Kennedy, the president uttered a single expletive "delivered more in anger than in relief." His supporters counted on increased defense spending, but now a major reason for it was gone. If Kennedy were to acknowledge that fact, it would torpedo a chief campaign charge that helped elect him.[21]

The missile gap was indeed heavily in America's favor. When Eisenhower's presidency ended, the United States had an overwhelming lead, with 160 operational Atlas ICBMs, compared with just four R-7s in the Soviet Union. In late 1961, Corona satellite intelligence showed that the Soviets had only six ICBMs. A year and a half into Kennedy's presidency, the United States still retained a commanding lead over the Soviet Union in ICBMs, 194 to 72. In fact, the U.S. lead in missiles motivated Khrushchev—always inclined to take big gambles—to place short-range missiles in Cuba, hoping in one stroke to achieve a kind of parity with the United States. Later in the 1960s, after Johnson became president, he spoke guardedly about surveillance from space and admitted that "we know how many missiles the enemy has and, it turned out, our guesses were way off. We were doing things we didn't need to do. We were building things we didn't need to build. We were harboring fears we didn't need to harbor." The admissions were cold comfort to Eisenhower, who still smoldered. In 1963, he commented that he was "really saddened by the readiness of some people who really don't know the facts, to go out charging and making this kind of allegation throughout the world, when it wasn't necessary to do it."[22]

But the missile gap had an impact because Americans believed in it, leading Eisenhower to call it "a useful piece of demagoguery." The allegation induced Congress to appropriate more money for defense spending than Eisenhower wanted (by $1 billion in the 1959 budget). By 1960, the term "missile gap" had firmly entered the American vernacular (even a New York Aqueduct racehorse was named "Missile Gap"). The term itself, and the fiction on which it was based, also gave Kennedy incalculable help in the presidential race. As a rule, during the Cold War Republicans enjoyed an edge over the Democrats in foreign policy, as voters trusted the GOP more in defense, thanks partly to Republicans' effectiveness in portraying themselves as tougher opponents of communism. In neutralizing that advantage, the missile gap charge gave Kennedy another way to tip the race in his favor.[23]

 ## Prestige and Economic Strength

Newsweek columnist Ernest Lindley remarked that the 1960 campaign featured two great innovations. One was television debates. The other was the concept of world prestige and Kennedy's charge that America's had slipped. At first, Lindley said, listeners reacted adversely to the idea. But as the senator stressed the theme, Nixon denied it, a hollow response that made the claim more cogent.[24]

Nixon stated that America's prestige stood at "an all-time high," whereas that of the Soviet Union had sunk to "an all-time low." Kennedy rejected this rosy view, saying that Americans "have been repeatedly assured by Mr. Nixon—in glowing, sugar-coated terms—that we have nothing to worry about in arms, science and space." Instead, Kennedy declared, "I have premised my campaign on the single assumption that the American people are uneasy at the present drift in our vitality and prestige."[25]

The television debates not only showcased Kennedy's celebrated poise and charisma but also became a forum in which the candidates tussled over America's standing. This topic surfaced in almost every one of their four face-offs. In the second debate, Kennedy said, "We have not maintained our position and our prestige," citing a February Gallup poll in which most respondents in eight of nine countries thought the Soviet Union would be ahead of the United States militarily and scientifically by 1970. In the third debate, Kennedy pointed to more indications that the country's status had slipped, such as "our being second in space," USIA polls, Soviet economic growth, and UN votes in which America lacked support from other nations. "So I would say our prestige is not so high," Kennedy concluded. "No longer do we give the image of being on the rise. No longer do we give an image of vitality."[26]

In the fourth debate, Kennedy continued the offensive, invoking space to illustrate his point. "I believe the Soviet Union is first in outer space. . . . We're first in other areas of science but in space, which is the new science, we're not first," he said. He painted a picture of a country frozen in amber, saying "we can no longer afford to stand still. We can no longer afford to be second best. I want people all over the world to look to the United States again, to feel that we're on the move, to feel that our high noon is in the future." Deploying a favorite campaign theme, Kennedy said that the next president had "to get this country moving again, to get our economy moving again, to set before the American people its goals, its unfinished businesses." Nixon countered, "America's prestige abroad will be just as high as the spokesmen for America allow it to be." As for space, he said, "Now, when we have a Presidential candidate—for example, Senator Kennedy—stating over and over again that the United States is second in space and the fact of the matter is that the space score today is 28-to-8—we've had twenty-eight successful shots, they've had eight."[27]

Nixon was right about the space race, but he was in a bind. By countering Kennedy's charge of declining prestige, he gave it credibility. It was as if Kennedy had sunk a hook into Nixon, and each time he twisted it, he elicited a response. As was true with any negative attack, answering it also kept the charge in the news, which created more damage. Throughout the campaign, Kennedy forced Nixon to react to charges about a slothful administration, and constantly on the defensive, the vice president never mounted an effective attack.[28]

Moreover, Kennedy had a point. On a personal level, he was more sensitive to image than Eisenhower or Nixon, and he took care to embellish his own appearance and prevent any untoward scene from blighting it. To keep his appearance fresh, Kennedy changed suits up to three times a day. Before his first television debate with Nixon, he sunned himself atop his Chicago hotel's roof to deepen his bronze tan. Although he liked golfing, he shied away from being photographed on the links to avoid the languid image that plagued Eisenhower. His campaign forbade photographers from taking pictures of him eating, and Kennedy whipped off a ceremonial Indian head-dress placed on him, remembering how foolish President Calvin Coolidge looked wearing one. Kennedy also had a superior understanding of the media and better relations with reporters than either Eisenhower or Nixon. Forced to assume the mantle of family politician after the death of his older brother Joseph, Kennedy had originally planned to become a journalist, and many of his best friends were reporters. (Jackie, who had also worked as a journalist, had similarly close relationships with members of the press.) He understood their craft, and he knew what made good copy.[29]

Kennedy translated his media savvy and solicitude about his image into a consciousness about the country's image—and how it had suffered. The *New York Times* conducted an ambitious survey of foreign government offi-cials, newspaper editors, and businessmen and found that while the United States still towered over the Soviet Union overall, America's prestige had waned during the Eisenhower years. Meanwhile, Soviet stature had risen, and a major cause was Sputnik. USIA director George Allen told Congress that the Soviet satellite "increased the prestige of the Soviet Union tremen-dously and produced a corresponding loss of United States prestige." A USIA international survey confirmed that the Eisenhower administration's posture of dismissing any "space race" was a poor tactic that suggested an in-ferior position in the race—and thus the reason to deny a competition.[30] Polls taken in 1960 showed the continued effect of Sputnik. More Ameri-cans continued to believe the Soviet Union, rather than the United States, was winning the "propaganda war." One survey showed that 41 percent of those questioned considered the Democratic Party best suited to enhance America's prestige, while just 25 percent thought the Republicans could do so. The USIA reported that worldwide people saw the United States lag-ging behind the Soviet Union, even though the scientific community knew that America actually led Russia in almost all science fields.[31]

The drop in America's image allowed Kennedy to talk convincingly of "Communist advance and relative American decline" worldwide and warn that "we have been slipping, and we are moving into a period of danger." Proof of communist gains came in Cuba, as Fidel Castro established a com-munist regime there in 1959. In truth, Cuba was one of only two countries that fell into communist hands during Eisenhower's presidency (the other, North Vietnam, was already under Ho Chi Minh's grip as Truman ended his term), but being close to America, Cuba magnified concerns of a sweeping communist tide. In light of such a danger, Kennedy ridiculed the Eisen-hower tenet that economic strength and a healthy consumer goods market should be the country's main concerns. America could not, he said, say to

Khrushchev that "you may be ahead of us in rockets, but we're ahead of you in color television." He added, "I'll take my television in black and white."[32]

That was the dilemma facing Americans: safety and security versus economic strength and consumer comforts. By charging that Eisenhower blindly pursued the latter, Kennedy implied that the seventy-year-old president was out of touch and failed to understand. He quoted Eisenhower as saying, "Being President is a very great experience . . . but the word 'politics' . . . I have no great liking for that." Kennedy observed, "The American people in 1952 and 1956 may well have preferred this detached, limited concept of the Presidency after twenty years of fast-moving, creative Presidential rule." But the country was in a new decade and era, and Kennedy warned that "a restricted concept of the Presidency is not enough. For beneath today's surface gloss of peace and prosperity are increasingly dangerous, unsolved, long-postponed problems." He stressed that America needed a leader who would act "first and fast." With such a leader, Kennedy promised, historians would look back on the 1960s and declare them "great years of the American Republic. These were the years when America began to move again."[33]

After Eisenhower's gray respectability, Kennedy seemed like a firecracker, and his promises of economic leadership offered even more dynamism. Here the fiscal conservatism of the Eisenhower administration, with its budget restrictions and vetoes, had an inherent disadvantage compared with promises of activism. Kennedy said he would pump more money into defense spending, and the Democratic platform targeted a gaudy 5 percent economic growth rate.[34]

Eisenhower told Nixon to follow the same course as he had on federal spending and economic growth if the vice president won the race. Be tough with Congress on a balanced budget, he advised. "If we don't do this and if you come to this chair," Eisenhower warned, "you will be the unhappiest man in the United States. If we don't begin to pay as we go, we'll be in a terrible spot and have no recourse except to desert liberty as we understand it." In real terms, this go-slow approach paid off. During the Eisenhower years, the economy registered a real GNP annual growth rate of 2.7 percent, a pace that reflected his gradual, incremental approach to governance. But in political terms, Eisenhower's policy seemed wan. By 1960, Democrats charged that this Eisenhower growth rate was a snail's pace, especially compared with historically higher rates, such as 3.72 percent for the 1879–1919 period, when America underwent titanic industrial growth.[35]

Ironically, it was the economy—sturdy for most of Eisenhower's presidency—that dealt the gravest blow to Nixon's campaign. In May 1960, a recession began, at a time when the economy had barely recovered from the 1957–58 slump. Indeed, the small gap between the two recessions marked the shortest period of recovery in the post–World War II era. Although the downturn proved mild, it lingered through the election, with unemployment reaching 6.3 percent in October. Only in May 1961 did recovery begin. Nixon was at the recession's mercy, and he was bitter. "All the speeches, television broadcasts and precinct work in the world could not counteract . . . [the] hard fact" of joblessness, he complained. Privately, he criticized "the standpat conservative economics that [treasury secretary Robert] Anderson and his crowd are constantly parroting." The economy might have been the race's deciding factor. Speechwriter Malcolm Moos recalled that "almost all people agreed that another month and the economy really cranking out of the recession, the result would have been different."[36]

Confident of a Republican victory, Eisenhower declined to propose a tax cut. The recession was mild, and the new administration—Nixon's, Eisenhower assumed—could cut taxes later, when it would reap the political rewards of such an action. In the meantime, postponing a tax cut would put the federal fiscal situation in better health. But politically, Nixon paid the price for the recession and the fiscal discipline that kept inflation low. Raymond Saulnier recalled that "we didn't have much that was helping us in 1959–60. . . . On the contrary, we had a whole set of situations and forces that were tending to retard the economy. And, well, the economy continued on a rather sluggish basis in 1959, in 1960, and we lost that election."[37]

 ## Nixon's Handicaps

Space, ebbing U.S. prestige, and the sluggish economy produced a trio of handicaps hampering Nixon's chances, magnifying the negative reactions he tended to elicit from voters. His running mate provided scant help. Eisenhower had urged Nixon to pick Henry Cabot Lodge, the former Massachusetts senator whose seat Kennedy had taken after beating him in the 1952 Senate race. Lodge, Eisenhower reasoned, would add assets such as valuable diplomatic experience to the ticket, especially since he was serving as Eisenhower's United Nations ambassador. The advice proved an Eisenhower miscue. Lodge was a bumbling campaigner—lethargic, wooden, and dull—who insisted on afternoon naps and mustered only enough energy to participate in one daily event. He was dead weight on Nixon's back.[38]

Eisenhower's ambivalence toward Nixon presented another burden. The president's coolness surfaced in an odd, damaging statement at an August 1960 press conference, when he let slip his ambivalence toward Nixon. As

FIGURE 11. Republican vice presidential nominee Henry Cabot Lodge, Vice President Richard Nixon, and Eisenhower campaigning in New York City during the 1960 presidential race. Eisenhower and Nixon had a complex relationship, and Nixon felt that the president's space and economic policies needed to be more aggressive. (Library of Congress, Prints & Photos Division, *U.S. News and World Report* collection)

Eisenhower was ready to end the questions, a reporter pressed him on Nixon's input into administrative decision making. Eisenhower grew testy, and when asked to give an example of a "major idea" that originated with Nixon, he replied, "If you give me a week, I might think of one. I don't remember."[39] It was an appalling gaffe.

What Eisenhower meant was hard to divine. He might have been trying to underscore that he himself held the reins at the White House, contrary to the image of him as detached, and he probably also meant that Nixon was more important in the day-to-day operations of an administration that prized conservatism and steadiness over major legislation. Since the question was the last one that day, his remark might also have been a quick way to end the session as well as an invitation for the reporter to repeat it at the press conference scheduled for one week later. At the same time, though, Eisenhower's doubts about Nixon likely had grown since 1956. Following Nixon's 1959 trip to Russia, Milton Eisenhower reported to his brother that after Nixon gave a special television address to the Soviet people, he attended a dinner at the U.S. embassy at which he gulped down several martinis and aggressively solicited reactions to his speech, lacing his comments with profanity. The incident sowed further doubt in Eisenhower's mind about Nixon.[40]

Eisenhower's damaging press conference retort seemed to cut down Nixon's stock-in-trade, his experience as vice president, and it hurt. Still, despite the unintended slight, Eisenhower desperately wanted Nixon to win, although Mamie disliked the idea of her husband's campaigning in 1960. "There was some vein in his head that would stand out a little bit when he was getting thoroughly into some speech. And she didn't like that. She talked to doctors about it," recalled Edward McCabe. "So there were people looking out for him, you know, [to] keep trying to cool [him] down a bit. But he was a scrapper. He was a battler. He didn't like to lose, and he wanted to do what he could to win." Toward the campaign's conclusion, the president threw himself into the race, telling voters on election eve that they faced "an easy choice between dedication and experience rather than an attitude of arrogance and inexperience." Privately, Eisenhower expressed bafflement that the Democrats had nominated an "inexperienced boy" and said he was "appalled" that anyone as "immature" as Kennedy could reach the White House.[41]

Diving into the campaign also allowed Eisenhower to rebut the charges of a diminished America, a concept he could no longer ignore because he felt personally affronted. His patriotism had always run deep, so much so that early in his marriage he said to Mamie, "There's one thing you must understand. My country comes first and always will. You come second." Where Kennedy might have wanted citizens to reach, strive, and shake things up, Eisenhower saw the American way of life as exemplary, not to be tampered with or traduced. To him, the political charges questioning America's stature bordered on treasonous. Accusations of a fading nation made it hard "to control my temper," he said during a televised October campaign appearance. He pointed out that the United States always found support in the United Nations, and he mentioned that one neutral nation's leader confided that he instinctively looked to the United States for guidance. At a campaign dinner in San Francisco, Eisenhower said, "When in the face of a bright record of progress and development, we hear some misguided people wail that the United States is stumbling into the status of a second-class power and that our prestige has slumped to an all-time low, we are simply listening to a debasement of the truth."[42]

The 1960 presidential race was the only one in history in which space policy and prestige combined to play prominent roles, and both sides were concerned with them up to election day. James Hagerty worried that the

Soviets would put a man in space just before the election to help defeat the vice president. Two weeks before the election, Johnson asked Glennan for a schedule of NASA launches for the rest of 1960—including those with animals or humans aboard—which Glennan suspected was LBJ's attempt to learn whether the administration planned a pre-election launch to boost Nixon's campaign. Indeed, NASA launched Explorer VIII, but it gave little extra lift to Nixon.[43]

The vice president lost by the dime-thin margin of 0.1 percent in the popular vote. The defeat stung Eisenhower as much as if he himself had been on the ballot. "All I've been trying to do for eight years has gone down the drain," he lamented. He later called Nixon's loss his "principal political disappointment" and said that "one of the biggest mistakes of my political career was not working harder for Dick Nixon in 1960." Many factors contributed to Kennedy's narrow victory: television debates, a superior staff and campaign organization, growing African American support for the Democratic Party, Fidel Castro's communist takeover of Cuba, Nixon's time-consuming and energy-wasting visits to all fifty states, and even the workings of Chicago Mayor Richard Daley's Illinois vote machine. There was Nixon himself: a polarizing, shifty-eyed politician who was notoriously poor at conversation and whom many voters never forgave for Red-hunting during the McCarthy era. Moreover, after eight years of one president, voters usually grow fatigued and often pick the incumbent's polar opposite; thus they preferred Warren Harding's insouciance to Woodrow Wilson's stern idealism and FDR's cheerfulness to Herbert Hoover's gloom. In Kennedy, they saw a young, dynamic replacement to a stodgy septuagenarian.[44]

The issues of space, economic strength, and world prestige also hung heavily over the country and permeated the campaign. On all three, the Democrats had the advantage, and they generated a powerful undertow that swept the Republicans out of the White House. Eisenhower's popularity might have still been strong, and he drew enthusiastic crowds when he stumped for Nixon. But the support stopped at the edge of his political penumbra; signs amidst the crowds proclaimed, "We like Ike—We back Jack."[45]

Ironically, had Nixon won, he likely would have deviated from Eisenhower's space paradigm. Given Nixon's reaction to Sputnik and the interest he showed in the political benefits of space, he would have pursued a policy more active and flashy than Eisenhower's. But now the Democrats were to have the White House, and Eisenhower was left to close out his term and assess his achievements—in space and on earth.[46]

CHAPTER 16

Eisenhower versus Kennedy

Eisenhower hated giving up the Oval Office to Kennedy. He mused over "what Joe Kennedy is going to try to get his son to do when he becomes President." He thought his successor inexperienced (although Kennedy had served six years in the House and eight in the Senate) and too young for the presidency. Kennedy cronies like Frank Sinatra baffled the old general, who wondered why Kennedy chose such company. Privately, Eisenhower made his feelings known. He used Charles Wilson's remark about a man's "flywheel being too big for his engine" to describe Kennedy and said he had "a minimum of high regard" for him. He called him "Little Boy Blue" and "that young whippersnapper." On Inauguration Day, Nixon sat next to Eisenhower and later said that he could hear the outgoing president's teeth grating during Kennedy's inaugural address. (The scorn was mutual. When later asked what her husband thought of Eisenhower, Jacqueline Kennedy replied, "Well, not much. You know, Jack saw that all that could have been done, I mean, how [Eisenhower] really kept us standing still. . . . I don't think he thought much of him.")[1]

Up to that time, Eisenhower was the oldest man ever to occupy the White House. At age 70, he was the last president born in the nineteenth century, and he was turning over the office to the youngest man ever elected president, just forty-three years old. Belonging to two different generations, raised in distant regions and under entirely contrasting family circumstances,

Eisenhower and Kennedy also offered different policy paradigms for America. The old general favored incremental initiatives; his young successor wanted an accelerated agenda. Space offered a critical example of their differences.

The Race to the Moon

Initially, Eisenhower and Kennedy shared similar visions on space exploration. In January 1961, Eisenhower and Kennedy delivered State of the Union addresses. Eisenhower called the United States "preeminent today in space exploration for the betterment of mankind" and said, "Americans can look forward to new achievements in space exploration. The near future will hold such wonders as the orbital flight of an astronaut, the landing of instruments on the moon, the launching of the powerful giant Saturn rocket vehicles, and the reconnaissance of Mars and Venus by unmanned vehicles."

Speaking just eighteen days after Eisenhower, Kennedy seemed finally to agree that the United States led the Soviet Union in space. He declared, "Today this country is ahead in the science and technology of space, while the Soviet Union is ahead in the capacity to lift large vehicles into orbit." Echoing Eisenhower's hope to explore other planets, Kennedy invited "all nations—including the Soviet Union—to join with us in developing a weather prediction program, in a new communications satellite program and in preparation for exploring the distant planets of Mars and Venus, probes which may someday unlock the deepest secrets of the universe."

But in other areas, differences between the two speeches were so stark that they could have been delivered eighteen years rather than eighteen days apart. Eisenhower proudly called the NDEA "a milestone in the history of American education." Kennedy mentioned "90,000 teachers not properly qualified to teach" and warned, "We lack the scientists, the engineers and the teachers our world obligations require. We have neglected . . . the basic research that lies at the root of all progress." Although Eisenhower admitted that "unemployment rates are higher than any of us would like," he pointed out that America's GNP stood at more than half a trillion dollars, almost 25 percent higher than when his presidency began. But Kennedy said, "the American economy is in trouble. The most resourceful industrialized country on earth ranks among the last in the rate of economic growth."

Eisenhower stressed fiscal discipline. He spoke of "the long pull" of defense spending and warned, "Every dollar uselessly spent on military mechanisms decreases our total strength and, therefore, our security. We must not

FIGURE 12.   December 6, 1960. John Kennedy's postelection visit to the Eisenhower White House. Although at this time the two men had roughly congruent views on human spaceflight, in 1961 Kennedy announced the ultimate prestige gambit, a manned mission to the moon. Eisenhower called it "nuts." (John F. Kennedy Library)

return to the 'crash-program' psychology of the past when each new feint by the Communists was responded to in panic. The 'bomber gap' of several years ago was always a fiction, and the 'missile gap' shows every sign of being the same." He promised, "I shall submit a balanced budget for fiscal 1962 to the Congress next week."[2]

Kennedy was more willing to spend on defense and pledged to meet the challenges of "a period of uncertain risk and great commitment." To that end, he announced that he would accelerate Polaris and America's entire missile program. He expressed his "current intention to advocate a program of expenditures which . . . will not of and by themselves unbalance the earlier Budget [submitted by Eisenhower]." But he qualified that pledge by adding that "we will do what must be done. For our national household is cluttered with unfinished and neglected tasks."[3]

In private, Kennedy's tone was less alarmist. Ensconced in the Oval Office, he said to Charles Bartlett, the Pulitzer Prize–winning journalist who years earlier had introduced Kennedy to Jacqueline Bouvier, "You know,

Charlie, this country is in really good shape. And we're lucky—really lucky—to get elected with this country as strong and as well-run as it is." Bartlett informed Roemer McPhee about the new president's remarks, and McPhee told Eisenhower, who flashed his cold blue eyes and asked, "Roemer, what then does your friend Charlie Bartlett think of his friend Jack Kennedy?" Eisenhower's acerbic question, McPhee remembered, showed his lingering resentment of Kennedy's campaign accusations.[4]

Ironically, the country's "good shape" and healthy economy allowed Eisenhower's successors, Kennedy and Johnson, to expand programs he had tried to restrain—space, education, health, and welfare. After the successful 1969 Apollo moon landing, Johnson reflected on what he thought had been the space program's national effect. He mentioned that it allowed the government to pass an education bill, which led to more legislation. Subsequently, Johnson said, the thinking was, " 'Well, if you do that for space and send a man to the moon, why can't we do something for grandma with medicare?' And so we passed the Medicare Act, and we passed forty other measures." He concluded, "And I think that's the great significance that the space program has had. I think it was the beginning of the revolution of the '60s." A signal for change came when Kennedy promulgated ambitious plans to project American power in space.[5]

That came as a surprise, for little in Kennedy's past suggested an interest in space. A bartender at a Boston-area tavern that Kennedy frequented recalled witnessing a conversation the senator had just after Sputnik. Kennedy scoffed at rockets, calling them a waste of money and questioning their use in space. He might have been playfully trying to provoke a debate, or he might have been serious. Keith Glennan was disappointed that Kennedy gave no direction to NASA before taking office, failing even to name a new director, whom Glennan hoped to work with to make a smooth transition. During his last weeks in office, Glennan ended multiple diary entries with the line, "No word from the Kennedy administration!"[6]

Kennedy was unfamiliar with space as a policy domain. *Time* magazine correspondent Hugh Sidey, a presidential observer who covered Kennedy closely, wrote, "Of all the areas of bafflement when Kennedy took office, space seemed more perplexing than the others. Kennedy seemed to know less about it, be less interested in it." When he devoted time to it, he tried to get his bearings. While president-elect, Kennedy asked Jerome Wiesner to head an ad hoc committee to study space policy. On January 10, the eight-man panel presented its findings, which doled out unsparing criticism of manned spaceflight. It regretted that "by having placed highest national priority on the MERCURY program, we have strengthened the popular belief that man in space is the most important aim of our nonmilitary space effort. The manner in which this program has been publicized in our press has further crystallized such belief. It exaggerates the value of that aspect of space activity where we are less likely to achieve success." In addition to its inherent problems, the manned program siphoned attention away from scientific areas "in which we have already achieved great success and will probably reap further success in the future." Human space travel not only diverted focus from substantive exploration, but it could also prove political poison, especially if an astronaut were to die in space. The best course was to concentrate on satellites and science, the committee recommended. Among the members of PSAC, Hornig recalled, "It was a gut feeling that this [moon mission] was more showmanship ahead of what you might call an orderly program."[7]

Once installed as presidential science advisor, Wiesner continued to espouse this thinking. In a February 1961 memorandum to Kennedy, he warned that competing in a space race would play to Russia's strengths. The United States would put the Soviets to shame in fields that really mattered; Wiesner wrote that "in almost any other area in which we would elect to compete, food, housing, recreation, medical research, basic technological competence, general consumer good production, etc., they would look very bad." Those were the arenas where the United States should choose to compete, Wiesner advised.[8]

Kennedy himself expressed another reason not to stake the nation's reputation in a space race. On February 8, 1961, at the second news conference of his presidency, he stressed astronaut safety. "We are very concerned that we do not put a man in space in order to gain some additional prestige and have a man take disproportionate risk," he said, "so we are going to be extremely careful in our work and even if we should come in second in putting a man in space, I will still be satisfied if when we finally do put a man in space his chances of survival are as high as I think that they must be."[9]

Still other considerations made Kennedy chafe at manned spaceflight. The price concerned him, as it did the director of the Bureau of the Budget, David Bell, who said that "the wisdom of staking so much emphasis and money on prestige that might or might not be gained from space achievements in the late 1960s and 1970s appears questionable." So he made no major revisions to the Eisenhower space program, including the $965 million NASA budget Eisenhower had proposed (for the fiscal year beginning in July 1961). In March 1961, when new NASA administrator James Webb asked for more money to speed up Project Apollo, Kennedy refused, agreeing only to Webb's request for more funding for the Saturn booster. As with Eisenhower, space ranked low on Kennedy's priorities. Theodore So-renson recalled that Kennedy "regarded his programs for education, con-servation, health and full employment to be more important than the space race." Foreign events were even more pressing. Kennedy devoted his entire inaugural address to foreign policy and once president focused his early at-tention on Laos, where the pro-American government seemed in danger of collapsing before the communist Pathet Lao.[10]

But a constellation of factors aligned to make a manned lunar mission a high priority for Kennedy. One was his competitive nature. Under patri-arch Joseph Kennedy, the Kennedy clan had always emphasized winning. Joseph Kennedy drilled into his children the idea that second place was unacceptable—it was as good as last. If the brothers failed to win a sailboat race, for example, their angry father demanded to know why. This ethic bred aggressive rivalries among the Kennedy brothers evident from their youth, even if the competition meant risk or injury. When John was a boy, he and older brother Joe played chicken on their bicycles, riding straight toward each other and smashing head-on. While Joe was unscathed, John needed twenty-eight stitches. For his entire life, Kennedy hated losing. Just after the 1960 election, he visited LBJ's ranch and went on a deer hunt with the vice president-elect and others. When aide Kenny O'Donnell proved more skilled at shooting deer than he was, Kennedy treated O'Donnell with cold silence for two hours. During the Cuban Missile Crisis, as Kennedy played checkers with Undersecretary of the Navy Paul Fay to release ten-sion, he deliberately upset the board when he realized he was losing. "One of those unfortunate incidents of life, Redhead," Kennedy cracked. "We'll never really know if the Under Secretary was going to strategically outma-neuver the Commander in Chief." (By contrast, during the D-Day inva-sion, when Eisenhower played checkers with naval aide Captain Harry Butcher, they played to a draw.) Racing the Russians seemed almost a natu-ral outgrowth of Kennedy's competitive instincts.[11]

But there was much more. Two events in April 1961 provided an impe-tus for a major policy change. One involved Major Yuri Gagarin. On April 12, the Soviet Union scored another space "first" when Gagarin became the first human to orbit the earth. Again, Khrushchev capitalized on the achievement's rich propaganda value. Calling to congratulate Gagarin, he exulted, "Let the capitalist countries catch up with our country!" Inspiring a national celebration, Gagarin received a parade through Moscow's streets and a reception in the Kremlin. Robert Seamans believed that the shock of Gagarin's orbit exceeded that of Sputnik. The latter was just a satellite, but a human in space represented a whole new order of achievement. "That was, to me, the big turning point. There wasn't any question then the [United States] was upset," Seamans recalled.[12]

Two days after Gagarin's triumph, Kennedy held a White House meeting with top advisors to discuss how to react to the Soviet coup. The president appeared tense. Sidey later recalled that Kennedy "kept running his hands through his hair, tapping his front teeth with his fingernails, a familiar nervous gesture." After despairing that the United States might not catch up to the Soviets, he implored, "Is there any place where we can catch them? What can we do? Can we go around the moon before them? Can we put a man on the moon before them? . . . Can we leapfrog?"[13]

As with Sputnik, Congress and the media exerted pressure after Gagarin's flight. Democratic congressman Victor Anfuso of New York said that he wanted "to see our country mobilized to a war-time basis because we are at war" and "to see some first coming out of NASA, such as the landing on the moon." Republican congressman James Fulton of Pennsylvania insisted that "we are in a race" and pledged to authorize as much money as NASA needed. *New York Times* military correspondent Hanson Baldwin criticized America's space program, writing that it had "cost the nation heavily in prestige and marred the political and psychological image of our country abroad." Baldwin warned that if the United States were to race the Russians in space "we must decide to do so on a top-priority basis immediately, or we face a bleak future of more Soviet triumphs."[14]

Just five days after Gagarin's flight came a second event, the Bay of Pigs invasion. CIA-trained Cuban rebels attempted to overthrow Fidel Castro's regime, but his army crushed them. The American-sponsored disaster left Kennedy's administration with a black eye, and White House morale sagged. Eisenhower believed that in world opinion, the Bay of Pigs made the United States look more foolish than the U-2 incident had, with nothing to retrieve from it. "Considering all the information we got out of the many, many U-2 flights, what happened at Paris fades into insignificance," he said. "But here we gained nothing, and it made us look childish and ridiculous." Although it might be an exaggeration to look for Project Apollo's roots in a craggy Cuban bay, the mission's abject failure left Kennedy scrambling to regain the high ground, and he looked to space. "I don't think anyone can measure it, but I'm sure [the Bay of Pigs] had an impact," Wiesner said. "I think the President felt some pressure to get something else in the foreground." Once again, America's image was on the line. Sorenson recalled that "the Soviets had gained tremendous world-wide prestige from the

Gagarin flight at the same time we had suffered a loss of prestige from the Bay of Pigs. It pointed up the fact that the prestige was a real, and not simply a public relations, factor in world affairs."[15]

The two events of April 1961 put the new president "in a mood to run harder than he might have" otherwise, said Wiesner. Rumors swirled that the Soviet Union would attempt to land a man on the moon in 1967 to coincide with the fiftieth anniversary of the Bolshevik Revolution. Like any president who finds his image sullied, Kennedy sought to redeem himself and prevent further damage, as Eisenhower did after Sputnik. As if in panic mode, Kennedy wrote a famous April 20 memorandum to Vice President Johnson in which he asked, "Do we have a chance of beating the Soviets by putting a laboratory in space, or by a trip around the moon, or by a rocket to land on the moon, or by a rocket to go to the moon and back with a man? Is there any other space program which promises dramatic results in which we could win?"[16]

Eager to magnify attention on space, the vice president asked Defense Secretary Robert McNamara for advice. The forty-year-old Pentagon "whiz kid" and number cruncher wrote back, "Major achievements in space contribute to national prestige. This is true even though the scientific, commercial or military value of the undertaking may . . . be marginal or economically unjustified. What the Soviets do and what they are likely to do are therefore matters of great importance from the viewpoint of national prestige." Other advisors whom the vice president consulted favored aggressive space showmanship. The Air Force's General Bernard Schriever supported an ambitious program "for prestige purposes, for those things we could see as having national security implications and because of the need for advancing technology." Wernher von Braun wrote to Johnson, "No, I do *not* think we are making maximum effort" in space, proposing, "Let's land a man on the moon in 1967 or 1968." His urgency was clear. He said that "in the space race we are competing with a determined opponent whose peacetime economy is on a wartime footing. . . . I do not believe that we can win this race unless we can take at least some measures which thus far have been considered acceptable only in times of a national emergency."[17]

The arguments for a lunar mission still fell flat with PSAC, but the scientists' opinions counted less than those of administration political advisors. Wiesner thought that Apollo had become "a political, not a technical issue. It . . . was a use of technological means for political ends. It was on these considerations that I did not involve PSAC." Kennedy knew that PSAC opposed a manned moon mission, but he was also aware that the entire issue had become framed as a political, not just a scientific, one.[18]

Space was to become an instrument of national policy, a means of enhancing world prestige, which mattered far more to Kennedy than it had to Eisenhower. Whereas Eisenhower worried over limited resources and budget deficits, Kennedy belonged to a generation of leaders who saw values like a balanced budget and small government as passé. Increased spending, the thinking in Kennedy's administration went, might help rather than hurt the economy. Both he and Eisenhower agreed that the United States competed against the Soviet Union in military might and economic strength, but Kennedy considered space another area of competition. Impatient, he wanted the United States to score a "first" in space before the Soviets did. "He felt this was tremendously important from a geopolitical standpoint," Robert Seamans recalled. Even though the United States actually led the Soviet Union in the space race, as measured by satellites and scientific knowledge, "I don't notice that that has any impact whatsoever on the world view of our position," Kennedy complained. "It's the manned program that incites world interest."[19]

Webb and McNamara prepared a final memorandum for the president, which Johnson approved in its entirety. The memorandum recognized image and manned spaceflight as factors in national undertakings and the world arena. "Dramatic achievements in space . . . symbolize the technological power and organizing capacity of a nation," the memorandum said. "It is for reasons such as these that major achievements in space contribute to national prestige." It stated bluntly, "The Soviets lead in space spectaculars which bestow great prestige." America's world standing justified a manned lunar mission, even if the scientific value of such a project was dubious. "*This nation needs to make a positive decision to pursue space projects aimed at enhancing national prestige,*" Webb and McNamara urged. They wrote, "We recommend that our National Space Plan include the objective of manned lunar exploration before the end of this decade. . . . The orbiting of machines is not the same as the orbiting or landing of man. It is man, not merely machines, in space that captures the imagination of the world."[20]

Alan Shepard's flight reinforced this thinking. On May 5, 1961, America sent Shepard, one of the Mercury Seven astronauts, into a suborbital flight aboard a Redstone rocket, yet the jaunt paled next to Gagarin's. Not only did Gagarin fly a month before and achieve orbit, but the rocket propelling him had ten times more power, and his space capsule was five times heavier. The Soviet news agency Tass called Shepard's fifteen-minute flight "very inferior" to Gagarin's, both scientifically and technically. Still, the Shepard flight captivated Americans and grabbed attention worldwide. An Australian tourist visiting New York City commented, "I think it's fantastic. It was thrilling—something the free world has been waiting for for several years." The *Times* of London wrote that the flight exorcised "the demon of inferiority" that plagued America. The USIA noted that observers worldwide gratefully contrasted the openness of Shepard's achievement with the secrecy surrounding Gagarin's flight. At a White House Rose Garden ceremony honoring Shepard, Kennedy said his flight "was made out in the open with all the possibilities of failure, which would have been damaging to our country's prestige. Because great risks were taken . . . it seems to me that we have some right to claim that this open society of ours which risked much, gained much."[21]

If Shepard's flight had come just ninety days earlier, Eisenhower might have left office cresting atop buoyant feelings about America's space program. The breakthrough helped to alter U.S. public perception. Just one month later, the percentage of Americans who believed that their country led the USSR in space research finally equaled those who believed Russia led, and Americans also appeared evenly split on which country would reach the moon first. Ever since Sputnik, polls had shown that Americans considered Russia ahead in space. For the first time, Americans saw the race as even. Shepard's flight—and perhaps the new president's tone—caused a dramatic shift in public opinion.[22]

Kennedy's Challenge, Eisenhower's Chagrin

In the wake of Shepard's flights and Johnson's memorandum, Kennedy approved a manned mission to the moon, even saying that "there is nothing more important" than winning the space race. As with the missile gap charge, Kennedy had been hoisted by his own petard. He had campaigned promising to inject dynamism and vigor into American life. Instead came Gagarin and the Bay of Pigs. "The world wanted to see results," Eugene Skolnikoff said. "So he had to make some decisions that might have been unwise from a technical or logical point of view but were wise for their political reasons." This president's new urgency reflected the prevailing ethos, when "everything [that] came up during those years was always couched . . . in terms of 'the Russians are going to get it first; we've got to do it,'" recalled Skolnikoff.[23]

Kennedy planned to unveil his new space initiative before a joint session of Congress. Before the speech, the Kennedy speech-writing team sent the first draft of the address to NASA for review. Seamans recalled, "We were aghast." The president was going to call for a moon landing by 1967, a time when Kennedy would be finishing a second term and Democrats could reap the rewards of such a feat. Webb urged the White House to change the wording to "by the end of the decade," a phrase Kennedy loosely interpreted to mean in 1969 or 1970, while hoping it would come while he finished a second term in 1968.[24]

On May 25, Kennedy went to Capitol Hill and made an unusual second State of the Union address, just four months after his first, on "Urgent National Needs." The speech contained the immortal line in which Kennedy challenged the nation to "commit itself to achieving the goal, before this decade is out, of landing a man on the moon and returning him safely to the earth. No single space project in this period will be more impressive to mankind, or more important for the long-range exploration of space; and none will be so difficult or expensive to accomplish." This was to be a national goal, and the president said, "it will not be one man going to the moon—if we make this judgment affirmatively, it will be an entire nation. For all of us must work to put him there."[25]

These sentences marked a sharp turnabout. As Seamans described it, "In less than five months the administration had gone from doubting the value of any human spaceflight (in the Weisner Report) to calling exploration of the Moon 'essential.'" It defined a new space goal and dramatically reordered presidential priorities. The decision was also controversial. It had little support from scientists, and it was brazen, building on a record of just fifteen minutes of human spaceflight. It was costly; estimates were that the federal government would have to spend $40 billion to send men to the moon, which averaged out to $225 per American (in 1960s dollars). It might divert the nation from more important priorities: National Urban League president Whitney Young commented, "It will cost thirty-five billion dollars to put two men on the Moon. It will take ten billion dollars to lift every poor person in this country above the official poverty standard this year. Something is wrong somewhere." As Kennedy returned to the White House in the presidential limousine, he commented on the restrained applause to his moon shot proposal.[26] After the speech, one poll showed that 58 percent Americans opposed money for such a venture; only 33 percent supported it. Yet just three months into his administration, Kennedy increased NASA's budget by 11.8 percent over Eisenhower's. By 1962, NASA's budget was greater than the combined sum of all its previous ones, and Kennedy continued to plug his goal. In a celebrated September 1962 speech at Rice University, he declared, "We choose to go to the moon in this decade and do the other things, not because they are easy, but because they are hard."[27]

While poetic and uplifting, these words hardly justified a major government program. Moreover, although analysts today credit Kennedy with giving the space program direction by issuing a clear, specific, and dramatic goal—which Eisenhower failed to do—Kennedy had trouble justifying it. At press conferences, he bobbed and weaved, assaying various angles as he strained to explain the moon effort. He warned that second-place status would spawn hand-wringing, predicting that "a year from now or 6 months from now, when the Soviet Union has made another new, dramatic breakthrough, there will be a feeling of why didn't we do more." He hinted at derivative applications such as "a good many industrial benefits" and likened space travel to Charles Lindbergh's transatlantic flight, which "demonstrated a competence in the field of air travel which could have significance in after years." He continued, "So it is with space. Space may be the means of transportation." On another occasion, he said, "This program in many ways is going to stimulate science." He also tacked toward defense, saying space was "an area which could affect our national security." At still another time, he suggested that "it is not a question of going to the moon. It is a question of having the competence to master this environment."

But Kennedy hit closest to the mark when he called a moon flight "essential to the United States as a leading free world power." His remarks at a June 1962 press conference, when he spoke at length about space, shone the best light on his calculus for a manned moon mission. "I do not think the United States can afford to become second in space because I think that space has too many implications militarily, politically, psychologically, and all the rest," he said. He then used his most concrete piece of evidence, a poll showing that more than two-thirds of French students believed the Soviet Union ranked first in science and technology. "I would not regard that as a very satisfactory statistic," he remarked. Space boiled down to a race for world prestige. Kennedy said it "had a tremendous impact upon a good many people who were attempting to make a determination as to whether they could meet their economic problems without engaging in a Marxist form of government. I think the United States cannot permit the Soviet Union to become dominant in the sea of space."[28]

Yet NASA insiders had reservations, and Kennedy's ambition had a cynical side to it. When a reporter challenged him about spending taxpayer money on a manned moon scheme, Kennedy replied, "Don't you think I would rather spend these billions on programs here at home, such as health and education and welfare? But in this matter we have no choice. The Nation's prestige is too heavily involved." In a dramatic November 21, 1962, White House meeting, Webb clashed with the president. Webb declined to label the Apollo program NASA's top priority because it would overshadow all of the agency's legitimate scientific projects, and he voiced worries about its dangers. Webb got on Kennedy's nerves; the president, who grew impatient with talkative aides, thought Webb "was rather a blabbermouth," Robert Kennedy confessed. On that day, as the two men locked horns, the president grew combative. He countered, "Jim, I think it is the top priority, I think we ought to have that very clear. . . . [T]his is important for political reasons, international political reasons. This is, whether we like it or not, in a sense a race." Kennedy said that NASA had to make Apollo a top priority and aim to beat the Soviets to the moon because "otherwise we shouldn't be spending this kind of money because I'm not that interested in space." He complained about "these fantastic expenditures which wreck our budget" and said that "the only justification for it in my opinion to do it in this time or fashion is because we hope to beat them." Webb believed that Kennedy's reasoning on prevailing over the Russians was askew. But the young president wanted more speed and drama, and his emphasis was clear. Beating the Soviets to the moon would, he believed, enhance U.S. prestige, and that in turn would bolster American power worldwide.[29]

Eisenhower's advisors were appalled. Killian thought that Kennedy "gave [the moon mission] too high a priority in relation to those undertakings that bear more directly on human well-being." Glennan called a manned flight to the moon "a very bad move," explaining that it forced the United States into a competition that would soak up a disproportionate share of the budget. Glennan "was very upset" with the new NASA administrators who intimated publicly that a moon landing was possible within a decade, Seamans recalled, and Glennan even complained to James Webb, telling him, "No, Jim, I cannot bring myself to believe that we will gain lasting 'prestige' by a shot we may make six to eight years from now. I don't think we should play the game according to the rules laid down by our adversary."[30]

Eisenhower agreed. The month before Kennedy gave his speech before Congress, the former president was visiting California, where reporters told him that the Russians might put the first man in space. "It is not necessary to be first in everything," he replied. After Kennedy's speech, he was more direct. On October 3, 1961, he spoke at the Naval War College in Newport, Rhode Island. His remarks remained a secret for a decade. He told faculty and students that someday "humans are going to circle the moon, take some pictures of it, and maybe even get to a planet and back if there's time—I don't know—but I believe those things ought to come about as a by-product of all the research we are doing today in missiles and in bigger engines and so on." Saying that the United States has "priority tasks and we ought to keep our minds on those tasks," he continued, "I think to make the so-called race to the moon a major element in our struggle to show that we are superior to the Russians is getting our eyes off the right target."[31]

During candid moments, Eisenhower's criticism was more pungent. He called Kennedy's pronouncement "almost hysterical." Visiting Washington and breakfasting with Republican congressmen, he declared, "Anybody who would spend $40 billion in a race to the moon for national prestige is nuts." In a letter to House minority leader Charles Halleck, Eisenhower wrote that he "never believed that a spectacular dash to the moon, vastly deepening our debt, is worth the added tax burden it will eventually impose upon our citizens. This result should be achieved as a natural outgrowth of demonstrably valuable space operations. . . . I suggest that our enthusiasm here be tempered in the interest of fiscal soundness."[32]

A revealing insight came during a January 1963 interview with CBS newsman Walter Cronkite, when the former president was spending the winter in Palm Desert, California. The archetype of a media space enthusiast, Cronkite described himself as "nuts about space" and expressed a desire to travel there (he even applied later to ride in NASA's space shuttle). He asked whether racing to the moon was "a stunt." Eisenhower replied that he had "no doubt that we're going to have the ability one day to go up to the moon and look it over and come back. But I don't see why we should do that, because I can see no military or other advantage in doing it now." Perplexed, Cronkite pressed Eisenhower, asking about the military value of getting to the moon first. "Maybe I'm just stupid on this thing," Eisenhower said. Mentioning satellites and scientific discoveries like the Van Allen belts, he continued, "But I don't see why we take this one thing and make it a stunt." He added fiscal concerns, questioning the value of putting "two or three more billion a year into your budget every year just for that one thing. I just don't see the point in us challenging someone, say, 'We're going to beat you to the moon.' That I just don't understand."[33]

And he continued to deprecate Kennedy's goal. Writing to NASA astronaut Frank Borman, who later commanded the 1968 Apollo 8 mission that orbited the moon, Eisenhower criticized the space program for the manner in which it was "drastically revised and expanded just after the Bay of Pigs fiasco in 1961." Under his administration, the objective had been "to do everything possible—and with a sense of urgency—to concentrate our efforts in space on projects that could yield definite benefits to the peoples of the earth." Spending for the program was pegged at "something like a level of 2 or 2½ billion dollars a year," Eisenhower said, a figure his scientists advised would serve national interests well. Now, he remarked with regret, costs "went up drastically" to serve "a race, in other words, a stunt." Eisenhower observed that Kennedy had "*challenged* the Russians to a race to the moon, implying that the prestige of the U.S.A. would be riding on the issue. This, I thought, unwise."[34]

The former president's objections reached a wider audience in articles he published in the *Saturday Evening Post*. Repeatedly, Eisenhower pummeled Kennedy's space initiative, calling it a "swollen program" bolstered by "hysterical fanfare." He acknowledged the stakes. "We didn't and don't want to be a second-best nation, not in any important field, and certainly not in total accomplishment. But can we," he asked, "best maintain our over-all leadership by launching wildly into crash programs on many fronts?" He admitted he was proud of the astronauts, adding, "Indeed, I personally approved the project for selecting and training our future space explorers. But why the great hurry to get to the moon and the planets? We have already demonstrated that in everything except the power of our booster rockets we are leading the world in scientific exploration." Rather than a race to the moon, Eisenhower argued for a "long-range" and "orderly, step-by-step" program to explore "the scientific, military, and industrial potentials in space." What Kennedy advocated instead, Eisenhower worried, was diverting "a disproportionate share of our brainpower and research facilities from other equally significant problems, including education and automation." He added, "We are breezily assured that the cost and dislocation brought about by this moon race are worthwhile for the new 'prestige' they will bring us. There is no way of telling how true that may be, but we can be sure of one thing: The voyage to the moon will set a new record for a trip taken on borrowed money."[35]

It was indeed expensive. Over the ten fiscal years leading up to the Apollo 11 moon landing, the federal government spent $25 billion on the space program (in 2010 dollars, that amount translated to $151 billion); in the mid-1960s, NASA accounted for 4.4 percent of the federal budget. By other measures, the sums were small. In the late 1960s, the United States spent more each year on the Vietnam War than the entire sum expended on Apollo. And as a Cold War instrument, the race to the moon had fewer long-term costs and more benefits to U.S. prestige than some of Eisenhower's own controversial initiatives, such as the CIA intervention in Guatemala to overthrow the left-leaning Jacobo Arbenz.[36]

Polling data through the 1960s showed that more Americans disapproved of Apollo than supported it, but as the first moon landing neared, the public rallied. A June 1969 Harris poll revealed that 51 percent of Americans favored the moon mission, with 41 percent opposed. Senator Barry Goldwater, a notorious fiscal tightwad but dedicated flyer himself, said that "the only national heroes we have today are the men in space," and he lauded them "for giving inspiration and hope to the young people of our country who are now beginning to realize that there is no such statement as 'it can't be done.'"[37]

On July 20, 1969, in New York City's Central Park, three large television screens broadcast the Apollo 11 moon landing, and a few hundred spectators showed up to watch despite a driving rain. Political irony also drenched the Oval Office that day. The president now was Richard Nixon, the vice president who had labored in Eisenhower's shadow, who early on had latched on to space's political importance yet lost the presidency to Kennedy, Apollo's champion. As the astronauts trundled along the lunar landscape, Nixon spoke to Buzz Aldrin and Neil Armstrong from the Oval Office, twice mentioning that their feat impressed "people all over the world." Always eager to bolster his image as a peacemaker, Nixon stretched to link "peace" with the moon mission, telling the astronauts that "as you talk to us from the Sea of Tranquility, it inspires us to redouble our efforts to bring peace and tranquility to earth."[38]

Nixon was always concerned with America's image abroad, and reporters in Europe said that the moon mission improved America's standing there. Media coverage of the Apollo mission was extensive, and the undertaking washed away some of the bitter feelings Europeans had about America's role in Vietnam. One Czechoslovakian broadcaster said that "this is the America we love, one so totally different from the America that fights in Vietnam." A Dutch commentator called his country "lunar crazy," and a German newspaper proudly noted that many of America's aeronautical scientists were German. The world audience watching the landing on television, estimated at one billion, included Queen Elizabeth and Pope Paul VI. At Tokyo's Shinjuku train station, a Japanese man voiced his opposition to the Vietnam War and American military bases in Okinawa yet expressed joy that the astronauts had reached the moon. He had political differences with America, he conceded, "But when I think of narrow Japan, and those men out there touching down on the moon, I wish I were with them." The Apollo mission, open and clearly civilian in nature, reaffirmed that America explored space peacefully. One State Department official even said, "There is no question that the success of [the] Apollo 11 mission did more to bolster prestige abroad than any single event since the termination of the Pacific War in 1945."[39]

That was the main aim. Contrary to popular lore, Apollo's derivative benefits—such as scientific spin-offs—were relatively few. Although people believed that civilian products such as Velcro, Teflon, and Tang drink mix numbered among manned spaceflight's useful by-products, they did not. But the moon landing did allow American scientists to share their work abroad. Foreign nations helped to track Apollo, and the six moon missions during 1969–72 brought back 842 pounds of lunar rock and soil, which NASA made available to schools, museums, and laboratories. Robert Seamans pointed out that the moon samples "went to 130 different laboratories, thirty of them over in foreign countries." Most of all, though, what America derived from Apollo was a boost in the prestige race. With one mission, the United States overshadowed all the propaganda gains of the Sputniks, Luniks, and Gagarin mission.[40]

America won the space race, and the victory magnified the country's world standing just as Olympic triumphs enhance a country's image or a professional sports championship adds a talismanic luster to a city's reputation. In a similar vein, intelligence analysts Albert Wheelon and Sydney Graybeal compared the prestige race in space to the importance of intercollegiate sports. Athletics had nothing to do directly with a school's academic reputation, yet "the coach is under relentless pressure to win games because his team, in some intangible sense, stands for the entire college." While they conceded that it was "neither rational nor desirable," they believed "our stature as a nation, our culture, our way of life and government are tending to be gauged by our skill in playing this game [in space]." The achievement likely brought tangible results, too: as economists have noted, much like "branding" in business, a better world reputation translated to increased trade, tourism, and investment in a nation. (Cape Canaveral's Kennedy Space Center alone has attracted thousands of tourists annually, many from abroad, bolstering the Space Coast economy; the main draw at the Space Center is, of course, the Apollo saga.)[41]

Even skeptics lauded the moon landing. Donald Hornig, who had chaired the panel that recommended against it, later praised the moon mission: "There's no question that the whole thing spurred the interest in scientists and science and spurred the Congress to much more attention to it, appropriating a lot more money. And in general, as a symbolic center for what this country was up to in a very dynamic period, I think it served its purpose very, very well." Hornig added that the manned lunar landing could "be justified, really, by just what I think it was meant to do: A symbol for the country of what was possible if you really tried." Arnold Frutkin later criticized manned spaceflight, saying that "my deepest sympathies are with Eisenhower because he knew that the substantive aspects were not there. . . . Sending men to the moon did not achieve anything very substantial in the world." Yet Frutkin conceded that when "you challenge [the Soviets] on their grounds, which was their space success . . . and carry it through to win, it is hard to argue against that. It was successful and it achieved its purpose." Eisenhower, too, might have viewed the Apollo missions more favorably after their successful completion.[42]

In a way, the space race came full circle, eliciting reactions as memorable as those when the first satellite was launched. David Beckler commented that "the psychological impact of [the moon landing] was just, again like Sputnik, unanticipated." But Beckler noted an important difference. The "psychological effects of Sputnik were kind of negative," he said. "The psychological effects of the manned lunar flight were confidence—[it] built confidence in people." Beckler noted that the moon landing was "a singular event. And there are not many singular events you can think of that would have that kind of [positive] effect." Instead, many singular events frozen in people's memories have been associated with unpleasant shocks—the Kennedy assassination, the space shuttle disasters, or the September 11, 2001, terrorist attacks.[43]

The Apollo missions dispelled any notion that the United States lagged behind the Soviet Union in the space race or science. Seamans said, "After we landed on the moon, there wasn't anybody going around saying that the Soviets had more scientific and technical capability than we did, which they had been saying." The moon race allowed the United States to play to its strengths in electronics, computerization, rocketry, and managerial talent. The Soviet Union's brute rocket power and state guidance of goals could not compete. Earlier in the 1960s, Khrushchev conceded that the Soviet Union had fallen behind the United States in space exploration. Still, he believed that his country "should send a man to the moon—both for the good of science and for the prestige of our country."[44]

But the Soviet effort to send men to the moon imploded, crushed by the same forces that eventually gutted its economic and political system. The military, the real raison d'être for Russian rockets, resented the civilian effort impinging on its turf. The regimented Soviet educational system failed to encourage innovation and creativity, perhaps best illustrated when the Soviet rocket designed for a moon mission, the N-1, repeatedly failed, and Russian engineers could neither make improvements nor find replacements. An ossified government bureaucracy lacked the managerial talent to bounce back from setbacks and guide a lunar mission, and a secretive space program suppressed the media and public support needed to sustain it. Moreover, an expensive moon race was foolhardy for a nation that failed to provide basic consumer goods for its citizens.[45]

For the United States, though, the Apollo moon landing added another gem to a Cold War technological record studded with successes, and this record led to unforeseen effects stretching decades into the future. In 1983, Ronald Reagan, the science fiction buff who speculated about an alien invasion of earth, gave a surprising speech broaching the vision of a space shield comprising high-tech laser and particle beams that would protect America from incoming Soviet missiles. Critics dubbed Reagan's so-called Strategic Defense Initiative (SDI) "Star Wars," but Soviet leaders were startled. Over the decades, they had witnessed a succession of American technological triumphs, and Soviet ambassador to the United States Anatoly Dobrynin singled out three as especially impressive: the atom bomb, the Apollo program, and the top-secret Project Jennifer, which created the *Glomar Explorer*, a special ship that in 1974 retrieved part of a Soviet submarine that lay three miles deep on the Pacific Ocean floor. Dobrynin recalled that upon hearing of Reagan's SDI, the Kremlin "feared that the United States had achieved a technological breakthrough," rendering Russian missiles useless. Dobrynin wrote, "Our leadership was convinced that the great technical potential of the United States had scored again and treated Reagan's statement as a real threat." The prospect of the SDI forced the Soviets to the bargaining table, leading Soviet president Mikhail Gorbachev to meet Reagan in two summits that culminated in the 1987 Intermediate Range Nuclear Freeze (INF) Treaty, a remarkable agreement that wiped out an entire class of atomic weapons, intermediate-range missiles, which had been born in the Eisenhower era. Ultimately, too, it was not just American technology but a relentless reality at home that forced Gorbachev's hand, a dichotomy that Eisenhower had emphasized. Gorbachev said he was ashamed to admit that the Soviet Union was rich with resources yet "couldn't provide toothpaste for our people." Those were the small but significant items that collectively would win the prestige race, Eisenhower believed, and their scarcity showed that the Soviet Union could not afford massive military spending and would lose the Cold War.[46]

The Long-Term View

Eisenhower never got to see men walk on the moon. In April 1968, after playing golf in California, he suffered a mild heart attack. First hospitalized at California's March Air Force Base, he subsequently flew to Walter Reed Army Hospital in Washington. Mamie moved into a room next to his suite, and Eisenhower remained hooked to a cumbersome apparatus that he called "the bulldozer," a machine that helped to keep him alive. In August, he suffered another heart attack.[47]

But the general soldiered on. Having endorsed Richard Nixon for the 1968 Republican presidential nomination, he was pleased to see his former vice president win the election, and he entertained the notion of becoming a senior counsel ex officio for the new administration. Perhaps even more gratifying to Eisenhower was a February 13, 1969, hospital visit from CIA director Richard Helms and other intelligence officials to show reconnaissance satellites' latest photographs of Soviet military facilities. The material was so sensitive that the visitors closed the window blinds and asked all medical personnel to leave while Eisenhower reviewed it. As he did, he expressed amazement at how much better the photographs were compared with those he saw while president. He was pleased; the technology had come a long way, and he had helped to induce its birth.[48]

That improvement in satellite surveillance was one of the last confirmations of his legacy that Eisenhower saw. Over the next month, his weight plummeted to 125 pounds, and his skeletal appearance shocked visitors who had known him as a robust soldier and president. The end came on March 28, 1969, when Eisenhower died of heart failure. Throughout his career, he had been unpretentious; moreover, he had always had a soft spot for foot soldiers, feeling more comfortable with them than with generals or heads of state. Thus it was no surprise that one of his last requests was that he be buried in a simple, eighty-five dollar, standard-issue soldier's casket rather than anything more regal.[49]

Eisenhower's modesty and quiet effectiveness had always been admirable. But he declined to take advantage of space in the ostentatious way that Kennedy did, and his enthusiasm for it as a political issue was palpably lower. "Kennedy understood the situation perfectly, as a political animal," Arnold Frutkin said. "He realized we'd lost the first round, and he was looking to see what the second round could be that we could win. . . . He understood the situation very well and was willing to act on it in a way that Eisenhower wasn't, because Eisenhower clearly underestimated the international impact" of space endeavors. Like his scientists, Eisenhower examined space efforts in a rational, highly analytical manner. As Nixon observed, when "Eisenhower looked at [a] crisis, he looked at it very coldly," which had the virtue of leading to choices "that did not have the liabilities that some decisions have when they're made at the top of the head, or emotionally. He never made an emotional decision." But while that cool analytical style helped Eisenhower correctly see robotic space missions as cost-effective, it prevented him from weighing the political or emotional benefits of manned spaceflight.[50]

In explaining Kennedy's dramatic new space policy, the age gap was likely more important than any perceived missile gap. As with any person, advancing years tended to make Eisenhower more focused on a limited metric of priorities, whereas Kennedy was twenty-seven years younger and more receptive to new ideas—and more willing to take risks. NASA engineer Robert Gilruth, a member of the Space Task Group that supervised Project Mercury, believed that Kennedy's youth was a significant factor behind his decision to aim for the moon. "He was a young man. He didn't have all the wisdom he would have had. If he'd been older, he probably never would have done it," Gilruth said.[51]

Political training was at play, too. More than Eisenhower, Kennedy had an ear attuned to politics, and he also had to think about an eventual reelection campaign, whereas Ike did not. But Kennedy articulated an inspiring vision, realizing that prestige and space were vital weapons in fighting the Cold War. Winning the Cold War required invincible national security, as Eisenhower knew, as well as soft power bulwarks such as economic strength and an efficient transportation network. These things acted as quiet showcases for capitalism. But the Cold War also involved instruments such as rhetoric, propaganda, and showmanship. Although these elements had a more transient impact than world economic leadership, they—like economic strength—were important. Kennedy expanded such efforts by initiating the Alliance for Progress, an aid program designed to help Latin American countries, and the Peace Corps, which enabled young Americans to serve in Third World countries by teaching, building infrastructure, and helping communities.

Right up to his death, Kennedy played the public relations card better than Eisenhower did, even while privately agreeing with his predecessor about a manned moon mission. At a September 18, 1963 Oval Office meeting with Webb, Kennedy noted that "right now space has lost a lot of its glamour," expressing the concern that sending astronauts to the moon would look like "a stunt" that involved "a hell of a lot of dough . . . when you can learn most of what you want scientifically through instruments." He stressed to Webb that they needed to rationalize the mission using national security reasons rather than the country's world image, explaining, "The most we can say is this has got some military justification and not just prestige. Otherwise Eisenhower, who's been kicking us around . . . he's going to look like he's probably right." At one point, he even asked Webb bluntly, "Do you think the [manned] landing on the moon is a good idea?" (Webb told him it was because it would show "a basic ability in this nation to use science and very advanced technology to increase national power. . . .") But in public, Kennedy masked his inner doubts and appeared a full-throated supporter of manned spaceflight. On November 16, 1963, one week before his assassination, he made a highly symbolic visit to Cape Canaveral and toured the facility. He thoroughly enjoyed it. Viewing scale-size models of the Saturn rocket next to smaller ones, he appeared astonished at the super-booster's proportions. He spent considerable time with Robert Seamans, asking pointed questions about how America's rocket thrust capabilities compared with the Soviet Union's. As he left, he walked up the ramp to board his plane and then came back down and said to Seamans, "Now, be sure that the press really understands this," mentioning one reporter by name. He repeated the request to a military aide and, before bidding farewell to Seamans, added, "I wish you'd get on the press plane that we have down here and tell the reporters there about the payload."[52]

During the 1960s, as the manned space program grew, former president Eisenhower never publicly conceded the link between America's space endeavors and world prestige. But he found himself caught up in the excitement over manned spaceflight and was proud of his role in it. In 1962, as astronaut John Glenn orbited the earth, Eisenhower was golfing in California. To monitor the historic flight, he listened intently to a portable radio that he attached to his golf cart. He hoped to hear acknowledgment that he had promoted America's space program and expressed disappointment when none came. The Kennedy administration soaked up all the credit.[53]

But in many aspects of America's space program, Eisenhower's views remained reasonable and wise, partly because he focused on the long term. He felt that view distinguished him from politicians, once saying, "I will make smarter political decisions than a lot of guys who are pros, because they have gotten used to the narrow quick advantage, rather than taking a look at the longer range." Indeed, Eisenhower's "orderly" approach to space had virtues. The rush to land men on the moon during the 1960s might have even endangered astronauts' safety, as engineers complained about the emphasis on speed over safety. Lynn Radcliffe, the manager of New Mexico's White Sands rocket facility, protested, "They say we are in a race with the decade. This is dangerous. If we do not change our attitude about schedule and start worrying more about quality, we're going to lose some astronauts." Over the long term, the spasm of focus on Apollo weakened other space projects. The manned lunar missions seemed the sole goal, and in the crush of preparing for them, NASA failed to develop other projects or an overarching mission after Apollo. The space agency became a classic one-trick pony.[54]

As Apollo diverted NASA's attention, America fell behind the Soviet Union in other space endeavors. By the early 1970s, it trailed the USSR in the satellite scorecard, an area where it had led throughout the 1960s. America's attention also faded after Apollo. During the 1970s, new, more urgent national priorities replaced space: fighting high inflation, ending the Vietnam War, ameliorating an energy crisis, and pursuing détente with the USSR and China. Noted scientists echoed Eisenhower's views in emphasizing unmanned spaceflight. James Van Allen and William Pickering saw Apollo as a plateau and urged a return to robotic exploration, which was more cost-effective and scientifically beneficial. Nixon administration members agreed. Members of budget director Robert Mayo's staff noted that "no defined manned project can compete on a cost-return basis with unmanned space flight systems. In addition, missions that are designed around man's unique capabilities appear to have little demonstrable economic or social return to atone for their high cost. Their principal contribution is that each manned flight paves the way for more manned flight." Space exploration spawned not manned moon bases or orbiting hotels, as 1950s science fiction dreamers envisioned, but rather hundreds of satellites orbiting the earth, performing functions ranging from communications to reconnaissance. It was precisely what Eisenhower foresaw.[55]

By the early 1970s, as the Nixon White House groped for a new national space mission, enthusiasm sank further. When Vice President Spiro Agnew recommended a manned mission to Mars, few members of Congress expressed interest. The Senate majority leader, Mike Mansfield, a Montana Democrat, urged "balance" in space projects, saying that "there are problems on planet earth that must be faced up to." Democratic senator Clinton Anderson of New Mexico, who chaired the Senate Space Committee, said that rather than a Mars mission, "We might find that the money can be better used on education, on building good homes and on supplying medical services around the country." Even Senator Ted Kennedy—whose brother symbolized the nation's goal of a manned moon landing—wanted to restrain NASA's budget, arguing that $3 billion per year was sufficient.[56]

Yet pressure for manned spaceflight continued. NASA deputy administrator George Low maintained that keeping men in space was vital to America's space efforts. Instead of a manned Mars mission, NASA advanced the space shuttle. A novel concept, it was to be a reusable space vehicle, with the name "shuttle" denoting utility in ferrying satellites and material between space and earth. Part of the argument for the shuttle was rooted in precisely what Eisenhower feared—the pressure to continue the manned space program and provide contracts for the aerospace industry. The big question facing NASA was "how do you keep your numbers and your people and your laboratories and budget numbers going?" said Eugene Skolnikoff. "A manned space capability was seen as the way to do that. That's what interests the public, that's what interests the Congress, that's what makes the big payoff to the companies and the districts and the congressmen." NASA needed a manned space project to maintain a public image consonant with the enormous space centers at Cape Canaveral, Houston, and Huntsville. Frutkin agreed that "you can't argue with Kennedy's success with the man-to-the-moon program," but he added, "look at the can of worms he opened" with an industrial complex depending on manned spaceflight for its sustenance.[57]

But the space race was over, and this time Congress pushed back. Shuttle opponents argued it would grab the lion's share of NASA's budget and leave little for unmanned projects (indeed, by the twenty-first century, manned spaceflight devoured two-thirds of the agency's budget). Democratic senator Walter Mondale of Minnesota called President Nixon's support of the shuttle "another example of perverse priorities and colossal waste in government spending." Democratic senator William Proxmire of Wisconsin stated, "The shuttle won't cure one sick child, it would [not] provide housing for indigents. It won't provide food for the hungry. And it won't educate our offspring." Calling the shuttle a "space age boondoggle," Proxmire said it was "a complete mystery to me what tangible benefits the shuttle is going to provide." Since NASA justified the new vehicle only as a way to "continue to have an active space program," he sarcastically concluded, "It will keep the NASA technicians occupied. And it will keep the aerospace industry happy."[58]

But Nixon promised that the shuttle "will take the astronomical costs out of astronautics," and with his administration's backing, NASA secured congressional approval, which might even have become a bureaucratic justification to keep NASA itself alive. When Robert Frosch became NASA administrator for President Jimmy Carter, he completed a study on whether to continue the project. Frosch recalled that "my conclusion was that if we dropped the shuttle we might as well scratch NASA." The agency's funding and political support rested on the shuttle, and Frosch believed that without it, "NASA would have gotten to be a smaller and smaller agency and tucked in under something else eventually."[59]

To attract congressional support, NASA dressed up the shuttle in efficient, economical garb, predicting that a shuttle fleet would fly 779 missions over twelve years.[60] Instead, during thirty years of service, it flew only 135 missions. NASA estimated that a shuttle flight would cost just $8 million (in 1972 dollars), but the reality turned out to be $1.3 billion per flight. Indeed, the shuttle failed to perform many of the functions that NASA envisioned. NASA thought it could retrieve malfunctioning satellites and return them to earth for refurbishing, but simply using rockets to send up new ones proved more cost-effective. Limited to an orbital ceiling of three hundred miles, the shuttle could not reach satellites in geosynchronous orbits of 23,000 miles. It engaged in no true space exploration, unlike unmanned vehicles that probed the solar system's far reaches. Frutkin called the shuttle "a gargantuan waste of money." Its only unalloyed success was in keeping America in the manned spaceflight game, which became largely a publicity program after Apollo. "It contributes nothing to knowledge, nothing to industrial capability, and very little now to national prestige," said Harold Brown, defense secretary for Jimmy Carter. "But that's because it's been done once. To be first gets you something. To keep doing it, I think, gets you very little."[61]

Regrettably, the shuttle became a costly way to keep American men and women in space. It brought national tragedies: two shuttles, *Challenger* in 1986 and *Columbia* in 2003, perished in accidents, killing fourteen astronauts. Even veteran astronaut Story Musgrave, who flew on all five shuttles, called the craft "very unsafe, very fragile." The Associated Press estimated that the program cost more than the Panama Canal construction, the Manhattan Project, and the Apollo program combined. In the end, the shuttle also diverted engineering attention from the most promising form of space travel. NASA's post-shuttle proposals for manned spaceflight all returned to the old standby of rockets and disposable capsules, making the shuttle a deviation from this standard. Former NASA administrator Michael Griffin confessed that the shuttle might have retarded the space agency's development by decades. In the end, the shuttle left no one completely satisfied, and Eisenhower would have likely fulminated against it.[62]

Decades earlier, critics had derided him as old-fashioned and out of touch. But as time passed, he seemed more bellwether than backwater, and a new appreciation of his presidency emerged.

Conclusion

Eisenhower practiced a disciplined leadership stressing tenets that seemed archaic and dull. Most of all, he resisted cries for expansive government programs and spending. As Herbert York judged, after Sputnik the administration "was able to deal successfully and sensibly with most of the resulting rush of wild ideas, phony intelligence, and hard sell." Eisenhower was a throwback to pre-Keynesian thinking that emphasized balanced federal budgets and limited spending; as the new Keynesian paradigm of deficit spending took hold, advocating government intervention to massage the business cycle, Eisenhower's way seemed outdated. In the wake of Sputnik, it was easy to grow impatient with his patience.[1]

Yet Eisenhower repaired to his arsenal of presidential powers. He gave television talks, reached out to scientists, approved a backup satellite, and beat back pressure for more space and defense spending. He accomplished all this while summoning the physical courage to rebound from a mild stroke. He consciously kept his political conduct elevated and only privately disparaged adversaries and rivals. At a 1959 press conference, a reporter noted that "in the last few months people have been jumping on you with more regularity. I wonder, sir, you never seem to hit back. Don't you ever feel like taking a retaliatory poke at these people?" Eisenhower expressed his desire "to preserve the dignity of the office" and said that it was "not a good business for me to get up and call people some of the names they call me." By behaving this way, Eisenhower avoided political polarization and made a rebound possible. All these actions, Eisenhower stressed, demanded calm rather than panic. Good leadership meant the ability to set aside frenzied emotions and judge an issue's importance based on its future value. It was no accident that Eisenhower's post-Sputnik legacy—such as a new civilian space agency and an orderly satellite and science program—had a positive long-term impact.[2]

Given a tense political situation, Eisenhower's achievements after Sputnik were impressive. For the last six years of his presidency, he partnered with opposition Congresses, the final one after the 1958 midterms being heavily Democratic and poised to frustrate him. Still, he worked with Capitol Hill on major post-Sputnik legislation, including the NDEA and the establishment of NASA. This cooperation entailed laying aside his distaste for politicians and instead working with legislators to forge a bipartisan response to Sputnik. In 1972, before historians began major reassessments of his presidency, journalist and erstwhile Eisenhower critic William White already praised the achievements of "what was in effect a coalition government," adding that "the farther it recedes into history the better it looks."[3]

➤● An Open Program

NASA's founding secured Eisenhower's legacy in space policy, and the organization flowered during the last two years of his presidency. It also highlighted the contrast between the public American space program and the closed Soviet one. Arnold Frutkin, who served as the U.S. representative to the United Nations Outer Space Committee, recalled hearing committee members from other countries express appreciation "at how open we were," and NASA's civilian nature and America's participation in international space activities showed "that we were indeed open and not just talking about it." Two tragedies, occurring worlds apart during the 1960s, underscored the difference. On March 23, 1961, Russian cosmonaut Valentin Bondarenko died when a fire consumed the oxygen-saturated chamber in which he trained. In 1967 a similar conflagration erupted in the pure oxygen environment of an Apollo 1 space capsule during training. That fire killed three of NASA's best astronauts: Virgil "Gus" Grissom, Edward White, and Roger Chafee. With more openness from abroad, and the information it would have provided, they might have been saved.[4]

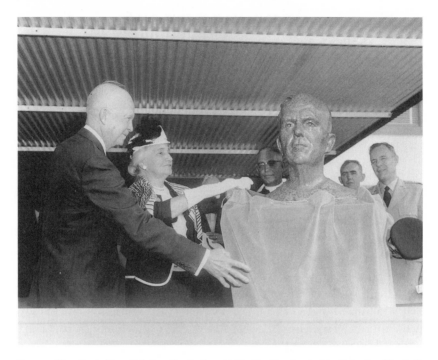

FIGURE 13. Huntsville, Alabama, September 1960. Eisenhower assists Katherine Marshall, widow of George C. Marshall, in unveiling a bust of her husband. The ceremony honored the renaming of the Huntsville space facility as the George C. Marshall Flight Center. (Dwight D. Eisenhower Library)

Eisenhower's involvement with an open space agency went on display during his last months in office. On September 8, 1960, he flew to Huntsville, Alabama. Keith Glennan had wanted to rename ABMA after George Marshall, and although the general had little connection with space, Eisenhower agreed and accepted Glennan's request to attend the dedication. Marshall had been his mentor during World War II, and with few pioneers in the U.S. space program, his name seemed as good as any to crown the space center. Whereas Glennan originally envisioned a modest affair, the ceremony mushroomed into a public relations event, as Eisenhower toured the facility for two hours. With Wernher von Braun and Karl Heimber, chief of the center's test division, he inspected a Saturn rocket booster. Eisenhower and von Braun shared a mutual antagonism; the president bristled at the scientist's grandstanding and pleas for more money, while von Braun bristled at Eisenhower's tight-fisted approach. But for the moment, they put aside their strained relationship, and the rocket scientist answered the president's "intelligent and penetrating questions," as Glennan observed, and showed him around the facility.[5]

FIGURE 14.   During the Huntsville visit, as rocket scientist Wernher von Braun points, Eisenhower gazes up at a model of the Saturn V rocket, designed to lift men into space. On this day, Eisenhower put aside his misgivings over manned spaceflight and his differences with von Braun. (Dwight D. Eisenhower Library)

In dedicating the Marshall Space Flight Center, Eisenhower unveiled a large bust of the general and spoke to ten thousand workers. He paid homage to the super-booster, saying, "No doubt this mighty rocket system makes its presence known loudly—possibly too loudly—in Huntsville. But it is a significant forward step in our conquest of space and for growth in human comprehension." He touted U.S. space achievements and emphasized, "All that we have already accomplished, and all in the future that we shall achieve, is the outgrowth not of a soulless, barren technology, nor of a grasping state imperialism. Rather, it is the product of unrestrained human talent and energy restlessly probing for betterment of humanity." In a felicitous inversion, the president who often overemphasized secrecy left a space legacy that was conspicuous for its open nature.[6]

Space Score: 31 to 9

Sputnik left a scar on Eisenhower and his reputation. In the larger view of America's space program, his response appeared insufficient. "My own assessment," James Van Allen wrote decades later, "is that Eisenhower was more of a 'follower' than a 'leader' in our early space achievements." He had never been a grand strategist or initiator, neither as a general nor as president. Instead, he assumed the role he had taken during World War II, acting as the final decision maker once plans came to his desk.[7]

Yet, as in World War II, Eisenhower made wise decisions during a vital contest. By 1960, like two giant prizefighters exchanging blows before a world audience, both the United States and the Soviet Union had scored impressive space shots. After a faltering start, the U.S. program accelerated and overtook the Soviet Union's. An administration report on space concluded that America's technical and scientific advances "exceed substantially" those of the Soviet Union. These achievements included the discovery of the Van Allen belts, the first satellite to use solar batteries, communications breakthroughs from SCORE to Echo I, and photography at 20,000 miles, including the first picture of the earth sent from space. (Later, in 1963, the United States scored yet another coup by launching the world's first geosynchronous satellite, settling in a fixed spot 23,000 miles above the earth, and the next year the country orbited the first geosynchronous communications satellite.) In guidance and tracking systems, the United States and the Soviet Union stood even. In electronics, miniaturization, instrumentation, and radio communication, the United States led. As the Eisenhower administration wound down and Glennan prepared to return to the Case Institute of Technology, the NASA administrator said that the United States was "once again preeminent" in space research. An American would orbit the earth in 1961, he predicted, and U.S. manned flights around the moon would take place between 1968 and 1970, followed by a manned lunar landing. Critics tagged the Eisenhower years as an era of "complacency" and scant domestic initiatives. But those years showed remarkable innovation, especially in space.[8]

By 1960, the American space program had earned worldwide respect. Soviet propaganda organs no longer stung it with satire, and at year's end, *U.S. News and World Report* said that the United States had "moved well ahead" of the Soviet Union in space exploration, both scientific and military. "A good case can be made," the magazine reported, "that the U.S. now has the over-all edge." Russia led in just two areas, manned spaceflight and the development of a super-booster.[9]

In January 1961, when Eisenhower left office, two numbers stood out: thirty-one and nine. The United States had sent thirty-one satellites into space; the Soviet Union, nine. The American vessels proved more durable and reliable, too. Fifteen of the American craft still orbited the earth; the Soviets had just two. While neither of the Russian satellites sent radio signals, nine of America's did. The only contested race continued to be in rocket horsepower. Here Eisenhower gave America a lift by pushing the Saturn super-booster. In January 1960, Eisenhower backed a doubling of funds for space projects as well as continued overtime for Saturn. In fact, Eisenhower authorized additional budget appropriations for NASA largely to accelerate Saturn. His efforts quickly saw results, as NASA successfully tested its first Saturn on October 27, 1961.[10]

Space provided welcome good news for Eisenhower's last year in office. A lame-duck president whose arms control momentum ignominiously failed at the Paris summit, Eisenhower initiated few programs in 1960. Ironically, in space research and flight—where he showed only muted enthusiasm—he enjoyed a steady pulse of achievements and spent more money than ever before. The truth was that the Eisenhower administration guided one of the most energetic, fast-moving scientific programs in history. Although his style was incremental, the sum of his achievements was monumental. When his presidency ended, the United States had gone from having no large rockets or measurable space program to having IRBMs, ICBMs, and space satellites. Eisenhower was especially interested in the satellite reconnaissance program that he began, the benefits of which silently continue to accrue. The spy satellites now in space, taking photographs and gathering intelligence that may not be public knowledge for decades, are the technological children of Corona and trace a pedigree back to Eisenhower.[11]

Despite his resolve to contain NASA's budget, Eisenhower allowed space activities to be one of the few areas where he increased spending. NASA's budget rose from $176.1 million in fiscal year 1959 to $468.6 million in 1960 to $744 million in 1961. As a share of total federal expenditures, NASA's budget jumped from 0.2 percent in 1959 to 0.9 percent in 1961. It was rare indeed that Eisenhower agreed to double an agency's funding, but he made exceptions with NASA. "You can't have Buck Rogers without the buck" was one expression about spaceflight's expense, and Eisenhower recognized it. Had he more effectively communicated his fiscal commitment to NASA and space, he could have touted this achievement along with the Interstate Highway System, the St. Lawrence Seaway project, Alaska and Hawaii statehood, the Civil Rights Act of 1957, ICBM and IRBM development, and the NDEA.[12]

At the end of Eisenhower's presidency, many Americans had gotten the message about the country's space surge, believing that the United States had almost caught up with Russia. A Gallup poll showed that nearly as many Americans—35 versus 40 percent—thought that their country, not the Soviet Union, would be the first to send a human into space (the balance had no opinion). Just a year earlier, the Soviet Union had led in that perception by a much larger margin, 44 to 34 percent.[13]

The "Space-Industrial Complex"

While presiding over the growth of America's space and rocket programs, Eisenhower closely monitored costs and results. Were he alive during the twenty-first century, Edward McCabe believed, Eisenhower would still support scientific endeavor. "He would not be lacking in imagination and gumption," McCabe said, "But also he would not be lacking in the wisdom to know when we might be overreaching as a country, either in terms of ability to pay, or ability to fight a war." The continuing cost of manned spaceflight would alarm him, and he would be entitled to let slip a reproachful "I told you so." As he foresaw, in the early twenty-first century, the space program's workhorses and pioneers continued to be unmanned vehicles, which explored Mars and probed far into the galaxy at a fraction of the projected cost of any human missions. And automated explorers get better every year.[14]

Eisenhower's leadership in space mirrored his generalship—moderate and cautious—and he kept NASA and its mission as he wanted, using the presidency to restrain expensive ideas for manned trips to the moon or beyond. In fact, he wanted private industry to shoulder more of the cost of space activities. A month before leaving office, he approved a space policy emphasizing private industry's development of communications satellites, with the federal government only providing assistance. His stance presaged the collaboration between NASA and private enterprise that has become more integral to the space agency's future.[15]

Yet Eisenhower's immortal farewell address, which he delivered on television on January 17, 1961, bore out his concerns over undue collaboration between industry and government. Though he warned specifically about a military-industrial complex, his words also applied to what could be termed a "space-industrial complex." He devoted most of the address to the Cold War. One of its ironies was that to protect American freedom, "a permanent armaments industry of vast proportions" combined with "an immense military establishment" to rob citizens of liberty. The ligament joining politicians and the defense industry made Eisenhower uneasy. "The total influence—economic, political, even spiritual—is felt in every city, every State house, every office of the Federal government," he said. Then came his warning: "In the councils of government, we must guard against the acquisition of unwarranted influence, whether sought or unsought, by the military-industrial complex. The potential for the disastrous rise of misplaced power exists and will persist." He went on to lament the other corrupting change he had witnessed in his lifetime. "Today, the solitary inventor, tinkering in his shop, has been overshadowed by task forces of scientists in laboratories and testing fields," he said. He cautioned that "public policy could itself become the captive of a scientific-technological elite." (Once, in opposing $350 million in federal money for medical research, Eisenhower remarked that the cure for cancer would likely come from "some little guy working in an attic without a federal grant.")

Eisenhower concluded the speech with his belief that economic freedom was inseparable from political liberty. He cautioned, "We cannot mortgage the material assets of our grandchildren without risking the loss also of their political and spiritual heritage. We want democracy to survive for all generations to come, not to become the insolvent phantom of tomorrow."[16]

The initial reaction was tepid. The *New Republic* wondered at his timing: "He had eight years to give this warning; why wait till a minute before midnight?" The *New York Post*'s William Shannon called the address "wooly and sentimental in its thought, undistinguished in its language, pretentious and in bad taste." The French newspaper *Le Monde* said it lacked originality and laid bare the failure of a man who wanted peace but "leaves his country at grips with a more terrifying menace than ever."[17] Yet the "military-industrial complex" became the best-remembered words of Eisenhower's presidency. Using an apposite phrase, he captured the dilemma presidents faced with national security on one hand and bloated budgets on the other. The defense industry sought to make profit, while the military's motive "is the security of the country," Harold Brown said. Together, the arms industry and Pentagon "tend—as Eisenhower made clear himself many times in his evaluation of the situation—to overinsure. Their job is to keep the country from losing a war. And because that is their job, they tend to underrate and undervalue the importance of fiscal prudence, which can be undermined by excessive military spending." In the final analysis, Brown said, "it's up to a decision maker above the military to strike the correct balance." Yet members of Congress, while overseeing the military and concerned with national security, also had constituent industries and jobs to serve through defense contracts. That left the president to act as the ultimate arbiter, preserving the delicate balance among many competing interests.[18]

Although Eisenhower had worried about the military-industrial complex for decades, a new phenomenon—the space race—lurked in the shadows of his address. The Sputnik uproar strengthened individuals, both in and out of government, who sought profit from it. "The people who irritated him were the hard-sell technologists who tried to exploit Sputnik and the missile-gap psychosis it engendered," wrote Herbert York. "We were to be wary of accepting their claims, believing their analyses, and buying their wares."[19] Eisenhower grasped the danger of a "scientific-technological elite" pushing public policy in the wrong direction, and that danger existed with space.

His warning could have been most directly applicable to the aerospace industry, which overemphasized manned spaceflight. Private companies had a huge stake in the venture. For example, twelve contractors vied to build the Mercury space capsule (which required seven miles of electrical wiring and human life support systems crammed into a compact, complex vessel). Farming out work to multiple corporations shared the wealth but increased the cost; other multimillion-dollar contracts involved the capsule's heat shield (made by Alcoa and the Brush Beryllium Company) and the global tracking network (which involved Bell Telephone, International Business Machines, Bendix Aviation, and other concerns).[20]

Once committed to manned spaceflight, a "space-industrial complex" would be difficult to contain. "The industries got so heavily into manned space [flight], so now one of the big arguments for continuing man in space is that you have industries to support," Arnold Frutkin said. "You have industries that are going to be badly hurt if they do not continue doing work on man in space." Like Pentagon budgets, space spending—especially for manned flight—competed for scarce national resources and crowded out private sector activity. Eisenhower feared such scenarios, and he believed that interests demanding more federal funding could endanger democracy without bringing dividends to science or even greater prestige. Indeed, the resulting deficits and sluggish economy would detract from the country's image. Both economic strength and global respect rested on meaningful investment rather than government contracts for defense and aerospace.[21]

Eisenhower and Economic Strength

In leading America through the early space race, Eisenhower strove for arms control with the Soviet Union and was fiercely proud of his foreign policy record. "The United States never lost a soldier or a foot of ground in my administration. We kept the peace." Irritated at critics who charged him with passivity, he added, "People ask how it happened—by God it didn't just happen, I'll tell you that." He also believed that his presidency established "a firm base" for future economic expansion. Raymond Saulnier said, "He didn't approach the business of government as a popular business [where gaining votes and playing with political symbols commanded his foremost attention]. He approached it as a business of doing what was important and essential to the development of a strong economy and a democratic system, which meant that general liberties, individual liberties, be maximized." America's space efforts paled next to his greater imperatives: balanced budgets and fiscal solvency.[22]

Eisenhower funneled money toward his priorities. The *Wall Street Journal* noted that during Eisenhower's eight years, Americans "built more roads, schools, hospitals and homes than in any comparable period. And if our foreign position has not fulfilled the hopes of eight years ago, it is nonetheless true that we face the Communist danger from a position of greater strength." Eisenhower, the paper concluded, gave "good government" to Americans. (Indeed, before his death, Eisenhower planned to write a book detailing his presidency's economic history, and he had even asked Saulnier to lay the groundwork for it by preparing a study on that topic.)[23]

Eisenhower's space achievements thus appeared more impressive against the backdrop of his tightly controlled federal budget. Despite pressure after Sputnik to spend more, his insistence on fiscal prudence helped to achieve his great objective, a balanced federal budget. During fiscal years 1956 and 1957, the budget ran modest surpluses of $1.6 billion and then had a $1.2 billion surplus in FY 1960. Over eight years, Eisenhower kept federal spending remarkably stable. During FY 1954, the federal budget came to $77.6 billion. The last budget that Eisenhower formulated before leaving office, FY 1962, was $80.9 billion. Federal spending was just 15 percent of the GNP, the lowest level since 1939, and deficits never exceeded 2.3 percent of the GNP. Eisenhower contained spending despite the federal government's growth, exemplified by new agencies such as NASA and ARPA, ambitious legislation such as the NDEA, and projects like the Interstate Highway System.[24]

Remarkably, against pressure to increase military spending, Eisenhower contained the defense budget, generally below his stated goal of $40 billion. For his last full year in office, 1960, defense spending was $35.8 billion, even less than the $38.0 billion for 1958, the year after Sputnik, when cries for military spending were loudest. That amount represented 59.1 percent of the total federal budget, down from the Korean War period high of nearly 70 percent. To keep the budget down and make defense cuts, Eisenhower faced vitriol from Democrats and arm-twisting from Republicans. He withstood constant coercion from the Pentagon for the newest weapons. The media questioned the wisdom of his defense posture. Stephen Ambrose noted, "Eisenhower was fighting virtually a one-man battle on holding down the costs of defense."[25]

But he was not entirely alone. In declaring Eisenhower its 1959 "Man of the Year," *Time* reserved its greatest praise for his post-Sputnik budgetary restraint. The president had "fought one of his hardest and most successful battles in 1959. In January, when he formally announced his determination to balance the budget at $77 billion, the lopsided Democratic congressional majority hooted and howled. Indeed, it seemed all but impossible at a time when recession and the challenge of the U.S.S.R.'s Sputniks had ballooned the deficit to some $12 billion. But Ike rammed across his point." He badgered members of Congress, vetoed bills, and publicly stressed government economy. "Eisenhower had performed the political miracle of making economy popular," *Time* noted, and the strong American economy "served as a springboard for vast creative forces," such as rebuilding Japan and West Germany and aiding Third World countries.[26]

Although the nation's GNP grew at 2.4 percent from 1953 to 1960, less than the 3–3.5 percent rate that characterized healthy expansions, Eisenhower's growth rate came while he tried to shrink defense spending. Had he tried to pump more money into the military—as Ronald Reagan did during the 1980s—the economy would likely have registered higher GNP growth, perhaps more than 3 percent. Instead, the GNP growth during Eisenhower's presidency reflected increased production of consumer goods. He believed that consumers, not the military, should enjoy the fruits of the free market. In the end, these years were, as Saulnier put it, "good times for the consumer." Indeed, Eisenhower had reason to be proud of his economic record. During his eight years in office, inflation—which he considered a paramount threat to national security and freedom—averaged just 1.4 percent. He closed out his term with the lowest inflation rate among all other outgoing postwar presidents. The average unemployment rate during Eisenhower's presidency, 4.8 percent, reflected the effect of three recessions but was still respectable. As budget director Maurice Stans observed, the Eisenhower prosperity carried over into the 1960s. "[W]age and price inflation was minimal," Stans said, "a balance between labor costs and productivity was achieved; interest rates were stabilized; the budget was in balance and a trade surplus was rebuilt. Prices increased less than one and one-half percent through 1965."[27]

Perhaps most important, Eisenhower remained true to his principles. During his last days in office, Eisenhower talked of leaving a "legacy of thought" for the new administration, and he stressed that one of the most important gifts he could give to the country was an emphasis on fiscal conservatism.[28]

● World Prestige

Blunders and scandals have sullied presidents during second terms; Nixon had Watergate, Reagan had Iran-Contra, Clinton had the Monica Lewinsky affair and impeachment, George W. Bush had a financial system meltdown and the ongoing Iraq War. During Eisenhower's second term, the worst scandals were Sherman Adams and the U-2 fiasco, which embarrassed him but never reached the magnitude of other presidents' calamities. Instead, his voyages abroad were resounding successes, reaffirming America's internationalism and amity with less developed nations. Eisenhower maintained the dignity of the office and was an effective diplomatic agent on the world stage.

The loss of U.S. prestige that Eisenhower's critics lamented was part of a larger trend that has been difficult to counter. The late 1940s and 1950s were a unique era in history when the United States, emerging victorious after world war, stood at an unnatural pinnacle. From there, the only way to go was downhill. By 1972, pollster George Gallup, testifying before the Senate Foreign Relations Committee, said, "Our prestige is at a low point around the world." The Vietnam War, domestic protests, soaring crime rates, economic troubles, and a media emphasis on bad news all had combined to damage America's image. In the decades since, the country's image has often slumped. A 2007 world poll showed that America ranked among the five countries with the least favorable images (along with Russia, North Korea, Iran, and Israel), and a 2011 Pew Research Center survey showed that pluralities in Britain, France, Germany, and Spain believed that China, not the United States, was the world's greatest economic power.[29]

Eisenhower's dignity helped to maintain U.S. prestige, but he also had a blind spot. He only halfheartedly conceded the connection between space and America's image. Historian David McCullough recalled working for the USIA during the Kennedy administration, when Edward Murrow instructed, "Find out what's bugging people." Learning what people value is vital, and in this respect, Eisenhower never treated space as a grand opportunity to be grasped; moreover, his distaste for politics prevented him from trumpeting America's lead in the space race. (He perhaps reflected most closely the paradigm of Japan's space program, which quietly launched its first satellite in 1964 and concentrated on unmanned space activities while its economic might captured world attention.) Nor did Eisenhower recognize that launching the world's first satellite would have made his presidency more consequential and inoculated him against pernicious political pressures. By failing to heed warnings of a first satellite's prestige, he made his job tougher and invited the attacks that came after October 4, 1957. The criticism following Sputnik weakened media support for Eisenhower and emboldened members of Congress to blame or beard him.[30]

For presidents, one lesson of Sputnik is that principles are indeed vital, and adhering to them prevents a politician from pandering. Yet a leader's priorities must be dynamic, responding to changing circumstances and new developments. Sweeping events might demand visible action and bold rhetoric, rather than the incremental shifts that Eisenhower preferred. Otherwise, a president will be tagged as a "reactionary fossil," as Eisenhower himself conceded. Eisenhower's failing was in the arenas of politics and perception. He never fully emphasized the truth that the United States far outpaced the Soviet Union in the satellite and science race, nor did he articulate why this preeminence mattered. According to McGeorge Bundy, a top advisor to Kennedy and Johnson, "Eisenhower did not adequately explain himself. . . . So while he did sensible things and resisted foolish ones, he allowed the ensuing public arguments to be led by men who did not understand matters as well as he did."[31]

In resisting space exploration's patriotic dividends, especially space "firsts" and manned spaceflight, Eisenhower appeared strangely insensitive to world opinion and politics, two areas where he claimed credentials and insight. Americans wanted inspirational leadership and progress. Eisenhower, the general who titled his World War II memoir *Crusade in Europe*, never as president generated a sense of a crusade. Thus, in reflecting caution and moderation, Eisenhower's space policy succeeded well. In demonstrating bold leadership, it did not. He had secured for America the two standards of presidential leadership, peace and prosperity, but he proved less successful in instilling a sense of the third "p"—progress. Even his definition of it was odd and tautological. When asked about his criteria for success at a summit meeting with Khrushchev, he stressed progress, saying, "My criterion is still progress that I can see as measurable progress."[32]

● Sputnik in the Twenty-First Century

More than a half-century after the Space Age began, magazine editor Aaron Robinson ruminated over the significance of space achievements like NASA's shuttle, using arguments that would have benefited Eisenhower. "Politicians often tell us that the U.S. is No. 1, but occasionally the rank and file needs proof with something besides the per capita consumption of chicken nuggets," he wrote. "Call us simplistic; say we're drunk on the tonic of superficial symbology, but We the People need occasional collective amazement. . . . We need feats and triumphs and technological wow moments, so we can point and say, 'We did that.'" Such defining moments galvanize new generations of Americans to pursue science careers and dream of breakthroughs in medicine, physics, and technology. Without such inspiration, Robinson argued, "How do you get a kid to look up from a Malaysian-made game console and consider becoming an engineer?"[33]

In the Soviet Union's seventy-four-year history, Sputnik represented a high point. Should the United States lose its world economic preeminence to a rival such as China, the manned moon landings will stand as a proud moment during its era of dominance. John Kennedy, not Dwight Eisenhower, will reap the historic benefit. Kennedy's May 1961 address to Congress and his September 1962 Rice University speech will remain famous presidential sound bites, and during moon landing anniversaries, the media will show footage of them. Centuries from now, when advanced rockets may enable astronauts to explore space's deeper reaches, the media may still show these speeches. Even that far into the future, Kennedy will seem a visionary who captured a moment when Americans believed in their abilities, trusted technology, and saw space as a vast new frontier.[34]

Likewise, the reverence for Kennedy at NASA will remain profound. Robert Seamans recalled NASA engineers thanking Jacqueline Kennedy effusively when she visited Cape Canaveral after her husband's assassination. "They wanted Mrs. Kennedy to know how much they appreciated Kennedy's support," Seamans said. Even though Eisenhower signed the legislation creating NASA, the agency's two major space centers are named after Kennedy and Johnson. By failing to lunge at the opportunities space offered, Eisenhower lost the chance to leave a larger and more visible legacy.[35]

Yet one of the most singular endorsements of Eisenhower's understated leadership came from former president Gerald Ford, who judged him the best president of the twentieth century, admiring his fiscal integrity, ability to set long-term goals, and concern for the nation's interests over instant political gratification.[36] Those principles are enduring. Even though space faded as an issue and never again loomed over political campaigns as in 1960, the tenets Eisenhower stressed amidst the apparent crisis—especially economic strength—allowed America to recover from the Sputnik panic. In 2008, the *Economist* marveled at how America bounced back after twentieth-century crises: "In the 1950s [the United States] went into a Sputnik-driven spin about Soviet power; in the 1970s there was Watergate, Vietnam and the oil shocks; in the late 1980s Japan seemed to be buying up America. Each time, the United States rebounded, because the country is good at fixing itself." The key was how America repaired itself: it did so by following many of the principles Eisenhower espoused—while ignoring others, such as restraining the federal debt, at its own peril.[37]

During the 1980s, in fact, Chrysler chairman Lee Iacocca became a national hero for breathing life back into his nearly defunct automobile company, and admirers even bandied his name about as a presidential contender. In his best-selling autobiography, Iacocca prescribed his formulae for keeping America competitive. He recommended infrastructure development and financial aid for students studying technology. He questioned the value of racing the Soviet Union in nuclear capabilities and wondered what virtues the atomic weapons protected, writing, "Without a strong, vital industrial infrastructure, we're a nation bristling with missiles that surround a land of empty factories, unemployed workers, and decaying cities. Where is the wisdom in this policy?" Three decades later, Iacocca echoed Ike, showing how durable Eisenhower's principles were.[38]

America's competitive standing will face challenges in the twenty-first century and beyond. The United States will find that it trails other nations in attention-grabbing areas. The country no longer boasts the world's tallest skyscraper, and its Olympic teams do not always haul in the most gold medals. Its economy and educational system endure stiff competition, and eventually, the yuan may challenge the dollar as the world's reserve currency. Someday, too, voyagers from other nations will leave footprints on the moon. Indeed, in 2011, when NASA retired its space shuttle fleet, commentators noted that U.S. astronauts would now depend on Russian Soyuz craft to fly to the International Space Station and bemoaned the blow to American pride.

Eisenhower would likely have scoffed, and he would have had a point. The country cannot be first in everything, he always said; instead, it should focus on vital areas. His priorities remain the urgent ones: the economy, low inflation, low taxes, free trade, defense, and federal debt. His warnings about deficits, especially from excessive military spending, were prophetic. Although it failed to capture media attention and the public's interest as Sputnik did, what Eisenhower called impending "fiscal calamity" remained his clarion call. In 1962, he stated, "I personally believe—with, I am sure, very little company in either Party—that the defense budget should be substantially reduced. At least, all America understands that every defense dollar wastefully expended, that every defense dollar needlessly appropriated, weakens this nation." More than sheer military might, this balanced approach helped America during the Cold War. As space historian Roger Launius has written, "In contrast to those who believe Ronald Reagan essentially won the competition by spending the Soviet Union into oblivion, Eisenhower's strategic vision did more to establish the conditions for success than any other single set of decisions during the forty-year conflict." The key was Eisenhower's insight that power built on debt is power that will crumble, that nations build greatness not on battlefields but in banks and brokerages. Today, the United States lacks the economic vibrancy of the 1950s, and as a cause for its woes, Eisenhower would likely point to one fact: the country spends more on the military than any other nation on earth, and it alone accounts for more than 40 percent of worldwide defense spending. Even more, Eisenhower would take fright at today's federal debt, measured in the trillions of dollars, which robs the country of prestige and economic power.[39]

Economic power bore a link with science, too. Under the economic system that Eisenhower cherished, science prospered, and Americans reached the moon. By contrast, state-run economies sometimes moved fast but veered off in impulsive directions or at erratic speeds. Under such conditions, science suffered. As Columbia University physicist John Dunning noted after the second Sputnik launch, "Fear, the high price of failure and the unscrupulous use of power by the mediocre take a heavy, if hidden, toll of research under dictatorship."[40] Eisenhower addressed this concept at a press conference during his last year in office. A reporter noted that Khrushchev had boasted, "Our flag is flying on the moon," asserting that it proved communism's superiority over capitalism. "I think it's crazy," Eisenhower exclaimed. He stressed that "in an industrial complex of the strength of Russia's . . . if it wants to put all of its strength in a particular field of activity—and remember, secretly undertaken—of course it can come out with spectacular achievements. . . . But my contention is we should not be hysterical when dictatorships do these things." Americans, by contrast, believe in "a broader and better type of civilization."[41] Perhaps the ultimate measure of Eisenhower's contrast rests in the Cold War's conclusion. For all the uproar and self-congratulation following Sputnik, just four decades after its launch, the Soviet Union was gone.

After Sputnik, George Field of Princeton University's Observatory wrote, "In the long run we shall be judged by our virtues and not by our rockets." That was Eisenhower's point. He complained to the media that almost all of their publications had pictures of rockets and missiles, which created the impression that "the only thing this country is engaged in is weaponry and missiles. And, I'll tell you we just can't afford to do that. The reason we have them is to protect the great values in which we believe." Eisenhower understood what others around him did not, that the focus should be less on the Soviet Union's military might and space successes and more on its internal frailties.[42]

Today the Kennedy and Johnson Space Centers, bearing the names of Eisenhower's flamboyant successors, continue to attract media attention and tourists. Americans more commonly see Eisenhower's name in a less spectacular yet more practical venue, on simple blue signs that dot his eponymous interstate system. The contrast is fitting. It speaks to Eisenhower's more subdued, often poor approach to public relations. But the blue markers bear silent tribute to Eisenhower's understanding of America's strengths and his attempts to reinforce them. They also reflect the principles that helped him through his "Sputnik moment." In an intense three-and-a-half-year period after the Soviet satellite launch, he endured crises and criticism, setbacks and successes, and progress both steady and staccato. In the end, he left the country in better shape than he found it and, indeed, in better shape than most observers recognized. Eisenhower's finest legacy, though, transcended the space race and the Cold War. It is his blueprint for a strong economy and world prestige—one that still gives guidance today.

ACKNOWLEDGMENTS

I began this work years ago, and many persons and institutions have helped to see it to completion. Generous institutional support came from Dowling College. Dowling's Faculty Development and Curriculum Committee for Social Sciences awarded me course releases to free up time for this project, and Dowling's travel and research funding helped to defray various expenses. I received help from dedicated Dowling undergraduate research assistants, including Catherine Ferguson, Jack Edelson, Carolyn Badalucco, and Cole Hall. In one of my Dowling courses, "The United States, 1945–68," students read early manuscript drafts, and their reactions and research for their own papers benefited me greatly. Maria Lovejoy and Greg Cespedes of Dowling's Duplicating Services bound versions of the work as it moved from amorphous mass to manuscript form; they were always cheerful—even when I showed up with more work for them. Chris Kretz and other colleagues at Dowling College's library gave indispensable aid with interlibrary loans and primary-source research.

An Abilene Travel Grant helped during one of my trips to the Eisenhower Presidential Library. There I received much assistance from the archivists, including Christopher Abramson and audio-visual specialist Kathy Struss. Audio-visual archivist Laurie Austin of the John F. Kennedy Library was a pleasure to work with during a visit there. The archivists at the Gerald R. Ford Presidential Library, always welcoming, helped in tracking down evidence of Ford's early interest in the space program and his congressional support for Eisenhower's policies. The *U.S. News and World Report* photograph collection at the Library of Congress is a marvelous resource, and the Library staff provided ample assistance in duplicating pictures for this book.

The persons whom I interviewed were wonderful. They showed unstinting generosity, taking time out of their schedules to meet me, many of them hosting me at their homes or sharing lunch. I have listed them all in the sources section; they made research a pleasure. I wanted to convey special gratitude to William Ewald, who met me on several occasions to share his thoughts on Eisenhower and recollections of working with him. Andrew

Goodpaster and Arthur Larson gave me key insights into Eisenhower's reaction to Sputnik and approach to governing, and they both inspired me to keep digging. Bud Reynolds of Cocoa Beach, Florida, introduced me to his friends, retired NASA engineers in the Cape Canaveral area, who recounted stories of the early space race to me. John Neilon shared his Vanguard recollections, directed me to colleagues, and supplied more details after he read an early manuscript version. David Beckler made excellent contributions with his insights into PSAC plus his unpublished article recounting science advice given to Eisenhower. I am extremely grateful to many other interviewees and correspondents who offered their time and memories, including Hans Bethe, Harold Brown, Arnold Frutkin, Caryl Haskins, Donald Hornig, Spurgeon Keeny, Edward McCabe, Roemer McPhee, Alice S. Ritchie, Raymond (Steve) Saulnier, Robert Seamans, Eugene Skolnikoff, and W. North Sterrett.

At its inception and early stages, this project received careful guidance from Alden Vaughan, to whom I remain extremely grateful. A telephone conversation with Stephen Ambrose was critical, as he offered suggestions on how to unearth fresh material. John Garraty's praise of an early manuscript draft meant much to me then and still does today. Alan Brinkley offered enormous support and wisdom that shaped this project and influenced me in ways far beyond research and writing. Other colleagues and friends who have helped immensely include J. D. Bowers, Mark Carnes, George Colburn, Joe Hamilton, Laura Kalman, Michael Krysko, Edward O'Donnell, Hervey Priddy, Carl Reddel, Andrew Rotter, William Shelton, and David Stebenne.

Ron Hoham of Colgate University sharpened the manuscript with a scientist's insights—along with great friendship. William Pickett shared his expertise on Eisenhower to strengthen Ike's presence in these pages. Tim Greene and an anonymous reviewer at Cornell University Press gave meticulous perusals and wise comments. This book is vastly improved because of Leo McCue, who generously applied his editorial skills and historical knowledge.

My editor at Cornell University Press, Michael McGandy, tracked this project for years, expressing interest and providing gentle encouragement. Sarah Grossman helped in arranging the photos, and copyeditor Julie Palmer-Hoffman did terrific work in copyediting the manuscript. I might add that I am a native Ithacan, a graduate of Ithaca City Schools and Ithaca High, where I had excellent teachers and classmates, many motivating me to study American history. I enjoyed returning to my hometown, discussing the manuscript with Michael, and seeing central New York again.

I owe a tremendous debt to Michael Green of the College of Southern Nevada. Mike proofread many manuscript iterations, supplied thoughts that otherwise would have eluded me, and directed me to new sources. He was there every step of the way.

Two people tower above all. My parents, Dr. Bogdan and Seiko Mieczkowski, inspired me with their own scholarship and writing, and as always, we shared many conversations about this work. They read various drafts, giving feedback at every stage; the final product reflects their care, knowledge, and disciplined thinking.

My wife, Vanessa, makes our home environment conducive to concentration and learning, and she accompanied me on research and interview trips. When she could not, she endured my absences; for her steadfast support, I am grateful.

You the reader make all the effort worthwhile, and I was flattered to get messages from readers of my other works who asked questions about them or expressed interest in my research. If you would like to contact me, please feel free to e-mail me at mieczkoy@dowling.edu.

Many and sincere thanks to all.

# Notes

Abbreviations for Sources

AKP	Arthur Krock Papers
ALP	Arthur Larson Papers
AS	Alphabetical Subseries
ASU	Arizona State University
AWAS	Ann Whitman Administration Series
AWDS	Ann Whitman Diary Series
AWF	Ann Whitman File
AWF NSC Series	Ann Whitman File National Security Council Series
BGP	Barry Goldwater Papers
BNS	Briefing Notes Subseries
BW	*Business Week*
CD	*Congressional Digest*
CUCOHC	Columbia University Center for Oral History Collection
DDE	Dwight D. Eisenhower
DDEL	Dwight D. Eisenhower Library
DDS	Department of Defense Subseries
DEDS	Dwight Eisenhower Diary Series
FIT	Florida Institute of Technology
GP	Gallup Poll
GRFL	Gerald R. Ford Library
GWU	George Washington University
HJP	Henry Jackson Papers
HSTL	Harry S. Truman Library
JFKL	John F. Kennedy Library
JJP	Jacob Javits Papers
JMP	John Medaris Papers
LBJL	Lyndon B. Johnson Library
LMS	Legislative Meeting Series
MLPU	Seeley Mudd Library, Princeton University
NASA HO	National Aeronautics and Space Administration History Office
NYHT	*New York Herald Tribune*
NYP	*New York Post*
NYT	*New York Times*
OCB Series	Operations Coordinating Board Subseries

OSANSA	Office of the Special Assistant for National Security Affairs
OSAST	Office of the Special Assistant for Science and Technology
OSS	Office of the Staff Secretary
PCM	Paley Center for Media
PP	Presidential Papers
PPP	Public Papers of the Presidents
SBU	Stony Brook University
SEP	*Saturday Evening Post*
SPI	Space Policy Institute
SS	Subject Subseries
USN	*U.S. News and World Report*
UW	University of Washington
WHO	White House Office
WHP	White House Presidents
WP	*Washington Post*
WPP	William Proxmire Papers
WSJ	*Wall Street Journal*

Introduction

1. PPP 1957, 719–32.

2. Ewald interview, 2010.

3. PPP 1957, 707.

4. WP, Jan. 11, 1961; *National Review,* Jan. 14, 1961, 8; *New Republic,* Oct. 10, 1960, 20.

5. *Newsweek*, Dec. 5, 2011, 58.

Chapter 1

1. Bille and Lishock, 65, 101; Burrows, 164; D'Antonio, 11.

2. *Newsweek* , Oct. 14, 1957, 38; Crouch, 141; Dickson, 105.

3. USN, Oct. 18, 1957, 32; *Newsday*, Oct. 5, 1957, 3; Launius, "Sputnik and the Origins of the Space Age," http://www.hq.nasa.gov/office/pao/History/sputnik /sputorig.html.

4. *Time*, Oct. 14, 1957, 45; *Newsweek*, Oct. 14, 1957, 38; Hardesty and Eisman, 66; Oakley, 343.

5. Reedy, 56–57; Brzezinski, 148; York, 107.

6. *Fortune*, August 1957, 94; N. Khrushchev, 37; Yeager and Janos, 259–62.

7. Bethe interview.

8. Keeny interview; Bowie and Immerman, 46.

9. Taubman, 382; B. Mieczkowski, 46; Pappalardo interview; *Air & Space Magazine*, Oct./Nov. 1957, 54.

10. McDougall, 267.

11. Bethe interview; Bille and Lishock, 27; Keeny interview.

12. Jackson notes on Russian trip, Box 230, Folder 23, HJP, UW; Brzezinski, 135; Dickson, 99.

13. Jackson address to National Guard, Box 3, Folder 26, HJP.

14. Clowse, 21; D'Antonio, 8; Hardesty and Eisman, 67; NYT, Oct. 6, 1957, E5; *Fortune*, Jan. 1958, 98. A ballistic missile, unlike a cruise missile, has no rocket propulsion for the latter part of its flight, just like a bullet fired from a gun, which is also "ballistic." It moves inexorably toward a predetermined target, with no change possible in its flight path.

15. WSJ, Nov. 8, 1957; GP, v. 2, 1521, 1526; Skolnikoff interview.

16. *Newsday*, Oct. 7, 1957, 3; Dickson, 116, 117; N. Khrushchev, 47; Letter from Boyd Milligan, Nov. 3, 1957, U.S. Senate, 1949–61, Committee on Armed Services, Box 355, LBJL.

17. GRF Congressional Papers, Press Secretary and Speech File, 1947–73, Box D15, Folder: Challenges of the Space Age 1959, GRFL; "Conversation with Gerald Seigel," "The Legislative Origins of the Space Act," workshop held on Apr. 3, 1992, SPI, GWU, NASA HO; Dickson, 127; Oakley, 344; Killian, 7; Stever, 125.

18. Memo from Reedy to Johnson, Oct. 17, 1957, U.S. Senate, 1949–61, George Reedy Files, 1951–55, Box 420, LBJL.

19. NYT, Nov. 15, 1957.

20. NYP, Oct. 6, 1957, 1; *Newsday*, Oct. 5, 1957, 17; WP, Nov. 12, 1957.

21. Dickson, 128; *Newsday*, Oct. 7, 1957, 2, 30; USN, Feb. 7, 1958, 34; Memo from Reedy to Johnson, Oct. 17, 1957, U.S. Senate, 1949–61, George Reedy Files, 1951–55, Box 420, LBJL; Dickson, 115.

22. Killian, 2; *Newsweek*, Oct. 14, 1957, 38; NYT, Oct. 5, 1957, A3; D'Antonio, 25; NYT, Oct. 5, 1957.

23. AWF: NSC Series; 339th Meeting of the NSC, Minutes, Oct. 11, 1957, DDEL; PPP 1957, 210; Eisenhower, *Waging Peace, 1956–1961*, 205; Conference in the President's Office, Oct. 8, 1957, WHO, OSS, DDS, Box 6, DDEL.

24. Brzezinski, 40; "U.S. Policy on Outer Space," Jan. 26, 1960, Box 7, SS, OCB Series, WHO, OSANSA, DDEL; Clowse, 7.

25. Brzezinski, 147; Dickson, 143; *Baltimore Sun*, Mar. 30, 1960; WSJ, Jan. 6, 1959.

26. Goodpaster interview, 1989; *Waco News-Tribune*, Oct. 22, 1957.

27. Hardesty and Eisman, 76; N. Khrushchev, 47; Rorabaugh, 24; Brzezinski, 177, 205, 269.

28. "U.S. Scientific Satellite Program: General Considerations," May 10, 1955, WHO, OSANSA, BNS, Box 7; WHO, OSS, Records, Cabinet Series C-39 (3); Meeting Notes, Oct. 18, 1957; Memo of conference with the president, Feb. 4, 1958, WHO, OSS, DDS, Box 6, DDEL.

29. Frankel, 179.

30. Frankel, 180; Bille and Lishock, 105; *Tyler Courier-Times*, Oct. 18, 1957; *Tyler Morning Telegraph*, Oct. 19, 1957.

31. Lewis, 55; *Sputnik Mania*, A&E Television, DVD, 2008.

32. Twigg interview; Mars interview.

33. *Newsweek*, Oct. 28, 1957, 31; Oct. 14, 1957, 37–38.

34. GP, v. 2, 1520, 1523, 1539, 1570; Memo for Neil McElroy from O. M. Gale, Apr. 14, 1958, Box: WHP, Eisenhower, Folder: Space Policy—Eisenhower, Correspondence (1958–60), NASA HO; Donald Michael, "The Beginning of the

Space Age and American Public Opinion," *Public Opinion Quarterly* (Winter 1960), 578, 579.

35. *Philadelphia Inquirer*, Nov. 20, 1959; "Conversation with Glen Wilson," in "The Legislative Origins of the Space Act," SPI, GWU, NASA HO.

36. NYP, Oct. 10, 1957; DNC Cartoon Clipping Files, Box 362, Folders: Space Program—Satellites 11/3/57–11/9/59; Space Program, General 12/8/57–3/21/60, JFKL.

37. *Newsday*, Oct. 5, 1957, 1; *Sputnik Mania*; Frutkin interviews, 2008 and 2010.

38. *Economist*, Nov. 9, 1957, 275.

39. Clowse, 19; NYP, Oct. 11, 1957; *Lewiston Daily News*, Oct. 8, 1957; *Time*, Dec. 16, 1957; *Newsweek*, Oct. 21, 1957; *Life*, Nov. 18, 1957, 26.

40. "CBS Television Special Report: Sputnik I" (Oct. 6, 1957), PCM.

41. Roger Launius, "Eisenhower and Space: Politics and Ideology in the Construction of the U.S. Civil Space Program," in Showalter, 166; *Sputnik Mania*.

42. Ewald, 285; Hughes, 121; Letter to E. E. Hazlett, Feb. 26, 1958, Eisenhower: Papers as President, 1953–61, AWF, DEDS, Box 30, DDEL; McCabe interview; see GP, v. 2, especially pp. 1351 and 1522; one brief exception saw Eisenhower hit 60 percent in Jan. 1958; Cox, 21.

43. Ambrose, *Eisenhower: The President*, 425; McDougall, 148; Brzezinski, 131–32.

44. Kalman, 284; NYT, Oct. 6, 1957; Oct. 11, 1957.

45. NYT, Oct. 8, 1957; Oct. 13, 1957.

46. Statement of Senator Jacob Javits, Oct. 6, 1957, Folder 10/6/57 Earth Satellite; Remarks of Senator Javits, Folder 10/11/57 New School for Social Research, Satellites; Remarks of Senator Javits, Oct. 17, 1957; all in Series 1, Subseries 1, Box 14, JJP, SBU.

47. Killian, 128; Bethe interview; York interview.

48. Dickson, 186; PPP 1959, 772.

49. *Aviation Week*, Oct. 28, 1957, 30.

50. Doyle, 80.

51. *The Nation*, Nov. 23, 1957, 381.

52. WP, Nov. 10, 1957.

53. Letter from Eisenhower to Loyd Swenson, Aug. 5, 1965, Box: WHP, Eisenhower, Folder: Eisenhower—Space Exploration (1955–63), NASA HO; NYP, Oct. 10, 1957.

54. Dickson, 139; Pach and Richardson, 47.

55. Perret, 382; NYT, Oct. 6, 1957, 43; Gould, 272; *Life*, Oct. 18, 1957, 128.

56. *Brown Daily Herald*, Oct. 9, 1957.

57. WP, Nov. 9, 1957; Nov. 12, 1957.

58. NYP, Oct. 8, 1957; PPP 1957, Nov. 13 speech.

59. Clowse, 24; D'Antonio, 44; "U.S. Policy on Outer Space," WHO, OSS, AS, Box 24, Folder: Space Council, DDEL; Democratic Advisory Council Position Paper on Space Research, Sept. 7, 1960, Research Coordinator Position and Briefing Papers, Box DNC 197, Folder: Space Research 10/21/59–9/7/60, JFKL; *Newsweek*, Oct. 28, 1957, 35.

60. "World Opinion and the Soviet Satellite," Oct. 17, 1957, WHO, OSANSA, BNS, Box 7, DDEL; original underlining of "détente" removed.

61. Beschloss, 157; Special Staff Note, Oct. 15, 1959, AWF, DEDS, Box 45, Folder: Toner Notes, Oct. 1959, DDEL; Dickson, 27, 140.

62. Brzezinski, 204, 207; Dickson, 130; Oberg, 330; Oakley, 343; *Time*, Oct. 21, 1957, 21.

63. *Time*, Jan. 6, 1958.

64. "A History of the Committee on Science and Technology" (2008), 23, available at http://science.house.gov/sites/republicans.science.house.gov/files/documents /Committee_History_50years.pdf; S. Khrushchev, 210.

65. Oberg, 35; WSJ, Nov. 8, 1957; Dickson, 131–32; Thompson, 96; *Newsweek*, Oct. 28, 1957, 35.

66. Ewald interviews, 2006, 2009.

67. Aitken, 265–66.

68. Sloan, 124.

69. Gibbs and Duffy, 105; Goodpaster interview, 2000; Ambrose, *Eisenhower:The President*, 601; West with Kotz, 139.

70. Larson, 10; Rorabaugh, 19; Doyle, 70.

71. Stebenne, 176; Hughes, 173; Beschloss, 154.

72. Thompson, 44.

73. Frankel, 181; Raymond Saulnier, "An Economist's-Eye View of the World," unpublished article in author's collection.

Chapter 2

1. Ambrose, *Eisenhower: Soldier and President*, 240–42; Brendon, 200–203; Perret, 381–84.

2. NYT, Oct. 6, 1957.

3. NYT, July 30, 1955, A7; Dickson, 76–77; Stever, 126.

4. Report of the Committee on the Law of Outer Space of the Section of International and Comparative Law, the American Bar Association, Series 3, Box 113, Folder 12, Space Law, 1958, JJP, SBU; Eisenhower, *Mandate for Change,* 491–92; Wright brothers comment in Memo of conference with the president, Sept. 23, 1959, AWF, DEDS, Box 44, DDEL.

5. Report of the Committee on the Law of Outer Space, JJB, SBU.

6. Letter from Alva Blanchard, Aug. 16, 1955, Central Files, General File GF 145-D, Box 1155, DDEL.

7. Larson letter; Larson interview.

8. Pickering interview, Apr. 22 and 29, 2003, conducted by Shirley Cohen, Caltech Archives, http://oralhistories.library.caltech.edu.

9. Frutkin interview, 2010.

10. Bille and Lishock, 18; Dickson, 53; DeGroot, 19; Hardesty and Eisman, 16; Lethbridge, 110; Halberstam, 612; McDougall, 43.

11. Brzezinski, 9; *American Weekly*, Aug. 3, 1958, 12; Dickson, 57–58; Hardesty and Eisman, 20.

12. Taubman, 196; Chronology of Significant Events in the U.S. Long Range Ballistic Missile Program (undated), WHO, OSS, DDS, Box 6, DDEL (hereafter

"Chronology"); *This Week*, Apr. 13, 1958; *Nashville Tennessean*, Oct. 10, 1957; *Newsweek*, Oct. 14, 1947, 40; *Time*, Feb. 17, 1958, 24; Bille and Lishock, 23; Crouch, 47, 72–73; Dickson, 59–63; Halberstam, 69; Lawrence, 29–30; Lethbridge, 2.

13. Hardesty and Eisman, 152.

14. NYT, July 8, 1957; *This Week*, Apr. 13, 1958; Bille and Lishock, 41; Crouch, 116–17, 128; Dickson, 73–74.

15. David Akens, Historical Origins of the George C. Marshall Space Flight Center (Huntsville, Alabama: Dec. 1960), MSFC Historical Monograph One, James Webb Papers, Box 173, HSTL (hereafter "Akens in Webb Papers"); Crouch, 129; DeGroot, 39; McDougall, 119; von Braun's italics are original.

16. Chronology, WHO, OSS, DDS, Box 6, DDEL.

17. *Cleveland Plain Dealer*, Nov. 14, 1957; WSJ, Nov. 11, 1957; McDougall, 105; Notes on meeting of ODM SAC with the president, Oct. 15, 1957, Box: White House Presidents, Eisenhower (hereafter WHP-E), National Aeronautics and Space Act (cont'd), NASA HO.

18. Launius and McCurdy, 34; Eisenhower, *Waging Peace,* 207–9; Ewald, 244.

19. GRF Congressional Papers, Campaign File 1948–74, Box 64, GRFL.

20. *Newsweek*, Oct. 19, 1959, 74.

21. Dickson, 80.

22. Chronology, WHO, OSS, DDS, Box 6, DDEL; Stever, 111; Crouch, 129; Stares, 31; Wang, 52–53.

23. Ambrose, *Eisenhower: The President,* 268.

24. Pickering interview; Sloan, 98; USN, Jan. 10, 1958, 67–68; Wang, 101; Hughes, 250.

25. Gibbs and Duffy, 123.

26. Bowie and Immerman, 248; Eisenhower, *Waging Peace*, 208; Launius and McCurdy, 23–24; Divine, *The Sputnik Challlenge,* 25

27. Chronology, WHO, OSS, DDS, Box 6, DDEL; *Birmingham News*, Oct. 15, 1957; Lethbridge, 6–7; Dickson, 87–88; Medaris, 119; Piszkiewicz, 99–100.

28. Wang, 53, 54.

29. Taubman, 202–5.

30. Hunley, 85; Dickson, 70; *Time*, Oct. 28, 1957, 18.

31. Ewald interview, 2006.

32. Lethbridge, 5; Dickson, 84.

33. Crouch, 131–32.

34. Lethbridge, 2.

35. Larson letter; Neilon interview; *Air and Space*, Oct./Nov. 1987, 48; *Fortune*, Feb. 17, 1958, 37; Brzezinski, 167, 168, 225; Crouch, 111; Dickson, 83; Kistiakowsky, 97; Lethbridge, 4–5; McDougall, 122; Callahan and Greenstein, 29; USN, Nov. 22, 1957, 37–38.

36. Stares, 34.

37. PPP 1957, 720; Akens in Webb Papers, HSTL; McDougall, 122; Lethbridge, 5; Dickson, 85.

38. Callhan and Greenstein, 23; *Fortune,* Jan. 1958, 100; Eisenhower, *Waging Peace,* 209; Dickson, 85.

39. Kenneth Osgood, "Before Sputnik: National Security and the Formation of U.S. Outer Space Policy," in Launius et. al., *Reconsidering Sputnik,* 202; Frutkin interviews, 2008 and 2010; Ellis, 111–12.

40. Frutkin interviews, 2008 and 2010.

41. McDougall, 120; Minutes of cabinet meeting, Oct. 18, 1957, AWF, DEDS, Box 27, DDEL; Letter from Eugene Emme, Aug. 6, 1969, Box: WHP-E, NASA HO.

42. Dickson, 153; Kistiakowsky, 68; Eisenhower, *Waging Peace,* 208; Bille and Lishock, 119.

43. Minutes, Oct. 11, 1957, AWF: NSC Series, 339th Meeting of the NSC, DDEL.

44. Meeting notes, Feb. 4, 1958, WHO, OSS: Records, LMS, L-44 (3), DDEL.

45. Larson interview; Neilon interview; Meeting notes, Feb. 4, 1958, WHO, OSS: Records, LMS, L-44 (3), DDEL. Eisenhower expressed similar sentiments in Meeting notes, Jan. 7, 1958, LMS, L-44 (1), DDEL.

46. Letter from Eisenhower to Charles Halleck, Mar. 26, 1963, Box: WHP-E, NASA HO; Roger Launius, "Eisenhower, Sputnik, and the Creation of NASA," *Prologue,* Summer 1996, 131; Osgood, "Before Sputnik," 219.

47. Memo for the President, Oct. 7, 1957, WHO, Office Conference in the President's Office, Oct. 8, 1957, OSS, DDS, Box 6, DDEL; *Time,* Feb. 17, 1958, 24; Hardesty and Eisman, 64.

48. *Fortune,* Jan. 1958, 100.

49. Letter from Eugene Emme, Aug. 6, 1969, Box: WHP-E, NASA HO.

50. Memo for the President, Oct. 7, 1957, WHO, OSS, DDS, Box 6, DDEL.

51. Ewald, 283, 284; Medaris, 135; *Time,* Oct. 21, 1957, 22.

52. Frutkin interview, 2008.

53. D'Antonio, 107; Brzezinski, 42–44, 152; Hardesty and Eisman, xi–xii; Dickson, 104–5; Bille and Lishock, 66. Cognizant of the superpower competition, Korolev feared America would launch a satellite before Russia, so at the last minute, he ordered Sputnik's launch date moved up by two days, to October 4.

54. Memorandum for William Elliott from David Z. Beckler, Apr. 18, 1956, Box 8, SS, OCB Series, WHO, OSANSA, DDEL

55. *Baltimore Sun,* July 28, 1957; *St. Louis Post-Dispatch,* Aug. 16, 1957.

56. PPP 1958, 6.

57. McDougall, 108

58. "U.S. Scientific Satellite Program: General Considerations," May 10, 1955, WHO, OSANSA, BNS, Box 7, DDEL; McDougall, 120; Turner, 16–17.

59. Schauer, 12; Dickson, 99; Killian, 14; Ewald, 284.

60. Letter to Arthur Flemming from Isadore Rabi, Oct. 10, 1956, WHO, OSANSA, BNS, Box 7, DDEL; *Huntsville Times,* July 1, 1957.

61. Memo from David Z. Beckler to Arthur Flemming, Jan. 23, 1957, Box: WHP-E, National Aeronautics and Space Act (cont'd), NASA HO; Hardesty and Eisman, 41.

62. Goodpaster interview, 1989.

63. Beckler interview, 2008; Callahan and Greenstein, 22.

64. Snead, 48–49; Dwayne Day, "A Strategy for Reconnaissance: Dwight D. Eisenhower and Freedom of Space," in Day et al., 126.

65. Morgan, 78; Memo of conference with the president, Feb. 4, 1958, WHO, OSS, DDS, Box 6, DDEL.

66. Memo from Andrew Goodpaster, June 7, 1956, WHO, OSS, DDS, Box 6, DDEL.

67. Ewald interview, 2006.

68. Memo for the assistant secretary of defense (R&D), June 22, 1956, WHO, OSS, DDS, Box 6; Memo from E. V. Murphree to the deputy secretary of defense, July 5, 1956, WHO, OSS, DDS, Box 6, DDEL.

69. Day, "A Strategy for Reconnaissance," 134; Ewald interview, 2006.

70. Memo of conference with the president, Oct. 9, 1957, AWF, DEDS, Box 27, Folder: Oct. 1957 Staff Notes (2), DDEL; Dickson, 123.

71. Eisenhower: Papers as President, LMS, Legislative Minutes 1958 (1), Supplementary Notes, Jan. 7, 1958, DDEL.

72. Doyle, 84; Divine, *The Sputnik Challenge,* 5; Letter from Donald Menzel, Sept. 7, 1960, Pre-Presidential Papers, Box 747, JFKL.

73. McDougall, 124; Frutkin interview.

74. Lethbridge, 6–7; Dickson, 87–88; Medaris, 136.

75. Brzezinski, 163; Divine, *The Sputnik Challenge,* 9–10.

76. Chronology, WHO, OSS, DDS, Box 6, DDEL; Akens in Webb Papers, HSTL; Crouch, 140; Lethbridge, 6–7; Dickson, 88–89; *This Week,* Apr. 13, 1958.

77. *St. Louis Post-Dispatch*, Aug. 16, 1957; Dickson, 86.

78. Divine, *The Sputnik Challenge,* 27; Chronology, WHO, OSS, DDS, Box 6, DDEL.

79. Neilon interview; DeGroot, 54.

80. Medaris, 155; NYT, Nov. 10, 1957; *Time,* Feb. 17, 1958, 24; Halberstam, 626.

Chapter 3

1. PPP 1955, 333.

2. Ewald, 11; Ambrose, *Eisenhower: Soldier and President*, 76, 184, 244; Goodpaster interview, 2000.

3. Thompson, 161; Greenstein, 19, 73, 68–69; Adams, 302; Perret, 437–38.

4. *Fortune*, Jan. 1958, 100; Minutes, Oct. 10, 1957, 339th Meeting of the NSC, AWF, NSC Series, DDEL.

5. Larson letter to author.

6. Arthur Larson Records, Presidential Speeches: Science and Security Background Material, Memo for President from McElroy, Oct. 28, 1957, DDEL.

7. *Newsweek*, Nov. 11, 1957, 36; NYT, Nov. 6, 1957.

8. Hughes, 246; Brendon, 348; NYT, Oct. 20, 1957, E20.

9. Pach and Richardson, 35; Ewald, 192; Secretary of Defense press conference, Nov. 16, 1954, Box 282, Folder 34, HJP, UW; Halberstam, 619, 623; USN, Oct. 18, 1957, 86.

10. Excerpt from hearings, 2/26/58, WHO, OSAST, Box 15, DDEL; DNC Clippings: Dulles, Box 5, JFKL; Nashville *Tennessean*, March 11, 1958; *Denver Post,* March 11, 1958.

11. Adams, 415.

12. Gaddis, 162–63.

13. Goodpaster interview. See also Eisenhower: Papers as President, AWF, DEDS, Oct. 1957 Staff Notes (1), Memo—Chesney to Whitman, Oct. 28, 1957, DDEL.

14. Letter from George Homans to Maxwell Rabb, Oct. 8, 1957 (emphasis original), Box: WHP-E, National Aeronautics and Space Act (cont'd), NASA HO.

15. Larson interview; GP, v. 2, 1523; Divine, *The Sputnik Challenge*, 45.

16. Letter from Eisenhower to Lloyd Swenson, Aug. 5, 1965, Box: WHP-E, NASA HO; Eisenhower, *Waging Peace*, 206; Brzezinski, 136.

17. Eisenhower, *Waging Peace*, 206; *Fortune*, Jan. 1958, 100. A similar statement can be found in Eisenhower's Papers as President, AWDS, Ann C. Whitman Diary entry, Dec. 30, 1957, DDEL.

18. Telephone calls, Nov. 21, 1957, AWF, DEDS, Box 29; Notes of Meeting, Oct. 18, 1958, WHO, OSS, Records: Cabinet Series, C-39 (3), DDEL.

19. PPP 1959, 244.

20. Larson interview; Detlev Bronk, "Science Advice in the White House," in Golden, *Science Advice to the President*, 256; Meeting with the President, 10/22/07, ALP, Box 22, DDEL.

21. NYT, Oct. 20, 1957, E7; *Fortune,* Jan. 1958, 100; Summaries of Discussions, Oct. 17, 24, and 31, 1957, Eisenhower: PP, NSC Series, DDEL.

22. Greenstein, 42, 232; Charles Maier, "Science, Politics, and Defense in the Eisenhower Era," in Kistiakowsky, *A Scientist at the White House,* xxviii; Larson, 14, 197.

23. Bethe interview; Mackey interview.

24. Clowse, 113; Goodpaster interview, 1989.

25. *Time*, Oct. 21, 1957, 22; Diary, Oct. 8, Eisenhower: PP, AWF, AWDS, Box 9, DDEL.

26. Conference in the President's Office, Oct. 8, 1957, WHO, OSS, DDS, Box 6; AWF: DEDS, Box 27, Folder: Oct. 1957 Staff Notes (2), Memo of Conference, Oct. 9, 1957, DDEL.

27. *Sputnik Mania*, A&E Television, DVD, 2008; Ambrose, *Eisenhower: The President*, 429; PPP 1957, 719–32; Eisenhower, *Waging Peace*, 211.

28. PPP 1957, 719–32.

29. Skolnikoff interview; Ewald interview, 2006.

30. NYP, Oct. 10, 1957.

31. *Time*, Oct. 28, 1957, 18; NYT, Oct. 15, 1957.

32. Ambrose, *Eisenhower: The President,* 53, 73; Pickett, 192; Divine, *The Sputnik Challenge,* 6.

33. Eisenhower, *Waging Peace*, 211.

34. *Fortune*, Jan. 1958, 101; Memo of conference, Oct. 15, 1957, AWF, DEDS, DDEL; David Z. Beckler, "Talk on Science in the Eisenhower Administration," Mar. 2005, unpublished paper in author's collection.

35. Memo of conference, Oct. 15, 1957, AWF, DEDS, DDEL; Notes on meeting of ODM SAC with the president, Oct. 15, 1957, Box: WHP-E, National Aeronautics and Space Act (cont'd), Folder: Eisenhower Administration—Space Correspondence, 1955–57, NASA HO; Killian, 17; David Z. Beckler, "Talk on Science in the Eisenhower Administration."

36. Bethe interview.

37. Witkin, 16.

38. Eisenhower, *Waging Peace*, 214.

39. West with Kotz, 180; Eisenhower, *Waging Peace*, 215; Hughes, 249. Similar sentiments of Queen Elizabeth and Prince Philip are recorded in Memo—Chesney to Whitman, Oct. 29, 1957, Eisenhower: PP, AWF, DEDS, Oct. 1957 Staff Notes (1), DDEL.

Chapter 4

1. Ambrose, *Eisenhower: The President*, 28; Ambrose, *Eisenhower: Soldier and President*, 240, 259; Brendon, 203; Ewald, 318; West with Kotz, 138.

2. Thompson, 147, 221.

3. Wukovits, 13; Gilbert, 76, 132; Larson, 3; Thompson, 42, 74.

4. WP, Nov. 9, 1957; *Tyler Courier-Times*, Oct. 18, 1957; *Tyler Morning Telegraph*, Oct. 19, 1957.

5. Caryl Haskins letter.

6. Wukovits, 109.

7. Oberg, 27; Witkin, 28, *Fortune*, Jan. 1958, 93; *Department of State Bulletin*, Nov. 4, 1957, 710.

8. Killian, xvii–xviii.

9. Killian, 97; Memo of conversation, AWF, DEDS, Box 27, DDEL.

10. Thompson, 176; AWF, DEDS, Box 46, Folder: Telephone Calls, Nov. 1959, DDEL; Kistiakowsky, 250.

11. Ewald, 16; Bethe interview.

12. Haskins letter; Halberstam, 617; PPP 1960–61, 403; York interview.

13. Bille and Lishock, 104; Brzezinski, 27; Cadbury, 85, 87, 89–90; D'Antonio, 7.

14. Ewald interview, 2006; Divine, *The Sputnik Challenge*, 41.

15. Ewald, 287; Regan, 252, 253.

16. PPP 1959, 512; Truman, 512–13.

17. WSJ, Nov. 8, 1957.

18. PPP 1960–61, 1041–42.

19. Ambrose, *Eisenhower: The President*, 229; Ewald interview, 2006; McPhee interview; McCabe interview.

20. Ambrose, *Eisenhower: The President*, 256; Weiner, 75.

21. Crouch, 129; Memo by Andrew Goodpaster, July 29, 1958, WHO, OSS, Records Subject Series, Alphabetical Subseries, Box 14, DDEL; Beschloss, 111–12; Dwayne Day, "Cover Stories and Hidden Agendas: Early American Space and National Security Policy," in Launius et al., 175.

22. Daniloff, 57; Hotz, "Radar in Turkey," in Witkin, 27–28.

23. D'Antonio, 41; Divine, *The Sputnik Challenge*, 30–31; Halberstam, 620, 621; Kistiakowsky, 313.

24. Beschloss, 150; Halberstam, 617.

25. Dickson, 100; Beschloss, 148–49, 152; Kistiakowsky, 312; Letter to E. E. Hazlett, Nov. 18, 1957, Eisenhower: Papers as President, 1953–61, AWF, DEDS, Box 28, DDEL.

26. Eisenhower, *Waging Peace*, 225; Divine, *The Sputnik Challenge*, 41

27. Dickson, 79; Hardesty and Eisman, 58.

28. Dickson, 101; "Proposed White House Release," WHO, OSS, DDS, Box 6, DDEL.

29. Eisenhower, *Waging Peace*, 210.

30. Dallek, 165–67; Gaddis, 181.

31. Pickett, 64; Letter to Carl Marsh, Feb. 6, 1957, Eisenhower, Dwight: PP, AWF, AS, Box 15, DDEL.

32. PPP 1958, 6–7; Ambrose, *Eisenhower: The President*, 381.

33. *Commonweal*, Jan. 17, 1958, 395; *Washington News*, Nov. 23, 1957.

34. Goodpaster interview, 1989; *Economist*, Dec. 14, 1957, 933.

35. *Economist*, Oct. 12, 1957, 99–101, and Dec. 14, 1957, 932.

36. PPP 1957, 387; Larson, 93; Morgan, 87; USN, Apr. 12, 1957, 121, and Jan. 17, 1958, 98; NYT, Jan. 3, 1957; Bowie and Immerman, 210.

37. USN, Jan. 17, 1958, 99; Thompson, 133; Larson, 72.

38. Ewald, 97–98; Kistiakowsky, 388; Morgan, 88; Pach and Richardson, 165, 166–67; Ewald interview, 2006.

39. Ambrose, *Eisenhower: The President*, 88; PPP 1957, 348; Kistiakowsky, 160; Hughes, 81.

40. Hughes, 28; WP, Dec. 20, 1957; Ambrose, *Eisenhower: The President*, 88, 389; Larson, 23; Ewald interview, 2006.

41. Gaddis, 188; Sloan, 15; Saulnier, 48–49; Snead, 24.

42. PPP 1959, 250; Thompson, 51; Sloan, 81.

43. Beschloss, 153; Hughes, 250; Glennan, 157.

44. Pach and Richardson, 53, 76; Sloan, 76; Testimony before Preparedness Subcommittee by Allen Dulles and Herbert Scoville, U.S. Senate, 1949–61, Committee on Armed Services, Box 355, LBJL; Comments Concerning Mutual Aid Speech, ALP, Box 16, DDEL.

45. Ambrose, *Eisenhower: Soldier and President*, 290, 440; Morgan, 82; Pickett, 145; *Time*, July 4, 1955.

46. Killian, 230; McPhee interview; Gaddis, 187–88; Kistiakowsky, 42.

47. Keeny interview; Ambrose, *Eisenhower: The President*, 457.

48. Ambrose, *Eisenhower: The President*, 395; Beckler interview, 2008; York, 70.

49. Wang, 119; Stever, 79, 83; McDougall, 341; Stares, 129–31; York, 129.

50. Hughes, 250; Charles Maier, "Science, Politics, and Defense in the Eisenhower Era," in Kistiakowsky, xxii; Sloan, 71; Snead, 19; PPP 1957, 722; Letter, Eisenhower to Altschul, Oct. 25, 1957, Eisenhower: PP, AWF, Box 28, DDEL.

51. Saulnier, 113; Eisenhower: PP, LMS, Legislative Minutes 1958 (1), Supplementary Notes, Jan. 7, 1958, DDEL.

52. Ambrose, *Eisenhower: The President*, 520.

53. McDougall, 113; Saulnier, 9.

54. McDougall, 139; PPP 1957, 343.

55. *Newsweek*, Nov. 14, 1960, 32.

56. Letter from Eisenhower to Charles Halleck, Mar. 26, 1963, Box: WHP-E, NASA HO; SEP, Aug. 11, 1962, 23, and May 18, 1963, 16.

57. SEP, May 18, 1963, 16; *Time*, Jan. 4, 1960; Ambrose, *Eisenhower: Soldier and President*, 30; Ewald, 11.

58. *Time,* Apr. 27, 1953; McPhee interview; Sloan, 80.

59. PPP 1958, 307, 308.

60. Speech in San Antonio, Oct. 10, 1960, Post-Presidential Files, Speech Files, General File, Box 731, HSTL.

61. Truman, 479; PPP 1959, 511, 512; Ewald, 292–93.

62. NYT, Oct. 15, 1957, A17; Morgan, 40.

63. Saulnier, 3.

64. Morgan, 23; Eisenhower, *Waging Peace,* 127–29; Larson, 142; Sloan, 67–68, 102–24, 145.

65. *Arizona Republic,* Nov. 16, 1957.

66. Morgan, 12; Eisenhower, *Waging Peace,* 217; PPP 1957, 714; Letter, Eisenhower to Altschul, Oct. 25, 1957, Eisenhower: PP (AWF): DEDS, DDEL.

67. SEP, May 18, 1963, 18; Saulnier, 2, 37.

68. Letter from Eisenhower to Saulnier, Mar. 4, 1964, personal papers of Raymond Saulnier in author's collection; Eisenhower, *White House Years,* 2:651.

69. Saulnier interview.

70. Sloan, 16; Saulnier, 22.

71. Ewald, 251; USN, Jan. 30, 1961, 69.

72. NYT, May 16, 1958; Preble, 50.

73. *Fortune,* Nov. 1957, 125, 126; Beschloss, 81.

74. Interview with Walter Cronkite, Jan. 23, 1963, DDEL: Papers, Post-Presidential, Speeches Series, Box 5; Letter to Arthur Larson, Jan. 23, 1964, ALP, Box 21, DDEL.

Chapter 5

1. Ambrose, *Eisenhower: Soldier and President,* 20–21, 26–28; Perret, *Eisenhower,* 24–25, 30; Brendon, 35–36.

2. Ambrose, *Eisenhower Soldier and President,* 88, 252–56.

3. Larson letter; NYT, Nov. 3, 1957, A1; Bille and Lishock, 114; Brzezinski, 214; D'Antonio, 91; DeGroot, 84; Dickson, 166.

4. Taubman, 427, 434, 437, 457; Brzezinski, 209–10; William Pickett, "Eisenhower, Khrushchev, and the U-2 Affair: A Forty-Six-Year Retrospective," in Clifford and Wilson, 141.

5. Christian Herter Papers, Presidential Telephone Calls 1957, Telephone Call Summary, Oct. 11, 1957, DDEL; NYT, Oct. 12, 1957, and Nov. 4, 1957.

6. Eisenhower, *Waging Peace,* 219; NYT, Nov. 5, 1957; Dickson, 141; *Time,* Nov. 18, 1957, 75; *Nation,* Nov. 23, 1957, 379; Stan Laurel to Marie Hatfield, Nov. 15, 1957, www.lettersfromstan.com.

7. Eisenhower: PP, AWF, NSC Series, 343rd Meeting of NSC, Summary of Discussion, Nov. 8, 1957, DDEL; NYT, Nov. 4, 1957, and Nov. 5, 1957; Memo by J. S. Earman, Mar. 18, 158, WHO, OSS, 1952–61, SS, AS, Box 7, DDEL; Brzezinski, 215.

8. D'Antonio, 92.

9. Dickson, 142; NYT, Nov. 10, 1957; *Time,* Jan. 6, 1958.

10. NYT, Nov. 4, 1957; McDougall, 149.

11. *Sputnik Mania,* A&E Television, DVD, 2008; NYT, Nov. 5 and Nov. 7, 1957. The American Aviation Publications printed *Missiles and Rockets Magazine, Missile Week, American Aviation, Aviation Daily,* and twelve other missile and aviation publications.

12. Ambrose, *Eisenhower: The President,* 519; Goodpaster interview, 1989.

13. Letter from Symington to Eisenhower, Oct. 8, 1957, Box: WHP-E, National Aeronautics and Space Act (cont'd), NASA HO; WSJ, Jan. 20, 1958; Memo of conference with the president, Feb. 15, 1958, AWF, DEDS, Box 30, DDEL.

14. Goodpaster interview, 1989.

15. Larson, 156; Larson interview; Brzezinski, 217.

16. Brendon, 218; Halberstam, 229–31; Aitken, 220; Oshinsky, 463.

17. NYT, Sept. 23, 1956; West with Kotz, 152–53.

18. Ambrose, *Eisenhower: The President,* 53; PPP 1957, 689–94.

19. Allen, 156; Goodpaster interview, 1989; Meeting with the president, 10/22/07, ALP, Box 22, DDEL; emphasis original.

20. Wukovits, 74, 110.

21. Ewald, 45, 146; McCabe interview; Pickett, 13, 179.

22. Nixon, *RN,* 378–79; *Time,* Jan. 4, 1960; Eisenhower, *Waging Peace,* 216.

23. *Time,* Oct. 28, 1957, 18; WSJ, Jan. 20, 1958. Other prominent senators supporting a Department of Science included Estes Kefauver of Tennessee and Mike Mansfield of Montana.

24. Memo of conference with the president, June 18, 1958, AWF, DEDS, Box 33; Letter from DDE to Charles Potter, Oct. 21, 1957, AWF, DEDS, Box 28, DDEL; Griffith, 54; Roger Launius, "Eisenhower, Sputnik, and the Creation of NASA," *Prologue,* Summer 1996, vol. 28, no. 2, 137.

25. Brinkley, 71.

26. Memo of conference with the president, June 18, 1958, AWF, DEDS, Box 33, DDEL; Larson interview; Larson letter; Larson, 155, 157.

27. Ambrose, *Eisenhower: The President,* 29; Ewald interview, 2006; McCabe interview; Meeting with the president, 10/22/07, ALP, Box 22, DDEL; Memo for Arthur Larson, Nov. 5, 1957, AWF, DEDS, Box 28, DDEL.

28. Wukovits, 45; Larson, 146; Thompson, 44; Meeting with the president, 10/22/07, ALP, Box 22, DDEL; Ewald, 41; McCabe interview.

29. Ambrose, *Eisenhower: Soldier and President,* 206–7; Memo for Arthur Larson, Nov. 5, 1957, AWF, DEDS, Box 28, DDEL; Divine, *The Sputnik Challenge,* 45; Ewald, 142.

30. WP, Nov. 9, 1957; Eisenhower, *Waging Peace,* 223.

31. Larson interview; Larson, 155–56.

32. Stebenne, 204; PPP 1957, 789–99.

33. WSJ, Nov. 18, 1957; Brzezinski, 222; WP, Nov. 9, 1957, and Nov. 10, 1957; Dickson, 146.

34. WP, Nov. 8, 1957, and Nov. 9, 1957; WSJ, Nov. 11, 1957.

35. Medaris, 166–67, italics removed; Larson interview.

36. Stebenne, 204.

37. PPP 1957, 807–16.

38. WSJ, Nov. 14, 1957.

39. Hughes, 252; Seamans interview.

40. WP, Nov. 12. 1957.

Chapter 6

1. Ambrose, *Eisenhower: The President*, 228, 288, 291.

2. West with Kotz, 172.

3. Eisenhower, *Waging Peace*, 223; Snead, 10.

4. Text of Javits address, Jan. 17, 1958, Series 1, Subseries 1, Box 14, Folder: 1/17/58 San Francisco Commonwealth Club, Missile Race, JJP, SBU; NYT, Jan. 17, 1960.

5. Killian, 96; McDougall, 151; Snead, 47; Keeny interview.

6. Keeny interview.

7. Ewald, 250; Wang, 81.

8. *Economist,* Jan. 4, 1958, 36.

9. WP, Dec. 20, 1957; McDougall, 151.

10. Eisenhower, *Waging Peace*, 219; Ewald, 249; Snead, 125; Keeny interview.

11. Letter from Johnson to Eisenhower, Dec. 4, 1957; Letter from Eisenhower to Johnson, Jan. 28, 1958, Box: WHP-E, National Aeronautics and Space Act (cont'd), NASA HO.

12. Killian, 97.

13. Snead, 144; Peebles, 202; Eisenhower, *Waging Peace,* 221–23.

14. Preble, 35; Divine, *The Sputnik Challenge,* 39; Ambrose, *Eisenhower: The President,* 494–95; Gaddis, 185; Keeny interview.

15. Launius and McCurdy, 19; Bowie and Immerman, 153–54.

16. Morgan, 93; Divine, *The Sputnik Challenge,* 83.

17. York, 132–33.

18. Snead, 187.

19. Ambrose, *Eisenhower: The President,* 441; Letter to E. E. Hazlett, Nov. 18, 1957, Eisenhower: PP, 1953–61, AWF, DEDS, Box 28, DDEL.

20. PPP 1957, 786; Letter from Burns to Eisenhower, Nov. 1, 1957, Box: WHP-E, National Aeronautics and Space Act (cont'd), NASA HO.

21. *Fortune,* Jan. 1958, 232.

22. Eisenhower, *Waging Peace,* 227–28.

23. Sterrett interview.

24. Eisenhower, *Waging Peace,* 227–28; West with Kotz, 182.

25. Gilbert, 108, 109; Stebenne, 209; Larson, 161; Memo of Staff Conference, Dec. 6, 1957, WHO, OSS, 1952–61, SS, AS, Box. 33; "A Black Day at the White House," 11/26/57, ALP, Box 16, DDEL.

26. Nixon, *RN,* 184; Ambrose, *Eisenhower: The President,* 441.

27. Larson interview.

28. Letter to Edward Hazlett, Feb. 26, 1958, Eisenhower: Papers, 1953–61, AWF, DEDS, Box 30, DDEL; Kistiakowsky, 213, 219; Eisenhower, *Waging Peace,* 229.

29. AKP, Works: Memoranda, Box 1, Book II: 1948–60, 309, MLPU; Divine, *The Sputnik Challenge,* 58.

30. Ambrose, *Eisenhower: The President*, 437; Larson, 175–76.

31. Brown interview; Divine, *The Sputnik Challenge,* 73; Dickson, 6.

32. Eisenhower, *Waging Peace*, 231–33; D'Antonio, 136; Larson, 175.

33. Ambrose, *Eisenhower: The President,* 275; Kistiakowsky, 347; Nixon, *RN*, 185; PPP 1957, 244–45.

34. Divine, *The Sputnik Challenge,* 132; Hughes, 131, 132.

35. Neilon interview; Dickson, 154, 155; Memo for the secretary of the navy, Oct. 29, 1957, WHO, OSAST, Box 15, DDEL.

36. York interview.

37. Neilon interview; Lethbridge, 9.

38. Neilon interview; Johnson, 271; *Newsweek*, Dec. 16, 1957, 66; S. Khrushchev, 262.

39. NYT, Aug. 18, 1958; Bud Reynolds interview; Welby Risler interview; Charlie Mars interview; Neilon interview.

40. Al Nagy e-mail to author, Aug. 23, 2005; NYT, Aug. 18, 1958; *Time,* Dec. 30, 1957; D'Antonio, 122, 125.

41. USN, Dec. 13, 1957, 33; Woods, 335.

42. USN, Jan. 10, 1958, 67.

43. *Time,* Dec. 16, 1957.

Chapter 7

1. Sloan, 135.

2. Saulnier interview; Morgan, 64; Pickett, 147.

3. Morgan, 61; Saulnier, 73.

4. Folder: Daily Journal, June 1957, Box: Daily Journal 1957, JMP, FIT; *Time,* Feb. 17, 1958, 25; *This Week*, Apr. 13, 1958; Divine, *The Sputnik Challenge*, 10; Lethbridge, 8–9; Medaris, 153; Dickson 148.

5. Goodpaster interview, 1989; Conference in President's Office, Oct. 8, 1957, WHO, OSS, DEDS, Box 6, DDEL.

6. Oct. 1957 Staff Notes (2), Conference Memo, Oct. 8, 1957, AWF, DEDS; Memo of conference with the president, Oct. 8, 1957, AWF, DEDS, Box 27, DDEL.

7. Medaris, 190; Lethbridge, 9.

8. *Huntsville Times,* Jan. 31, 1968; NYT, Feb. 1, 1958; D'Antonio, 142; Dickson, 171.

9. Medaris, 212; NYT, Feb. 1, 1958; D'Antonio, 163–64.

10. Eisenhower, *Waging Peace*, 256; Dickson, 175; Bille and Lishock, 133–34; NYT, Feb. 2, 1958, and Oct. 25, 1959.

11. Bille and Lishock, 137; GRF Congressional Papers, Press Secretary and Speech File 1947–73, Box D15, Folder: Challenges of the Space Age 1959, GRFL; Letter from Eisenhower to Lee DuBridge, Jan. 31, 1968, Box: WHP-E, Folder: Eisenhower—Space Exploration (1955–63), NASA HO.

12. *Time,* Mar. 31, 1958, 11–12; NYT, Mar. 18, 1958; DeGroot, 94; Dickson, 179.

13. Bille and Lishock, 157, 174; Dickson, 180.

14. Clowse, 112–23; Killian, 144.

15. Brendon, 353; Killian, 234.

16. WSJ, Mar. 17, 1958; *Newsweek,* Mar. 10, 1958, 27, 29; Divine, *The Sputnik Challenge,*118; NYHT, Mar. 11, 1959.

17. *Economist,* Jan. 16, 1960, 203; PPP 1957, 782; Letter from Burns to Eisenhower, Nov. 1, 1957, Box: WHP-E, National Aeronautics and Space Act (cont'd), NASA HO.

18. *Economist,* Dec. 1, 2001, 74; *Newsweek,* Mar. 10, 1958, 27, 30; Morgan, 93, 99, 100; Sloan, 52; *Cleveland Plain Dealer,* Mar. 23, 1958.

19. Ewald, 288; *New Republic,* Nov. 3, 1958, 5; Preble, 39.

20. Morgan, 100, 102, 103; Woods, 337; Sloan, 144; Pach and Richardson, 177; Saulnier, 110–11.

21. Morgan, 106; Ewald, 289; *Time,* Oct. 13, 1958.

22. NYT, Jan. 6, 1958; quote refers to the fiscal year ending June 30, 1959; *New Republic,* Sept. 12, 1960, 3.

Chapter 8

1. Donaldson, 24, 34–35.

2. Brendon, 397; Glennan, 208; Pach and Richardson, 234; Nixon, *RN,* 286–87; Larson, 166; Ambrose, *Eisenhower: The President,* 499.

3. Donaldson, 24; Brzezinski, 183.

4. McCabe interview; Ambrose, *Eisenhower: The President,* 649; Eisenhower with Nixon Eisenhower, 221.

5. Rorabaugh, 65; Y. Mieczkowski, 51; Thompson, 151.

6. Larson, 12; Ewald, 27; Kessler, 18–19.

7. Pickett, 181, 183.

8. *Time,* Feb. 17, 1958; Woods, 1020; Ewald, 27.

9. Ewald interview, 2006.

10. Johnson, 272.

11. "Conversation with Gerald Seigel" and "Conversation with Eileen Galloway," "The Legislative Origins of the Space Act," NASA HO.

12. Conversation with George Reedy, in "The Legislative Origins of the Space Act," NASA HO; George Reedy, Memo, U.S. Senate, 1941–61, George Reedy Files, 1951–55, Box 421, LBJL.

13. Memo from Reedy to Johnson, Oct. 17, 1957, U.S. Senate, 1949–61, George Reedy Files, 1951–55, Box 420, LBJL.

14. USN, Jan. 17, 1958, 101; NYT, Feb. 9, 1958; Morgan, 91.

15. Caro, 1021; Memo from Reedy to Johnson, Oct. 17, 1957, and George Reedy, Memo, U.S. Senate, 1941–61, George Reedy Files, 1951–55, Boxes 420 and 421, LBJL, emphasis original.

16. *Tyler Courier-Times,* Oct. 18, 1957; *Tyler Morning Telegraph,* Oct. 19, 1957; George Reedy interview with John Logsdon, May 20, 1992, http://www.space -settlement-institute.org/Articles/reedyinterview.htm; Brzezinski, 183–84.

17. "Conversation with Glen Wilson," NASA HO; Clowse, 59.

18. Woods, 335; D'Antonio, 133.

19. Wang, 177; D'Antonio, 131; Divine, *The Sputnik Challenge,* 64; Clowse, 60.

20. Robert Dallek, "Johnson, Project Apollo, and the Politics of Space Program Planning," in Launius and McCurdy, 70; Dwayne Day, "Invitation to Struggle: The History of Civilian-Military Relations in Space," accessed at http://history.nasa.gov /SP-4407/vol2/v2chapter2-1.pdf; Roger Launius, "Eisenhower, Sputnik, and the Creation of NASA," *Prologue,* Summer 1996, vol. 28, no. 2, 132.

21. Launius, "Eisenhower, Sputnik, and the Creation of NASA," 136; USN, Jan. 17, 1958, 100–102; Logsdon, *The Decision to Go to the Moon,* 22.

22. Glen P. Wilson, "How the U.S. Space Act Came to Be," Appendix to "The Legislative Origins of the Space Act," NASA HO; Divine, *The Sputnik Challenge,* 79; Griffith, 10–11; USN, Jan. 31, 1958, 56; Clowse, 59.

23. *Time,* Feb. 17, 1958, 20; Stever, 131.

24. Wicker, 151; *Dallas Morning News,* Nov. 12, 1958; NYHT, Nov. 18, 1958; "Conversation with Eileen Galloway."

25. Dickson, 151–52; McCabe interview.

26. Nixon, *RN,* 368–69; West with Kotz, 337, 389; Oral history interview of James Killian by E. M. Emme and A. F. Roland, July 23, 1974; NASA HO; "Conversation with George Reedy."

27. Letters from John Christian, Mar. 7, 1959, and J. R. Aston, Feb. 5, 1959, U.S. Senate, 1949–61, Subject Files 1959, Box 730, LBJL.

28. Wilson, "How the U.S. Space Act Came To Be."

29. NYT, May 25, 1958; Larson, 92; Gaddis, 133.

Chapter 9

1. Memo of conference with the president, June 18, 1958, AWF, DEDS, Box 33, Folder: June 1958—Staff Notes (2), DDEL.

2. Bowie and Immerman, 183; Thompson, 250.

3. Thompson, 87.

4. Snead, 59; Keeny interview; Beckler interview, 2008.

5. WP, Nov. 14, 1957; Divine, *The Sputnik Challenge,* 48–49.

6. WSJ, Nov. 11, 1957; Skolnikoff interview.

7. Ewald interview, 2006; Killian, 227–28, 241.

8. Killian, 65–66; Ewald, 284–85.

9. Wang, 64; Jefferson-Jackson Day Dinner, Nov. 1, 1957, Post-Presidential Files, Speech Files, Reading Copies, Box 715, HSTL.

10. David Z. Beckler, "Talk on Science in the Eisenhower Administration," March 2005; PPP 1957, 551.

11. Roger Launius, "Eisenhower and Space: Politics and Ideology in the Construction of the U.S. Civil Space Program," in Showalter, 169; Wang, 86; NYT, June 12, 1960; Killian, 107; Beckler interviews.

12. Killian, 247; Keeny interview.

13. *Fortune* , Jan. 1958, 94; West with Kotz, 187–88.

14. Snead, 73; Stever, 129; Kistiakowsky, 242.

15. Ambrose, *Eisenhower: The President,* 19; Ewald, 72; Skolnikoff interview.

16. Killian, 29–34, 36–37.

17. http://history.nasa.gov/sputnik/16.html; PPP 1958, 269–73.

18. Discussion at the 357th Meeting of the NSC, March 6, 1958, DDE website (from Ann Whitman File); "Introduction to Outer Space" accessed at www.fas.org /spp/guide/usa/intro1958.html; Divine, *The Sputnik Challenge,* 106–7.

19. *Washington Star,* Apr. 16, 1958; Killian, 212; Kistiakowsky, 123, 188; SEP, May 18, 1963, 19.

20. Killian, 220.

21. Kistiakowsky, 339; Divine, *The Sputnik Challenge,* 124.

22. Kistiakowsky, 243; Bowie and Immerman, 255; Reeves, 395.

23. Hornig interview.

24. *Economist,* Jan. 10, 2009, 69; Haskins letter.

25. Avosso interview.

26. *Time,* Nov. 18, 1957.

27. Pach and Richardson, 106; NYT, Dec. 13, 1959; *Time,* Feb. 17, 1958; NYHT and NYT, Nov. 22, 1957.

28. NYT, Apr. 1, 1956; BW, Apr. 19, 1958, 156.

29. USN, Jan. 15, 1954, 46; Remarks of Sen. Javits, Oct. 17, 1957, Series 1, Subseries 1, Box 14, JJP, SBU.

30. *Providence (RI) Sunday Journal,* Nov. 17, 1957; NYT, Feb. 8, 1958; Brendon, 232; WP, Feb. 4, 1958.

31. Seamans interview; *Time,* Nov. 25, 1957; Clowse, 63.

32. NYT, Aug. 9, 1959; *Time,* Apr. 26, 2010, 4; Clowse, 35–36; George Reedy, Memo, U.S. Senate, 1941–61, George Reedy Files, 1951–55, Box 421, LBJL.

33. *Time,* Feb. 17, 1961; Divine, *The Sputnik Challenge,* 53; Clowse, 108, 123.

34. NYT, Apr. 5, 1977; Diary, Mar. 17, 1958, Eisenhower: Papers, 1953–61, AWDS, Box 9, DDEL; Ewald interview, 2010.

35. Notes on meeting of ODM SAC with the president, Oct. 15, 1957, Box: WHP-, National Aeronautics and Space Act (cont'd), NASA HO; NYT, Sept. 14, 1958.

36. Remarks of Sen. Javits, Oct. 1, 1957, Series 1, Subseries 1, Box 14, JJP, SBU; WSJ, Jan. 20, 1958.

37. CD, Sept. 1961, 194; *Time,* Apr. 30, 1965.

38. PPP 1957, 243; USN, Apr. 12, 1957, 120.

39. Clowse, 49–51; 54–57.

40. Letter from DE to Charles Potter, Oct. 21, 1957, AWF, DEDS, Box 28, Folder: Oct. 1957 DE Dictation, DDEL; PPP 1957, 776, emphasis original.

41. WP, Nov. 14, 1957; PPP 1957, 794–95; 814; Minutes of Cabinet Meeting, Dec. 2, 1957, DDEL website, www.eisenhower.archives.gov; Clowse, 63; Divine, *The Sputnik Challenge,* 90.

42. PPP 1958, 127, 519, 528; NYT, Aug. 22, 1958; *Time,* Aug. 11, 1958; Clowse, 136–38; Killian, 195.

43. CD, Apr. 1965, 40; NYT, Aug. 22, 1958; NYT, Mar. 27, 1966; *Time,* Sept. 1, 1958; USN, Sept. 12, 1958, 78.

44. USN, Sept. 12, 1958, 79, and Nov. 7, 1958, 71; NYT, Aug. 22, 1958.

45. CD, Apr. 1965, 40, 64; PPP 1958, 131; NYT, Aug. 22, 1958.

46. Clowse, 126, 128, 136.

47. *Time,* Nov. 30, 1959.

48. Memo from N. M. Pusey, Nov. 25, 1959, Eisenhower, PP, AWF, Name Series, Box 13, DDEL; *Science,* Feb. 1960, 488; *Time,* Feb. 16, 1959.

49. *Science,* Feb. 1960, 488; Letter to Nathan Pusey, June 1, 1959, Eisenhower, PP, AWF, DEDS, Box 42, DDEL.

50. PPP 1959, 793; *Time,* Feb. 16, 1959, and Nov. 30, 1959; NYT, June 30, 1959, and Nov. 20, 1959; Clowse, 154.

51. CD, Apr. 1965, 40.

52. Citizens' Committee for Extension of the NDEA, Aug. 7, 1961, Flemming, Arthur: Papers, 1939–75, Box 41, DDEL; CD, Apr. 1965, 40; Clowse, 151.

53. Divine, *The Sputnik Challenge,* 166; NYT, June 29, 1961; Clowse, 154–55.

54. Clowse, 147, 157–58.

55. Brendon, 312; *Economist,* Feb. 13, 1960, 620; R. N. Smith, 228–29, 285, 287; Crapol, 80.

56. Clowse, 140; PPP 1960–61, 925; Killian, 196; Thompson, 242.

Chapter 10

1. Bowie and Immerman, 53, 89; Doyle, 82; Ewald, 63, 64, 65; Gaddis, 199; Larson, 198; Pach and Richardson, 39; Perret, 437; Pickett, 187; Thompson, 24.

2. Larson interview; Larson, 154; Goodpaster interview, 1989.

3. D'Antonio, 228; Dickson, 194; Griffith, 11.

4. Memo of conference with the president, Feb. 4, 1958, AWF, DEDS, Box 30, DDEL; WHO, OSS, Records, LMS, Supplementary Notes, Feb. 4, 1958, DDEL; Steve Garber, "NASA's Origins as a Civilian Agency," Box: WHP-E, NASA HO.

5. WHO, OSS, Records, LMS, Supplementary Notes, Feb. 4, 1958, DDEL; Dwayne Day, "Invitation to Struggle: The History of Civilian-Military Relations in Space," 249, accessed at http://history.nasa.gov/SP-4407/vol2/v2chapter2-1.pdf.

6. Medaris, 243; NYT, Mar. 15, 1958.

7. Day, "Invitation to Struggle," 249; McDougall, 166.

8. "Conversation with Paul Dembling," in "The Legislative Origins of the Space Act," NASA HO; Griffith, 53; Launius, *NASA,* 30.

9. Stares, 41, 43; WSJ, Nov. 13, 1959.

10. Wang, 94; Dickson, 187; Griffith, 8–9.

11. WHO, OSS, Records, LMS; Supplementary Notes, Feb. 4, 1958; Minutes of Cabinet meeting, Feb. 7, 1958, Eisenhower, PP, 1953–61, AWF, DEDS, Box 30, DDEL; Speech to the National Nuclear Energy Congress, March 19, 1958, WHO, OSAST, Box 14, DDEL.

12. Memo of conference with the president, Feb. 4, 1958, WHO, OSS, DDS, Box 6, DDEL; Memo of conference with the president, Feb. 4, 1958, AWF, DEDS, Box 30, DDEL; WSJ, Feb. 5, 1958; Dickson, 178.

13. Garber, "NASA's Origins as a Civilian Agency"; NYT, Feb. 5, 1958; McDougall, 171; Interview with James Killian by E. M. Emme and A. F. Roland, July 23, 1974, NASA HO; Divine, *The Sputnik Challenge,* 101; Wang, 97.

14. Goodpaster interview, 1989; Ewald, 202–3.

15. Interview with James Killian, NASA HO; Goodpaster interview, 1989; Day, "Invitation to Struggle," 248; Memo from Eugene Emme, Aug. 6, 1969, Box: WHP, Eisenhower, NASA HO; WSJ, Feb. 5, 1958; Frutkin interview.

16. PPP 1959, 772; Beckler interview, 2008.

17. James Killian, Memo on Organizational Alternatives for Space Research and Development, Dec. 30, 1957, http://history.nasa.gov/sputnik/iv1.html.

18. First Semiannual Report to the Congress, Oct. 1, 1958–Mar. 31, 1959, NASA, WHO, OSANSA, OCB Series, SS, Box 7, DDEL; WSJ, Feb. 5, 1958; Killian, 132, 133, 283; Griffith, 57.

19. First Semiannual Report to the Congress, Oct. 1, 1958–Mar. 31, 1959, NASA, WHO, OSANSA, OCB Series, SS, Box 7, DDEL; WSJ, Feb. 5, 1958; McDougall, 75.

20. WSJ, Feb. 5, 1958; McDougall, 164. Unlike with the later "NASA," which was pronounced as a word, the "NACA" enunciated each individual letter; "Conversation with Paul Dembling," NASA HO.

21. Goodpaster interview, 1989; Robert Piland, interview by Summer Chick Bergen, Aug. 21, 1998, accessed at the Johnson Space Center website, www.jsc.nasa.gov; Bilstein, 47; Suggested remarks by the president, Sept. 18, 1958, AWF, DEDS, Box 36, DDEL; White House statement, Apr. 2, 1958, Box: WHP-E, National Aeronautics and Space Act, Folder: NASA Act of 1958; Garber, "NASA's Origins as a Civilian Agency."

22. Memo of conference with the president, Mar. 5, 1958, AWF, DEDS, Box 31, DDEL; "Conversation with Eileen Galloway," in "The Legislative Origins of the Space Act," NASA HO.

23. McDougall, 175–76; Killian interview, NASA HO; Piland interview by Bergen, Aug. 21, 1998; Launius, *NASA*, 31; Skolnikoff interview.

24. Memo for Record, July 7, 1958, Eisenhower, PP, AWF, DEDS, Box 35, DDEL; Interview with James Killian, NASA HO; Glen P. Wilson, "How the U.S. Space Act Came to Be," NASA HO; NYT, Feb. 7, 1958.

25. Griffith, 96–97; Memo of conference with the president, July 17 and July 25, 1958, AWF, DEDS, Box 35, DDEL; NYT, July 30, 1958.

26. *Cleveland Plain Dealer*, Jan. 11, 1959; NYT, May 7, 1961; Hunley, 5; Memo of conference with the president, Sept. 23, 1959, AWF, DEDS, Box 44, DDEL.

27. Griffith, 96–97; Gerald R. Ford Congressional Papers, Press Secretary and Speech File 1947–73, Box D15, Folder: Challenges of the Space Age 1959, GRFL; "Conversation with Eileen Galloway" and "Roundtable Discussion," "The Legislative Origins of the Space Act," NASA HO.

28. *NASA: 50 Years of Exploration and Discovery*, 49; Griffith, 98; Launius and McCurdy, 39.

29. WSJ, Oct. 2, 1958; Dickson, 192; NYHT, Oct. 22, 1959; *Time*, Nov. 2, 1959, 10; *Baltimore Sun*, Oct. 22, 1959; NYT, Oct. 22, 1959; *Cleveland Plain Dealer*, Oct. 25, 1959; Logsdon, *The Decision to Go to the Moon*, 74.

30. NYHT, Oct. 22, 1959; Medaris, 244; Kisiakowsky, 100; WSJ, Oct. 22, 1959.

31. Eisenhower, *Waging Peace*, 258; PPP 1958, 269–73; NYT, Oct. 25, 1959; Memo for Loomist, Mar. 24, 1958, WHO, OSAST, Box 15, DDEL.

32. Day, "Invitation to Struggle," 248.

Chapter 11

1. Divine, *The Sputnik Challenge,* 143; Pickett, 113–14; Wang, 104.

2. Ewald, 241; McCabe interview; Larson, 86; Pach and Richardson, 192–95; Pickett, 128.

3. Larson, 38.

4. Ambrose, *Eisenhower: The President,* 467; Larson, 22; Ewald, 162.

5. Notes dictated by the vice president, July 15, 1958, Eisenhower, PP, 1953–61, AWF, AS, Box 28, DDEL; Brzezinski, 169.

6. NYT, Aug. 6, 1958; *Time,* Jan. 6, 1958.

7. www.brain.gallup.com, GP #604, Sept. 15, 1958; The precise percentage was 0.26.

8. *Time,* Sept. 1, 1958, 8; Snead, 173; WP, Aug. 15, 1959.

9. *Commonweal,* Aug. 29, 1958, 531.

10. The four American satellites were Explorers I, III, and IV and the Vanguard. NYT, Oct. 5 and Oct. 15, 1958; D'Antonio, 219.

11. Larson, 35; NYT, Nov. 1, 1958.

12. Pach and Richardson, 183; Speech in New Castle, Oct. 21, 1958, Post-Presidential Files, Speech Files, General File, Box 730, HSTL.

13. Adams, 168; Ambrose, *Eisenhower: The President,* 218–19; Brendon, 92–93; Pickett, 95; USN, Feb. 21, 1958, 52.

14. Moore, 569; Divine, *The Sputnik Challenge,* 198; Ewald, 292; Morgan, 125.

15. Sloan, 60–61; Pach and Richardson, 183–84.

16. Ford, 72; *Time,* Nov. 10, 1958; McDougall, 176.

17. Cannon, 671; Pach and Richardson, 184; PPP 1958, 827–32.

18. Divine, *Eisenhower and the Cold War,* 131–32.

19. Ambrose, *Eisenhower: The President,* 486; First Semiannual Report to the Congress, Oct. 1, 1958–Mar. 31, 1959, NASA, WHO, OSANSA, OCB Series, SS, Box 7, DDEL; Stever, 135; NYT, Jan. 4, 1959; Dickson, 194.

20. Bille and Lishock, 163–64; Dickson, 195.

21. Memo for the secretary of defense, Aug. 15, 1958, WHO, OSAST, Records, 1957–61, Box 15, DDEL; Dickson, 197.

22. *Time,* Dec. 29, 1958, 7–8, 31.

23. Untitled speech draft and text of message by the president, Dec. 19, 1958, WHO, OSANSA, OCB Series, SS, Box 8, DDEL; D'Antonio, 243.

24. *Time,* Dec. 29, 1958, 8; Dickson, 201.

25. Information plan for Project SCORE, WHO, OSS, AS, Box 18, DDEL; Successful U.S. and Russian satellites, U.S. Senate, 1949–61, Committee on Aeronautics and Space Sciences, Box 359, LBJL.

26. NYT, Jan. 18, 1959; D'Antonio, 244.

27. USN, Dec. 26, 1958, 27.

Chapter 12

1. Wukovits, 9, 10, 52; Brendon, 71.

2. Beschloss, 225.

3. *Time,* Jan. 19, 1959; Conference memo, Sept. 30, 1959, AWF, DEDS, Box 44, DDEL.

4. Haskins letter; Beckler interview, 2008.

5. 357th Meeting of the NSC, Mar. 6, 1958, DDEL website, www.eisenhower .archives.gov (from Ann Whitman Files); Telephone calls, Mar. 17, 1958, Eisenhower, Papers, 1953–61, AWF, DEDS, Box 31, DDEL; Hunley, 291.

6. Conference. memo, Sept. 23, 1959, AWF, DEDS, Box 44, DDEL; Goodpaster interview, 1989.

7. *Time,* Jan. 6, 1958; Oberg, 36, 37.

8. WSJ, Nov. 5, 1959; Kistiakowsky, 81, 100.

9. Goodpaster interview, 1989; Supplementary notes, Feb. 4, 1958, WHO, OSS, Records, LMS, DDEL; NYT, Jan. 7, 1959, and Feb. 4, 1960.

10. Killian, 137; *Economist,* Oct. 3, 1959, 44; Kistiakowsky, 191.

11. Memo on Presidential Proclamation on Outer Space, Oct. 31, 1958, WHO, OSANSA, OCB Series, Administrative Subseries, Box 1; Memo to General Goodpaster et. al., from Karl Herr, Oct. 31, 1958, and Memo to the president from Karl Herr, Nov. 25, 1958, Box 8, SS, OCB Series, WHO, OSANSA; Memo for the President, Nov. 25, 1958, WHO, OSS, 1952–61, SS, AS, Box 22, DDEL.

12. Brendon, 139; Doyle, 85.

13. U.S. Policy on the Control and Use of Outer Space, Series 3, Box 113, Folder 12, Space Law, 1958, JJP, SBU; Goodpaster interview, 1989.

14. WSJ, Nov. 5, 1959; PPP 1957, 721–22; Killian, 124; Memo for the National Aeronautics and Space Council, Mar. 26, 1959, WHO, OSANSA, OCB Series, SS, Box 7, DDEL; Kistiakowsky, 125.

15. Larson, xii; Letter to E. E. Hazlett, Nov. 18, 1957, Eisenhower: Papers, 1953–61, AWF, DEDS, Box 28, DDEL.

16. Letter to Paul Hoffman, June 23, 1958, AWF, DEDS, Box 33, DDEL; Pach and Richardson, 78.

17. Seamans interview; NYT, Sept. 17, 1959.

18. Conference memo, Feb. 4, 1958, AWF, DEDS, Box 30; also in WHO, OSS, DDS, Box 6; Conference memos, Sept. 23 and Sept. 30, 1959, AWF, DEDS, Box 44, DDEL; WSJ, Oct. 22, 1959; *Hartford Courant,* Aug. 3, 1955.

19. *Time,* Feb. 1, 1960; Kasey S. Pipes, "More Like Ike: The Eisenhower Example, and the Lessons for Today's GOP," Jan. 18, 2009, www.themoderatevoice.com; Morgan, 17.

20. McPhee interview; Ambrose, *Eisenhower: The President,* 76; NYT, Feb. 23, 1955.

21. PPP 1958, 88–89; Pach and Richardson, 58.

22. Conference memo, Sept. 30, 1959, AWF, DEDS, Box 44, DDEL; Conference memo, Feb. 24, 1959, WHO, OSS, AS, Box 18, DDEL.

23. Conference memo, Nov. 17, 1959, WHO, OSS, 1952–61, AS, Box 24, DDEL; Kistiakowsky, 100; Seamans, *Project Apollo,* 7; Richard Brastaad, "NASA's Share of Total Federal Government Expenditures since 1958," http://www.richardb .us/nasa.html#graph.

24. NYT, Nov. 6, 1959; Brastaad, "NASA's Share"; Gerald R. Ford Congressional Papers, Box D15, Folder: House Speech: On President's Budget Message, Jan. 19, 1959, GRFL; Hunley, 40. In late 1959, Eisenhower said that Sputnik cre-

ated a bulge in defense spending, the effects of which continued. If he had to run another deficit, he declared, he would regard his administration as discredited; see Conference memo, Nov. 17, 1959, WHO, OSS, 1952–61, AS, Box 24, DDEL.

25. WSJ, Oct. 7, 1959; Dec. 19, 1960; and Aug. 9, 1962.

26. USN, Jan. 16, 1959, 116.

27. SEP, Aug. 11, 1962, 24.

28. Democratic Advisory Council Position Paper on Space Research, Sept. 7, 1960, Box DNC 197, JFKL.

29. Logsdon, *The Decision to Go to the Moon*, 110–11.

30. Pach and Richardson, 9, 10; Ambrose, *Eisenhower: The President,* 177.

31. Larson, 97; Conference memo, Feb. 4, 1958, AWF, DEDS, Box 30, DDEL; Launius and McCurdy, 21; Ambrose, *Eisenhower: The President,* 112.

32. PPP 1957, 694; Frankel, 180. A century earlier, Abraham Lincoln had already worried about the blight on America's international standing that racism caused, writing in 1858, "I hate [slavery] because it deprives our republican example of its just influence in the world." From Guelzo, 4.

33. NYT, Oct. 5, 1957, and Mar. 23, 1958.

34. Logsdon, *The Decision to Go to the Moon,* 12; Ewald interview, 2006.

35. McPhee interview; Ambrose, *Eisenhower: Soldier and President,* 88; Launius, "Eisenhower and Space: Politics and Ideology in the Construction of the U.S. Civil Space Program," in Showalter, 157.

36. PPP 1960, 127.

37. Kistiakowsky, 336.

38. NYT, Oct. 29, 1960, and Jan. 23, 1960.

39. Sloan, 97; Memo to General Goodpaster, WHO, OSS, AS, Box 17, DDEL.

40. PPP 1955, 554; Kistiakowsky, 227.

41. Stebenne, 201; Memo from R. V. Mrozinski, Jan. 9, 1958, and also CIA Suggestions Relating to the International Posture of the U.S., Jan. 1958, both in WHO, OSANSA, OCB Series, Administrative Subseries, Box 5, DDEL.

42. "World Opinion and the Soviet Satellite," Oct. 17, 1957, WHO, OSANSA, BNS, Box 7, DDEL; Frutkin interview, 2010; *Newsweek,* Feb. 15, 1960, 35; GP, v. 3, 1653.

43. *Newsday,* Oct. 7, 1957, 31; "U.S. Policy on Outer Space," Dec. 17, 1959, accessed at http://www.marshall.org/pdf/materials/808.pdf.

44. Letter from Glennan to the president, Nov. 16, 1959, WHO, OSS, 1952–61, AS, Box 24, DDEL.

45. WSJ, Nov. 5, 1959; Logsdon, *The Decision to Go to the Moon,* 142; Conference memo, Sept. 9, 1959, AWF, DEDS, Box 44, Folder: Staff Notes—Sept. 1959 (2); Conference memo, Sept. 21, 1959, WHO, OSS, AS, Box 18, DDEL; Kistiakowsky, 74; NYT, Oct. 2, 1960; *Nation,* Nov. 23, 1957, 381.

46. Wang, 99; Larson, 95–96.

47. *Time,* Mar. 28, 1960, 44, and Apr. 6, 1959, 58; *Newsweek,* Feb. 9, 1959, 84; NYT, Oct. 2, 1960; *Time,* June 6, 1960, 56; Bille and Lishock, 159; USN, Oct. 17, 1960, 66.

48. NYT, May 3, 1960.

49. Conference memo, Feb. 24, 1959, WHO, OSS, AS, Box 18, DDEL; N.S.C. 10/10/57, ALP, Box 16, DDEL.

Chapter 13

1. The Ovi Team, "The Kitchen Debate Transcript," www.ovimagazine.com; Aitken, 265; Ambrose, *Nixon:The Education*, 520–25; Eisenhower, *Waging Peace*, 408, 410; Taubman, 416. Nixon's version of this meeting differs from the president's, recounting that Eisenhower said he planned to invite Khrushchev to the United States and asked Nixon to discuss a prospective visit. See Nixon, *Six Crises*, 242–43.

2. Stebenne, 23, 208, 216–20, 231; Two sessions with the president (11/5/57), ALP, Box 16, DDEL; Reminiscences of Malcolm Moos (1973), on page 18, in the Columbia University Center for Oral History Collection (hereafter CUCOHC).

3. NYT, May 29, 1959.

4. *Washington Daily News*, Mar. 8, 1961; Stever, 91; Conference memo, Feb. 4, 1958, AWF, DEDS, Box 30, DDEL; Beard, 184; Koller, 6.

5. Stever, 120; Koller, 7, 8; Divine, *The Sputnik Challenge*, 26–28.

6. Keeny interview.

7. Wang, 108.

8. Ewald interview, 2006.

9. NYT, Jan. 4 and Jan. 11, 1959; Hardesty and Eisman, 90–91.

10. Crouch, 154; Keith Glennan interview in *Space Race: Race to the Moon* (vol. 1, DVD), Allegro Corporation, 2007; NYT, May 29, 1959; Hardesty and Eisman, 93–94; Akens in Webb Papers, HSTL.

11. Hardesty and Eisman, 91; *Time,* Sept. 21, 1959; NYT, Sept. 20, 1959; USN, May 25, 1959, 40–41; N. Khrushchev, 53.

12. AKP, Works: Memoranda, Box 1, Book II, 1948–60, 318A, MLPU; Beschloss, 177–78, 184.

13. Taubman, 422, 424.

14. Beschloss, 188–89, 190, 202; Kistiakowsky, 84–85, 90; Pach and Richardson, 208; Taubman, 425.

15. Taubman, 407; *Discover Presents:The History of Space Travel*, Fall 2007, 38; Kistiakowsky, 149; NYT, Dec. 7, 1959, 30; Beschloss, 214; Bowie and Immerman, 54; Frankel, 182; Gaddis, 159–60, 196; Pach and Richardson, 208–9.

16. Kistiakowsky, 69; NYT, Sept. 19, 1959.

17. WSJ, Jan. 5, 1959.

18. WSJ, Jan. 5 and Jan. 6, 1959.

19. *Time,* Oct. 19, 1959; BW, Oct. 17, 1959, 130–31, 133; USN, Oct. 19, 1959, 41.

20. Status Report on National Space Program, Oct. 13, 1959, WHO, OSS, AS, Box 18, DDEL; Beschloss, 193.

21. *Aviation Week*, Apr. 11, 1960, 30; NYT, May 22, Oct. 2 and Nov. 24, 1960; WSJ, Feb. 23, 1962; USN, Dec. 19, 1960, 52; *Time,* Apr. 11, 1960, 62; *NASA: 50 Years of Exploration and Discovery*, 175; *Economist,* Apr. 23, 1960, 330.

22. *Newsweek,* Oct. 21, 1957, 33; USN, Apr. 13, 1959, 73, and Dec. 19, 1960, 52.

23. Democratic Advisory Council Position Paper on Space Research, Sept. 7, 1960, Box DNC 197, JFKL; *Economist,* Aug. 20, 1960, 730; *Fortune*, Aug. 22, 1960, 20–21; PPP 1960–61, 630; NYT, Aug. 13, Aug. 14, 1960; Hunley, 49.

24. Seamans interview; Memo from David Z. Beckler to Victor Cooley, Oct. 8, 1957, WHO, OSAST, Box 3, DDEL.

25. Divine, *The Sputnik Challenge*, 110, 154; www.theblackvault.com/documents /spysatellites/PoppySatellite.pdf; *Baltimore Sun*, June 18, 1998, http://articles.balti moresun.com/1998-06-18/news/1998169123_1_spy-satellites-grab-naval-research; DeGroot, 92.

26. Brzezinski, 251; Divine, *The Sputnik Challenge*, 189; Memo from Richard Bissell, Nov. 5, 1958, WHO, OSS, Records Subject Series, AS, Box 14, DDEL; R. Cargill Hall, "Postwar Strategic Reconnaissance and the Genesis of Corona," in Day et al., 113; Taubman, 238–39, 266–67.

27. "CORONA and the U.S. Presidents," in Day et al., 174–75.

28. *Newsweek*, Aug. 22, 1960, 78; NYT, Aug. 13, 1960; Taubman, 258, 295; PPP 1960–61, 632; *Time*, Aug. 22, 1960; Dwayne Day, "The Development and Improvement of the Corona Satellite," in Day et al., 38.

29. Brzezinski, 270; Dickson, 213; Hardesty and Eisman, 96–97.

30. Logsdon, *John F. Kennedy and the Race to the Moon*, 9, 13.

31. "CORONA and the U.S. Presidents," 177–78, "Introduction," 3, 5, 6; and Albert Wheelon, "CORONA: A Triumph of American Technology," 47; all in Day et al.; Taubman, 326.

32. Akens in Webb Papers, HSTL; WSJ, Oct. 21, 1959; NYHT, Oct. 22, 1959; NYT, Oct. 9, 1959; Conference memo, Oct. 23, 1959, AWF, DEDS, Staff Notes, Oct. 1959 (1), Box 46, DDEL; and Conference memo, Sept. 30, 1959, AWF, DEDS, Box 44, DDEL.

33. *Cleveland Plain Dealer*, Oct. 25, 1959; NYT, Feb. 3, 1960; *Chicago Tribune*, Mar. 24, 1962; *Economist*, Oct. 31, 1959, 423; *Newsweek*, Aug. 3, 1959, 69.

34. Conference memo, Oct. 23, 1959, AWF, DEDS, Staff Notes, Oct. 1959 (1), Box 46, DDEL; Meteorological Satellite Program, Apr. 1959, and Memo for the National Aeronautics and Space Council, Dec. 17, 1959, both in WHO, OSS, 1952–61, AS, Box 24, DDEL; Conference memo, Sept. 23, 1959, WHO, OSS, AS, Box 18, DDEL; Neufeld, 346.

35. PPP 1960–61, 37; Conference memo, Jan. 11, 1960, WHO, OSS, AS, Box 18, DDEL; *Economist*, Feb. 6, 1960, 522; NYT, Jan. 15 and Feb. 9, 1960.

36. *Newsday*, Oct. 7, 1957, 30; Launius, "Eisenhower, Sputnik, and the Creation of NASA," 130; Conference memo, Feb. 10, 1958, Eisenhower: Papers, 1953–61, AWF, DEDS, Box 30, DDEL.

37. *Fortune*, Dec. 1959, 95; *Reporter*, Apr. 27, 1961, 21.

38. NYT, Oct. 2, 1960, and July 17, 1969; Killian, 144; *Washington Star*, Sept. 24, 1960; Conference memo, Oct. 13, 1960, WHO, OSS, Box 18, DDEL.

39. National Aeronautics and Space Council meeting, Dec. 3, 1958, Box 6, and U.S. Policy on Outer Space, Jan. 26, 1960, Box 7; both in SS, OCB Series, WHO, OSANSA, DDEL; Crouch, 154–55; USN, June 27, 1960, 43.

40. Logsdon, *The Decision to Go to the Moon*, 31, 55; WP, Apr. 10, 1959; Crouch, 156; Accomplishments of NASA, 1958–1960, Eisenhower: Papers, 1953–61, AWF, AS, Box 15, DDEL.

41. Launius and McCurdy, 40–41; Seamans, *Project Apollo*, 9; Democratic Advisory Council Position Paper on Space Research, Sept. 7, 1960, Box: DNC 197, and

Position Paper on Space Research, Aug. 31, 1960, Papers of President Kennedy, Pre-Presidential Papers, Box 993, JFKL; Memo from Eugene Emme, Aug. 6, 1969, Box: WHP-E, NASA HO.

42. Seamans, *Project Apollo,* 9; U.S. Policy on Outer Space, Jan. 26, 1960, DDEL; Hunley, 180.

43. Michael Beschloss, "Kennedy and the Decision to Go to the Moon," in Launius and McCurdy, 53; Logsdon, *The Decision to Go to the Moon,* 34–35; Wang, 97.

44. Eisenhower with Nixon, 69; Memo of meeting, Jan. 4, 1961, WHO, OSANSA, Special Assistant Series, Presidential Subseries, Box 5, DDEL; Seamans, *Aiming at Targets,* 94; NYT, Jan. 17, 1961.

45. NYT, Nov. 10, 1957; *Economist,* Feb. 8, 1958, 486; Medaris, 187.

46. Legislative leadership meeting, Mar. 18, 1958, Supplementary Notes, Eisenhower: Papers, 1953–61, AWF, DEDS, Box 31, DDEL; *Time,* Nov. 23, 1959, 18; Logsdon, *The Decision to Go to the Moon,* 26, 56–57.

47. Memo of conference with the president, Sept. 23, 1959, AWF, DEDS, Box 44, DDEL; Legislative leadership meeting, Mar. 18, 1958, Supplementary Notes, Eisenhower: Papers, 1953–61, AWF, DEDS, Box 31, DDEL; Ewald, 287; Glennan, 292.

48. Memo of conference with the president, Oct. 13, 1960, WHO, OSS, Box 18, DDEL; Glennan interview in *Space Race: Race to the Moon*; NYT, June 17, 1958; Saulnier interview.

49. Hunley, 269; Conference memo, Oct. 13, 1960, WHO, OSS, Box 18, DDEL; Seamans, *Project Apollo,* 7.

50. Democratic Advisory Council Position Paper on Space Research, Sept. 7, 1960, JFKL.

51. *Time,* Feb. 8, 1960, 19; *Economist,* Aug. 20, 1960, 730; WSJ, Aug. 1, 1960.

Chapter 14

1. NYT, Aug. 16, 1959; *Time,* Jan. 4, 1960.

2. NYT, Jan. 10, 1960; *Time,* Aug. 24, 1959, 11; WP, Dec. 25, 1960.

3. Thompson, 160; PPP 1960–61, 198.

4. *Newsweek,* Nov. 4, 1960, 34; Ambrose, *Eisenhower: The President,* 552–53; Blaine with McCubbin, 111.

5. McPhee interview; Bowie and Immerman, 208.

6. GP, v. 3, 1649, 1651; Brendon, 312; Pach and Richardson, 47; Rorabaugh, 28.

7. GP, v. 2, 1570, and v. 3, 1653; http://brain.gallup.com, question qn28b, GP #639.

8. USN, Oct. 19, 1959, 41; Letter from Donald Menzel, Sept. 7, 1960, Pre-Presidential Papers, Box 747, JFKL.

9. *Time,* Oct. 12, 1959, 21; *Chicago Sun-Times,* Jan. 8, 1960; *Newsweek,* Feb. 15, 1960, 35; NYT, Oct. 2, 1960; NYT, Jan. 7, 1960.

10. McPherson, 57; *New York Daily News,* May, 6, 1961; Seamans, *Project Apollo,* 45.

11. Hunley, 79, 67, 212; NYT, Oct. 6, 1959.

12. NYT, Dec. 9, 1959.

13. Hunley, 67; DNC Cartoon Clipping Files, Box 362, Folder: Space Program, General 12/8/57–3/21/60, JFKL.

14. Hughes, 132–33.

15. Wukovits, 75–76.

16. Brendon, 83, 117; Wukovits, 99–101.

17. Beschloss, 48; Ewald interview, 2010.

18. Ambrose, *Eisenhower: Soldier and President*, 47, 73; Ambrose, *Eisenhower: The President,* 53.

19. White, 112; Reston, 190–91. The other generals who became president were George Washington, Andrew Jackson, William Henry Harrison, Zachary Taylor, Franklin Pierce, Ulysses Grant, Rutherford Hayes, James Garfield, and Benjamin Harrison. Besides Eisenhower, the only other general with no political experience was Taylor.

20. Truman, 187; Brendon, 10; Hughes, 149; Sloan, 16; Larson, xii; Skolnikoff interview.

21. Adams, 84; Brendon, 4, 264; Kennedy, 134; PPP 1957, 214–15; Nelson, 34–35; Van Atta, 56–78; Updegrove, 35; West with Kotz, 157–58; *Newsweek*, Oct. 28, 1957, 32.

22. Divine, *The Sputnik Challenge*, 16–17.

23. Memo for Governor Adams, Oct. 8, 1957, WHO, OSS, 1952–61, SS, AS, Box 23, DDEL.

24. PPP 1960–61, 166, 330; McPhee interview.

25. Memo of Staff Conference, Dec. 6, 1958, WHO, OSS, 1958–61, SS, AS, Box 22, DDEL.

26. NYT, Nov. 20, 1960; Hunley, 212, 286, 289, 290.

27. Hunley, 32; Letter, Glennan to D. E., Nov. 16, 1959, and Conference memo, Nov. 17, 1959, WHO, OSS, 1952–61, AS, Box 24, DDEL.

28. PPP 1960–61, 643–44; Kistiakowsky, 330.

29. Ambrose, *Eisenhower: Soldier and President*, 73; Pickett, 4; Boller, 290, 291; Nelson, 30; McCabe interview.

30. Minutes of cabinet meeting, Oct. 9, 1958, Eisenhower: Papers, 1953–61, AWF, DEDS, Box 26, DDEL; Divine, *The Sputnik Challenge,* 191.

31. Gilbert, 94 and 132–41; McPhee interview; Reminiscences of Malcolm Moos (1973), on page 28, in the Columbia University Center for Oral History Collection; Larson, 174–75; Medaris, 165–66, 196. After suffering his heart attack, Eisenhower also failed to thank any of his cabinet officers for ensuring that the executive branch functioned smoothly in his absence.

32. Medaris, 165–66, 196.

33. NYT, Jan. 17, 1960.

34. PPP 1959, 576; Ambrose, *Eisenhower: The President,* 625.

35. Ambrose, *Eisenhower: The President,* 542–43.

36. NYT, Jan. 17, 1960; Pickett, 193; Brendon, 23.

37. Position Paper on Space Research, Pre-Presidential Papers, Box 993, JFKL (italics removed).

38. Hughes, 144; White, 134; Edwards, 132; Wagner, 26.

39. Cannon, 42–44, 214; Gerald R. Ford Congressional Papers, Press Secretary and Speech File, 1947–73, Box D15, Folder: Challenges of the Space Age, GRFL; Perret, 596–97.

40. Eisenhower, *Waging Peace,* 652.

Chapter 15

1. Beschloss, 7.

2. Conference memo, April 11, 1959, WHO, OSS, Records Subject Series, AS, Box 15, DDEL; Gromyko, 220; Reston, 197; *Newsweek,* Nov. 14, 1960, 34.

3. Medaris, viii; Stares, 51.

4. *Time,* July 11, 1960; GP, v. 3, 1672; Rorabaugh, 69.

5. Beschloss, 254; Kistiakowsky, 375.

6. Ewald, 284–85.

7. Democratic Advisory Council Position Paper on Space Research, Sept. 7, 1960, Box DNC 197, Folder: Space Research, 10/21/59–9/7/60, JFKL

8. Gretchen Van Dyke, "Sputnik: A Political Symbol and Tool in 1960 Campaign Politics," in Launius et. al., *Reconsidering Sputnik,* 386; *Moberly Monitor-Index,* July 12, 1960; John Kennedy, Democratic National Convention Nomination Acceptance Speech, July 15, 1960, www.americanrhetoric.com; NYT, Nov. 14, 1959.

9. Logsdon, *John F. Kennedy and the Race to the Moon,* 8.

10. NYT, Oct. 26, 1960; McDougall, 222; Letter from JFK to Bruce Pickering, Oct. 23, 1959, Pre-Presidential Papers, Senate Files, Legislation Files, 1953–60, Box 726, JFKL.

11. Rorabaugh, 92–93; Draft of science speech, Position and Briefing Papers: Science, JFKL.

12. Olsen, 358–59; Kennedy, 85–86; NYT, Oct. 31, 1960; *Economist,* Jan. 2, 1960, 36; Logsdon, *The Decision to Go to the Moon,* 66.

13. McDougall, 222; NYT, Oct. 26, 1960, and Sept. 14, 1959; Hughes, 316; NYT, Oct. 7, 1959.

14. USN, Aug. 29, 1960, 31, and Oct. 17, 1960, 66; NYT, Nov. 4, 1960.

15. Donaldson, 128; Preble, 4.

16. Beschloss, 326; Kistiakowsky, 250; Kennedy, 133–34; Beard, 3; D'Antonio, 5; Divine, *The Sputnik Challenge,* 177.

17. Thompson, 173; Ambrose, *Eisenhower: The President,* 560; Andrew Bacevich, "The Tyranny of Defense Inc.," *Atlantic* (Jan./Feb. 2011), 74–79.

18. Divine, 183; Donaldson, 128; Killian interview, NASA HO; Beschloss, 366.

19. Donaldson, 128; Hardesty and Eisman, 108; Preble, 104, 114; Edwards, 133.

20. Preble, 106.

21. Hardesty and Eisman, 110; Reeves, 249; Preble, 154.

22. Brzezinski, 269; Ernest May, "Strategic Intelligence and U.S. Security," in Day et al., 25; McDougall, 251; Dickson, 213; Interview with Walter Cronkite, Jan. 23, 1963, DDE: Papers, Post-Presidential, Speeches Series, Box 5, DDEL.

23. Eisenhower, *Waging Peace*, 390; Divine, *The Sputnik Challenge*, 177–78; NYT, Sept. 8, 1960; Van Dyke in Launius et al., 393–94.

24. *Newsweek*, Nov. 14, 1960, 34.

25. NYT, Oct. 31, 1960, and Oct. 2, 1960.

26. See debates.org for debate transcripts.

27. NYT, Oct. 22, 1960; debates.org.

28. Larson, 118.

29. Gaddis, 199; Mears, 17; West with Kotz, 237, 256.

30. NYT, Oct. 31, 1960, and Oct. 29, 1960.

31. GP, v. 3, 1678, 1704; Summary of meeting, April 30, 1960, WHO, OSAST, Box 14, DDEL.

32. Gaddis, 164; NYT, Oct. 19, 1960.

33. NYT, Jan. 15, 1960, and Sept. 21, 1960.

34. NYT, Sept. 18, 1960; BW, July 16, 1960, 26, 27.

35. Pickett, 160; Sloan, 50.

36. Saulnier, 128; Morgan, 169; Pach and Richardson, 229; The Reminiscences of Malcolm Moos (1973), on page 16, in the CUCOHC.

37. Pach and Richardson, 228; Saulnier, 126; Saulnier interview.

38. Rorabaugh, 115–16.

39. PPP 1960–61, 658.

40. Rorabaugh, 122; Beschloss, 183–84.

41. McCabe interview; *Time*, Nov. 16, 1960; AKP, Works: Memoranda, Box I, Book II: 1948–60, 335, and Book III: 1960–65, 339, MLPU.

42. Wukovits, 23–24; Gibbs and Duffy, 104; *Newsweek*, Nov. 14, 1960, 34; WP, Oct. 11, 1960; *Time*, Oct. 31, 1960.

43. Kistiakowsky, 385; Hunley, 252.

44. Pach and Richardson, 229; Gibbs and Duffy, 111.

45. Rorabaugh, 171.

46. Eisenhower, *Waging Peace*, 652; McDougall, 225.

Chapter 16

1. McCabe interview; Seamans, *Aiming at Targets*, 74; Goodpaster interview, 2000; Gibbs and Duffy, 109; Rorabaugh, 196; Kennedy, 133–34.

2. PPP 1960–61, 913–20; PPP 1961, 19–28.

3. WP, Jan. 31, 1961; PPP 1961, 22, 23.

4. McPhee interview.

5. Sloan, 157; McDougall, 407; Morgan, 181.

6. Dickson, 19; Hunley, 296, 300, 302, 304, 306, 309.

7. Hardesty and Eisman, 110–11; Kennedy, Pre-Presidential Papers, Box 1072, JFKL; Logsdon, *The Decision to Go to the Moon*, 73; McDougall, 309; Hornig interview.

8. Logsdon, *John F. Kennedy and the Race to the Moon*, 62.

9. PPP 1961, 70.

10. Logsdon, *John F. Kennedy and the Race to the Moon*, 65; Kistiakowsky, 409; Hardesty and Eisman, 119; NYT, July 17, 1969; Logsdon, *The Decision to Go to the Moon*, 95.

11. Martin, 12; Parmet, 21; Reeves, 219; O'Brien, 807; Wukovits, 118.

12. Logsdon, *The Decision to Go to the Moon*, 101; Hardesty and Eisman, xvi; Seamans interview.

13. Hardesty and Eisman, 120.

14. Logsdon, *The Decision to Go to the Moon*, 102, 103.

15. Beschloss, 387; Logsdon, *The Decision to Go to the Moon*, 111, 112.

16. NYT, Apr. 15, 1961; Seamans, *Aiming at Targets*, 87.

17. Launius and McCurdy, 57; Logsdon, *The Decision to Go to the Moon*, 114.

18. Logsdon, *The Decision to Go to the Moon*, 118.

19. Gaddis, 204; Logsdon, *The Decision to Go to the Moon*, 150, 164; Seamans interview.

20. "Recommendations for Our National Space Program: Changes, Policies, Goals," Papers of President Kennedy, President's Office Files, Special Correspondence, Box 30, JFKL.

21. Hardesty and Eisman, 125; NYT, May 6 and May 7, 1961; Logsdon, *John F. Kennedy and the Race to the Moon*, 96; *Newsweek,* July 28, 1969, 27.

22. GP, v. 3, 1720. According to the survey, the percentage of those thinking the United States or the USSR led in space both was 38. Thirty-four percent believed Russia would reach the moon first; 33 percent thought America would.

23. Logsdon, *The Decision to Go to the Moon,* 136; Skolnikoff interview.

24. Seamans, *Aiming at Targets*, 91; Sorenson, 525.

25. Speech transcript available at www.history.nasa.gov.

26. Seamans, *Aiming at Targets,* 88; DeGroot, 142, 200; Sorenson, 17.

27. GP, v. 3, 1720; NYT, Apr. 15, 1961; Launius and McCurdy, 61; John Kennedy, Rice University, Sept. 12, 1962, transcript available at www.jfklibrary.org.

28. PPP 1962, 485; PPP 1963, 350, 568, 832,

29. DeGroot, 152; *NASA: 50 Years of Exploration and Discovery*, 229; Seamans, *Project Apollo*, 44–45, 46; Logsdon, *John F. Kennedy and the Race to the Moon*, 45, 227.

30. Killian, 143; Seamans interview; Launius and McCurdy, 62

31. NYT, Apr. 15, 1961; *(Washington, D.C.) Sunday Star,* June 13, 1971.

32. Launius and McCurdy, 61; NYHT, June 13, 1963; Letter from Eisenhower to Charles Halleck, Mar. 26, 1963, Box: WHP-P, NASA HO; Roger Launius, "Eisenhower and Space: Politics and Ideology in the Construction of the U.S. Civil Space Program," in Showalter, 174.

33. Interview with Walter Cronkite, Jan. 23, 1963, DDE Papers, Post-Presidential, Speeches Series, Box 5, DDEL.

34. Letter to Major Frank Borman, USAF, June 18, 1965, DDE Papers, Post-Presidential, 1961–69, "Convenience" File, Box 1, DDEL, emphasis original.

35. SEP, Aug. 11, 1962, 24; May 18, 1963, 19; and Apr. 11, 1964, 19.

36. NYT, July 21, 1969; *Economist,* July 2, 2011, 67; Logsdon, *John F. Kennedy*, 2–3; Pach and Richardson, 93.

37. NYT, July 15, 1969; Goldwater to Colonel Tom Stafford, June 20, 1969, Folder: Goldwater: Personal, Alpha Files, Stafford, Thomas, BGP, ASU.

38. NYT, July 21, 1969; Ambrose, *Nixon: The Education*, 284; PPP 1969, 520.

39. DeGroot, 239; NYT, July 16 and July 21, 1969; Logsdon, *John F. Kennedy and the Race to the Moon*, 238.

40. DeGroot, 149; *USA Today,* Dec. 9, 2011; Seamans interview; Logsdon, *John F. Kennedy and the Race to the Moon,* 238.

41. DeGroot, 144.

42. Hornig interview; Frutkin interview, 2008.

43. Beckler interview, 2008.

44. Seamans interview; Dickson, 217; N. Khrushchev, 56.

45. Hardesty and Eisman, 222–23.

46. Dobrynin, 528; D'Souza, 179; Bunch, 84.

47. Eisenhower with Nixon, 260.

48. Eisenhower with Nixon, 263; Taubman, 323–24.

49. Wukovits, 75, 111–12; Updegrove, 49.

50. Frutkin interview, 2010; *The Eisenhower Legacy* (Starbright Media Corp., 2007).

51. DeGroot, 142.

52. Meetings: Tape 111, James Webb, Sept. 18, 1963, audio accessed at www.jfklibrary.org; Seamans interview; Seamans, *Aiming at Targets,* 115.

53. Eisenhower with Nixon, 68.

54. Doyle, 73; DeGroot, 215.

55. McDougall, 422, 430; NYT, July 27, 1969; DeGroot, 245; *Economist,* Sept. 29, 2007, 16.

56. NYT, July 30, 1969; *Newsweek,* July 7, 1969, 63.

57. Skolnikoff interview; John Logsdon, "Shall We Build the Space Shuttle?" *Technology Review,* Oct./Nov. 1971, 49, 51; Frutkin interview, 2008.

58. Letter to the *Milwaukee Journal,* Jan. 11, 1972, Box 127, Folder 23; "Space Shuttle Should Be Deleted from NASA Appropriations," Box 127, Folder 22; and Space Shuttle Fact Sheet, National Taxpayers Union, Box 127, Folder 23; all in WPP, UW; *Economist,* July 26, 2008, 91; WP, Jan. 14, 1972.

59. "Space Shuttle: Commemorating 30 Years of Exploration and Discovery, 1981–2011," *Florida Today* (2011), 28, see FloridaToday.com/shuttlelegacy; Frosch interview.

60. "Space Shuttle Should Be Deleted from NASA Appropriations," WPP, UW.

61. "Space Shuttle: Commemorating 30 Years of Exploration and Discovery," 29; Frutkin interview, 2008; Brown interview.

62. *Time,* July 18, 2011, 64; *Economist,* July 2, 2011, 67.

Conclusion

1. York, 12; WP, Oct. 17, 1990.

2. PPP 1958, 303–4.

3. White, 136.

4. Frutkin interview, 2010; Hardesty and Eisman, 212.

5. Hunley, 214, 226.

6. PPP 1960–61, 690; NYT, Sept. 9, 1960.

7. James Van Allen letter, July 21, 2005; NYT, Dec. 6, 1959; Brendon, 254.

8. Status Report on National Space Program, Oct. 13, 1959, WHO, OSS, AS, Box 18, DDEL; American Accomplishments, U.S. Senate, 1949–61, Committee on

Aeronautics and Space Sciences, Box 359, LBJL; USN, Oct. 19, 1959, 42; *Baltimore Sun,* Dec. 30, 1960; McDougall, 128.

9. USN, Dec. 19, 1960, 52–53.

10. *This Week,* Jan. 1, 1961; WP, May 6, 1961; see also USN, Dec. 19, 1960, 52, which reported that by December 1960, the United States had launched thirty-two satellites, while the Soviet Union had put up nine; NYT, Jan. 17 and Feb. 3, 1960.

11. *Time,* Dec. 15, 1958, 15.

12. *Budget of the United States Government: 1961,* 162; *Budget of the United States Government: 1962,* 175; *Budget of the United States Government: 1963,* 72; Richard Brastaad, "NASA's Share of Total Federal Government Expenditures since 1958," http://www.richardb.us/nasa.html#graph; Sloan, 53.

13. GP, v. 3, 1702–3 and v. 4, 1650–51.

14. McCabe interview; *Economist,* July 26, 2008, 91.

15. NYT, Dec. 20, 1960.

16. AKP, Works: Memoranda, Box 1, Book II: 1948–60, 318A, MLPU; PPP 1960–61, 1038–39.

17. *New Republic,* Jan. 30, 1961, 3; *Time,* Jan. 27, 1961; WP, Jan. 19, 1961.

18. Brown interview.

19. York, 11.

20. First Semiannual Report to the Congress, Oct. 1958–March 31, 1959, NASA, WHO, OSANSA, OCB Series, SS, Box 7, DDEL; NYT, Jan. 13, July 15, and July 16, 1959. Once the McDonnell Aircraft Corporation won the competition to build the space capsules, it ran continuous shifts and employed thirteen thousand on the project; see DeGroot, 102–3.

21. Frutkin interview, 2010; PPP 1960–61, 1039.

22. Doyle, 92; Saulnier, 235.

23. WSJ, Jan. 20, 1961; Saulnier interview; Eisenhower to Saulnier, Mar. 4, 1964, letter photocopy in author's collection.

24. Sloan, 79–81; Stebenne, 187; Saulnier, 228.

25. Sloan, 81; Ambrose, *Eisenhower: The President,* 561.

26. *Time,* Jan. 4, 1960.

27. Saulnier, 224–25; *Economist,* Nov. 8, 2008, 37; WP, Oct. 17, 1990; Thompson, 217.

28. Hunley, 175, 176.

29. NYT, Oct. 4, 1972; *Time,* Mar. 26, 2007, 16–17; Richard Wilke, "From Hyperpower to Declining Power: Changing Global Perceptions of the U.S. in the Post-Sept. 11 Era," pewglobal.org/2011/09/07/from-hyperpower-to-declining-power/.

30. *Harvard Business Review,* Mar. 2008, 48.

31. Snead, 175.

32. PPP 1959, 574.

33. *Car and Driver,* May 2010, 42.

34. Logsdon, *John F. Kennedy and the Race to the Moon,* 244.

35. Seamans interview.

36. "Presidential Approval Ratings, Gallup Historical Statistics and Trends," gallup.com. Among all post–World War II presidents, Eisenhower's average was second only to Kennedy's 70 percent; Y. Mieczkowski, 82–83.

37. *Economist*, July 26, 2008, 15.

38. Iacocca with Novak, 327, 332–33.

39. Pickett, 194; Address to a Republican congressional dinner, June 22, 1962, DDE Papers, Post-Presidential, Speeches, Series, Box 2, DDEL; Roger Launius, "Eisenhower and Space: Politics and Ideology in the Construction of the U.S. Civil Space Program," in Showalter, 152; *Economist*, June 11, 2009, 22.

40. NYT, Nov. 10, 1957.

41. PPP 1960–61, 172.

42. NYT, Dec. 12, 1957; PPP 1960–61, 1045–46.

BIBLIOGRAPHY

Archives

Columbia University Center for Oral History Collection, New York, New York
Dwight D. Eisenhower Presidential Library, Abilene, Kansas
Gerald R. Ford Presidential Library, Ann Arbor, Michigan
Barry Goldwater Papers, Arizona State University, Tempe, Arizona
Henry Jackson Papers, University of Washington, Seattle, Washington
Jacob Javits Papers, Stony Brook University, Stony Brook, New York
Lyndon B. Johnson Presidential Library, Austin, Texas
John F. Kennedy Presidential Library, Boston, Massachusetts
Arthur Krock Papers, Seeley Mudd Manuscript Library, Princeton University
John Medaris Papers, Florida Institute of Technology, Melbourne, Florida
National Aeronautics and Space Administration History Office, Washington, DC
Paley Center for Media, New York, New York
William Proxmire Papers, Wisconsin Historical Society, Madison, Wisconsin
Harry S. Truman Presidential Library, Independence, Missouri

Interviews, Letters, and Unpublished Sources

Personal Interviews

Louis Avosso, Feb. 8, 2006
David Beckler, Jan. 9, 2007; Jan. 18, 2008
Hans Bethe, June 7, 1990
Harold Brown, Apr. 22, 2010
William Ewald, Mar. 23, 2006; Nov. 24, 2009; Nov. 18, 2010
Robert Frosch, May 16 2006
Arnold Frutkin, Apr. 6, 2010
Andrew Goodpaster, June 12, 2000
Donald Hornig, Sept. 14, 2006
Spurgeon Keeny, Aug. 28, 2007
Robert Mackey, Aug. 24, 2005
Charlie Mars, July 21, 2005
Edward McCabe, Aug. 29, 2007
Roemer McPhee, Aug. 29, 2006
John Neilon, July 22, 2005
Gene Pappalardo, Oct. 15, 2002, by Michael Pappalardo
Bud Reynolds, July 21, 2005

Welby Risler, July 20, 2005
David Z. Robinson, Feb. 8, 2007
Raymond Saulnier, May 26, 2006
Robert Seamans, May 15, 2006
Eugene Skolnikoff, May 22, 2008
W. North Sterrett, Sept. 15, 2005
John Twigg, Aug. 23, 2005
Murphy Wardman, July 21, 2005

Telephone Interviews

Arnold Frutkin, June 20, 2008
Andrew J. Goodpaster, Mar. 1, 1989
Arthur Larson, Apr. 11, 1989
Herbert York, May 29, 1990

Letters to Author

Caryl P. Haskins, May 10, 1990
Arthur Larson, Nov. 22, 1988
James Van Allen, July 21, 2005

Unpublished Papers in Author's Possession

Beckler, David Z., "Talk on Science in the Eisenhower Administration"
Eisenhower, Dwight, Letter to Raymond Saulnier, Mar. 4, 1964
Saulnier, Raymond, "An Economist's-Eye View of the World"

Audio-Visual Sources

The Eisenhower Legacy. Starbight Media Corp. DVD. 2007.
Space Race: Race to the Moon. Vol. 1. Columbia River Entertainment Group. DVD.
    2007.
Sputnik Mania. A&E Television Networks. DVD. 2008.

Series Cited

Air and Space Magazine
American Weekly
Atlantic
Aviation Week and Space Technology
Baltimore Sun
Brown Daily Herald
Business Week
Car and Driver
Cleveland Plain Dealer
Commonweal
Congressional Digest

Congressional Quarterly
Dallas Morning News
Denver Post
Department of State Bulletin
Discover Presents
Economist
Florida Today
Fortune
Hartford Courant
Harvard Business Review
Huntsville Times
Invention and Technology
Lewiston Daily News
Life
Moberly Monitor-Index
Nashville Tennessean
Nation
National Review
New Republic
New York Daily News
New York Herald Tribune
New York Post
New York Times
New Yorker
Newsday
Newsweek
Philadelphia Inquirer
Prologue
Providence Sunday Journal
Public Opinion Quarterly
Public Papers of the Presidents of the United States
Reporter
Saturday Evening Post
Science
St. Louis Post-Dispatch
Technology Review
This Week
Time
Tyler Courier-Times
Tyler Morning Telegraph
U.S. News and World Report
USA Today
Waco News Tribune
Wall Street Journal
Washington Daily News
Washington News

BIBLIOGRAPHY

Washington Post
Washington Star
Washington Sunday Star

Books

Adams, Sherman. *Firsthand Report: The Story of the Eisenhower Administration*. New York: Harper and Row, 1961.

Aitken, Jonathan. *Nixon: A Life*. Washington, DC: Regnery Press, 1993.

Alexander, Charles C. *Holding the Line: The Eisenhower Era, 1952–1961*. Bloomington: Indiana University Press, 1977.

Allen, Craig. *Eisenhower and the Mass Media: Peace, Prosperity, and Prime-Time TV*. Chapel Hill: University of North Carolina Press, 1993.

Ambrose, Stephen. *Eisenhower: Soldier and President*. New York: Simon & Schuster, 1990.

——. *Eisenhower: The President*. New York: Simon & Schuster, 1984.

——. *Nixon: The Education of a Politician, 1913–1962*. New York: Simon & Schuster, 1987.

——. *Nixon: The Triumph of a Politician, 1962–1972*. New York: Simon & Schuster, 1989.

Barbree, Jay. *"Live from Cape Canaveral": Covering the Space Race, from Sputnik to Today*. New York: Smithsonian Books, 2007.

Beard, Edmund. *Developing the ICBM: A Study in Bureaucratic Politics*. New York: Columbia University Press, 1976.

Beschloss, Michael. *Mayday: Eisenhower, Khrushchev, and the U-2 Affair*. New York: Harper and Row, 1986.

Bille, Matt, and Erika Lishock. *The First Space Race: Launching the World's First Satellites*. College Station: Texas A&M University Press, 2004.

Bilstein, Roger. *Orders of Magnitude: A History of the NACA and NASA, 1915–1990*. Washington, DC: NASA Office of Management, Scientific and Technical Information Division, 1989.

Blaine, Gerald, with Lisa McCubben. *The Kennedy Detail: JFK's Secret Service Agents Break Their Silence*. New York: Gallery Books, 2010.

Boller, Paul. *Presidential Anecdotes*. New York: Penguin Books, 1981.

Bowie, Robert, and Richard Immerman. *Waging Peace: How Eisenhower Shaped an Enduring Cold War Strategy*. New York: Oxford University Press, 1998.

Boyle, Peter. *Eisenhower*. Harlow, England: Pearson, 2005.

Brendon, Piers. *Ike: His Life and Times*. New York: Harper and Row, 1986.

Brinkley, Alan. *The End of Reform: New Deal Liberalism in Recession and War*. New York: Alfred Knopf, 1995.

Brownstein, Ronald. *The Second Civil War: How Extreme Partisanship Has Paralyzed Washington and Polarized America*. New York: Penguin Press, 2007.

Brzezinski, Matthew. *Red Moon Rising: Sputnik and the Hidden Rivalries That Ignited the Space Race*. New York: Times Books, 2007.

Budget of the United States Government: 1961. Washington, DC: U.S. Government Printing Office, 1960.

Budget of the United States Government: 1962. Washington, DC: U.S. Government Printing Office, 1961.

Budget of the United States Government: 1963. Washington, DC: U.S. Government Printing Office, 1962.

Bunch, Will. *Tear Down This Myth: The Right-Wing Distortion of the Reagan Legacy.* New York: Free Press, 2009.

Burrows, William. *This New Ocean: The Story of the First Space Age.* New York: Modern Library Paperbacks, 1998.

Cadbury, Deborah. *Space Race: The Epic Battle between America and the Soviet Union for Dominion of Space.* New York: HarperCollins, 2006.

Cannon, Lou. *President Reagan: The Role of a Lifetime.* New York: Simon & Schuster, 1991.

Caro, Robert. *The Years of Lyndon Johnson: Master of the Senate.* New York: Alfred Knopf, 2002.

Clifford, J. Garry, and Theodore Wilson (eds.). *Presidents, Diplomats, and Other Mortals: Essays Honoring Robert H. Ferrell.* Columbia: University of Missouri Press, 2007.

Clowse, Barbara Barksdale. *Brainpower for the Cold War: The Sputnik Crisis and National Defense Education Act of 1958.* Westport, CT: Greenwood Press, 1981.

Cook, Blanche Wiesen. *The Declassified Eisenhower: A Divided Legacy of Peace and Political Warfare.* New York: Penguin Books, 1984.

Cox, Donald. *The Space Race: From Sputnik to Apollo . . . And Beyond.* Philadelphia: Chilton Books, 1962.

Crapol, Edward. *John Tyler: The Accidental President.* Chapel Hill: University of North Carolina Press, 2006.

Crouch, Tom. *Aiming for the Stars: The Dreamers and Doers of the Space Age.* Washington, DC: Smithsonian Institution Press, 1999.

Dallek, Robert. *An Unfinished Life: John F. Kennedy, 1917–1963.* New York: Back Bay Books, 2003.

Damms, Richard. *The Eisenhower Presidency, 1953–1961.* Harlow, England: Pearson, 2002.

Daniloff, Nicholas. *The Kremlin and the Cosmos.* New York: Alfred Knopf, 1972.

D'Antonio, Michael. *A Ball, a Dog, and a Monkey: 1957, The Space Race Begins.* New York: Simon & Schuster, 2007.

Day, Dwayne, John M. Logsdon, and Brian Latell. *Eye in the Sky: The Story of the Corona Spy Satellites.* Washington, DC: Smithsonian Institution Press, 1998.

DeGroot, Gerard. *Dark Side of the Moon: The Magnificent Madness of the American Lunar Quest.* New York: New York University Press, 2006.

Dickson, Paul. *Sputnik: The Shock of the Century.* New York: Walker, 2001.

Divine, Robert. *Blowing on the Wind: The Nuclear Test Ban Debate, 1954–1960.* New York: Oxford University Press, 1978.

———. *Eisenhower and the Cold War.* New York: Oxford University Press, 1981.

———. *The Sputnik Challenge: Eisenhower's Response to the Soviet Satellite.* New York: Oxford University Press, 1993.

Dobrynin, Anatoly. *In Confidence: Moscow's Ambassador to America's Six Cold War Presidents.* New York: Times Books, 1995.

Donaldson, Gary. *The First Modern Campaign: Kennedy, Nixon, and the Election of 1960*. Lanham, MD: Rowman and Littlefield, 2007.

Doyle, William. *Inside the Oval Office: The White House Tapes from FDR to Clinton*. New York: Kodansha International, 1999.

D'Souza, Dinesh. *Ronald Reagan: How an Ordinary Man Became an Extraordinary Leader*. New York: Free Press, 1997.

Dulles, Allen. *The Craft of Intelligence*. New York: New American Library, 1965.

Edwards, Lee. *Goldwater: The Man Who Made a Revolution*. Washington, DC: Regnery, 1995.

Eisenhower, David, with Julie Nixon Eisenhower. *Going Home to Glory: A Memoir of Life with Dwight D. Eisenhower, 1961–1969*. New York: Simon & Schuster, 2010.

Eisenhower, Dwight. *Mandate for Change, 1953–1956: The White House Years*. Garden City, NY: Doubleday, 1963.

——. *Waging Peace, 1956–1961: The White House Years*. Garden City, NY: Doubleday, 1965.

Ellis, Richard. *Presidential Travel: The Journey from George Washington to George W. Bush*. Lawrence, Kansas: University Press of Kansas, 2008.

Ewald, William. *Eisenhower the President: Crucial Days, 1951–60*. Englewood Cliffs, NJ: Prentice-Hall, 1981.

Ford, Gerald R. *A Time to Heal: The Autobiography of Gerald R. Ford*. New York: Reader's Digest, 1979.

Frankel, Max. *The Times of My Life and My Life with the Times*. New York: Delta Trade Paperbacks, 1999.

Gaddis, John L. *Strategies of Containment*. New York: Oxford Press, 1982.

Gallup, George. *The Gallup Poll: Public Opinion, 1935–1971*. Vols. 2 and 3. New York: Random House, 1972.

Gavin, James M. *War and Peace in the Space Age*. London: Hutchinson of London, 1959.

Gibbs, Nancy and Michael Duffy. *The Presidents Club: Inside the World's Most Exclusive Fraternity*. New York: Simon & Schuster, 2012.

Gilbert, Robert. *The Mortal Presidency: Illness and Anguish at the White House*. New York: Fordham University Press, 1998.

Golden, William (ed.). *Science Advice to the President*. New York: Pergamon Press, 1980.

Gould, Lewis. *Grand Old Party: A History of the GOP*. New York: Random House, 2003.

Green, Constance McLaughlin, and Milton Lomask. *Vanguard: A History*. Washington, DC: Smithsonian Institution Press, 1971.

Greenstein, Fred. *The Hidden-Hand Presidency: Eisenhower as Leader*. New York: Basic Books, 1982.

Griffith, Alison. *The National Aeronautics and Space Act: A Study of the Development of Public Policy*. Washington, DC: Public Affairs Press, 1962.

Gromyko, Andrei. *Memories*. London: Arrow Books, 1989.

Guelzo, Allen. *Lincoln's Emancipation Proclamation: The End of Slavery in America*. New York: Simon & Schuster, 2004.

Gunnell, John. *Standard Guide to 1950s American Cars*. Iola, WI: Krause Publications, 2004.

Halberstam, David. *The Fifties*. New York: Villard Books, 1993.

Hardesty, Von, and Gene Eisman. *Epic Rivalry: The Inside Story of the Soviet and American Space Race*. Washington, DC: National Geographic, 2007.

Hirsch, Richard, and Joseph John Trento. *The National Aeronautics and Space Administration*. New York: Praeger Publishers, 1973.

Hoopes, Townsend. *The Devil and John Foster Dulles*. Boston: Little, Brown, 1973.

Hughes, Emmet John. *The Ordeal of Power: A Political Memoir of the Eisenhower Years*. New York: Atheneum, 1975.

Hunley, J. D. (ed.). *The Birth of NASA: The Diary of T. Keith Glennan*. Washington, DC: National Aeronautics and Space Administration, 1993.

Iacocca, Lee, with William Novak. *Iacocca: An Autobiography*. New York: Bantam Books, 1984.

Johnson, Lyndon. *The Vantage Point: Perspectives on the Presidency*. New York: Holt, Rinehart, and Winston, 1971.

Kalman, Laura. *Right Star Rising: A New Politics, 1974–1980*. New York: Norton, 2010.

Kennedy, Jacqueline. *Historic Conversations on Life with John F. Kennedy: Interviews with Arthur M. Schlesinger, Jr., 1964*. New York: Hyperion, 2011.

Kessler, Ronald. *In the President's Secret Service: Behind the Scenes with Agents in the Line of Fire and the Presidents They Protect*. New York: Crown Publishers, 2009.

Khrushchev, Nikita. *Khrushchev Remembers: The Last Testament*. Boston: Little, Brown, 1974.

Khrushchev, Sergei. *Nikita Khrushchev and the Creation of a Superpower*. College Station: Pennsylvania State University Press, 2000.

Killian, James. *Sputnik, Scientists and Eisenhower: A Memoir of the First Special Assistant to the President for Science and Technology*. Cambridge, MA: MIT Press, 1977.

Kinnard, Douglas. *President Eisenhower and Strategy Management: A Study in Defense Politics*. Lexington: University of Kentucky Press, 1977.

Kistiakowsky, George. *A Scientist at the White House*. Cambridge, MA: Harvard University Press, 1976.

Koller, Al. *A History of Cape Canaveral and the John F. Kennedy Space Center*. Titusville, FL: U.S. Space Walk of Fame Foundation, 2004.

Krock, Arthur. *Memoirs: Sixty Years on the Firing Line*. New York: Funk & Wagnalls, 1968.

Larson, Arthur. *Eisenhower: The President Nobody Knew*. New York: Charles Scribner's Sons, 1968.

Launius, Roger. *NASA: A History of the U.S. Civil Program*. Malabar, FL: Krieger, 1994.

Launius, Roger, John M. Logsdon, and Robert W. Smith. *Reconsidering Sputnik: Forty Years since the Soviet Satellite*. New York: Routledge Press, 2000.

Launius, Roger, and Howard McCurdy (eds.). *Spaceflight and the Myth of Presidential Leadership*. Champaign-Urbana: University of Illinois Press, 1997.

Lawrence, Richard (ed.). *The Mammoth Book of Space Exploration and Disasters*. New York: Carroll and Graf, 2005.

Lethbridge, Cliff. *The Story of Explorer: America's First Satellite*. Cocoa, FL: Air Force Space and Missile Museum Foundation, 1998.

Lewis, Richard S. *Appointment on the Moon: The Inside Story of America's Space Venture*. New York: Viking Press, 1968.

Logsdon, John. *The Decision to Go to the Moon: Project Apollo and the National Interest*. Cambridge, MA: MIT Press, 1970.

———. *John F. Kennedy and the Race to the Moon*. New York: Palgrave MacMillan, 2010.

Logsdon, John, et al. *Exploring the Unknown: Selected Documents in the History of the U.S. Civilian Space Program*. Vol. 2. Washington, DC: NASA, 1996.

Martin, Ralph. *Seeds of Destruction: Joe Kennedy and His Sons*. New York: G. P. Putnam's Sons, 1980.

McDougall, Walter A. *. . . The Heavens and the Earth*. New York: Basic Books, 1985.

McPherson, James. *Drawn with the Sword: Reflections on the American Civil War*. New York: Oxford University Press, 1996.

Mears, Walter. *Deadlines Past: Forty Years of Presidential Campaigning: A Reporter's Story*. Kansas City: Andrew McMeel Publishing, 2003.

Medaris, John. *Countdown for Decision*. New York: G. P. Putnam's Sons, 1960.

Mieczkowski, Bogdan. *Personal and Social Consumption in Eastern Europe: Poland, Czechoslovakia, Hungary, and East Germany*. New York: Praeger, 1975.

Mieczkowski, Yanek. *Gerald Ford and the Challenges of the 1970s*. Lexington: University of Kentucky Press, 2005.

Moore, John. *Elections A to Z* (2nd ed.). Washington, DC: CQ Press, 2003.

Morgan, Iwan. *Eisenhower versus "The Spenders": The Eisenhower Administration, the Democrats, and the Budget, 1953–60*. New York: St. Martin's Press, 1990.

NASA: 50 Years of Exploration and Discovery. Tampa, FL: Faircount Media Group, 2008.

Nelson, Dale. *The President Is at Camp David*. Syracuse, NY: Syracuse University Press, 1995.

Neufeld, Michael. *Von Braun: Dreamer of Space, Engineer of War*. New York: Knopf, 2007.

Nixon, Richard. *RN: The Memoirs of Richard Nixon*. New York: Touchstone, 1990.

———. *Six Crises*. Garden City, NY: Doubleday, 1962.

Oakley, Ronald. *God's Country: America in the Fifties*. New York: Dembner Books, 1986.

Oberg, James. *Red Star in Orbit*. New York: Random House, 1981.

O'Brien, Michael. *John F. Kennedy: A Biography*. New York: Macmillan, 2005.

Olsen, James. *Stuart Symington: A Life*. Columbia: University of Missouri Press, 2003.

Oshinsky, David. *A Conspiracy So Immense: The World of Joe McCarthy*. New York: Free Press, 1983.

Pach, Chester, and Elmo Richardson. *The Presidency of Dwight D. Eisenhower*. Lawrence: University Press of Kansas, 1991.

Parmet, Herbert. *Jack: The Struggles of John F. Kennedy*. New York: Dial Press, 1980.

Peebles, Curtis. *Shadow Flights: America's Secret Air War against the Soviet Union*. Novato, CA: Presidio Press, 2002.

Perret, Geoffrey. *Eisenhower*. Holbrook, MA: Adams Media, 1999.

Pickett, William. *Dwight David Eisenhower and American Power.* Wheeling, IL: Harlan Davidson, Inc., 1995.

Piszkiewicz, Dennis. *Wernher von Braun: The Man Who Sold the Moon.* Westport, CT: Praeger, 1998.

Preble, Christopher. *John Kennedy and the Missile Gap.* DeKalb: Northern Illinois University Press, 2004.

Public Papers of the President: Dwight D. Eisenhower, 1953–1961. 8 vols. Washington, DC: U.S. Government Printing Office.

Public Papers of the President: John F. Kennedy, 1961–1963. 3 vols. Washington, DC: U.S. Government Printing Office.

Public Papers of the President: Richard M. Nixon, 1969. Washington, DC: U.S. Government Printing Office, 1970.

Reedy, George. *The Twilight of the Presidency.* New York: New American Library, 1970.

Reeves, Thomas. *A Question of Character: A Life of John F. Kennedy.* New York: Free Press, 1991.

Regan, Donald. *For the Record: From Wall Street to Washington.* New York: Harcourt Brace Jovanovich, 1988.

Reston, James. *Deadline: A Memoir.* New York: Random House, 1991.

Roman, Peter. *Eisenhower and the Missile Gap.* Ithaca, NY: Cornell University Press, 1995.

Rorabaugh, W. J. *The Real Making of the President: Kennedy, Nixon, and the 1960 Election.* Lawrence: University Press of Kansas, 2009.

Saulnier, Raymond. *Constructive Years: The U.S. Economy under Eisenhower.* Lanham, MD: University Press of America, 1991.

Schauer, William. *The Politics of Space: A Comparison of the Soviet and American Space Programs.* New York: Holmes and Meier, 1976.

Seamans, Robert. *Aiming at Targets: The Autobiography of Robert C. Seamans, Jr.* Washington, DC: NASA History Office, 1996.

——. *Project Apollo: The Tough Decisions.* Washington, DC: NASA History Division, 2005.

Shelton, William. *Soviet Space Exploration: The First Decade.* New York: Washington Square Press, 1968.

Showalter, Edward (ed.). *Forging the Shield: Eisenhower and National Security for the 21st Century.* Chicago: Imprint Publications, 2005.

Skolnikoff, Eugene. *Science, Technology, and American Foreign Policy.* Cambridge, MA: MIT Press, 1967.

Sloan, John. *Eisenhower and the Management of Prosperity.* Lawrence: University Press of Kansas, 1991.

Smith, Martin, and Patrick Kiger. *Poplorica: A Popular History of the Fads, Mavericks, Inventions, and Lore That Shaped Modern America.* New York: Harper Resource, 2004.

Smith, Richard Norton. *Patriarch: George Washington and the New American Nation.* Boston: Houghton Mifflin, 1993.

Snead, David. *The Gaither Committee, Eisenhower, and the Cold War.* Columbus: Ohio State University Press, 1999.

Sorenson, Theodore. *Kennedy.* New York: Harper and Row, 1965.

Stares, Paul. *The Militarization of Space: U.S. Policy, 1945–1984*. Ithaca, NY: Cornell University Press, 1985.

Stebbins, Richard, et al. *The United States in World Affairs, 1957*. New York: Harper and Brothers, 1958.

Stebenne, David. *Modern Republican: Arthur Larson and the Eisenhower Years*. Bloomington: Indiana University Press, 2006.

Stever, Guy. *In War and Peace: My Life in Science and Technology*. Washington, DC: Joseph Henry Press, 2002.

Stiglitz, Joseph. *The Three Trillion Dollar War: The True Cost of the Iraq Conflict*. New York: Norton, 2008.

Strauss, Lewis. *Men and Decisions*. Garden City, NY: Doubleday, 1962.

Taubman, William. *Khrushchev: The Man and His Era*. New York: Norton, 2003.

Thompson, Kenneth (ed.). *The Eisenhower Presidency: Eleven Intimate Perspectives of Dwight D. Eisenhower*. Lanham, MD: University Press of America, 1984.

Truman, Harry. *Years of Trial and Hope, 1946–1952*. Garden City, NY: Doubleday, 1956.

Turner, Stansfield. *Burn Before Reading: Presidents, CIA Directors, and Secret Intelligence*. New York: Hyperion, 2005.

Updegrove, Mark. *Second Acts: Presidential Lives and Legacies after the White House*. Guilford, CT: Lyons Press, 2006.

Van Atta, Don. *First off the Tee: Presidential Hackers, Duffers, and Cheaters from Taft to Bush*. New York: Public Affairs, 2003.

Wagner, Steven. *Eisenhower Republicanism: Pursuing the Middle Way*. DeKalb: Northern Illinois University Press, 2006.

Wang, Zuoyue. *In Sputnik's Shadow: The President's Science Advisory Committee and Cold War America*. New Brunswick, NJ: Rutgers University Press, 2008.

Weiner, Tim. *Legacy of Ashes: The History of the CIA*. New York: Doubleday, 2007.

West, J. B., with Mary Lynn Kotz. *Upstairs at the White House*. New York: Warner Books, 1973.

White, William. *The Responsibles: How Five American Leaders Coped with Crisis*. New York: Harper and Row, 1972.

Wicker, Tom. *JFK and LBJ: The Influence of Personality upon Politics*. Baltimore: Penguin Books, 1968.

Wiesner, Jerome. *Where Science and Politics Meet*. New York: McGraw-Hill, 1965.

Wilson, Robert (ed.). *Character Above All: Ten Presidents from Reagan to Bush*. New York: Simon & Schuster, 1995.

Witkin, Richard (ed.). *The Challenge of the Sputniks: In the Words of President Eisenhower and Others*. New York: Doubleday, 1959.

Woods, Randall. *LBJ: Architect of American Ambition*. New York: Free Press, 2006.

Wukovits, John. *Eisenhower*. New York: Palgrave MacMillan, 2006.

Yeager, Chuck, and Leo Janos. *Yeager: An Autobiography*. New York: Bantam Books, 1985.

York, Herbert. *Race to Oblivion: A Participant's View of the Arms Race*. New York: Simon & Schuster, 1970.

INDEX

Page numbers for figures are in italic.